THE TONGUES
OF ITALY

THE TONGUES
OF ITALY

PREHISTORY AND HISTORY

Ernst Pulgram

GREENWOOD PRESS, PUBLISHERS
NEW YORK

Preface

It may seem audacious for a linguist to wander so far outside of his domain as I have done in this book, and for anyone to try to encompass so long a span of mankind's history. If nonetheless I have undertaken to do so, it is because I felt that such a unified linguistic history of Italy, which now exists only in so many unconnected portions, was needed, as was, I believed, an attempt to correlate its linguistic with its nonlinguistic cultural components. Language is but one part of the cultural baggage of a society, and it influences, and is influenced by, all the others. Hence it is instructive to discover in what way, generally and specifically, this interrelation operates and manifests itself.

Experts in the various subjects with which this book deals may well disagree with some things I am saying. While I ask no indulgence for factual mistakes, it should be borne in mind that this is a work of synthesis whose parts had to be fitted together into a reasonable, compact whole, and that therefore on occasion details dear to the specialists had to be remodeled or discarded owing to the overriding exigencies of the total design. I have not done this anywhere lightly or willfully, of course, but only after long study and deliberation.

I have, I trust, nowhere propounded linguistic views that clash with established theories of anthropology, archaeology, history, and other sciences; indeed it has been my aim to accustom students of linguistics to utilize fully, though critically, the data provided by nonlinguistic research. But it was, by the same token, equally my purpose to persuade scholars of other fields to take full cognizance of the facts and requirements of linguistic science and not to propose, in their turn, hypotheses ostensibly deduced from pseudo-linguistic considerations which modern linguistics cannot accept, least of all as the only possible answers, or to uphold opinions incompatible with those of the linguistic scientist.

But in addition to being helpful to students and scholars con-

cerned with the prehistory and history of Italy, and in particular
with her languages, this book will, I hope, also appeal to the lay
reader. Of course, it is difficult to please both the expert and the
amateur with the same text. But rather than popularizing the work
in content and size in order to satisfy the latter, I am instead asking
him not to be deterred by the necessary bulk of the scholarly discussion and all the apparatus that goes with it, and to be patient
through those sections which are addressed mainly to the specialist.
I did not think I ought to shorten or omit these portions. A quicker
turning of the pages will carry the reader less interested in detail
over these spots without discomfort or loss of continuity of the
story.

In the task of preparation and in writing this book I have been
aided immeasurably by fellowships, and furloughs from my teaching and other academic duties. And upon completion of the manuscript I was given funds that saw it through the press. With
pleasure and gratitude I list the Institutions to which I am deeply
obliged for assistance:

American Council of Learned Societies, for a Faculty Study
    Fellowship, 1951–52;

University of Michigan, for granting a leave of absence in
    1951–52, and a Sabbatical Leave in 1954–55;

John Simon Guggenheim Memorial Foundation, for a Fellow-
    ship in 1954–55, and for financial aid toward the publica-
    tion of this book;

Horace H. Rackham School of Graduate Studies, University
    of Michigan, for a grant to cover travel expenses in 1954–
    55, and for financial aid toward publication of this book;

American Academy in Rome, for giving me guest privileges in
    1951–52, 1954–55, and 1956–57.

To all those persons who, individually or on behalf of the Institutions they represent, helped me in so many ways to educate
myself and to write down what I had learned, and to the Director
and staff of the Harvard University Press, I express my profound
and heartfelt thanks.

The magnitude of my indebtedness to each of numerous scholars and to my teachers is best measured in my bibliography, and I
shall refrain from invidiously singling out any person.

Last but not least I thank Italy, that fascinating and enchanting land, and I thank its good people, friends and strangers, in the city and in the country, learned and unlettered, because of whom my labor has always been one of joy and love.

Rome, January 1957   E. P.

CONTENTS

BOOK THREE. ROMAN ITALY

BOOK FOUR. MEDIAEVAL ITALY

MAPS

The Tongues of Italy

Note

The Bibliography at the end of the book is arranged by Parts. The bibliography for each Part consists of two sections: books and articles cited, and additional titles. Neither is exhaustive, but both are purposely large enough to show the enormous amount of work that has been done by other scholars and to lead readers to further research, both on major and minor points. The first list by its nature cannot be selective, but the second is.

All translations from foreign languages are my own, unless otherwise stated in the footnotes.

Passages from the following are reproduced with the permission of the publisher: L. R. Palmer, *The Latin Language* (London: Faber and Faber Limited, 1954); Arthur E. R. Boak, *A History of Rome to 565 A.D.* (4th ed., New York: The Macmillan Company, 1955); Earnest A. Hooton, *Up From the Ape* (New York: The Macmillan Company, 1946); Joshua Whatmough, *The Foundations of Roman Italy* (London: Methuen & Company Limited, 1937); Massimo Pallottino, *Etruscologia* (Milan: Ulrico Hoepli, 1955); Giacomo Devoto, *Gli antichi Italici* (2nd ed., Florence: Vallecchi Editore, 1951).

INTRODUCTION

Italy, it is often said, in the past two millennia has thrice ruled the western world in three different domains of human endeavor: once in government and law, once in religion, and once in art.

Under the Roman emperors well nigh the entire known world was governed by Romans and guided by Roman laws, and to this day a fair number of nations base their corpus iuris on the experience and tradition of the Roman state, from the venerable Twelve Tables of 450 B.C. to the gigantic Theodosian Code of A.D. 438.

Although Jesus Christ was a Palestinian, Christianity conquered from Rome, the Roman Pope competed with the Holy Roman Emperor for the rule over the world and over men's loyalties, and to this day millions look to the Holy See of Rome for spiritual guidance.

In the middle of our millennium there flourished in the cities of Italy the Renaissance which was not merely a renascence of antiquity but indeed heralded the birth of a new art for Europe and the world, and to this day the giants of Italian painting and sculpture and architecture are the masters and teachers of countless disciples who come to Italy as on a pilgrimage.

But there is yet a fourth domain in which Italy ruled, namely, its language, and to this day the Neo-Latin languages are spoken by ever more persons from the Balkans to the Andes. It is the story of this fourth phenomenon, but only as it occurred on Italian soil, which this book proposes to tell, from the beginnings in a misty past to the time when the modern Italian language was formed; from the prehistoric era of which we know little more than that the denizens of Italy by virtue of being human could talk, through the period of the arrival of Indo-European idioms, through the years when one of them, Latin, spoken first by a mere handful of peasants of Latium, came to conquer all of Italy and later the Romanic-speaking world, until finally Dante gave Italy its national tongue.

I have written this book because I felt that the story of man in Italy, having been told many times by political historians, church historians, and art historians, might now be narrated from the point of view of the linguistic historian, or the historical linguist, for in languages also there is laid down testimony to the fate of the men who spoke them. The beginnings, the spread, and the retrenchments of a language have much to tell, in a very peculiar fashion, about its speakers. And, as "all the world's a stage, and all the men and women merely players," the play's historical events in which man participates, in majesty and in misery, are in turn the warp and the woof that weave not only the stuff of his speeches, but also the texture and the pattern of his speech.

BOOK ONE

MODERN ITALY

Part One. Introduction to Italy

MODERN ITALY

The Land Italy is a very mountainous country; only one-fifth of its surface is flatland. With the exception of the center of the Po plain and the southern end of the Apulian tableland, the hills and mountains are always within sight of the farmer tilling his fields in the plains and valleys. But more frequently the fields spread upon the very slopes, occupying every foot of cultivable ground, no matter how thin the layer of fertile soil.

Very little of the total land of Italy is, or need be, uninhabitable. And one may well say that much of the country that lies barren, fallow, eroded, and sterile, has become so through human use and abuse. Ruthless deforestation, overgrazing of pastures, lacking river control, failure to drain in some places and irrigate in others, the wasteful and inefficient agricultural methods of the great estate, these and other causes account to a greater extent than nature's often contrary ways for the impoverishment of the land. For Italy is a poor country today.

The traveler who comes to Italy from the north must at some point cross the mountainous barrier of the Alps that separates Italy from the rest of Europe. However, this mightiest mountain chain of Europe turns its less accessible and steeper front toward Italy, whereas the ascent to its heights and passes from Central Europe is generally milder and less wearisome, though of course longer. For example, the river Po descends five thousand feet from its springs to the plain over a length of twenty-five miles. But the Rhine drops the same height from its springs to the Bodensee over a distance of one hundred miles.

The roads over most Alpine passes are made impassable by snow and ice from six to nine months a year. In our day communication is maintained the year round through railroad tunnels, the longest in Europe (Mont Cenis, St. Gotthard, Simplon, and one through the Mont Blanc in the planning stage), and by air.

Only the lowest passes (Brenner, Tarvisio) can be kept open for rail and road traffic. But until a century ago transalpine connections were likely to be completely severed from one-half to three-fourths of the year, or at best restricted to hazardous crossing on foot which could be undertaken only by hardy mountaineers; and before the roads were paved the deep mud that followed the snow made ascent or descent impossible for wheeled vehicles long into the spring and early summer. Armies did cross the Alps during the winter months on very rare occasions and only when absolutely necessary. The risks for such an enterprise were incalculable, as Hannibal, toward the end of the third century B.C., and Napoleon, two thousand years later, were to discover.

Today, sixteen viable passes lead over the Alps. Some of them were known in antiquity, a few probably also in prehistoric times. The *Tabula Peutingeriana* shows nine.[1] In general the height of the passes decreases from west to east. The highest among them, probably not used in antiquity (it does not figure on the *Tabula Peutingeriana*) is the Stelvio, or Stilfser Joch, on the Swiss border, at the upper end of the Adda Valley, the Valtellina, where the road rises to 9050 feet. The most useful and most traveled, ever since prehistory, is the Brenner Pass, because of its low elevation (4500 feet) and its location on the most important thoroughfare connecting Munich, Innsbruck with Verona, Bologna, that is, western and northern Europe with Italy. There the Romans laid out an important military road, which was subsequently used by many hostile invaders, as it was by the armies of the German emperors on their marches against Italy. A carriage road was built as early as 1772, and the railroad line was completed in 1867.

All eight passes to the west of the Brenner are free of snow only three to five months of the year. Only three of them (St. Gotthard, Bernina, Stelvio) were unknown to the Romans.

---

[1] The *Tabula Peutingeriana* is an eleventh- or twelfth-century copy, now deposited in the Nationalbibliothek in Vienna, of an original fourth-century Roman map, drawn by one Castorius. It is not really a map in our sense of the word, but merely a graphic, schematized itinerary containing the roads of the Roman Empire. It is not oriented to the points of the compass, has no scale (distances may be gathered from the figures along the roads between the various localities), and gives but the most rudimentary picture, only in a left-right dimension, of the relative location of places. Nonetheless it is one of the most important ancient geographic documents in our possession. Cf. Miller 1916.

To the east of the Brenner, the most important and lowest is the Peartree Pass (so called after an ancient Roman inn *ad pirum* 'The Peartree'), only 3000 feet high, by the Romans called Mons Ocra. It lies north of the Istrian peninsula. In prehistoric times it served as a trade route along which precious amber was carried all the way from the Baltic Sea to the Mediterranean, along the valleys of the Oder, March, Danube, Save, hence across the pass into the Isonzo Valley and the plain. It may also have been the pass across which the Argonauts carried their ship "Argo," thus closing the circle that had led them from the Black Sea into the Adriatic Sea and back to Greece again.[2] In Roman times the passroad was protected by the foundation of the colony Aquileia in 186 B.C.[3]

Many times foreign invaders, of whom I shall speak in the proper place, crossed, or attempted to cross the Peartree Pass in order to reach Italy: the Kelts (179 B.C.), the Germanic Kimbri (113 B.C.), the Visigoths under King Alaric (A.D. 402 and 408), the Huns under Attila (452), the Ostrogoths under Theodoric (488), the Langobards (568), the Mongolian Avars (610), the Magyars (899, 921, 924). Throughout the Middle Ages the pass and the country around it were hotly contested because of their strategic importance. And one may also be certain that various prehistoric invasions and immigrations of Italy, in addition to the amber trade, used this route. The neolithic and the Metal Age cultures, and the Indo-European languages, came at least in part this way.

The question one inevitably asks is whether the Alps provided Italy and her peoples with an effective bulwark against incursions from the north. Apparently they did not, formidable as the barrier may seem on a map. In prehistoric times when the Stone Age people of Italy offered no concerted resistance to invaders, many Central Europeans, in small groups and in tribes, seem to have marched into Italy in search of an easier life. They brought with them the cultures of Central Europe and the Danube basin, including Indo-European dialects. In Roman days, only four really dangerous invasions occurring before the crumbling of the Empire are note-

[2] Cf. Semple 1931, 225–226.
[3] Cf. the map of Roman fortifications on the Carso plateau and the Peartree Pass in Semple 1931, 220.

worthy: that of the Kelts (in the fifth century B.C.), two forays
by the Carthaginians under Hannibal (218 B.C.) and Hasdrubal
(207 B.C.), and finally the irruption of the Kimbri (101 B.C.). Until the period of continuous onslaughts by the barbarians upon an
already weakened empire from the fourth century after Christ on,
the Romans and Italy seemed safe enough behind that natural
obstruction — but surely not because the mountains were an in-
superable obstacle by themselves but rather because human defenders were willing and able to make use of them. Reliance on a natural
defense of this kind cannot but lead to a Maginot-Line complex and
to national disaster. Hence a modern historian speaks of "that . . .
splendid traitor, the Alpine frontier of Italy." [4]

The other great mountain chain of Italy, the Apennines, does
not constitute a natural boundary line but runs the whole length
of the Italian boot, from the straps to the tip of the toe. Although
the whole mass is geologically neither uniform nor of equal age, it
presents the appearance of a continuous unit, but without a unique
principal longitudinal range. Instead it is composed of a very
irregular series of chains and massifs which give the relief of the
peninsula that improvised, helter-skelter arrangement of heights
and lowlands, broad valleys and narrow gorges, and that ever-
changing and variegated landscape whose many parts are singularly
difficult of access and have therefore hindered internal communication. This accounts for the many enduring cultural and linguistic
subdivisions in Italy, of which more will have to be said.

Throughout the whole length of Italy, from the Po through
Sicily, runs a line of volcanic rifts. They begin near Padua in the
Euganean Hills, whose hot sulphur springs have been known since
antiquity for their therapeutic virtues, then can be traced along a
string of extinct volcanoes (Monte Amiata in Tuscany, Monti Ci-
mini north of Rome, the Alban or Latin Hills, with sulphur springs
near Tivoli) and crater lakes (the Trasimeno of Hannibalic fame,
Bolsena, Vico, Bracciano, Albano, Nemi). From this point south,
volcanic activity still continues in our days: on Vesuvius, the Phleg-
rean Fields and Solfatara, the island of Ischia (all near Naples),
Stromboli and the other Liparian islands, Mount Etna, and on the
little island of Pantelleria. Earthquakes have been frequent and im-

⁴ Myres 1953, 117.

portant in Italy's history, as have volcanic eruptions and tidal waves. Volcanoes play a notable part in ancient mythology, and the workshops of Hephaistos, or Vulcan, were located severally on the isle of Lemnos, under Mount Etna, and on the island of Hiera (now Volcano) in the Lipari group. The shaking of the earth and the subterranean roar which preceded or accompanied volcanic eruptions were thought to be due to the writhing and bellowing of the giants imprisoned and bound beneath the surface of the earth. No myths were attached to Vesuvius, because it was recognized as a living volcano only when, after a warning quake in A.D. 63,[5] it became disastrously active in A.D. 79, and destroyed in an outbreak of extreme violence two flourishing cities at its feet, covering Herculaneum under a stream of molten lava, and smothering Pompeii under a rain of ashes and pumice.

Yet Italy owes much of the fertility of her plains, especially of Campania, to their volcanic soil, for weathered lava contains naturally and abundantly the elements (phosphorus and potash) which elsewhere must be added to the soil through artificial fertilizers. And one of the most common building materials of the Romans, the tufa, widely used in ancient Rome because it could be quarried right outside the city, is an agglomeration of volcanic cinders. It is hard and durable, yet it can be easily quarried, cut, and sculptured. It is the tufaceous soil in and around Rome that made it possible for the early Christians to cut the labyrinths of miles and miles of catacombs.

The plains of Italy occupy, as I mentioned, only one-fifth of the country's surface. Two-thirds of this total is accounted for by the plain of the Po River and its tributaries alone, a vast triangle in the north, outside the peninsula proper. The other flatlands of Italy are relatively small, crammed in mostly between either side of the Apennines and the seashore. Starting in the northwest, one may mention the Maremma of Tuscany, the Roman Campagna, the Pontine plain, Campania, the plain of Paestum, the plains of Santa Eufemia and Gioia. Beyond the southwestern tip of the peninsula, the next flat area is the plain of Sybaris, then that of Metaponto. In the southeast stretches the Apulian tableland, from the heel of the boot

[5] Tac. *Ann.* 5.33–34, and Suet. *Nero* 30, report how the earth quivered (in ecstasy or agony?) while the emperor Nero was making his Neapolitan debut as a singer.

all the way to the foothills of the Monte Gargano and the Abruzzi. Along the rest of the Adriatic coast as far as Rimini and the Po country the mountains crowd upon the sea, and only the numerous short valleys issuing from the Apennines, and the flat-topped ridges between them are cultivable land. I have already mentioned the valleys within the Apennines, of which some are so wide and fertile as to be classed with the arable plains.

All geographic boundaries of Italy are natural barriers, in the north the Alps, and for the rest the sea. The peninsula itself is so narrow that no point on it is farther than sixty-seven miles from the sea, and even in the continental provinces of the north the shore is nowhere more than one hundred miles distant. For this reason the coastline is very long in relation to the total area. Nonetheless the Italians have never been a really seafaring nation like the Greeks and Phoenicians, or like the Vikings and British. The Romans themselves were farmers and cattlebreeders throughout their history, and their wars were fought mainly, and by preference, on land. Whenever they did venture out upon the water it was generally through necessity, either to fight a maritime nation (for example, the Carthaginians, in the three Punic Wars of the third and second centuries B.C.) or pirates which threatened the lifelines of the Empire (compare Pompey's spectacular naval victories in 67 B.C.). In part this neglect of the sea is due to the paucity of good harbors along the extended coastline. Rome herself never had a good maritime port, despite the elaborate installations of the emperors Claudius (41–54) and Trajan (97–117) at Ostia. The harbors of Genoa, La Spezia, Naples (where Puteoli, founded as the Cumaean colony of Dicaearchia, now Pozzuoli, was the true port of Rome for a long time and maintained itself even after Claudius' works at Ostia) on the west coast, and on the east coast Trieste (sluggish since it ceased to be the first port of the dissolving Habsburg Empire, in 1918), Venice (a location unused until the sixth century after Christ), Ancona, Bari, Brindisi, and Taranto, are the only acceptable ports of Italy. But they do not bear comparison with the Piraeus (Athens), or the estuaries of the Thames (London), the Rhine (Rotterdam), the Elbe (Hamburg), the Weser (Bremen), the Tajo (Lisbon), and many others. And one should not forget that finally, through the discovery of America, the Mediterranean, the gathering focus and the radiating hub of civilization for many centuries, was reduced to a relatively quiet pool whose drowsiness was enlivened only by local concerns, while the life and business of the globe were inevitably lured to the coast and harbors of the Atlantic Ocean. Only the opening of the Suez Canal, in 1869, brought new international movement to the Mediterranean — but by then the nations whose shores it laved had spent their strength, and Italy had long since ceased to be the mistress of the world.[6]

Of the two coasts of Italy, the Tyrrhenian and the Adriatic, the latter has always been less favored culturally, possibly because the Adriatic Sea has always been outside the main traffic lanes of the Mediterranean, particularly before and since the golden age of Venice, and also because the climate and the soil are less inviting on the eastern side. The greatest civilization of ancient Italy lay also along the west coast: the Greeks, the Etruscans, and the Romans founded their principal cities there.

The rivers of Italy, too, do not lend themselves to teaching a nation the mastery of the waterways. Apart from the Po, the Tiber, and the Arno, Italian rivers are too short, too violent, and too capriciously irregular for river traffic in any ships beyond small barges. The Ofanto of Apulia, for example, may carry as little as 1.5 cubic meters per second, or it may roar along at a rate of 2300 cubic meters per second. Most streams dry up nearly or wholly during the long drought seasons, while in the rainy season they become destructive torrents, their floods periodically carrying off bridges and houses, and silting up the cultivated land of their valleys. These irregular qualities, fortunately lacking in the more steady Alpine streams which are nourished by the eternal ice and snow of the glaciers, make the peninsular watercourses also unsuitable for the generation of hydroelectric power. Although the nature of Italy's rivers is to a large degree caused by the deforestation of the watersheds, whose denuded and eroded hillsides cannot store any underground water, it seems that even under optimal conditions, as they

[6] Today it is cheaper and more convenient to have ships with merchandise from the Far East destined for Central Europe continue the long voyage through the Straits of Gibraltar to the ports of France, England, Holland, and Germany, rather than transfer the cargo from ship to railroad at one of the Mediterranean ports. Hence Switzerland, for example, receives more eastern imports through Rotterdam than through Genoa.

may have prevailed some 2500 years ago, the waterways of Italy were never apt to form a net of usable lanes for traffic and commerce.

We might now familiarize ourselves with the major provinces and regions of Italy whose names will occur many times in the following pages.[7]

Beginning in the northwest, Piedmont lies, as its name implies, at the foot of the mountains. Descending from the highest peaks of the Alps, one distinguishes the mountainous, the hilly, and the flat region. All rivers stream fanlike toward the Po, and many of them are harnessed to run the generating turbines of hydroelectric plants. The focal point of the whole district is the prosperous industrial city of Turin, known for its automobile manufacture. The hills and valleys bear fruit, their wines are famous, and the wet lowlands are planted to rice.

To the east of Piedmont is Lombardy, whose name recalls the Langobards who held the country from 568 to 774, with their capital at Pavia. The present center is the thriving, bustling city of Milan, the second city of Italy after Rome. The landscape resembles that of Piedmont, and the agricultural and horticultural products are largely the same. Lombardy occupies the second place in Italy (after Liguria) in the generation of hydroelectric power. The drained and irrigated (an indispensable combination) plain provides fat pasturage for a growing dairy industry.

Between Lombardy and the Adriatic lie the three Venetian provinces, Venezia Tridentina, Venezia Euganea, and Venezia Giulia (of which the last, however, now belongs in part to Yugoslavia). Venezia Tridentina, so called after the Roman town Tridentum, now Trento, covers mainly the area of the river Adige,

---

[7] The division of Italy into regions that I shall employ here does not correspond to a governmental or administrative sectioning of the country. They are rather, like the French provinces (Normandy, Ile de France, Provence, Burgundy, etc.) or like 'New England,' 'Dixie,' 'the Midwest,' historical and traditional regions. The boundaries and names of some of them go back to Roman times, in particular to the *regiones* of Augustus. (However, to satisfy local aspirations, the compartments of Sicily, Sardinia, and Venezia Tridentina, have been accorded political autonomy under the new postwar Constitution.) The true administrative units of local government are the ninety provinces, which correspond to the French Départements.

Statistical data, unless otherwise indicated, are taken from the *Annuario Statistico Italiano* and the *United Nations Statistical Yearbook*.

the formerly Austrian South Tirol. The country is important for its fruit, lumber, and hydroelectric power. The famous Dolomites, a tourist paradise in summer and winter, belong partly to this province, partly to the adjoining Venezia Euganea.

Venezia Euganea is the largest of the three Venezias. It contains at least five great cities, Verona, Vicenza, Padua, Treviso, and Venice. The Venetian part of the Po valley is called the Polesine, a rainy and humid area (the local dialect has about forty terms for rain and wetness), but rich and fertile. It is easily ravaged by flooding of the Po River which flows between enormous dikes and whose normal level is higher than that of the surrounding countryside. There is little industry in this province, and practically no mineral wealth.

Venezia Giulia occupies the Istrian peninsula and the land to the north of it. It is the region of the lowest passes, the backdoor to Italy. It is also the land of the arid, calcareous, sterile Carso. Since the main occupation of the inhabitants is nonetheless farming, poverty is inevitable.

Returning westward, we now come to the narrow strip of land east of the French border, between Piedmont and the Ligurian Sea. This is Liguria, completely occupied by the western Apennines, a once heavily wooded but now deforested country, unlovely except for the shoreline, the beautiful Riviera, the playground and the flower garden of Europe. Besides tourism Liguria has one other major economic asset: its great ports of Genoa and La Spezia. Agriculture hardly counts in Liguria, unless one so considers the miles and miles of flowerbeds along the sea, producing roses and carnations for all Europe. Among industries only shipbuilding around Genoa is of importance.

The province which occupies the Po plain south of the river, and the adjacent northern slopes of the Apennines is called Emilia, after the ancient Roman Via Aemilia which ran from Fanum (Fano) to Mediolanum (Milan), skirting the edge of the mountains, and stringing together, as does the modern road, all the principal cities of the region — Rimini, Forlì, Faenza, Bologna, Modena, Reggio, Parma, Piacenza. Another great center of the province is Ravenna, formerly a seaport, now four miles inland due to the silting up of the Po delta. It was once the capital of the fading Roman Empire, then the seat of Theodoric, king of the Goths. The hilly zone of Emilia bears fruit, the plain cereal crops.

South of the line that connects La Spezia and Rimini we enter upon the peninsula proper. We shall later see that this natural and administrative boundary constitutes also an important linguistic frontier, separating northern from central and southern Italian dialects, indeed the so-called Western from the Eastern Romanic languages.

Here the Apennines begin the long curve which deflects their main course from a west-east to a north-south direction. To the south and west of the northern part of this arch spreads Tuscany. It is mainly a mountainous and hilly province, with some flatlands near the coast, recently regained for agriculture after a long malarial sleep, but all of it intensely and fruitfully cultivated. Tuscany is also richer in minerals than the provinces discussed so far, and this may have been one of the principal attractions that lured prehistoric and protohistoric settlers of Iron Age culture particularly to this part of Italy, as we shall see, above all the Etruscans. The towns of Tuscany — Florence, Siena, Pisa, Lucca, Pistoia, Arezzo — are among the brightest jewels of Italy, all renowned because of their mediaeval and Renaissance rather than classical associations.

On the eastern side of the Apennine crest, descending toward the Adriatic, are situated the mountainous Marche. The principal cities lie along the coast: Pesaro, Fano (fishing), Senigallia (named after the Keltic Senones), Ancona (a harbor), and many summer resorts with beaches. Farther south and a little inland stand the towns of Macerata and Ascoli Piceno, the latter's name recalling the ancient Picenes, of whom we shall hear later.

Wedged in between the Marche and Tuscany, but west of the main ridge of the Apennines, lies the landlocked province of Umbria, often called *Umbria verde*, 'Green Umbria,' whose more durable and richer verdure is due to favorable geological conditions. Most of Umbria, except the wide and fertile Clitunno Valley, is mountainous and hilly, with little room for agriculture. The prominent cities are Perugia (an Etruscan foundation), Assisi (the city of St. Francis), Spello, Bevagna, Foligno, Trevi, Orvieto (also of Etruscan origin), and Spoleto, all of them on hilltops, and all of them very ancient. Industry is insignificant, except at Spoleto and

Terni. (Near the latter the industrial installations have destroyed the once beautiful cascades of the Marmore, praised and sung in verse by earlier travelers.)

South of Tuscany and Umbria extends Latium. (It should be noted that the modern Latium, or Lazio, occupies really double the area of what the Romans called Latium, which corresponds mainly to the modern Roman Campagna south of Rome.) Latium is less hilly than its neighbors, and its plains, the Campagna and the Pontine marshes, once were, and are slowly becoming again, important agricultural districts. Until recently, the Roman Campagna, just outside the gates of Rome, traversed by the venerable Via Appia, was a desolate, malaria-ridden wasteland, populated only by semi-nomadic shepherds, which despite its vicinity to Rome was culturally so remote an area as to induce the Vatican to organize it, in 1897, as a missionary district.

Latium is the heartland of Roman and Italian history, and of the Latin language, because it was the home of the Latin tribes and of the Romans themselves, who set out from their Seven Hills to conquer the world.

The eastern half of the peninsula in the latitude of Latium is occupied by the province of Abruzzo e Molise. This is the most mountainous and wildest tract of Italy and from it rise the highest peaks outside of the Alps: the Maiella (8500 feet) and the Gran Sasso (9000 feet). Despite this the region is mainly an agricultural one, thanks mainly to three relatively extensive plains, that of Aquila, that of Sulmona, and the vast basin of the former Lake Fucino which was completely drained toward the end of the last century. Sheep are the principal animal product. They are led twice a year on long treks, the so-called transhumance: descending from the heights in the winter when deep snow covers the mountain pastures, they feed in the humid and warmer valleys; but as the drought dries out the plains, they ascend again for the summer into the highlands. This type of nomadic flocks is found all over Italy where the climate and the soil require it. Industry in the Abruzzi is inconsequential.

Below Latium and the Abruzzi we enter the Mezzogiorno, Italy's southland, a national problem much for the same economic reasons as was and in some degree still is the South of the United

States, but by no means so far on the road to economic and social recovery. Its misery has been endemic for centuries, and all its troubles are man-made, producing a discouraged, indolent, ignorant, and fatalistic population, weakened by hunger and disease.

The transition from north to south is of course a gradual one, since there is no trenchant political or racial or cultural boundary that could cause an abrupt break. In fact on one's way from southern Latium into the plain of Campania one enters upon one of the most thriving and fertile agricultural districts of Italy, called *terra di lavoro* 'the land of tillage.' Its ancient capital Capua (now Santa Maria di Capua Vetere, modern Capua lying some two miles distant) was before Rome one of the most opulent towns of Italy. The earth is good and lavishes triple crops upon the farmers, and the land is thickly settled. Yet the inhabitants, while they do not go hungry, are still quite poor among the riches, for more often than not they do not own the land they cultivate, wages are small, families are large. The modern capital of the province, Naples, is a poor, squalid city, in one of the most beautiful natural settings anywhere in the world. Around it is concentrated the industry of Campania, which covers under a gloomy pall of smoke the places where in the old days wealthy Romans came to spend the summer in their luxurious villas of Puteoli, Baiae, Cape Misenum.

As the counterpart of Campania on the Adriatic shore, though reaching farther north and south, stretches the long, narrow province of Apulia, or Puglia. It consists in the north of a low tableland, the Tavoliere di Puglia, in the center of the higher and hilly Murge, and in the south of the lowlands of the Sallentine peninsula. The main cities are on the seashore, Bari, Brindisi, and Taranto being ports of more than local importance. The inland center in the north is Foggia, where the north-south and the east-west railroad lines intersect. The Apulian plain is not nearly as rich as the Po plain, and very dry, lacking both perennial rivers and sufficient precipitation, though there is evidence that in ancient days, especially before the Roman occupation of the land, the soil was more fertile.

Between Apulia and Campania is wedged in the province of Lucania, which has only a narrow outlet to the sea on the Gulf of Taranto. It is probably the poorest and most backward region of Italy. Only 4.8 per cent of its soil is productive. As the railroad from

Salerno to Taranto follows the Basento River it does not touch any center of habitation over a stretch of nearly seventy miles, which is unique in a country as densely settled as is Italy.

The last province to be mentioned is the forefoot and the toe of the Italian boot, called Calabria now, Bruttium by the Romans. It is mountainous throughout, but has preserved some of its forests, which are favored also geologically by a granitic instead of limestone soil. This region seems to have changed in natural aspect less since antiquity than any other of Italy, but it also has been more laggard in finding its way back to civilization since the Greeks deserted it. Calabria was once a flourishing part of Magna Graecia, and on its seashore arose Temesa, Hipponium, Rhegium, Locri, Scylletium, Croton, Sybaris, Siris, whose very names suffice to evoke past splendors and opulence. Now the coastal areas are barren and swampy, just barely awakening from a centuries old malarial slumber, the rivers are untamed destructive torrents.

This, then, in a nutshell, is Italy, the *Italia* of the Romans. But the familiar name did not always refer to the entire peninsula.[8] Until about 500 B.C. the Greeks called ϝιταλία only the southernmost part of Calabria, from the straits of Messina north as far as the isthmus between the Gulf of S. Eufemia and the town of Squillace. The word can be compared with Latin *uitulus* 'calf,' so that ϝιταλία was perhaps the 'cattle country.'[9] In the middle of the fifth century the designation was extended northward to include all of ancient Bruttium, approximately as far as the present boundary between Lucania and Calabria. From then on the name moves gradually north to include more and more of the peninsula: by the middle of the fourth century one finds it applicable as far as Paestum along the coast, but inland the line is difficult to establish; a hundred years later, at the beginning of the Punic Wars, Italia refers to all of the central and southern peninsula, but with Latium still excluded; at the end of the First Punic War, in 241 B.C., the wording of a treaty between Rome and Carthage makes it clear that Italia now includes the entire peninsula; only after the Second Punic War, which ended in 201 B.C., and after the permanent subjugation of the Kelts of Gallia Cisalpina

[8] Cf. Wikén 1937; Wistrand 1952; Klingner 1941; Ducati 1948, 6–8.
[9] Cf. Altheim 1951, 44–45; Sergi 1922, 9. A different interpretation is suggested by Ribezzo 1920.

on both sides of the Po, which terminated in 191 B.C., can the name Italia be used to designate continental as well as peninsular Italy to the foot of the Alps. Polybius seems first to have employed it geographically with that extent in the middle of the second century B.C. But the official political use of it in this sense appears only in the days of Augustus (31 B.C.–A.D. 14), a century and a half later.[10] From the reign of Caracalla (211–217) on, in consequence of the emperor's gift of citizenship to all inhabitants of the provinces, the name Italia designated just one of the several provinces that constituted the empire. The administrative division of the state under Diocletian (284–305) made of Italia one of the four *praefecturae*, which included Italy proper, Illyricum, and Africa. After the fall of the empire the name did not again refer to a single political unity and reality, governed by the Italians as a nation, until 1870.[11] But, despite this lack of political meaning, the name Italy was generally known and used throughout these centuries to describe the total area of the sixteen provinces.

[10] Cf. Plin. *N.H.* 3.46.
[11] On the proposed etymologies of *Italia* and the spread and the varied meaning of the name see Rauhut 1946.

CHAPTER II

The Climate To travelers, and conquerors, from the north, Italy is the land of warmth and sunshine. In relation to northern climes this may be true, but it is not true that all of Italy enjoys always a balmy air. In the hills and mountains it can get very cold indeed; even Naples may have, though rarely, freezing temperatures; and the dark, foggy cold of the Po plain goes to the marrow of one's bones. But on the whole the country has what is called a Mediterranean climate, which, though its summers are apt to be unpleasantly hot and droughty, has mild winters.

Since most rain-bearing winds in Europe come from the west, and since the long chain of the Apennines hinders their progress across Italy, they unload their content of moisture on the western slopes of the mountains. This leaves the eastern half of the peninsula, facing the Adriatic Sea, with considerably less precipitation even during the rainy season. The cities of Venice, Bologna, Ancona, Foggia, Bari may receive in the course of the year only two-thirds of the amount of rain that falls on Genoa, Florence, Livorno, Rome, Naples. Adding these climatic advantages of the west to the already mentioned geographic superiority, that is, closeness to the lines of traffic and communication of the Mediterranean as compared with the Adriatic cul-de-sac, we see one more reason for the continued cultural superiority that has characterized the western provinces. From this generalization one may except some purely local phenomena, such as Ravenna, Venice, Rimini, which despite their eastern location became great centers, albeit impermanently, through some specific political or commercial causes.

Statistics on precipitation have little meaning, however, unless some information is provided on the manner and the extent in which the quantity of rain that falls benefits the land. In large parts of Italy, where bedrock comes to the surface or where the thin layer of topsoil is unprotected and not knit together and held in place by the roots of trees and other vegetation, the blessings of adequate precipitation may well be wasted because the water not only runs simply off the surface but indeed washes away the soil. And if an evenly spread annual rainfall of twenty-three inches is sufficient to keep the lawns of southern England rich and green throughout the year, the same amount of rain, if concentrated in seven months and followed by five months of merciless heat and drought, as is the case in large tracts of Italy, cannot have equally beneficial effect upon the vegetation. It will also make a considerable difference whether twenty-three inches of water pours down upon the country in ten violent storms or gently waters the earth in fifty or a hundred rainy days. Therefore, although in statistics the annual rainfall of Italy looks good, when broken down into monthly precipitation it appears less favorable, and if set side by side with temperature charts matters seem even worse. Furthermore, when one considers the soil of Italy, especially the wide expanses of porous limestone and the bare, deforested hillsides, which cannot hold and store humidity, the picture will be fairly unpleasant in many districts, and fully disastrous in some.

In addition, rainfall may vary greatly from year to year throughout the Mediterranean basin, and the biblical story of the seven lean years and the seven fat years, so cleverly managed by Joseph for Pharaoh, may have, as do many mythological tales and legends, a factual basis. In the period between 1938 and 1947, the yearly rainfall of Turin, for example, vacillated between 20 and 40 inches, that of Rome between 20 and 44, that of Genoa between 33 and 54, and that of Palermo between 16 and 52 inches.

The winter temperatures vary greatly from place to place. As mentioned before, the winter climate of Italy is generally mild. However, this does not apply to the Po plain, and to elevations in the Apennines and Alps above three thousand feet, where the cold may be severe and a fair amount of snow can be expected. It is not surprising, then, that the hospitable coastal and lowlying regions of Italy should have been prey not only to the incursions of northern foreigners, but also to periodic invasions by the inhabitants of the harsh mountainous districts of the Apennines themselves. Indeed the history of pre-Roman Italy and of the early days of the Roman republic is studded with the contests between the dwellers of the plains and the fierce, rugged highlanders of the Sabine mountains and the Abruzzi. "He who has ever descended from the snow-clad highlands of Samnium and Lucania, when the north-wind, penetrating to the bones, howls over the ridges, to the sunny shores of the Tyrrhenian Sea which bloom in eternal spring, will comprehend how the Aequi and the Volsci, Samnites, Lucanians, or whatever they may be called, again and again fell upon the plain and the Romans like beasts of prey whom hunger and cold drive to attack human habitations."[1]

Rome may have mild, rainy weather, while skiers romp in the snow on Mount Terminillo, sixty miles away. The Monte Sila in Calabria may be snowbound, while the oranges ripen farther north around the Bay of Naples. And the inhabitants of Milan may leave their city, shrouded in a cold fog or lashed by icy winds, to seek the warmth and sunshine of the Riviera on the other side of the Apennines, eighty miles distant.

In the summer, such striking discrepancies do not exist. All of Italy is rather warm and often fiercely hot. Smaller local variations come into play, such as, for example, have throughout the ages prompted the inhabitants of broiling Rome to seek the breezes of the Alban Hills, either, in former times, to spend a whole summer in a villa of the ancient resort of Tusculum, now merely a romantic site of ruins, or, more modestly in our days, to take the bus to Tivoli of a Sunday afternoon.

One may well ask whether the same climatic conditions prevailed throughout the prehistory and history of Italy, for a climate different from that of today or of the recent past would surely have had grave repercussions upon the landscape, the economy, the lives of the people, in short, upon history itself. But here the opinions diverge greatly. Nissen gathered from ancient testimony that in Roman antiquity the period of summerly drought, for instance, began later and ended earlier than it does today; that there was more rainfall, due in part to heavier forestation, which in turn caused a better retention of moisture in the soil, so that the rivers of Italy, even those of limestone regions, were more regular, carried more water, and were less torrential in the rainy season; that the snow on the Apennines lasted longer; that on account of all this the

[1] Nissen 1883, 1.227–228.

harvesting dates were later than they are now; and that the winters were colder.[2]

Since the days of Nissen, some climatologists have developed a theory of climatic changes running in cycles.[3] In the absence of direct records beyond accidental allusions, and because of the complete lack of any climate statistics for the remote and even more recent past, inferences are made by Huntington on the basis of archaeological evidence, historical records, and botanical research. Among the first are the ruins of towns and cities, in Asia and America, located in desert areas where, had past climate conditions been similar to those prevailing now, no habitation centers of such size could have flourished or even originated.[4] Among the second are historical records of migrations from dry lands, or lands that were becoming desiccated due to lack of rain, into more favored areas. Among the third are studies of the growth of the very ancient sequoia trees of California, the relative width of whose yearly growing-rings indicates either favorable, that is, wet, or unfavorable, that is, dry, growing conditions. From all this evidence Huntington derives a number of climatic correlations and chronological sequences which, he believes, allow him to establish a number of conclusions on the climate of a given region, whose validity is then tested — in the case of Italy, for example, by the known facts of Roman economic history: favorable climatic conditions of sufficient humidity for abundant growth of vegetation and such seasonal variation of weather as is stimulating to humans, find their historic expression in sound economic conditions and a progressive, industrious, searching attitude of man; unfavorable conditions, or lack of precipitation and the monotony of warmth and aridity tend to bring about a weaker economy and a less active and vigorous humanity.[5]

Huntington applies his theory of climatic cycles to Roman history in such a way that he can explain events and the changing of conditions as they occur within very brief periods of time. It is

[2] Nissen 1883, 1.397 ff.
[3] Cf. especially the works of Ellsworth Huntington listed in the bibliography.
[4] It is suggested by Menghin 1941, that the vast glaciation of the last Ice Age in the middle and upper zone of the northern hemisphere had, as its parallel phenomenon in the Mediterranean area, a pluvial age. Therefore the present desert areas of the Near East and North Africa used to be fertile lands during the Stone Age.
[5] Huntington 1945, 562 ff.

questionable whether the evidence for cyclic changes of climate provides really sensitive enough a scale for what one might call micro-history, and one cannot help wondering whether the author of this daring hypothesis has not perhaps allowed his hypothetical climatic cycles to fit the known facts of Roman history, especially since the major burden of the chronological correlation of climate and history of Italy is borne by the growth of the sequoia trees of California. Other scholars have indeed found other cycles, hence different periods of rise and decline of Roman Italy. I am willing to accept the thesis of climatic macro-cycles which outline and circumscribe long eras, but I am wary of theories which can interpret practically all the details of history on such a basis, tracing and explaining political events within the short spans of a century or less.[6]

The contention that the Mediterranean climate in classical times was by and large moister and cooler than nowadays, more like that of modern Central Europe than that of Italy, is, according to some, not fully supported by the facts we know. The general desiccation of the soil may be due, they say, not to reduced precipitation but to human failure to preserve and use economically what moisture there is.

Deforestation is certainly responsible for the aridity of vast areas of Italy, regardless of the natural drought season. The earlier harvest time of our days may well be due not to less humidity but to the development of earlier ripening types of grain. The description of severe winters and wet summers which ancient authors have left us, may be precisely indicative of the unusualness of such phenomena. For, were they normal, would writers make a special point of mentioning them? And, finally, the lines of plant limits, in terms of geographic latitude and elevation, are the same today as in antiquity, as far as we know.[7] At least one anthropographer assures us that the large majority of climatologists deny the cycle theory, that it is often a pet subject of archaeologists and historians not competent to deal with it, and that Huntington is quite wrong. "The

[6] Cf. Brooks 1922, 141; Whatmough 1937, 37 ff. Curry 1928, 298, believes to discern cycles of climate and migrations every 640 years. Myres 1953, 129–130, accepts the principle of climatic cycles for Italy but assigns an optimum climate with more than average rainfall to the entire long period from the seventh century B.C. to the second century after Christ.
[7] Cf. Cary 1949, 3.

causes of decline [of Rome] are to be sought not in a changed climate, but in denudation of the hillside soil, deforestation with the failure of springs, destruction of irrigation works by barbarian or nomad attack, collapse of orderly government under repeated barbarian inroads, and possibly in the exhaustion of the soil, causing agricultural decline."[8]

I have already referred to man-wrought ruin of a particular tract of land, or at least to man's failure to continue or reactivate improvements installed in ancient times. This human failure appears to be proven by the fact that within recent times human effort, and not a new climate, has again improved the yield of the land in many places which had lain desolate and barren since antiquity, for example, the Pontine Marshes, dreaded and abandoned already by the Romans, and the sizable plains around ancient Metapontum and Sybaris in the south, which are under our very eyes being awakened to new life, thanks to a redistribution of the land which is taken, against payment, from the uninterested absentee owners of immense holdings and parceled out to small peasants who will till their own soil and care for it.

I should suggest that we do not emphasize too much, certainly not beyond the limits proposed by Whatmough,[9] the variations of the climate of Italy in the past 2,500 years as a decisive factor of the history which we shall have to tell. In fact, we could do nothing worse than subject ourselves voluntarily to the stifling restrictions and inhibitions of any monolithic philosophy of history and human evolution, be it climatic, economic, or racial. But we must, and shall, endeavor to examine all the natural and cultural aspects of man, his surroundings, his civilization, with the aim of finding which ones were at any given moment or era responsible for man's history in Italy and, in this book especially, for his languages.

[8] Semple 1931, 99–100.
[9] Whatmough 1937, 33 ff.

CHAPTER III

The People In physical appearance there is no true national 'Italian' type, although the dark haired and relatively short are in a majority, especially in the south. Concerning the Italian's alleged vivacity and talkativeness, one may admit that the inhabitants of cities and metropolitan areas more often than not are blessed with both, though vast numbers of mountaineers and peasants, who painfully and with the sweat of their brow barely support themselves, are no more gabby and light-minded than a dour Scotch farmer.

Indeed, the description of the country and of its climate should have made it quite clear that such a variety of natural surroundings and human conditions, coupled with the absence of intense communication and national unity from the fifth century after Christ down to the recent past, will be anything but conducive to developing and maintaining a single national type in physical, cultural, and linguistic terms.

I prefer not to put much trust into the pseudo-scientific racial theories and divisions of Italy, past and present, based on cranial measurements and cephalic indexes, labial and cacuminal habits of articulation, tallness and shortness, blondness and brunetteness, regional physiognomies, suffixes of ethnic and local names, usage of the article, linguistic developments from Latin to Italian, intellectuality, state of health, criminality, martial spirit — most of them as unmeasured as they are unmeasurable, all marshalled in order to concoct a veritable witch's brew of unpalatable hypotheses and theories which can prove almost anything one might care to prove.[1] Nor do I wish the reader to succumb to the fond theories of some modern Italian patriots and educators, that contemporary Italy and her inhabitants owe it to themselves to be in all respects continuators and heirs to the heritage of Caesar and Augustus, or even the Grac-

[1] For an example of this 'method' see Pullè 1927.

chi and Cicero, on the basis of an alleged, though of course spurious, racial and ethnic continuity; that the Italian child somehow (one wonders how) sucks from his mother's breast the spirit of ancient Rome; that thereby Italians are the keepers and promoters of culture and civilization par excellence. Fortunately some Italians are wisely and stoically immune to such propaganda.

We must, to begin with, guard against the notion that Rome, the city, the state, and the center of Christendom, is or ever was Italy to any greater extent than, say, New York is America. Hence to claim 'Roman' descent for all Italians is biologically and historically ridiculous, and even to claim Roman culture for all of Italy is wrong. For there existed in Italy before Rome, and outside the city of Rome and Latium, tribes and nations of whom, though we may not know much else, it is at least certain that their local culture, including their language, was quite different from what the Latins themselves claimed as their heritage. "The belief which is enshrined in ancient historians of Rome, and which is only just beginning to disappear from their modern successors, that Rome was all but a heaven-sent power whose mission it was to civilize both Italy and the world, is untrue. The provinces of Italy, with hardly an exception, already had remarkable civilizations of their own before Rome conquered them."[2]

We shall subsequently see what these civilizations were and what kind of people created them. But there is no evidence that Roman practical politics and political practice deemed the remodeling of the nations of Italy in Rome's image either worthwhile or opportune. Rather the contrary was true. Whatever equalization did take place was due to the exigencies of the daily living together of Romans and non-Romans and to administrative pressures, which in many respects united the conquerors and the vanquished and caused them to conform and adjust to one another. If Italy did not become Romanized under the compulsion of the Roman Empire, not even in language, as thoroughly as one might think, it could hardly thereafter become culturally unified in the course of its checkered and largely unhappy history. Yet, conversely, Rome herself received much from the provinces; physically through the immigration of provincials into the great city, culturally through

[2] Whatmough 1937, 9.

the reception and propagation of imported ideas. Hence "Rome without Italy is unintelligible."[3]

But it is not my meaning, since I reject the thorough mixture of Romans with Italians, that there existed at any time, or continued to our days, somewhere in Italy any unmixed, pure races. True, the so-called Mediterranean anthropological type is perhaps dominant in most parts of Italy today, and very likely was even more so in the era before transalpine, transadriatic, and transtyrrhenian invasions. Later on, Roman admixture, through the settling all over Italy of Roman veterans and administrators and their families, further complicated matters, without ever leading to complete ethnic equalization. The result is that today any attempted racial typology is at least as hopeless in Italy as it is elsewhere in Europe. True racially pure types may possibly be discovered outside of crowded Europe, where protracted isolation of a group might have led, through ethnic inbreeding, to the development and continuity of a relatively homogeneous somatic type. Obviously, that condition of isolation cannot be claimed for Italy at any time since the Palaeolithic Age. "Attempts to classify the population of the peninsula and of its islands by racial criteria have always met with failure. . . The 'Italian type' is the product of pure speculation and scientific dilettantism, of charlatanism or demagogy."[4]

The number of the population of Italy has undergone extraordinary variations in the course of history. Any estimates concerning population in prehistoric times are, to say the least, daring. And for the Roman Age also, though we are in a better position for guessing, we are a long way from certainty. However, it is as sure as can be that the prehistoric dwellers of Italy were comparatively few, a fraction of today's figure. It also seems fairly certain that the successive infiltrations and immigrations, of which we shall have to speak in detail, brought over the centuries a fair number of new settlers to Italy who apparently thrived and multiplied.

The early history of Rome and Latium must have been a prosperous period. It is claimed that the population increased to such an extent that exhaustion of the soil of Latium ensued as early as the fourth century B.C., whereupon the Romans felt compelled to em-

[3] Whatmough 1937, 9.
[4] Olschki 1949, 17.

bark upon a series of imperialist ventures of expansion, beginning with the first war against the Samnites, 343–341. During the next century conquered territory was relatively easy to come by, thanks to the superiority of Roman arms and organization. But the third century, with its colossal drain on Roman resources in the fight for life against Carthage, showed already shortages in many respects, including manpower. After the fortunate outcome of the Second Punic War, Rome could again rally her strength and recuperate to some extent. Then followed the unhappy second century with all its internal troubles and new demands upon manpower in the Second Macedonian War (200–197), the Syrian War against Antiochus III (192–189), the Third Macedonian War (171–168), the Third Punic War (149–146), the Achaean War (146), the Numantine War (143–133), the hateful civic disturbances under the Gracchi (133–121), the Jugurthine War (111–105), the war against the Kimbri and Teutons (113–101). What an account of expense of natural resources, money, and human blood! Then came the first century with its sanguinary internal strife until Augustus established peace — at the cost of the republican form of government: the Social War against the Italian allies (91–88), the First Mithridatic War (88–84), the bloody civil war between Marius and Sulla (88–82), the Second Mithridatic War (83–81), the war against the usurper Sertorius in Spain (80–72), the War of the Gladiators and the Third Servile War (73–71), the war against the pirates to keep the lifelines of the empire open (78–67), the Third Mithridatic War (74–64), the conspiracy of Catilina and the near-civil war in consequence thereof (66–62), the conquest of Gaul by Caesar (58–51), the civil war between Caesar and Pompey (49–46), the war in Africa (47–46), the war against Pompey's sons (46–45), the civil war of Mutina (44–43), the civil war of Perusia (41–40), the Sicilian war (38–36), the war between Octavian and Marc Antony (31–30).

For Rome to emerge from all this bloodshed without mortal wounds was miraculous. The wounds and the continued bloodletting were indeed mortal at least to the republic, although under the wise leadership of Augustus, the state, now a principate, was given a chance to recover. Luckily Rome's external enemies were beaten, or at least sufficiently exhausted to give the Romans a breathing spell. But during the Principate and the subsequent Dominate there is sufficient indirect evidence that the state and its leaders had to contend with a continuing and worsening manpower shortage. It was to play a decisive part in weakening the country economically and militarily so as to make it in the end a comparatively easy victim to usurpers of the imperial power and to invading barbarians, especially since, in her desperate search for soldiers, Rome had admitted and encouraged a kind of fifth column of non-Italian mercenaries and officers in its armies, with disastrous results to the efficiency and the morale of the once unconquerable legions.[5]

Throughout the early Middle Ages the old Italian population lay prostrate. The vigorous German invaders from the north — Ostrogoths, Visigoths, Langobards — did mix to some extent with the natives, though not as intensively as one might expect, and rejuvenated Italian civilization in some degree, especially in the northern provinces. In the south new cultural vigor was imported through the Normans and the Moslems. Given the political condition of the peninsula in the succeeding centuries, with its lack of national unity and national purpose, it is not surprising that statistics on a national scale should be lacking even for the recent past. On the whole, however, it seems that the population continued to increase until it reached, in 1900, about 32,000,000.

Today, something over half a century later, despite two world wars and the bloody, futile Mussolinian enterprise of the Abyssinian conquest, Italy's involvement in the Second World War and, until recently, a vast emigration to the New World,[6] Italy numbers

[5] On the causes and consequences of the manpower shortage during the Empire see Boak 1955.

[6] In 1913, the heaviest emigration year for Italy, no less than 560,000 persons migrated overseas to America, of whom 380,000 came to the United States, over 1,000 per day. To this figure must be added another 310,000 persons who left Italy for other European countries. During that year, then, about 2,400 persons left Italy each day to seek a better life elsewhere. (It must be noted here that in the same year also 190,000 repatriations occurred. But the repatriated, though of some value to Italy for the savings they brought home, scarcely made any impact on the country's economy and ethnography since most of them were past the prime of life and retired into the idleness of old age.)

In 1938, the last normal prewar year, the corresponding figures were these: 28,000 persons migrated overseas, of whom 12,000 came to the United States; 72,000 went to other European countries; and 90,000 settled elsewhere in the Mediterranean basin, mainly in North Africa. (Repatriations from overseas that year amounted to 1,300 persons only.)

By 1949 the figure had risen to 155,000 overseas migrations, of whom only

47,000,000 inhabitants, and the population growth continues at an increasing rate, as of course it does in the rest of the world. The density of population has increased between 1871 and 1947 from 90 to 150 persons per square kilometer.

Today there could be no economic desire on any invader's part to settle in this country, unless he planned to enslave completely or partly exterminate the native population. While the climate is as pleasant as ever, the natural resources, including a considerable proportion of the vital topsoil, have diminished to a disastrous degree, and only a long-term program of reforestation, watershed protection, and soil conservation would restore them for future generations. In the meantime, the land cannot nourish the teeming and ever-increasing masses. Birth control is not practiced widely or intelligently in Italy, partly because of ignorance of proper methods, partly because of the violent opposition of the Catholic Church.

Out of 18,000,000 persons who constitute the working population of Italy, no fewer than 8,000,000, or 44 per cent, derive their livelihood from agricultural pursuits. At present, 47 per cent of the entire productive surface (and only 8 per cent of Italy is reckoned totally unproductive) is agricultural.[7] Considering the rapid growth of industrialization and the increase in the number of nonagricultural workers all over the world, it is safe to assume, in the absence of national statistics for Italy, that the percentage of agricultural workers and persons who derive their livelihood from the soil directly, increases as we recede in history. As far as Roman and pre-Roman Italy are concerned, the bounty of the earth alone sustained the nation, although during the later republic and the empire an economy tending toward commercialism reduced the importance of the products of the Italian soil since imports from abroad were cheaper.

Outside of the cities and large metropolitan areas, Italians prefer to congregate in villages of various sizes rather than dot the countryside with single farms. The latter mode of dwelling is practiced only in Umbria and Tuscany to any extent. Even in completely new

---

11,000 went to the United States, but 98,000 to Argentina. There were 16,000 repatriations in that year.

[7] The percentage of arable land is approximately the same in France, Germany, and Czechoslovakia; it is higher, in Europe, only in Denmark, Hungary, Poland, and Rumania.

districts of rural resettlement such as the Pontine Marshes, towns and villages were created in which the farmers live together in preference to dwelling in dispersed homesteads and isolated estates. To be sure, landholdings are for the most part so small (and often peasants do not own the land they till) that building a farmhouse on one's acreage would be uneconomical and impractical. Besides, it used to be essential to form a community for common defense against raiders and foreign enemies, and farmers congregated for their own protection behind the walls and bastions of their towns. Last but not least, the lowlands where the fields lie are, or at least were until quite recently, often infested by malaria, hence the farmers shunned the plains and huddled together on the hilltops in crowded, grey stone villages with narrow, steep streets.

Some geographers and ethnologists say that Italians, and Mediterranean peoples in general, are fearful of isolation and love gregarity, hence move together in densely settled communities.[8] It will be difficult to prove this, or the contrary. I venture to suggest that the exigencies imposed by the surroundings and the conditions of life were the causes for creating that sense of gregarity, if it exists, and that it is not a racial trait. And this is not the only instance in this book where it will be necessary to point out that what are often called, fondly or disparagingly, common racial traits which of biological necessity produce certain results, are for the most part acquired characteristics and peculiarities in response to outside pressures.

[8] Cf. Sorre 1934, 52.

CHAPTER IV

Wealth and Poverty   Contemporary Italy is a poor country. It is poor in natural resources and because of an antiquated socio-economic system dominated by an agricultural and industrial capitalism of outmoded philosophy and behavior, based on small production and high profits per unit of product. In the course of time this has led to a catastrophically lopsided distribution of wealth and income, and to the progressive decay of the bourgeois middle class. Yet it has also become clear, I trust, that this land is so favored by its fortunate location and climate that, were it not for man's own undoing, the country could much better nourish and sustain its population. But, since 92 per cent of Italy's soil is already productive in some way, amelioration must needs come through intensification and modernization, there being obviously no room for areal extension.

We find no indication in pre-Roman days, or even during the early republic, that Italy's earth did not sufficiently provide for all its people. But there is no question that in modern Italy the productive land is not always and everywhere wisely and economically managed so as to yield a maximum crop. This is due in part to antiquated methods, to the absence of good artificial fertilizers, and perhaps mainly to the lack of interest on the farmer's part in land he does not own — land which belongs to an absentee landlord who, holding enough acreage to derive a considerable income without running his farms at full efficiency, does not particularly care to improve the output per acre, a reform which would involve great expense for reorganization and experimentation and research.[1]

While statistics showing that only 8 per cent of the entire country is unproductive and that 47 per cent is given to agriculture look impressive, the figures are fairly meaningless unless some statement is made as to precisely how much, or how little, each acre produces.

[1] Cf. also Sorre 1934, 38–39.

Hence Nissen, who certainly knew Italy, declared bluntly that "no rhetoric can refute the fact that half of Italy's soil is unplanted or unplantable, that the working population literally goes hungry despite industry and skill."[2] Although this was written three quarters of a century ago and conditions have since somewhat changed for the better, no really important progress has been made except in scattered areas.

Today, an equitable and, even more urgent, economically efficient redistribution of the soil is still one of the most pressing problems facing the government. The new Constitution of 1946 provides, in Article 44, that out of a total of 53,000,000 acres of arable land 3,700,000 should be redistributed, that is, taken away from large landowners, especially the latifundists, and turned over to small proprietors. It is provided, however, that exemption from expropriation be granted to those large landholders who can prove that their land is efficiently utilized *pro bono publico*. Of course, owners who thus lose their land receive indemnities in cash or in securities from the government, the expense to be charged to the public debt. Conversely, the new owners are not given the land outright but must pay for it. To insure that no speculation is indulged in whereby the newly distributed land would, for cash paid to the new owner, immediately revert to the latifundist and the old situation be restored (which is exactly what happened after land distributions in ancient Rome where no decree prevented resale), the law provides as part of the contract between the government and the farmer that he may not sell the land for thirty years. In order to help the new proprietor even further, perhaps sometimes against his will, he is also obliged to join government cooperatives. The demands of land-hungry peasants for a piece of ground of their own far exceed the available supply. The final selection of the lucky candidates must be made by lot.

It is necessary to mention one of the most serious causes of the decline of the economy in ancient and modern Italy, which is indeed at the bottom of much of Italy's misery and poverty. This is deforestation.

The surface occupied today by forests is given as approximately 20 per cent of the total area of Italy. However, this is an optimistic

[2] Nissen 1883, 2.1.81.

figure which includes not only true forests but also districts of shrub and maquis, which are economically unprofitable and which geographically and climatically cannot fulfill the functions of real woods. There can be no question but that in ancient Italy, through the early Roman republic, the picture was totally different, though worsening with the progress of time and the waxing power of imperialistic Rome. The older history of Rome is full of references to the wealth of forests of Italy, inherited from prehistoric times. Unrelenting deforestation without insurance of sustained yield, similar to the depredations inflicted upon the virgin forests of the American Midwest and Northwest, was initiated only by the Romans of the later republic.[3] The Monte Cimino, a short distance north of Rome, now a bare and scrubby district with some new growth, was feared as late as the third century B.C. by those Roman legions which had to cross it on their way north.[4] In the middle of the second century B.C. extensive oak forests were still standing in the Po country, where acorn-fed hogs constituted a rich source of income for local farmers.[5] No trace of such forests remains today. Even in the last century of the Roman republic the situation had grown so bad that pine for ships and other woods had to be imported from the distant regions of the Caucasus (the famous Pontic pines, named after the Pontus Euxinus, the Black Sea), and the emperor Tiberius (14–37) had to obtain his building timber from the Alps.[6] And whatever low-grade lumber for firewood had been left standing around Rome and in the Apennines down to the early Empire was given the *coup de grâce* by the immense demands for fuel consumed in the vast and numerous bathing establishments of Rome and other cities, with their hot water pools and sweating rooms,[7] and by the central heating system of the better houses, in which the hot air coming from a central heating plant was conducted under the double floors and into the double walls of the rooms.

[3] Cf. Pais 1933, 1.20.

[4] Liv. 9.36–38 reports that in 310 B.C. the Roman consul Quintus Fabius Rullianus entered this forest in the course of a war against the Etruscans, in defiance of an order from headquarters in Rome forbidding him to risk so grave a danger. Cf. Deecke 1888, 8–9.

[5] Pol. 2.15.3.

[6] Verg. *Georg.* 2.440–445; Hor. *Carm.* 1.14.11. Cf. also Nissen 1883, 1.434.

[7] In the early third century of our era there were 800 baths in Rome alone, of which the largest, the Thermae of Caracalla, could accommodate 1,600 visitors at once.

It seems that within two centuries or less the forests of Italy were burnt down to provide pastures, cut down, plundered ruthlessly, but never restored. To this day, vast tracts of the Apennines are rugged, denuded landscapes, whose soil has long since been washed away.[8]

As the eroded earth is deposited by the streams in the lowlands at the foot of the mountains along the seashore, it silts up river mouths and harbors and causes swamps. These must be drained if the country is to be made fertile and spared the ravages of malaria. Moreover, the bare mountains and hills contribute considerably to the worsening of the local climate and to prolongation and intensification of the inevitable yearly drought, since the water vapor given off by forests and falling as rain is eliminated,[9] and since the hot air rising from the barren, heated earth during the summer prevents any condensation of vapor which might lead to precipitation, such as occurs where cooler air arises from wooded areas.[10]

There is excellent evidence that the sterile area of the Roman Campagna and other parts of Latium, whose barrenness and solitude I mentioned, now fallow for two millennia, was once a fertile and

[8] Cf. Sion 1934, 299, on the frequent *frane* 'landslides' and large *calanchi* 'eroded badlands' of Italy.

[9] According to a report of the United States Forest Service in the *New York Times* of 20 August 1926, quoted by Frank 1927, 56 fn.2. In addition, Italy's present prevailing type of vegetation is, like the vegetation of all arid areas, adapted to hold and store water within the plant rather than release whatever little humidity is available: foliage does not look fat and green, but thin and greyish and yellowish, the leaves of deciduous trees are small and leathery rather than large and fleshy. The olive tree is the prototype of this sort of vegetation; its extreme form are the thorny, frugal cactuses, ubiquitous in Italy.

[10] Cf. Visintin 1947, 56. I am reminded of how Plato, *Critias* 111 B–D, describes the decay of Attica: ". . . there are remaining only the bones of the wasted body . . . all the richer and softer parts having fallen away, and the mere skeleton of the land being left. But in the primitive state of the country, its mountains were high hills covered with soil, and the plains, as they are termed by us, of Phelleus were full of rich earth, and there was abundance of wood in the mountains. Of this last the traces still remain, for although some of the mountains now only afford sustenance to bees, not so very long ago there were still to be seen roofs of timber cut from trees growing there, which were of a size sufficient to cover the largest houses; and there were many other high trees cultivated by man and bearing abundance of food for cattle. Moreover, the land reaped the benefit of the annual rainfall, not as now losing the water which flows off the bare earth into the sea, but, having an abundant supply in all places, and receiving it into herself and treasuring it up in the close clay soil, it let off into the hollows the streams which it absorbed from the heights, providing everywhere abundant fountains and rivers . . ." (Translation by B. Jowett, 3rd ed., Oxford 1892, vol. 3, p. 532.)

populous district of Italy. We know this in part from traditional and historical sources,[11] in part from archaeological exploration.

In southern Etruria and in the Roman Campagna, especially near Velletri, the ancient Velitrae, were found the remnants of a very old pre-Roman system of subterranean canals, the *cuniculi*.[12] Some scholars consider them drainage canals, designed to gather excessive moisture in the plain and to channel and regulate the water coming down from the neighboring hills for the purpose of preventing erosion of the hillsides and swamping of the lowlands. Others see in them irrigation canals. Whichever theory may be correct (I am inclined to think that, like the system of canals of the modern Po plain, the *cuniculi* served both purposes), the fact remains that Latium and the Campagna were once thriving areas, diligently worked, nourishing a numerous population which inhabited cities, many now known by name only. The capital of these Latian tribes seems to have been Alba Longa, whose exact location is not certain (it stood possibly on the ridge above Lake Albano, perhaps near the present Castel San Gandolfo). The ritual center of the people was a temple dedicated to *Iuppiter Latiaris*, which crowned the loftiest peak of the Alban Hills, now called Monte Cavo, to which they climbed in a yearly solemn procession on a road whose remnants one may still follow to the summit. The inhabitants of Alba Longa probably sent out a colony into some low hills on the left bank of the Tiber, possibly in order to guard the river which at that point was easily crossed by friend and foe since a small island divided the broad stream into two narrow branches, and in order to keep an

[11] Speaking of the Latins' war of 385 B.C. against the Volscians, who sat in the mountains and in the lowlands between the mountains and the sea to the south of Rome, Livy wonders how a tribe which occupied so small an area could muster so many and such fierce soldiers. He comes to the conclusion that ". . . there was an immeasurable multitude of freemen in those regions which in our days scarce afford a scanty seed plot for soldiers, and are only saved from becoming a waste desert by gangs of Roman slaves." (Liv. 6.12.5, *LCL*, translated by B. O. Foster.) Cf. also Liv. 1.30.33; Plin. H.N.16.10.15; Theophrastus, *Hist. Plant.*4.5.5 and 5.8.3: "The country of the Latins is well watered, the lowland contains bay, myrtle and wonderful beech: they cut timbers of it of such a size that they will run the whole length of the keel of a Tyrrhenian vessel. The hill country produces fir and silver fir. The district called by Circe's name [Circean Cape] is, it is said, a lofty promontory, but very thickly wooded, producing oak in abundance and myrtle." (*LCL*, translated by Sir Arthur Hort.)

[12] Cf. Daremberg — Saglio, the article *s.v. cuniculi*, by De La Blanchère; Koch — Mercklin — Weickert 1915, 185–190; Frank 1919, 270. See also the recent report on the cuniculi around Veii by J. B. Ward Perkins in Van Buren 1956, 394.

eye on the Etruscans who looked down, for the time being without envy or concern, from the Ianiculum Hill on the right bank of the Tiber. Below they saw a mean little village on the Palatine Hill, that beggarly hamlet that was to be Rome, the future mistress of Latium, Italy, and the world.

The swampy alluvial plains at the foot of eroded mountains and at the seashore have also been responsible for one of the greatest scourges of Italy whose influence upon the physical and psychological condition of the country and its population has been immeasurably destructive — malaria. Some of the regions that harbored the greatest cities of Greek antiquity are only now slowly awakening from the drowsy somnolence in which endemic malaria has kept them for two thousand and more years. And at least one modern authority considers this dread disease the cause of the decline and fall of the Roman Empire itself.[13] He also claims that it was first imported into Italy by Hannibal's soldiers. The cause and the nature of the disease and ways of combating it were unknown until our own days, and during all these centuries it was allowed to ravage the land.[14]

[13] Jones 1907. Concerning Greece see Jones 1909.

[14] As late as the 1880's Nissen admonishes the traveler in Italy thus: "But in many places, together with the cool air of the evening, evil miasmas penetrate into the pores of the skin, which are enlarged in consequence of the heat of the day. Experience teaches that stagnant water produces, at the height of the summer, certain diseases which are endemic in the lowlands of practically the entire world . . . The infectuous matter is furnished by the organic substances which rot in the water, and it spreads over the surrounding territory . . . [The poison] crawls along the ground . . . It is more likely to attack a sleeping than a waking person, because during sleep the activity of the vessels of the skin is intensified . . . The best protection against the poison consists first of all in a moderate, sober way of life, then in a type of warm, woolen clothing which insures against humidity and catching of cold, and finally the open fire of the hearth, and communal settlements." Nissen 1883, 1.434-444. Note the insistence upon woolen clothing and the open fire. It has sometimes been claimed that the traditional woolen toga of the Romans and the sacred, ever-burning fire in the temple of the goddess Vesta, are early indications of sanitary precautions against malaria. However, if malaria was unknown in Rome before the third century, the much older worship of Vesta and the equally ancient wearing of the toga can have nothing to do with the disease. Moreover the toga was abandoned in spite of the prevalence of malaria — though this could be explained by the fact that in the course of time its original purpose was forgotten. But also the fire of Vesta may well be a vestige of an ancient cult of the fire, that gift of Prometheus to man, snatched from the gods, which is curiously dreadful and beneficent at the same time. (See Jones 1907, 68.)

For ancient medical theories on malaria see especially Col. De re rust. 1.5.6 and Varr. De re rust. 1.12.3.

Throughout its mediaeval and modern history, the ancient *Italia* of the Romans could not again attain national or economic unity. The detriment to the people, in physical and moral terms, the detriment to the economy and productivity of the land, is obvious and is immeasurable. But since its unification some eighty years ago, Italy has made vast economic advances.

Italy is today, as no doubt it was in antiquity, particularly after the decline of grain production, the producer par excellence of grapes, olives, and all kinds of fruits. It is the Garden of Europe, its orchard and its vineyard. Grapes are grown almost everywhere in Italy, but the wines are for the most part not as renowned and widely exported as those of France and the Rhine and Mosel districts.

Olives are considerably more important to the Italian economy, not because of exportation, which is, in effect, of small account (although Italy produces one fourth of the world's yield of olive oil), but mainly because oil is, unlike wine, nutritive and cheap food, so that even home consumption has considerable beneficial effects upon national health. The size of the harvest is subject to extraordinary yearly variations (for example, it was nearly three times higher in 1947 than in 1948), which of necessity causes difficulties to growers and merchants.

Italy grows and exports a vast quantity of fresh fruits and vegetables, mainly to central and northern Europe, where they are lacking through many months of the year. It should not be forgotten, however, that some of the principal fruit and vegetable crops of today are not native to Italy and were unknown to ancient Italy and in part even during the Middle Ages. The vine and the fig tree are not really autochthonous in the Apennine peninsula, although their introduction goes back to prehistoric times. The plane tree and the pomegranate were brought to Italy by the ancient Greeks. The Romans imported the truffle from Asia Minor, radishes and walnuts from Syria, apricots, almonds, and cherries from the Near East. The mulberry tree which, as the feeder of silkworms, is the foundation of Italy's great silk industry, came from the Levant in the thirteenth century; tobacco, now a state monopoly, is a native American plant; and palm trees are African by origin. Citrus fruits were imported from Persia, India, and the Far East only in the sixteenth century. Potatoes, tomatoes, and corn (maize) came from America about the same time.[15]

What seems to have been in short supply in Roman as it is in our time, is an adequate stock of meat, especially beef, at prices which all strata of the population can afford. This may be one of the reasons why in terms of the nutritive value of the national diet, Italy is ranked in twenty-second place among thirty-two nations of the world (first is New Zealand, the United States is third, China is last), and fifteenth among eighteen European countries (Switzerland is in first place, France is ninth, the Soviet Union last).[16] What with meat prices currently (1956) in Italy on a par with those in the United States, but with wages for workers at one-fourth, and lower, of those in the United States, no relief can be expected by the natural play of the market.

Now that the population of Italy is steadily increasing whereas emigration has been radically curtailed, the only hope for Italy seems to be to make the land more fertile so that it may nourish the masses of people. This is not a program to be accomplished in a short span of time, but one that will require several generations. Forests do not grow quickly, and lands now wasted and fallow and in the hands of uncooperative owners cannot be reclaimed from one year to the next.

[15] Cf. also Olschki 1949, 13 f.
[16] Huntington 1945, 441. The information was derived from statistics of the League of Nations, but no date is given.

Part Two. The Italian Language

THE DIALECTS OF MODERN ITALY

CHAPTER V

The Dialects of Italy If to the preceding physi-
cal description of Italy and to the few shreds of its history I merely
added that, before the peninsula was united by the ancient Romans,
it was occupied by speakers of a great variety of dialects mostly unintelligible to one another, that the Romans never really forced
anyone to learn the Latin of Rome, that after the fall of the Roman
Empire the country dissolved into a kaleidoscopic shifting patch-
work of kingdoms, principalities, dukedoms, city-states, bishoprics,
and the Church State, among which communication was poor for
both geographic and political reasons, and that this disunity ended
only less than a century ago when Italy was painfully welded
into one nation: if I said merely that much, it would easily follow
from it that today the land still resounds with a bewildering multi-
formity of dialects, still to a great extent mutually unintelligible.
There does exist a standard Italian language, the one that is taught
in Italian (and foreign) schools; nonetheless a fair (though decreasing) number of Italians, possibly able to understand it and
read it, must admit that they cannot speak 'Italian,' or speak it
haltingly and with a strong regional accent.

Italian immigrants to the United States also brought with them
and continued to use among themselves their local dialects rather
than the national language. This they employed only, if they knew
it at all, on formal occasions or to communicate with speakers of
other dialects. It has even been said that newly arrived Italians
settled in America as regional and dialectal groups rather than as
national Italians.[1] Many Italo-Americans of the second generation
who come to Italy as soldiers or tourists find to their surprise that
they have learned a dialect at home; they too cannot speak 'Italian.'

To Americans and even to some American linguists the matter

[1] Vaughan 1926.

of dialects is apt to remain somewhat puzzling, unless and until they are startlingly brought to realize that it is possible, in Italy and elsewhere in Europe, for localities belonging to the same nation and no farther apart than Boston and Providence, to use pronunciations and a vocabulary which severely hinder or render impossible conversation, unless one of the interlocutors is bilingual or both use some standard idiom, be it an interregional *lingua franca* or a national standard language. If one compares, for example, the entries in the *Linguistic Atlas of the United States* with those of the *Sprach– und Sachatlas Italiens und der Südschweiz*, one wonders whether the word dialect has really been employed unambiguously and in the same sense if it serves to distinguish American English of Chicago from that of Atlanta as well as Turinese from Neapolitan. Thus, the term dialect is weakened by the elasticity of its meanings; indeed, some students would accept it only for the American example just quoted, but not for the Italian, where they would prefer to speak of different languages.

This brings us face to face with the vexed terminological problem of the difference between dialect and language. It would lead too far afield to deal with this question here. I shall, in any event, speak of Italian dialects rather than languages, perhaps for no better reason than that all of Italy once was and now is again a political unit, and does possess a national standard language.

Dialect areas can be determined by means of isoglosses, that is, lines on a map which connect points of selected identical linguistic features, thus indicating boundaries of usage. Where we are dealing with a language boundary that coincides with a national frontier, isoglosses may run in thick, concentrated bundles in such a manner that few, if any, will diverge very much from the majority. This will be rare since political boundaries are fixed more often than not with little regard for bundles of isoglosses. But coincidence of the two types of boundary can occur where the border between two fundamentally allogloss states has been stable for a long time, and where on either side the government has persistently furthered and enforced linguistic nationalization.

But within a nation, and even between two states, a dialect boundary will rarely be of such a radical type that it will actually require the natives on either side to be bilingual if they wish to talk to one another, even though the international traveler who at best has mastered national standard languages, may be obliged to switch languages between two customs houses on the highway. On the whole, dialect areas are more likely to shade over gradually, to merge into each other. This is true also within Italy, although for nearly a millennium and a half after the collapse of the Roman Empire it was torn into a number of small disparate political units. Partly it is so because for almost a thousand years previously it had been a united nation under one strong central government, partly because during its political disunity many of the local governments were imposed by unwelcome foreigners who could not, and would not, instill a sense of narrow local, dynastic allegiance in the inhabitants of Italy, and also because the boundaries of the smaller governmental units within Italy's history were fixed and undone frequently, and never enjoyed the stability which is a condition for eventual isoglossic strengthening along a political boundary.

Since the isoglosses of Italy for the most part do not run in such a way as to give unambiguous boundary lines and to obviate special problems and disputes, different scholars have proposed different dialect classifications. My presenting one rather than another is a matter of personal preference and of confidence in its author.[2]

Yet, there is one dialect boundary on which practically all scholars have agreed, though endowing it with various degrees of importance, the one that runs roughly from La Spezia on the Tyrrhenian to Rimini on the Adriatic Sea, approximately separating continental from peninsular Italy. It concerns not only Italian but Romanic dialectology as a whole, because it separates the so-called Eastern from the Western dialects of the Romania. Among the first are Rumanian, the extinct Romanic language of Dalmatia, and the dialects of Italy south of this boundary, whereas all other Romanic dialects and languages belong to the second group.[3]

[2] I am following in the main Migliorini, Storia, 1948, 60–62.
[3] The question whether there exists or not such a boundary, and whether there are or are not Eastern and Western Romanic dialects is purely one concerning terminology and not facts, and it should not be presented and argued about as one of facts. That a rather thick bundle of isoglosses forms something of a boundary along this line cannot be denied. What can be denied, but only as a matter of taste or conviction, is that the bundle is significant enough to serve for an important division of the Romanic linguistic area.

The Italian speech between the La Spezia-Rimini line and the Alps is generally called Gallo-Italian, the name itself indicating one of the reasons for its peculiarities, that is, the Gallic (Keltic) linguistic substratum of the region which the Romans called Gallia Cisalpina.[4] The entire area can be divided into four dialectal subdistricts which are all named, as is generally true in Italy, after geographic or historic regions. They are the areas of the Piemontese, the Ligurian, the Lombard, and the Emilian dialects. Only the easternmost part of the Po plain, and Istria, are occupied by dialects belonging to the second large northern group called Venetian, the name again recalling the pre-Roman inhabitants of the country, the Veneti. To this group belong Venetian proper, Trentine, and Istrian.

Crossing the La Spezia-Rimini line at the Tyrrhenian coast we come upon the Tuscan dialects, among which are Florentine, Western Tuscan (Lucca, Pisa), and Southern Tuscan (Siena, Arezzo). The Corsican dialects are closely related to Tuscan. But as the island is a French possession (since 1768), the French standard language is of necessity gaining ground, especially among the educated, at the expense of the native dialects.

The fifth group of peninsular dialects, those of Central Italy, lies to the east and south of Tuscan and comprises Northern Latian, Umbrian, Marchigiano (the idioms of the Marche), and Modern Roman. (Old Roman, until the sixteenth century, was rather a southern type of speech.)

The remainder of the peninsula and Sicily belong to the southern Italian dialects: Southern Latian, Abruzzese, Campanian, Calabrian, Apulian, and Sicilian, each further divisible into a great number of local speech forms.

Certain idioms within the confines of the present Italian state and spoken by relatively few persons are linguistically not considered Italian proper. On the island of Sardinia one distinguishes northern (Gallurese), central (Logodurese), and southern (Campidanian) dialects, all of them belonging to what most scholars prefer to call the Sardinian, or Sardic language, which is an independent branch of the Romanic family and too different from the dialects of Italy to be classed with them.

[4] For a discussion of substrata see Chapter XXIVb.

In Friuli, and in the Alto Adige and some valleys of the Dolomites, as also in the Swiss canton Grisons (Graubünden), a relatively small number (about half a million) of persons speak dialects usually classified together (for no good reason of historical or descriptive dialectology) under the heading Raeto-Romanic (for no better terminological reason; some prefer to call them Ladin). But these dialects seem to many scholars sufficiently different from the surrounding Romanic idioms so as to merit a separate category. They may be subdivided into three more easily manageable and justifiable subgroups: Friulian (in Friuli, the region between the Alps and the head of the Adriatic Sea, with the capital at Udine), Ladin (in the Alto Adige and the Dolomites), and, in Switzerland, Romansh (in the upper Rhine and Inn valleys).

Provençal and Franco-Provençal are spoken in regions along the Franco-Italian frontier from Ventimiglia northward toward Turin, and in the numerous valleys descending toward the Po River. A Franco-Provençal speech island exists also in the localities of Faeto and Celle S. Vito, in the province of Foggia in Apulia.

Rumanian is spoken by some 2,500 persons in Istria. But this Istro-Rumanian has undergone considerable changes under the influence of its powerful neighbors, Italian and Slovene.

As for Italian dialects outside of Italy one should mention Ticinese, spoken in the Swiss canton Ticino, south of the St. Gotthard Pass. On the Balkan side of the Adriatic, Dalmatian and Vegliotic (of which the former died out at the end of the fifteenth, the latter at the end of the nineteenth century), though by some classified as Italian dialects, are generally regarded as independent languages.

The number of speakers of non-Romanic dialects in Italy today is very small, and political and cultural influences combine to force such persons to be at least bilingual if not to give up gradually their native idioms altogether. German is spoken by many of the inhabitants of Venezia Tridentina, in what was formerly the Austrian South Tirol, with Merano and Bolzano as its centers. The Fascist regime exerted enormous pressure to Italianize the Tirolians in speech, aiming for a resultant transfer of political allegiance in this recently ceded territory. After World War II, these none too successful attempts were abandoned, and today the region is officially bilingual. Because of its prosperity and progress it is attracting a great number of native speakers of Italian, especially Southerners, so that the relative number of speakers of German is bound to decrease.

In the extreme south, in a number of villages of southern Calabria and in the Terra d'Otranto of the Sallentine peninsula, Greek is spoken. The controversy as to the provenance of this idiom in southern Italy has been going on for three quarters of a century. Some say that the Greek now used in these villages goes back to the settlements of Byzantine Greeks in the early Middle Ages;[5] others insist that it is a direct continuation of the Greek spoken in Magna Graecia of pre-Roman days.[6] The problem is of interest far beyond its local importance because it touches upon questions of principle. On the whole, it seems to me that Rohlfs and his followers, who claim an ancient Greek continuity, have made a better case.[7] As one would expect, Greek is declining with increasing speed: it prevailed in forty-nine villages in the sixteenth century, in twenty-nine about 1750, and in twelve, according to Rohlfs's count, in 1928.[8]

There is also a number of Albanian settlements in Lucania, Apulia, Calabria, and Sicily, whose language was brought to Italy in the fifteenth and sixteenth centuries by refugees fleeing the Turkish occupation of their country. But, for Italy as a whole, the speakers of neither Greek nor Albanian are of linguistic importance.[9]

Sloveñe is spoken in Istria, and Serbo-Croatian by a few Slavic settlers in the province of Campobasso in the Molise.

In the history of the Italian language since Dante, two closely allied facts stand out: the tenacity and importance of local dialects, and the ineffectiveness and tardiness of linguistic standardization through the use of an official literary language. Just as the political

[5] Morosi 1870, 1878, 1890; Alessio 1934, 1938, 1939, 1941, 1943; Maccarrone 1926; Battisti 1927, 1930, 1933.

[6] Rohlfs 1926, 1928, 1933, 1937, 1947.

[7] Migliorini, Manuscript chapter I, suggests a compromise: the two factions are not really so far apart since even Rohlfs admits that the hold of Greek had become very tenuous by the time it was in fact invigorated through fresh Byzantine immigrations.

[8] Rohlfs 1928, 130.

[9] Rohlfs 1926, 135 ff.

history of the land is rather that of its different parts and of the continuous struggle over them by the great European powers — France, Spain, Germany, and the Church State — so the linguistic history of Italy, if it were to be told in full, would be the history of the various dialects. Italy, unfortunately, was not only the coveted prize in these conflicts but also the battlefield, and Italians were forever put to fight against each other under foreign emperors and generals. And whenever Italy did not contribute the blood of its citizens, it did waste its resources and wealth on enterprises that were neither undertaken in its interest nor terminated to its advantage. Moreover, and especially in the late Middle Ages and during the Renaissance, the lack of national guidance and direction led to an exaggerated separatism among the small Italian republics and city-states of the north, which bled and destroyed one another in hateful internecine wars, sometimes on their own initiative to gain economic advantage, but more often under the prodding of popes and emperors, as pawns in the unending contest for power between the secular and spiritual masters of Europe. The wars of Ghibellines and Guelphs, the raging feuds of Milan, Genoa, Pisa, Florence, Siena, Venice, are among the most distressing chapters of Italian history.

In addition, straight across the peninsula the Church State cut a big swath out of the land, cleaving Italy into two regions which remained removed from and little known to one another, living under different governments and developing different social and economic systems.

At no time since Rome, and later Ravenna, had ceased to be the capital of the Western Roman Empire, did Italy have a national capital and a national dynasty until the second half of the nineteenth century. Hence it also lacked an intellectual center of national prominence whose dialect could outshine and set itself above other types of local speech. One should compare this with France, which has been a compact nation ever since it became, after the division of Charlemagne's empire (843), the property of one of his grandsons. The royal court established itself not long thereafter (987) in Paris, it attracted the nobility, scholars, artists, persons of learned and social prestige. Thus the language of Paris and the Ile de France, as used by the court and the illustrious persons of the capital, set the tone and became the standard in speech and writing, slowly but inexorably overcoming its rival dialects, among which especially Provençal for a time threatened the northern hegemony. Deviations from Parisian standard French are still considered, by the purity-conscious Frenchmen, as provincialisms, of which everyone aspiring to social and intellectual prominence tries to rid himself, as he does of all the other appurtenances and behavior that might stamp him a boor and a bumpkin.

Compare the Italian situation with that of Spain which also, as Christendom painfully reconquered the Iberian peninsula after the long Moslem occupation (755–1492), took its linguistic cue from the reigning house and its capital, first at Burgos, then at Madrid, where the political, intellectual, and artistic center of the land came into being and whence Castilian derived its dominance over the other dialects of Spain.

Compare this with Germany where, although the country as a whole labored long under political disunity, linguistic standardization at least found the necessary prestige centers at the court of the Habsburg emperors. In addition, Germany had Luther who in his translation of the Bible (1522–1534) provided a model that could not fail to become familiar to millions and around which a literary language could grow. And it also had its forceful and fortunate language reformers and guardians, like Gottsched (1700–1766) and Klopstock (1724–1803), who, unlike their overly garrulous and ineffective Italian counterparts, of whom I shall speak, were less given to theoretical wrangling but instead, by their own literary work in prose and poetry, showed the way to the establishment of a *Schriftsprache*.

In Italy, during the same period, communications were poor for geographical, political, but also intellectual reasons. The reading public remained small, and literary works could not find a great national audience which would eventually imitate their language. Since political questions of course did not concern a national audience either, debates on a nation-wide scale on questions of government and politics were lacking also. Philosophical and scientific treatises and discussions not only did not interest the unlettered masses but indeed, if they found their way into manuscripts and printed books, were published until Galileo's time (1564–1642) and even thereafter in Latin, which was particularly tenacious in Italy for learned intercourse, partly because speakers of Italian in one form or another can learn Latin more easily than others, partly because of the pervading and immediate influence of the Roman church with its strong Latin tradition.

In the absence of unifying agencies, indeed in the presence of so many disunifying forces of a geographic, political, and intellectual nature, it is not surprising that the dialects of Italy retained, each in its own district, an unusual degree of vigor and distinctiveness down to our times. Whether this is good or bad, whether one should deplore the linguistic disjointedness of the nation or rejoice in the wealth of its tongues, is a matter of taste, depending on one's point of view. No judgment need be attempted here. In any event, future developments, whether they bring a continuation or a leveling off of dialects, will in no wise be determined by any linguist's opinion but will be entirely guided by the shaping of cultural forces.

CHAPTER VI

The Italian Standard Language

The creation and rise of the Italian standard language by no means coincided with the birth of the national state in 1861. Its creator (for there is one, oddly enough) was not Garibaldi but Dante, nearly six centuries earlier.[1]

In his *De vulgari eloquentia*, written at the beginning of the fourteenth century, Dante surveyed the languages of Europe (dividing them into three families, Greek, Germanic, and Romanic), of the Romania (where he established *oc*, *oil*, and *si* dialects, corresponding to the three words for 'yes'), and of Italy. Here he distinguished fourteen major different dialects, seven on either side of the Apennines, each further subdivided (1.8–10). Among these he found none suitable for literary use because of varied intrinsic shortcomings (1.11–15). What Italy needed, he thought, was a noble literary language which was constructed out of all the dialects, preserving a core of common features and discarding local peculiarities. This new language he would call *volgare illustre*, or *cardinale*, or *aulico*, or *curiale*.

The theory of peeling off, as it were, dialectal vagaries like the petals of an artichoke until there remains the small but delicious heart, may possibly look intriguing at first sight. But if viewed realistically, flaws appear to the critical eye of the linguist.

First of all, as the heart of the artichoke is not a whole artichoke, so a de-dialectalized language, incorporating only the common denominator of all related dialects of a nation, would be a poor thing indeed, surely not one that Dante himself would have employed. And he did not. It would remind one, *mutatis mutandis*, of Basic English, which, useful though it may appear for purposes of rudimentary communication and commercial correspondence,

---

[1] Cf. Devoto 1954, 56–61.

could scarcely obtain or even claim the title of an English *volgare illustre*.

Second (though this is a point which Dante himself could hardly have perceived), in the history of a great number of languages out of whose dialects a literary standard was to emerge, the process never occurred as Dante envisioned it. Rather, it came about in such a way that one of the existing dialects, for cultural, geographic, political, or intellectual reasons attained prestige and supremacy over the others to such a degree that it became the model, the standard for all formal linguistic expression, be it literary or learned, prosaic or poetic. Its stuff and its style came to be exalted among the everyday, humdrum, and often 'vulgar' types of speech.

This is the main reason why, in most areas of diversity between dialect and standard language, there attaches a social prestige to the latter. Hence it is generally taught and used in the schools(except in German Switzerland where the use of Swiss German, unintelligible to users of other kinds of German dialects, bears no social stigma but is indeed encouraged), and why children are instructed carefully on when to talk 'nicely,' that is, not in the local dialect. And in some circles the young are even shielded from contamination by the non-standard speech (except again in Switzerland).

But, of all these social and cultural conditions and implications in the selection and the spread of a standard language Dante knew nothing. His prescription for the creation of a *volgare illustre* (so called of course not in the sense of 'vulgar' but only in opposition to learned Latin) therefore runs counter to what one would consider the normal formation of a literary standard language, that is, one arising in accordance with the norms of human social and cultural, including linguistic, behavior.

Third, and most importantly, the language Dante himself used in his *Divina Commedia* (though not in all other writings) was not at all his theoretical *volgare illustre*, but his own native dialect, though stripped of some local peculiarities. It was, in fact, Florentine.[2]

The beginnings of another literary language had been discern-

[2] Bertoni 1938, 122, calls it a "fiorentino . . . smunicipalizzato, sregionalizzato, nazionalizzato," 'a dismunicipalized, disregionalized, nationalized Florentine.'

ible before Dante, that of the Sicilian School, which found its best expression at the court of Frederick II, at Palermo, in the first half of the thirteenth century. Himself a German of the house of Hohenstaufen, Frederick had assembled around him with a remarkable display of national, racial, and religious tolerance unusual for his day, Italians, Germans, Normans, Moslems, who imparted to his court a unique brilliance and intellectual animation. But the fall of the Hohenstaufen dynasty signified also the termination of this noble if untimely experiment, and with it the end of the Sicilian School of poetry. Palermo fell into the hands of the house of Aragon, as Naples became the property of the French royal house of Anjou, and with them narrowness, intolerance, and jealous parochialism shrouded the South for centuries to come.

Unfortunately we cannot be certain as to what the language of the Sicilian School was like because all manuscripts which transmit its poetry to us come from Tuscany and were generously Tuscanized. But this in itself is significant, for it was apparently to Tuscany that the spark passed from Sicily. In the free cities of ancient Etruria southern poetry flourished anew, somewhat changed and liberated from the strict exigencies of a courtly style, exigencies, however, which had contributed, as they had in Provençal poetry, greatly to its charms. Even at that early time, Florentine was so much in the ascendancy that Guido Guinizelli, the first lyric poet of the new direction, though himself Bolognese, gave his language a decidedly Florentine coloring. After him came the poets of the so-called *dolce stil nuovo*, 'the sweet new style,' all Florentines, and finally Dante himself, also a true Florentine, no matter how much he, the Ghibelline and imperialist, came to abhor and revile his home town because it went Guelphic and papist. So it is true that even before Dante, Tuscan, particularly Florentine, had acquired great prestige. But whether without Dante it would have enjoyed the fate of but transient glory like the language of the Sicilian School it is difficult to say. To me, at least, it seems that it would.

There can be little doubt that the modern Italian standard language is still fundamentally and principally the dialect of Tuscany, especially of Florence (again, as in Dante's use of it, without peculiar localisms such as, for example, the *gorgia toscana*, 'Tuscan throat,' because of which *la casa* is pronounced *la hasa*). The question which some have raised is whether this supremacy of Tuscan is due to Dante, and Boccaccio and Petrarch, or to certain qualities inherent in the dialect itself. As a linguist, I recoil almost instinctively from arguments pleading the intrinsic excellence of a language. To my mind, a language, being a feature and a vehicle of culture (in the anthropological and sociological sense; see below, Chapter VII), exists in the shape of, and performs according to the demands put upon it by this culture and its bearers. A judgment on the quality of language is therefore by implication one on the quality of a culture, and it is at least doubtful whether in the present context, in the comparison of the various dialect and culture areas of Italy, 'good' and 'bad' are appropriate terms. Nor can aesthetic impressions of linguistic quality, a language's beauty or ugliness,[3] concern us here, because such canons vary from man to man and from era to era.

However, in the case of Tuscan, something can be said in favor of arguing from its quality, but not, as we shall see, from an absolute but only from a relative, period-bound, culture-bound point of view. I have already mentioned how, among the welter of dialects of mediaeval Italy, it was Latin that furnished an unperturbed point of reference for all cultural endeavors on a higher plane, that Latin was the *lingua franca* of the intelligentsia of Italy and the western world. Dante, the mediaeval man par excellence, and all the others of his time and long after him to whom the education of the mind and the soul were dear, formed part of this intelligentsia. Hence he was, as they all were, imbued with a reverence and love for Latin as the vessel in which all secular and spiritual wisdom was contained. Whoever wanted to quench his thirst had to drink from it and no other. When there arose a desire, or a need, whatever its deeper roots, to create or discover a vulgar tongue equally worthy and capable of lofty thoughts and words, it was not unnatural that in the search for this tongue nearness to Latin should be an important criterion.

Now it is obvious that no Italian dialect, of the thirteenth century any more than of today, could really in grammar, syntax, hence

---

[3] Kristeller 1946, 57 finds in Tuscan "clarity, beauty" — which is irrelevant, and "proximity to Latin" — about which I shall speak presently.

also in style, imitate Latin in a significant degree. Above all, the wealth of Latin inflexions had been severely curtailed, necessitating certain adjustments which distanced Italian from Latin — without of course, in our eyes, making it a worse or poorer language, though one of a fundamentally different structure. Where Latin had been able to say, guided by aesthetical preference alone, *pater amat filium, pater filium amat, amat pater filium, amat filium pater, filium amat pater, filium pater amat,* all of them meaning, thanks to sufficient morphemic signaling devices and regardless of word order, 'the father loves the son,' Italian, like English, having lost most of the Latin inflexional equipment, can express the same meaning only as *il padre ama il figlio,* all deviations from this construction being virtually impossible in prose, and tolerable in poetry only if the context furnishes sufficient information as to who is the grammatical subject and who is the object. This withering of signaling suffixes alone sufficed to render all but impossible in Italian the majestic sweep of a long Classical Latin period with its array of rhetorical and stylistic artifices, especially those built on word order and rhythm (compare Cicero's *clausulae*), so highly prized by ancient and modern literati. In this respect, then, all Italian dialects must have seemed to lovers of Latin equally impoverished and irremediably and dismally inelegant.

Hence nearness to Classical Latin had to be sought in other features of the future Italian language: in its sounds, its vocabulary, and possibly in idiomatic expressions and phrases. The question we must ask ourselves, therefore, is whether Tuscan qualified on these grounds above other Italian dialects, at least in the eyes and to the ears of laymen. I am inclined to think that it did, and does.[4] But I arrived at this conclusion not by way of a scientific, statistical investigation (for which it would be virtually impossible to devise a method), but through a pragmatic rule of thumb which is purely impressionistic. Yet for this very reason, it seems to me, it corresponds to the pragmatic, nonscientific approach and judgment open to mediaeval Italians who were learned but not linguists, and is therefore admissible for my present purpose. It is simply this: as among speakers of Romanic idioms those native to Italy learn Latin more easily than the rest, so among native

[4] Cf. Devoto 1954, 61.

speakers of Italian dialects those of Tuscan speech have the advantage of their fellows. This statement can easily be confirmed by teachers of Latin. From this one can conclude, I believe, that there is a closeness between Tuscan and Latin greater than that between Latin and other dialects.[5]

However, I cannot believe that for reasons of closeness to Latin, Tuscan was also more easily intelligible to speakers of a greater number of Italian dialects than another living dialect would have been, as a sort of *lingua franca*, and that it was therefore singled out.[6] Indeed it seems to me that the two claims are incompatible: the dialect nearest to Latin was *ipso facto* less, not more, comprehensible to speakers of dialects farther removed from Latin. Therefore, if my argument on the relationship of Latin and Tuscan is valid at all, as I think it is, only those few who knew Latin could be cognizant of it, and only they could favor Tuscan over the other Italian dialects for this particular reason. The ordinary speaker of Tuscan knew nothing of any closeness of his dialect with Latin, or of any remoteness of other dialects from it, and the same goes for the speaker of other Italian idioms. Hence there can be no question of a popular preference, and Dante, in calling his a *volgare illustre, aulico, curiale, cardinale*, indicated by this very choice of epithets that he was aiming chiefly for noble and courtly qualities rather than amenities and advantages appealing to the masses.

It is an interesting question to ponder whether Tuscan could have become Italian par excellence also without Dante and the other two great Florentines, Boccaccio and Petrarch, the triad of greatest luster in Italian literary history. In a hypothetical question of this kind opinions are not easily supported by facts.[7] But,

[5] This runs counter to a basic tenet of the Neolinguistic school according to which Italian, being of a central area in relation to Latin, should exhibit a greater tendency toward innovation than the other Romanic languages which belong to peripheral areas (see Bonfante 1943). But this theory is open to a number of serious objections when it deals with linguistic areas which do not have one common socio-cultural center, in relation to which alone the terms 'central' and 'marginal' are definable. For Roman Italy this center was Rome; for mediaeval Italy and the Romania no such unique center exists. Cf. Palmer 1954, 26–28.

[6] Wartburg 1943, 203.

[7] This may explain (though not excuse) a single author's giving two contradictory answers in the same book; see Bodmer 1944, 312 and 348, respectively: "Modern Italian, as the accepted norm for Italy as a whole, is based on the dialect of Florence, which owes its prestige to the works of Dante, Petrarch, and Boccaccio and their sponsors, the master printers." "The dominant dialect was

judging again by what we learn from other language areas and the behavior of standard languages, together with what we know of the reaction to and consequences of pure theorizing on linguistic reforms without the setting up of a real model and without the imposition of nonlinguistic pressures, I should venture to say that without Dante, at least, Tuscan would have had no greater chance than Roman or Neapolitan or Lombard. Indeed I should go so far as to suggest that if Dante had been a child of Naples, and, providentially, Boccaccio and Petrarch also, Neapolitan and not Tuscan would have become Italy's national language.

Although Tuscan most likely occupied a favored position because of certain intrinsic qualities, and though perhaps the constellation of Dante, Boccaccio, and Petrarch was a singularly brilliant and propitious one, I should not for a moment believe that Tuscan made Dante, as some scholars seem to think, but that on the contrary Dante made Tuscan into Italian. Unlike in other European countries, in which a concatenation of cultural and physical circumstances exalted a local dialect above the others to become the tongue of the nation, in Italy this was the feat of a man, no less impressive and gigantic for being succored by factors outside him. If this touches upon a larger question in the philosophy of linguistics and history, and if my opinion concerning Dante is taken to imply that I believe, though not necessarily in a Carlislean or Nietzschean sense, that great men shape history to a more important degree than history moulds heroes to do its purposes, then let me be so counted.

Given the cultural situation of Italy, and the scholarly temper of the times, it was to be expected that Dante's language would not be rapidly and universally accepted.

As for the first, during the fourteenth century Italy was far from needing or being able to use efficiently a single national tongue for everyday intercourse. Besides, the works and ideas of Dante neither spread quickly nor did they penetrate deeply among the common people. Only in 1470 were books first printed in *volgare*, starting of course with an edition of the Bible, and followed by three editions of each of Dante's *Commedia*, Boccaccio's *Decam-*

---

that of Florence, which owed its prestige less to the poems of Dante, Petrarch, and Boccaccio than to a flourishing textile industry and wealthy banking houses."

erone, and Petrarch's *Canzoniere*. (It is known, however, that of these Great Three, Petrarch himself prized his works in Latin, a language he had mastered superbly, much higher than those in the 'vulgar tongue.') Once books in the new language were printed, the need for some orthographic standardization and for a grammatical codification became pressing. Both requirements were met before long by the Venetian Pietro Bembo, the first legislator of Italian, in his *Prose della volgar lingua* of 1525. But the struggle had merely begun.

As for the second, the scholarly temper of the times, the rise of the Tuscan language fell into a time of retrospection toward classical antiquity, expressed in the ideas and works of the Humanists.[8] To them, infused with a predilection for ancient culture, the intended enthronement of a vulgar tongue side by side with, or even above Queen Latin seemed an indignity and an outrage. Typical of their sentiments is a passage from a letter of the outstanding Florentine Humanist, Niccolò de' Niccoli (1363–1437), concerning Dante whom he calls the "poet of shoemakers and bakers": "Therefore I should exclude this poet of yours [Dante] from the company of literary men and should leave him with the girdle-makers, bakers, and that kind of crowd; for he talks in such a way that it seems he would rather want to be associated with that sort of people." Poetry seemed to these scholarly souls a mere trifling with words unless it were done in Latin. But Classical Latin had by then become a thoroughly dead language, a beautiful mummy, which even the sweet voices and most passionate entreaties of the Muses could not resuscitate. So the fourteenth century later earned for itself the name of *Secolo senza poesia*, the Century without poetry. The anti-volgare faction found its first vociferous spokesman in Leon Battista Alberti, in the middle of the fifteenth century.

Thus Italians girt themselves for the great battle of the *Questione della lingua*, which in some measure, though with less acrimony, occupies some Italians, scholars and amateurs, even in our day.[9] The basic problem was to decide in theory, first, whether Italian or Latin was more worthy of becoming the national lan-

[8] Cf. Devoto 1954, 69–86.
[9] For a full history of it see Labande-Jeanroy 1925; Hall 1942; Migliorini, *Questione*, 1948.

guage of Italy, and second, if it was to be Italian, which dialect should be chosen and by what means it should be propagated.

It surely can be said with full justification, and this is the measure of its futility, that this controversy carried on for centuries among the learned and pseudo-learned has scarcely deflected the course of linguistic history in Italy. Previous and subsequent events show decisively that the answers to all these questions had in practice been anticipated and started on their unremitting way toward realization with Dante's *Commedia*. Nonetheless, the fight dragged on, gathering as it went, not speed, but a plethora of subsidiary issues: Tuscanism versus Anti-Tuscanism (with Dante anomalously the titular head of both factions, for the first as a practitioner of Tuscan, for the second as an anti-Tuscan theoretician); Archaism versus Anti-Archaism (from the sixteenth century on); the Gallicists, or imitators of French, versus the Anti-Gallicists (a problem arising in the eighteenth century in the wake of French artistic and intellectual leadership, at issue equally in Spain and Germany). Within these basic positions a variety of combinations was possible, so that one could be Tuscanist and Anti-Archaist, but also Anti-Tuscanist and Archaist, and so forth.[10]

In France, the year 1539 brought forth the Ordinance of Villers-Cotterets which established French in the place of Latin as the language of the law courts, of state records, and of all official business. For Italy as a whole no such royal fiat was possible, nothing of the kind took place in any section of the country anywhere near that date (although in Florence at least, the vulgar tongue was made obligatory in the *tribunali commerciali* as early as 1414[11]). Yet over all the opposition briefly outlined, Tuscan did make headway. When the famous Jacopo Sannazaro (1458–1530), a Neapolitan, whom some overly enthusiastic admirers called the Christian Vergil, first wrote his *Arcadia* between the years 1481 and 1496, his language was naturally strongly colored by his native linguistic habits; but the *editio princeps* (1504) of the enormously successful pastoral romance in prose and verse was thoroughly Tuscanized. In 1525, the already mentioned *Prose* by Bembo made the

[10] Hall 1942, 3–7; see also *ibid.* the bibliography, 57–61, listing eighty-five primary works dealing with the *Questione della lingua.*
[11] Kristeller 1946, 58.

Three Great Tuscans the official models for Italian writing. In 1582, the *Accademia della Crusca* was founded in Florence with the aim, like its successors and imitators, the French and Spanish Academies, to watch over the purity and propriety of usage of the national tongue. Not long after its foundation, the Accademia began the publication of an Italian dictionary, which also was to become the model for dictionaries of the French (1694) and Spanish (1726–39) Academies, as well as for Samuel Johnson's *Dictionary of the English language* (1747–1755). But owing to the quarrels over the *Questione della lingua*, the problem of what the national language should be, and how it should be named, had become so embattled that the first suggestion for the title of the dictionary, of 1608, *Vocabolario della lingua toscana degli Accademici della Crusca*, and the second, of 1610, *Vocabolario della lingua toscana cavato dagli scrittori e uso della città di Firenze* ("Dictionary of the Tuscan language by the A.d.C.," and "Dictionary of the Tuscan language compiled from the writers and the usage of the city of Florence," respectively) were laid aside as too biased in favor of Florence. The first edition of 1612 appeared with the innocuous title *Vocabolario degli Accademici della Crusca*, which of course in no wise changed the Tuscan orientation of the work nor its influence.[12]

It is remarkable that among the three most important Romanic countries Italy was the first to produce a dictionary of a model language yet the least successful in propagating this language among its people. Neither in Spain nor in France did the standard language remain for as long as it did in Italy the prerogative of the learned and literary, a *Schriftstellersprache* much more than a *Schriftsprache*, the medium of expression of the literati much more than of the mere literate. The explanation for this precocity in codification is the rise and the enormous influence of the three great Tuscan stars, and the illustrious and nostalgic precedent of Classical Latin, so much closer to the hearts and eyes and ears and tongues of Italians than of other speakers of Romanic. And the reason for the sluggishness of Tuscan toward becoming a national language lies of course in the absence of political national unity, which both France and Spain enjoyed much earlier.

[12] Cf. Migliorini, Lingua, 1948, 96.

During the seventeenth century the use of Tuscan, or Italian, as one may well call it now, began finally to encroach upon the sciences, thanks above all to the Italian writings of Galileo Galilei and his disciples.

But ever since Dante it had been emphasized that this *volgare* was meant to be *illustre*, that it should serve the higher forms of literate and literary endeavors and should acquire a linguistic dignity, not to say ponderousness, commensurate with its lofty purposes. Italian followed this line of development all the more easily since its use was, as I have repeatedly noted, pretty much restricted to an intellectual clientele, with the common people in the small geographic, political, and dialectal subdivisions of Italy continuing their local speech habits, and feeling neither an urge nor a need for a thorough linguistic standardization. It was only the nineteenth century that slowly began to crush the shell of pedantry and academicism that had been progressively encasing written Italian and threatened to alienate it, another Classical Latin, completely from the everyday usage of even the literate and intelligent classes.

The impetus toward a reform came first from writers who followed the rise of romanticism, realism, and naturalism in French and German literature. It became quite impossible to do justice to the subjects and styles of the new schools through the medium of a formal, stiff, cranky language such as written Italian had become. One way out of the difficulty was for writers to turn to local dialects as the most suitable, indeed the only available form of unimpeded expression. Hence the century brings forth an important production in dialect literature.[18] The danger of this trend was of course that Italy reached the verge of creating literatures, instead of a national literature, and of continuing and strengthening local particularism.

Fortunately Tuscan found a reformer, indeed perhaps a savior, in the person of the novelist Alessandro Manzoni (1785–1873). His theoretical writings on linguistic matters extend through some fifty years of his long life; their practical application is laid down in his great novel, *I promessi sposi*, 'The Betrothed.' In the first edition, of 1825–26, the three volumes of the work could not

---

[18] See Tilgher 1930, 5–10.

deny the authorship by a Lombard who only with some effort had learned to handle Tuscan; but the much changed and improved second edition, of 1840–42, appeared, not unlike Sannazaro's second *Arcadia* nearly two hundred and fifty years earlier, in new Tuscan garb. While Manzoni thereby acknowledged the supremacy of Dante's idiom, he also insisted that, the first and foremost requirement for a language being its usability and appropriateness, borrowing from other dialects and even foreign languages, and above all a rapprochement with the spoken vernacular were not only permissible but indeed mandatory for the health of the living tongue.

Manzoni's pursuits were furthered by a political climate, embodied in the term *risorgimento*, 'resurgence,' which tended toward an awakening and progressive strengthening of national consciousness, and which was to culminate in the final attainment of Italian national unity in 1861. In the *Promessi sposi*, the description of Lombardy's plight under Spanish domination in the seventeenth century was but a thinly disguised lament over the province's contemporary misfortunes under the rule of France, and the effect was not lost upon the readers. It was a time in which a democratic tendency, showing itself all over Europe in the epidemic revolutionary outbreaks of 1848, a desire to shake off tyranny, and, in Italy, a will to political liberation and unification, not only favored and bolstered the establishment of a national language accessible to all classes, but indeed rendered necessary the new readable and pliable Manzonian prose in the place of the old Dantesc *volgare illustre*. That language was now hoary and gouty with age, its strength having been sapped by time and by the quacks who had all but embalmed it.

Again, as in the case of Dante, one is left to wonder what would have been the fate of Italian if Manzoni had not entered the hustings ever clamorous and dusty with the battle of the *Questione della lingua*, championing his worthy cause not only by words but also by deeds. Obviously Manzoni is not in any measure or sense as important a figure as Dante, but it is nonetheless thinkable that Dante's Italian might have shared the fate of Cicero's Latin, that is, become a petrified classical language completely out of touch with modern requirements and out of reach of the ordinary man. The rise of dialect literature just mentioned was a portent of this deficiency and danger.

Perhaps without Manzoni, though this is entirely hypothetical, the dialect of the Eternal City would have become a new literary standard, owing to the emergence of Rome as the capital of a united nation, and Tuscan relegated to the honored but sterile role of a classical language.

And this brings us to the last act, or in any event the latest, of the *Questione*, concerning the part which the idiom of Rome, now the political and intellectual center of Italy, was to, or should be made to play. Dante, reviewing the dialects in *De vulgari eloquentia*, called Roman a *tristiloquium*, a dismal kind of talk, the vilest of all Italy (1.11). Though his judgment was no doubt colored by the personal antipathy which a Ghibelline and imperialist felt toward papist Rome, it seems that the once greatest city on earth had then fallen so low economically, politically, and culturally, and had suffered such a loss of prestige in Italy, that there was little chance for its dialect to conquer a position of prevalence even if there had been no Florentine like Dante.[14] Because of this and in consequence of the later rise of Tuscan, the Romans became the victims of a linguistic inferiority complex. As late as 1861, the Roman popular writer Gioacchino Belli, a truly fine poet who wrote in the Roman vernacular (and whose monument stands, appropriately, in the populous Trastevere quarter), said he dared not translate the Gospel of St. Matthew into the lowly Roman dialect because he feared it would be an act of irreverence toward the Holy Book.[15] But the linguistic self-confidence of Rome increased with the city's ascendancy as the capital of the nation, and voices have been heard to demand that the Roman dialect take its "rightful place," that, at least, the Roman way ought to take precedence and become standard wherever it did not agree with Florentine. It should also be remembered that Rome now (in 1957) has well over one million inhabitants, as compared with some 200,000 in 1870.

Unfortunately, much of the reasoning on linguistic preference

[14] Cf. below, end of Chapter XXIX.
[15] Belli 1906, I.ccxxix. See also Migliorini 1933, 375–377.

and prestige is still in good *Questione* style, that is, irrelevant and irrational. Does Roman deserve the crown because of its "beautiful and warm accent"? Do arguments on age and reverence and patriotism have any pertinence? Does linguistic legislation by linguists and academies and parliaments make much sense in our time? Until another Dante arises, and until the same cultural and linguistic conditions repeat themselves, the linguistic history of Italy will be determined, literally, by *uox populi* [16] — although popular decision may be aided and given a direction by the endeavors of scholars like Migliorini, who takes a fully reasonable position and has suggested *glottotecnica* as a name for this technique of applied linguistics.[17]

In our days of steadily improving communication through increased literacy, the press, radio, television, the talking pictures, and of greater mobility of the population through a more dense and more rapid system of transportation by road, rail, and air, and, last but not least, the mingling of speakers of many dialects in military service both in peace and war, the leveling of dialectal divergencies and the spread of the national language in Italy is bound to progress apace, barring such cultural changes as we have recognized as capable of retarding, impeding, or fully reversing the trend.

[16] Cf. Devoto 1954, 145–158. From an article by Aldo Valori on the *terza pagina* 'the third (that is, the literary and critical) page' of the Roman newspaper *Il Messaggero* of 1 February 1955, I am quoting the following passages: "The new Dictionary will undoubtedly solve 99,000 out of 100,000 cases [of doubtful pronunciation], but there will always remain that 100,000th case in which uncertainty will be not only permissible but indeed obligatory. And precisely this case will leave to the pronunciation, indeed to the Italian language as a whole, this margin of arbitrariness which will convert it into an imperfect but live, rather than perfect but embalmed thing. . . . If the Dictionary of 200,000 words will be able to induce a Neapolitan to pronounce *collegio* rather than *collèggio* and *nobile* instead of *nòbbile*, it will mean that San Gennaro has accomplished one more miracle. . . . Let us unify, Gentlemen, if possible, but let's not get stomach ulcers and ruin our livers (*fegato*, with closed *e*) over it. . . . There are these doubtful words: *règime* or *regìme*? *Sclèrosi* or *scleròsi*? We'll see how the Dictionary makes out with those: no doubt its counsel will be inspired by a scientific criterion; but that is not always enough in confrontation with that capricious tyrant, usage — the only tyrant suffered in a democracy. . . ."
[17] Migliorini 1942.

BOOK TWO

PRE-ROMAN ITALY

Part Three. Prehistoric Background

CHAPTER VII

Language, Race, and Culture   The age of
the earth has been estimated as three billion years, whatever that
figure is worth, and man made his appearance on it from 1,000,000
to 500,000 years ago. The Age of Man coincides with what geol-
ogists call the Quarternary Era, the archaeological stages of which
are the Palaeolithic, the Neolithic, the Copper, Bronze and Iron
Ages. The most ancient human type of remains is a jawbone discovered in Kanam, in Kenya, whose age has been estimated as
about 600,000 years. The owner of the jaw would then have
lived at the time of the first of the four European Ice Ages (commonly termed Günz, Mindel, Riss, Würm), the last of which
ended only 20,000 years ago. Traces of man in Italy are no older
than the last glaciation, though of course absence of finds so ancient
and of an animal so relatively rare as man then was does not pre-
clude earlier existence.

To make these figures more palpable and put them in the proper
relative perspective, let us equate the age of the earth with one
calendar year. Then man would make his entrance upon the scene
between 9 and 10:30 P.M. on December 31, the oldest remains of
man in Italy would show up no earlier than three and one-half
minutes before the end of the year, and the real history of Italy
would commence about twenty seconds before the stroke of mid-
night.

Various early types of man, such as Pithecanthropus, Sinan-
thropus, Eoanthropus, and even the European Neanderthal man
are not the linear ancestors of the true *homo sapiens*, the species we
ourselves belong to, but represent different branches of evolution
which died out. They are generally named hominids or anthropoids. (No chronological sequence is implied. Hominid and *homo
sapiens* could have existed at the same time on earth, in different

places, possibly not even far apart, just as animals of different stages of evolution exist side by side today.)

As concerns western Europe and Italy, it is generally assumed that *homo sapiens* did not evolve in this part of the world but must have migrated there, allegedly from Africa across then existing land-bridges where now spreads the Mediterranean Sea. I mention this because it will have repercussions on the use of the term autochthonous as employed by some anthropologists and archaeologists. In an absolute sense, then, man may not be autochthonous in Europe. In a relative sense, however, if the word is employed at all, it means merely that one may possibly call autochthonous those persons who occupied an area before someone else. And if one is obliged to ask always, "Autochtonous with reference to whom, to what people?" the usefulness of the term becomes questionable at least.

Humanness is generally defined by anthropologists as the faculty of creating extracorporeal tools and language. Whatever animal uses tools and language as part of its cultural equipment is human, and tools and languages are, by definition, possessed by humans only.[1] "Man began his career as an anthropoid who was just learning to talk. He was distinguished from all other animal species by the faculty of articulate speech. It was this faculty which transformed the discontinuous, nonaccumulative, nonprogressive process of tool-using among the anthropoids into a continuous, cumulative, and progressive process in the human species. Articulate speech transformed, also, the social organization of this gifted primate, and by the inauguration of cooperation as a way of life and security, opened the door to virtually unlimited social evolution. And, finally, language and speech made it possible for man to accumulate experience and knowledge in a form that made easy transmission and maximum use possible . . . It was the ability to use symbols — of which articulate speech is the most important and characteristic expression — that made the origin and subsequent growth of culture possible." [2]

So-called animal-language and animal-societies based on co-

[1] Koppers 1952, 70, suggests that the use of tools implies teamwork, and since teamwork is impossible without language, tools and language are of contemporaneous, causally connected origin.
[2] White 1949, 240.

operation do not invalidate this argument, because the 'societies' and 'cultures' and 'languages' of animals refer to things which differ from the corresponding human phenomena not just in degree but also in kind. "Monkey culture, for example, differs from human culture because the psychological potentialities and needs of the monkey organism differ from those of man." [3] An animal cannot participate in the same manner as does man in a cultural system.[4] As for language, "words are both signs and symbols to man; they are merely signs to a dog," that is to say, animals have a sign behavior, man possesses a symbol behavior.[5] And only humans can make linguistic negative statements ("Something is *not*"), and only humans can lie.

Of the languages of palaeolithic and neolithic man we know nothing. The suggestion that they were 'primitive' is not meaningful, especially since this quality is associated by some with great simplicity and deficiencies, by others with great complexity and redundancies. To say, for example, that "primitive races are indeed not fully provided with the elements of language — the vowels and consonants" is unprovable as a statement of facts and absurd as a hypothesis; and to explain that such languages "are deficient in the modified vowels *oe* and *ue* (the German *ö* and *ü*); the fricative sounds *s*, *f*, and *ch*; and in the distinction between *k* and *g*, *t* and *d*, *p* and *b*" [6] is consummate phonetic and phonemic nonsense.

The case for primitive speech has also been made by some on the basis of physical primitiveness. Foremost among these anatomical and biological shortcomings were the absence of a chin and the smallness of the brain in early man. And someone even figured out that the men of the palaeolithic Acheulian culture in western Europe (about 430,000 to 180,000 years ago) either could not talk at all or produced only labial sounds; that during the subsequent Mousterian culture (about 180,000 to 100,000 years ago) dental sounds were added, and during the Aurignacian (about 100,000 to 75,000 years ago) palatal sounds finally joined the rest.[7] Of course, there is not the slightest linguistic evidence for such a

[3] Bidney 1953, 132.
[4] Bidney 1953, 133.
[5] White 1949, 27, 31.
[6] Schmidt 1935, 55.
[7] Franke 1913.

theory (if it can be called that), and the biological argument, in this case the absence of a chin and hence freedom of action for the *musculus genioglossus*, does not hold water, to say nothing of the fact that skeletal evidence is so scanty as not to allow much generalization on the physical makeup of the species concerned in the first place. To put it succinctly: "There is nothing about a snout that prevents its possessor from speaking, but there is something about the brain that goes with a snout that makes speech impossible." [8]

Now concerning this brain whose small size was thought to harbor a primitive mind and primitive language, experiments and measurements have recently shown that the mere physical properties of the brain, its size, the number of convolutions and fissures and wrinkles, and its shape, have nothing to do with human intelligence.[9] And of course, "studies made on skeletons alone will never enable us to make statements about either the mentality of the individuals concerned or about the mental change or progress over a period of time." [10] Or, to put it differently, "man's exceptionally rapid 'improvement' is due to the accumulation of experience and tradition rendered possible by speech, and subsequently accelerated by writing, not to accumulated mutations in his biological make-up." [11]

If we wish to penetrate in some measure the darkness that conceals man's early speech, we cannot follow any path that leads us to an assumption of primitiveness based on biological hypothesis or pure linguistic speculation. Indeed we are obliged to presume, and we have sufficient contemporary evidence for it, that human speech of all times, regardless of the vast differences in vocabulary and structure among the many languages, is essentially and potentially, by definition, of the same type and can perform all the tasks which the nonlinguistic culture of its users requires it to perform. Consequently, I shall at no point in this book argue from mental and physical, and therefrom demonstrable linguistic primitiveness.

It is necessary to discuss the term race, both on its own and in reference to language. I shall not enter upon all the intricacies and

[8] Hooton 1946, 162.
[9] Weidenreich 1948, 105–107.
[10] Weidenreich 1948, 109.
[11] Childe 1933, 413.

ramifications presented by this problem, but, rather, outline briefly the stand I am going to take on this question whenever the subject and my discussion on theories require a programmatic position.

Anthropometry has frequently been the pseudo-scientific refuge of various racial classifications of humanity. Modern anthropology has largely abandoned this method, at least for the determination of races, particularly prehistoric races.[12] But among those archaeologists and linguists who have an axe of their own to grind, anthropometry, especially craniometry, dies much harder. The notorious division of humanity into dolichocephalics, mesocephalics, and brachycephalics is scarcely any longer indulged in by reputable anthropologists for racial purposes.[13]

As far as we can trace back the history and prehistory of man in Europe, there has occurred throughout, ever since palaeolithic times, a continuous moving and migrating and mixing of persons. This excludes a priori the existence, at the present time, of any pure race that can derive its physical inheritance from a prehistoric or early historic pure race. However, it can of course happen, though instances are rare enough, that some group of racially mixed persons finds itself, because of an historical accident, for several generations or even centuries in such social and connubial isolation that during that period all progenation within this group will occur through inbreeding. The result is a physically rather homogeneous ethnos which will retain its common physical characteristics until its isolation is broken and mixture permitted.[14] Whether such a homogeneous unit should be called a race is largely a matter of terminology.[15] Perhaps the differences between Europeans,

[12] Weiner 1954.
[13] On the instability of head-form within constant heredity see the revolutionizing paper by Boas 1912. The methods and results are further refined by Shapiro 1939, and Lasker 1946. Cf. also Herskovits 1953, 39–42.
[14] Coon 1950, 3: "Race is a collection (basically a group) of individuals of both sexes, definitely associated with a place or region, habitually interbreeding, and possessing an historical continuity in the reproduction of a general type; these individuals tend not only to look alike but also to behave alike."
[15] Coon 1950, 85: "When one group has become sufficiently distinct from another group so that the majority of its members are easily identifiable, we call it a race." One of the principal troubles with the word race is that it has become odious because of the abuse perpetrated in its name. That is why Boas preferred to use the word 'type' in the manuscript for his publication of 1912; but he found the term 'race' substituted throughout by the United States Immigration Commission for which the report was originally written; cf. Boas 1912, 550 fn. 1.

African Negroes, and Mongolians are vast enough to warrant the term racial. Whether the word should still be used with reference to the distinction, still obvious enough to the naked eye, between Swedes and Sicilians is another matter. But to throw together into a Latin race all the speakers of Romanic languages is preposterous.

At best one can say that, as regards prehistoric anthropological evidence, if a radical change of culture is also accompanied by an abrupt change of physical type, then chances are that the new culture was imported by somatically different immigrants or conquerors. "Otherwise anthropometry is of little use in tracing prehistoric migrations." [16] The new orientation of anthropologists concerning anthropometry is well illustrated by these words: "My long and extensive experience in the fields of skeletal raciology and of the racial classification of living peoples has made me very critical of my own efforts and those of other anthropologists. If I have achieved neither competence nor confidence, I have, at any rate, acquired candor." [17]

Another superstition with which some of the following chapters of this book will be concerned, is the continuity and tenacity of the racial purity over centuries if not millennia, through prehistory and history. To illustrate this position I could cite Gobineau, Chamberlain, and their Nazi successors. But they have been thoroughly discredited in any event. It is considerably more alarming and insidious if such myths are contained, implicitly or explicitly, in learned works whose primary purpose is not, or not obviously, propagandistic. I shall give but one example out of many possible ones.

It may well be that the humans known by their distinctive culture as Cro Magnon men, living in western Europe, especially in France, about 70,000 years ago according to some,[18] 30,000 years ago according to others,[19] were of a fairly homogeneous racial type, for reasons such as mentioned, even though they were apparently of mixed origin. But it is quite impossible that any modern inhabitants of France are direct unmixed descendants, or even biological throwbacks, of that — using the term in a relative

[16] Childe 1950, 2. Cf. also Childe 1933, 193–195.
[17] Hooton 1946, 575.
[18] Ashley-Montagu 1951, chart facing p. 218.
[19] Taylor 1937, 158 ff.

sense — race. From these Cro Magnon people we have a number of implements, some remarkable cave paintings, and a few bones and skulls. On the whole, we know much better how they lived than what they looked like. Yet a sculptor, aided by an anthropologist, has fashioned a bust of a Cro Magnon man. The only real fact on which to base his sculpture was the shape of the skull, but the artist filled the gaps by using a fertile imagination. His Cro Magnon man has long, tidily brushed hair, a beard, a mustache, and wears an ornamental wreath of bones and teeth around his head. All in all he looks like a benign old fellow who contemplates with a sensitive facial expression a piece of handiwork, held in slim and delicate fingers. Examining this almost wholly imaginary bust our anthropologist then declares earnestly that the Cro Magnon gentleman is the "representative of a race which is still distinguished in many parts of Europe." [20] The only racial feature which Cro Magnon men and modern Europeans can provedly be said to have in common is their humanness. But to clinch the argument there is elsewhere in the same book a photograph of five peasant women from the village of Les Eyzies, in the valley of the Vézère, near the site of an authentic Cro Magnon rockshelter. The woman in the center is a round-faced, fat, jolly old lady, whose traits, we are solemnly told, "resemble those of the Old Man of Cro Magnon," [21] the old man, that is, fashioned at the pleasure of the sculptor and the anthropologist.

Although that kind of anthropology has theoretically reached its deserved demise, in practice it is not quite as dead as one would wish. Even Hooton, whom I just quoted approvingly as speaking out against anthropometric reconstruction and classification of races, finds that most whites in the Mediterranean area belong to the so-called Mediterranean race: this we might let pass if race is properly understood in a relative sense. But when he goes on to say that this racial type, exemplified by longheadedness and brunetteness, "retains the full pigmentation of hair, skin, and eyes that was characteristic of the early *Homo sapiens*," [22] we are left to wonder whence comes this clairvoyant intelligence concerning the pigmentation of early *Homo sapiens*.

[20] Elliot 1920, picture facing p. 174.
[21] Elliot 1920, picture facing p. 168.
[22] Hooton 1946, 582.

But racial myths are embraced also by some linguists, because certain authors figure for some reason that racial unity can be used to prove linguistic unity, or vice versa, that like language denotes like race. Why this premise, rejected by most scholars, should enjoy an air of greater authenticity with reference to prehistoric times than to the present, where its application is obviously quite out of the question, remains an enigma, unless we come to the caustic conclusion that lack of factual evidence not only fosters unfounded theorizing, but indeed excuses it and renders it respectable. "The principle that it is dangerous to infer the descent of an individual, the shape of his skull, or the colour of his skin from his language (which may not have been that of his parents), or to argue that his language must have been this or that because his skull was of a particular shape and his weapons of a particular pattern, is generally recognized, but is not always acted upon. No one would dream of applying such tests in the case of a living man; and the mere fact that the object of investigation has been dead for thousands of years, and that no other test *can* be applied, cannot make the results of this method any more convincing." [23]

For example, we know the Etruscans, an ancient nation of Italy of which much will have to be said, as a social group possessing a characteristic language and culture. Racially, anthropometrically we cannot isolate any 'Etruscans.' Attempts at doing so have led to astounding discrepancies. Examining 'Etruscan' skulls, one Italian scholar found that 72 per cent are dolichocephalic or mesocephalic, 28 per cent brachycephalic.[24] Another reckoned that 22.61 per cent are dolichocephalic, 77.39 per cent brachycephalic.[25]

Obviously the two were not measuring the same skulls, or did not call the same skulls 'Etruscan.' Indeed it would have been a mere coincidence had they done so, for the very simple reason that a body's being buried in a tomb with an Etruscan inscription, or together with implements and ornaments which are part of what is generally called Etruscan civilization, in a place where Etruscan civilization and language are predominantly attested (and I do not say 'predominated' with good reason), at a period when Etruscan

[23] Fraser 1926, 264. Cf. also Kretschmer 1896, 34–42, for a trenchant critique of craniometry.
[24] Sergi 1898.
[25] Scabia 1910.

rule is vouchsafed, does not mean that the body is of Etruscan race. Nor is all this proof for the existence of such a race.

In this book, then, I shall employ the term race, if I do so at all, in a purely relative sense, bound to a time and a place, without inference or implication regarding racial purity and linguistic heritage.[26]

The third term the use of which I must clarify is culture. This is relatively easy because there prevails general agreement on the meaning of the word. I shall apply it in the anthropological and archaeological sense (where Frenchmen speak of *civilisation* and Italians of *civiltà*), and not restrict it (in the sense of German *Kultur* and French *culture* and Italian *cultura* or *civilizzazione*) to only such physical or spiritual features of civilization and progress which have been found admirable and worth emulating and perpetuating. Culture is, then, the sum of "all those historically created designs for living, explicit and implicit, rational, irrational, and nonrational, which exist at any given time as potential guides for the behavior of men." [27] Another definition with more emphasis on the paraphernalia than on human behavior, and more concerned with archaeological evidence runs like this: "A culture is defined as an assemblage of artifacts that occur repeatedly associated together in dwellings of the same kind and with burials of the same rite." [28]

Each culture is communicable to all human beings. But an intransigent stand on cultural spread which asserts that all cultural change is due to migrations of cultures and their bearers [29] is as unfortunate as the opposite uncompromising assumption that cultural change is always a matter of internal development and evolution.

It has been observed, however, that culturally primitive socie-

---

[26] Cf. the article concerning races and languages of Anatolia by Furlani 1929, containing also a severe and deserved censure of Sergi 1926, for completely confusing the terms and beclouding the issues.

[27] Kluckhohn 1945, 97.

[28] Childe 1950, 2.

[29] This school is exemplified most radically in the writings of G. Elliot Smith and his disciples. In one of his works (1915) Smith rejects what he considers the meaningless dogma of the similarity of the human mind everywhere as an explanation for the identity of cultures. To make his point he attempts to prove that the embalming methods practiced by the Papuans of New Guinea were actually borrowed or learned from the mummy-making ancient Egyptians.

ties are rather conservative and do not show the same incentive and speed in producing cultural changes as do more civilized groups. Perhaps this is the reason why the Stone Ages lasted several hundreds of thousands of years with minimal progress (the Old Stone Age, during which man lived in a stage of food-gathering savagery, aided only by the most primitive tools in his fight for survival, comprises no less than 98 per cent of humanity's sojourn on this earth), whereas the development of civilization in the Metal Ages has been progressively more rapid. Because of this innate conservativeness it has been thought by some that "cultural change, however well it corresponded to the changed needs of a society, was often effected by a shock from without." [30]

In the matter of cultural spread by migration of the bearers of a culture, the appearance alone of a cultural change in a given area will give hardly an indication of the intensity and duration of the migration, or on the size of the migrating body. I venture to suggest, however, that the speed and the thoroughness with which a change of culture takes place may be a criterion of the number of its human transmitters involved.

If the cultural shift is gradual, undestructive of the old stratum but merely superseding it, if the development and advancement, while probably accelerated, remain on the whole linear and evolutionary, the migrating body of newcomers, if any, is small. In such a case I shall speak of spread by infiltration. But if the cultural conversion is abrupt, rapid, destructive of the old culture, if the innovations testify to a break and a revolution, then the immigrants bearing the new civilization have arrived in relatively, though not absolutely, great numbers, smothering under their weight, possibly annihilating, their less numerous and less dynamic predecessors. For this type of cultural spread I shall use the term of expansion by migration. Therefore, organic evolution of culture is not necessarily proof for purely local development with total absence of immigration, nor is each change of culture, gradual or swift, superficial or profound, sufficient proof of vast migrations involving whole tribes and nations. Each case has to be examined on its own terms, and the evidence must be drawn from available sources of *all* kinds.

[30] Childe 1950, 10.

However, although the cultural realia, such as pottery, arms, and implements, even new raw materials together with new techniques of converting them into objects, can possibly be transmitted from one region to another by means of trade and cultural borrowing along and across a cultural boundary without a permanent transfer of population, a process which I shall call expansion by diffusion, it is scarcely possible to imagine the transfer of a whole language over a large area previously occupied by another language, by the same means. Anthropologists know that nonlinguistic cultural traits are more easily borrowed and transferred than linguistic ones.[31] "More easily" means that the sum total of energy spent in the process needs to be greater for the second than for the first, energy being defined by a formula which incorporates the quantity and kind of things transferred, the number of carriers, the time expended, and the distance traversed.[32] Accordingly, if an entire social unit, a tribe or a nation, is to acquire a new language to the extent that within a few generations the old native dialect is actually fallen into disuse or wholly forgotten, as happened in the countries conquered by the Romans where Romanic languages are spoken today, the linguistic change must needs be effected, I believe, by a number of permanent new dwellers who actually settle and become naturalized in the new land, that is, by infiltration or migration. The exigencies of trade and intercultural and international intercourse lead at best to the acquisition of a foreign tongue, as a second language, by a few, and not to the complete displacement of the primary one. Also, diffusion across a cultural-linguistic boundary is not potent enough a force to penetrate deeply into a foreign dialect area; it may propel a number of items of linguistic inventory throughout such an area, but structural features can scarcely be thus propagated, least of all a totality of structures making up a language.[33] I shall therefore assume that wherever a complete substitution of idioms occurs, a permanent

---

[31] Cf. Hoijer 1948, 335.

[32] See Pulgram, On prehistoric, 1956. As regards prehistoric pottery in particular, Hencken 1955, 3, thinks that, since it is made by women, appearance of a new type indicates some kind of migration rather than mere conquest by arms. Yet it seems to me that the strength of the displacement of persons is again indicated by the mass of the finds; it need not be what I call migration, but only infiltration. (Query: Is it certain that pottery is generally made by women?)

[33] For details see Pulgram, On prehistoric, 1956.

ethnic transfer of a certain size, small though it may have been, must have taken place.[34]

With certain restrictions, the same can be said of ancient burial rites. It is true, of course, that funerary customs may, like realia, more easily than language be a matter of readily transferable fashion.[35] But more often the attitude toward death has deeper psychological roots which are generally to be sought in religion. Again it is true that religion can be spread like other cultural items: Roman legionnaires brought dozens of non-Italian cults home with them from various theaters of war, and missionaries carried, sometimes singlehanded like Saint Patrick, Christianity to the unbelievers. But since in prehistoric Italy we can reckon neither with a far-flung and mobile soldiery, nor with traveling missionaries, nor with xenophile tourists, I should rather think that the important distinction between cremation and inhumation rites, being more deeply and firmly anchored within a culture than the shape of pots and pans, is likely to have ethnic significance. In other words, although I do not mean to attach axiomatically a rite to a race nor intend to elevate this then-and-there useful criterion to general validity, the replacement of one funerary rite by another has a fair chance of being due to permanent human displacement, though again the number of migrating persons need not be great, if only their prestige and social organization be powerful. In this sense the transfer of burial rites has more in common with linguistic expansion than with the spread of archaeological realia.

Certainly wherever changes of linguistic and ritual evidence occur together, I should safely assume some degree of movement of persons even though the material culture may register no revolution.

From the preceding discussion of language, race, and culture it should have become clear that few generally valid rules on

[34] This is also, in the main, the opinion of Devoto 1931, 55, which is unfavorably criticized by Terracini 1933, 748, but restated by Devoto 1951, 65.

[35] So argues Laviosa-Zambotti 1947, 138, with reference to the so-called urn-fields. Note the remark on her stand concerning migration by Devoto 1950, 175. Randall-MacIver 1927, 196, thinks that the type of tomb depends not only on beliefs and rites but also on the kind of soil prevalent: for example, elaborate rock-hewn chamber tombs cannot be cut into clay or sandy soil. But there is no type of soil that will prohibit cremation of dead bodies. (However, the scarcity or absence of fuel, primarily wood, might do so.)

linguistic, racial, and cultural origins, spread, and changes can be postulated a priori, but that each instance has to be probed on its own terms, on the basis of whatever records are available.

It is, of course, very tempting to combine this triple evidence into a unified story, and a portion of this book will be concerned with such endeavors.[36] But the pitfalls are many and fatal. I have already pointed out that racial and linguistic unity are not necessarily conterminous or congruent. The same applies to racial and cultural, and cultural and linguistic unity. True, language is but one of a number of cultural features of a society. But this does not imply, in historic or prehistoric ages, that language and culture always occur in complete congruence. A single type of speech may comprise several material cultures, and a single material culture may have more than one linguistic vehicle.

In scrutinizing the records linguists are naturally at a disadvantage. Anthropologists and archaeologists discover at least testimony that has withstood the passage of time, consisting of bones, stone and metal implements and weapons, pottery, and other nonperishable remains. But there are no linguistic remnants that precede the art of writing, except such fossils as may be gleaned from local names that turn out to be much older than the language of which they came to form a part, or from artificial reconstructions. And as far as Italy and much of Europe are concerned, this kind of sure, though at least phonetically often enough still uncertain linguistic evidence, is very recent, taking us back into the past no farther than six or seven centuries before Christ, and remaining sketchy and untrustworthy for several hundred years yet.

"A few swords of a peculiar shape are dug up in the valley of the Seine; some skulls of approximately the same craniological character are found somewhere in the neighbourhood; it is known that at a date several centuries later than that previously assigned to the swords and skulls, a Celtic language was, in fact, spoken by a people settled in that region. With that material and no more, the archaeologist constructs a fairly circumstanial, and even moving, narrative of the invasion of the Seine Valley about 1000 B.C. by a Celtic-speaking people provided with swords and skulls of the pattern and shape of those just dug up from the earth. The

[36] For a model in method and execution see Speiser 1933.

reasoning here is somewhat difficult to follow. In the absence of all other evidence, it would seem that all that can be reasonably inferred from the presence of a number of swords and skulls in a particular spot is that at some time they were brought there, by human agency or otherwise. In favourable circumstances it may be possible to say with some degree of assurance that they were deposited at roughly the same time; but it is very difficult to see how it can be confidently assumed that the swords were the weapons actually used by the owners of the skulls. To go still farther and claim that the latter spoke a Celtic language is simply to wander into romance." [37]

Yet much wandering of this kind has been done: partly from wanderlust and for the innocent pleasure of the journey — though the travelogues published afterwards described a largely imaginary landscape; partly to prove an ulterior point, such as the excellence and tenacious permanence of a race together with its language and culture. If such voyages into the unknown are further encouraged by a national propensity to romanticize and sublimate a people's past and to eulogize the purity and virtues of its ancestors, and if moreover such pseudo-scientific frauds are sustained for political and demagogic purposes, and rewarded by the state, the inquiries cannot but result in senseless, tumid, and turgid fustian.[38]

It will be necessary to apply in this book better sense on such problems, and models are not lacking. "In dealing with prehistoric problems of Europe, when it is a question of passing on to the ethnic identification of the various groups, much more caution must be employed than has been done hitherto: the fact is that one was often wont to identify an ethnos on the basis of a culture." [39] "Only quite exceptionally do the skeletal remains associated with a given culture belong exclusively or even predominantly to a

[37] Fraser 1926, 262.

[38] I shall give only one example, but refrain from translating it into English, partly to preserve unmitigated its bombast, partly because I dare not translate lest I traduce it by trying to give it any kind of good sense lacking in the original. I am quoting Menghin 1936, 47–48: "Das Verhältnis von Sprache, Kultur und Rasse anlangend ist der Grundsatz, dass jedem Stammes- oder Volkstum eine geschlossene Verständigungs-, Gesittungs- und Blutgemeinschaft entspricht, aus den Tatbeständen ohne weiteres abzulesen." This author's vocabulary includes, on the subsequent page, such items as *blutmässig, Inwendigkeit eines Volkstums, fremdes Blut, rassische Umwandlung*.

[39] Laviosa-Zambotti 1950, 104–105.

single physical type. . . . A culture need not correspond to a group allied by physical traits acquired by heredity. Culture is a social heritage; it belongs to a community sharing common traditions, common institutions, and a common way of life. Such a group may reasonably be called a people. . . . Language goes not with race but with the group we term people; and so it is generally linked with culture. . . ." [40] (I scarcely need to add once more here the amplification that sameness of culture, however, is not necessarily indicative of sameness of language.) Elsewhere, too, Childe suggests that what has frequently been referred to as race might better be called people, indicating a cultural rather than a physical unity because "in the prehistoric past as obviously today, culture was independent of physical race, was not a matter of biological heredity but of social tradition." [41]

Without wanting to quibble over words, I shall not use the term people as indicating a group sharing the same material culture *and* language, as Childe proposes, because that might lead logically to an a priori correlation of culture and language. I shall, therefore, for better or for worse, but surely for good pragmatic reasons, dissociate language from culture, and apply the term people only in the sense of cultural unit, regardless of linguistic inheritance. I realize, of course, that language is but one facet of culture. But it is so peculiar and so unlike the other cultural phenomena that this separation is surely justifiable.

On the interrelation of race, culture, and language it will consequently be my postulate that equating and confusing evidence from these three areas must be avoided and rejected wherever it is found, because the three phenomena may possibly, but do "only exceptionally reflect an homogeneous unity preserved through millennia. . . . Only in very special geographic and environmental circumstances [of protracted isolation] can one observe and admit the phenomenon of the nearly unaltered conservation and association of the three factors engaged in the process of the creation of an homogeneous society." [42]

To conclude this rapid exposition on postulates and methods,

[40] Childe 1933, 198–200.
[41] Childe 1933, 417.
[42] Laviosa-Zambotti 1950, 103.

I must briefly mention one other poisoned source of errors, the freely flowing fount of proper names, local, tribal, national, and linguistic, from which ancient authorities and modern philologists have taken many a deep draught, with toxic if not fatal results. Such terms as Umbrian(s), Ligurian(s), Pelasgian(s), Aborigines, and many others are used by a great number of scholars, antique and recent, with unrestrained laxity and romantic impetuousness. But on closer scrutiny we find that not all of them call the same item by the same name, and that therefore their discussions and quarrels as likely as not are not over referends but merely over names. In addition, as we have seen already, a word like Umbrian may severally attach itself to linguistic, cultural, or ethnic evidence. Any author who uses the word, then, should make it clear to his readers whether he uses the term with regard to a language, to a culture, or to an ethnos; whether he has reference to an area currently called Umbria, or to one of Augustus' eleven regions, or to the district from which come the inscriptions in the so-called Umbrian dialect; whether he believes that the name Umbrians should designate speakers of Umbrian, or inhabitants of 'Umbria,' or the possessors of the Villanovan culture, or the people called 'Ομβρικοί by the Greeks, or the ones Pliny speaks of as the oldest nation of Italy.[43] For if author A claims that the 'Umbrians' are Villanovans, and author B that Umbrians speak an Indo-European dialect, whereupon author C concludes from this that the Villanovans are ethnically 'Indo-Europeans,' and that therefore either Pliny is wrong or the 'Indo-Europeans' are autochthonous in Italy, then nothing has been accomplished beyond a correlation of the occurrences, in different authors, of a mere name 'Umbrian,' that refers to different realities at different times. Obviously some conciliation of the refractory and often contradictory evidence is necessary, and it shall be one of the principal aims of this book; but it cannot be accomplished by juggling names and performing feats of onomastic legerdemain. "The Bronze and Iron Ages began to be loaded with tendentious names like Phoenician, Ligurian, Iberian, Celtic, and Teutonic, and archaeologists began to add to their already difficult problems the gratuitous difficulty of saying what language had been spoken by the people of their groups and

[43] Plin. *H.N.*3.9.112.

epochs." [44] "The archaeologist thinks of one series of ideas, the philologist of another, maybe totally different, when they speak of, say, Ligurians or *Italici* or Kelts." [45]

On the whole, names imposed in antiquity by known or unknown authors tend to enjoy a considerably greater longevity than the realia that go with and by them. Hence it is safe to state that the 'Umbrians' of the tenth century B.C. and those of the first century B.C. have little more in common than the name. Any conclusions concerning the race or the culture or the language of these 'Umbrians,' that apply and mingle, indeed mangle, the evidence of the whole intervening period, as dished up by any odd author who uses the name 'Umbrian' uncritically and indiscriminately, must needs be false. [46]

My relative reluctance to cite ancient authorities on these intricate problems can therefore, I hope, be readily understood. Unless I can persuade myself that I comprehend precisely whom or what Strabo meant by his Λίγυης, for example, I shall begin from a *tabula rasa* in preference to wrestling with the decipherment of onomastic usage by authors who not only meant different things by the same name, or the same thing by different names, but who also further confounded matters by imputing their own meanings upon each other's texts — which they were wont to copy from one another in the first place. [47]

Ancient historians and ethnographers, whom many present-day scholars choose to quote with more enthusiasm than discretion for confirmation or refutation of one or the other theory, do not necessarily invest the events and facts they discuss with greater authority and veracity solely because they are ancient and by a few centuries nearer than ourselves to the dates in question. Indeed the modern anthropologist and archaeologist, so long as they employ scientific and unprejudiced methods of inquiry, may come considerably closer to the truth than did their tradition-bound and legend-inspired predecessors. [48]

[44] Daniel 1950, 150.
[45] Whatmough 1927, 2–3.
[46] Cf. Pinza 1923, 45–46.
[47] For theoretic details see Pulgram, Names, 1956. The application of these principles occurs *passim* in the present book.
[48] Cf. Myres 1907, 170–171.

It is not surprising if anything but unanimity reigns among scholars concerning details as well as general trends in the prehistory of Europe. At the end of an outstanding work on the subject, Childe candidly admits this: "Our survey of prehistoric Europe has disclosed a fragmentary mosaic of barbaric cultures — or rather several imperfect mosaics one on top of the other. All are so incomplete that the pieces can be fitted to make different patterns. It is often doubted to which mosaic an individual fragment belongs. . . . The pattern here [in the chronological charts on pp. 331–333] adopted has frankly been determined as much by a subjective thesis as by the interdigitation of its component parts." [49]

If, therefore, on the basis of the evidence available, consisting mainly of crockery, arms, utensils, and adornments, a considerable number of learned, competent, and reasonable investigators come to widely divergent, indeed sometimes contradictory conclusions, one cannot but deduce that either the record does not suffice or that it is misread through a fundamental error in methodology.[50] But in any event, as long as adherence to a proposed thesis is a matter of personal choice even to the expert, who in fairness cannot accuse all of his dissenting colleagues of downright ignorance, the intelligent layman, or the scholar to whom the findings of prehistorians serve as corroborative testimony to dispel or lighten the doubts in his own field, will not easily commit himself fully and wholeheartedly to any one view. However, if he chooses, after due examination of all theories, the one or ones which dovetail with the reputable discoveries and postulates in his own area, he will not, I trust, be charged with shallowness or credulity for taking sides in controversies outside his full scholarly competence.

[49] Childe 1947, 330.
[50] Merhart 1942, 70, points out, "how weak are the methodological brakes which counteract subjective interpretations."

CHAPTER VIII

Prehistoric Europe I have alluded to the difficulties and discrepancies of opinion that plague the absolute prehistoric chronology of Europe. To begin with, the physical evidence, as gathered and interpreted by anthropologists and archaeologists, is restricted in both kind and volume. Only materials which have lasted through millennia, such as bones and stones, pottery and metal, can come to view. Of the way in which human beings used wood, leather, textiles, and other perishable stuff we know almost nothing apart from a few rare finds preserved by sheer accident. And the total bulk of remains of any type is necessarily small, not only because the scholar's spade can dig only so deep and turn over so much ground, but also because of a low density of population.[1]

The recently discovered process of radiocarbon dating, though still in its infancy, is promising and may well lead to refinements in the absolute chronology of prehistory.[2] But also with regard to a relative chronology, which does not date events but merely establishes their order of succession, there prevails anything but unanimity. At least the terms Stone Age, Copper Age, Bronze Age, and Iron Age, identifying four major divisions, have been generally accepted. This classification (minus the Copper Age) was first used by the Danish scholar J. C. Thomsen in 1836 in the arrangement of a prehistoric exhibition in the National Museum of Northern Antiquities in Copenhagen. But, whether it was known to Thomsen or not, there is in fact a passage in Lucretius where a similar sequence of phases in the development of civilization is related.[3]

[1] The reason for this lies in that at a stage of savagery or food gathering each human needed a greater area to feed off than do members of more progressed societies. The phenomenon called territoriality by biologists with reference to modern animals is applicable also to noncivilized man. It consists in the staking out and taking possession of a piece of territory by the male animal (an act that is loudly proclaimed by the male bird, for example, to the other birds by his singing) in preparation for acquiring a female and raising young.
[2] See Johnson 1951.
[3] Lucr. *De rer. nat.* 5.1282–1286: "The weapons in ancient times were the

The nearer we approach the dawn of history, the easier will become the task of dating, but also the more pressing the necessity to be accurate within a smaller margin of error. History, which by definition rests upon written records, does not commence in all parts of the inhabited world at the same time. In Italy, in fact, it begins quite late as compared with other regions of the Mediterranean basin. But since prehistoric Italy, as Europe in general, derived much of her culture from areas, such as Mesopotamia, Anatolia, Egypt, in which the same kinds of cultures are historically attested and can be connected with datable events, the prehistory of Europe from 3000 B.C. or thereabouts onward will prove to be less unyielding and obdurate than preceding ages. Nonetheless, our evidence, as far as Italy is concerned, will still be largely anthropological, archaeological, and legendary until the sixth century B.C., which means that it will lend itself to varying interpretations. Written historical records, fragmentary and untrustworthy though they may be, speak to us in the tongue of man; prehistoric monuments are but a sign language.[4]

The European Stone Age is generally subdivided into the Palaeolithic (Lower, Middle, and Upper), the Mesolithic, and the Neolithic. The first traces of man are some primitive stone tools that go back possibly to the interglacial period between the First (Günz) and Second (Mindel) Ice Age.[5] The Palaeolithic is, to date, by far the longest single cultural era of humanity, extending from the first appearance of man, perhaps half a million or more years ago, to about 8000 B.C. Accordingly, in about half a million years man learned no more than to improve slightly his technique of chipping and polishing rocks to fashion them into crude tools. His way of life was, much like that of the nonhuman animal, the tracking and killing of prey and the gathering of vegetable food for immediate consumption.

From this protracted age of palaeolithic savagery man finally

---

hands and claws and teeth, also *stones* and pieces of branches from the forest, then flames and the fire, once their nature was understood. Later the power of iron and bronze was discovered, but the use of *bronze* was realized before that of *iron*."

[4] The most usable and reliable comparative chart for prehistoric dating is Burkitt 1932.

[5] According to Hencken 1946, 341. Some scholars suggest other dates.

progressed to neolithic barbarism. There intervened a period, lasting perhaps some six thousand years, that has been termed Mesolithic and during which, most scholars believe, no great progress was made beyond the adaptation of life and the paraphernalia of living to new climatic conditions: the ice cap of the Upper Palaeolithic had finally receded toward the pole, and in its place grew thick, wild forests, new surroundings for man which demanded adjustments.

But the cultural changes that occurred in Europe from 2500 B.C. on, with the rise of neolithic cultures (note that we have now entered upon a period which is already historical in Egypt and Mesopotamia), are considerably more striking and radical; they are not merely a measured development of the preceding stage but constitute something of a revolution in human life and behavior. Chief among the changes is the conversion from a food-gathering to a food-raising economy. And since the earliest traces of agriculture are found in the Near East as far back as the fourth millennium B.C., since various neolithic implements and utensils uncovered in Europe were no doubt of Near Eastern provenance or were at least imitations of Near Eastern equipment, the conclusion is virtually inevitable that the Neolithic Age in Europe was not a mere indigenous development of the Palaeolithic and Mesolithic but a revolution due to cultural importation and, quite certainly, human migration.

Physical anthropology and anthropometry is of small assistance in determining whether or not the neolithic revolution in Europe was accomplished by a veritable Völkerwanderung, or mass migration, because the evidence of skulls and bones is rather scanty. But whatever facts are available, and the degree to which their interpretation is trustworthy, tend to favor very strongly a migration hypothesis.

Further corroborative data for large migratory movements of humans out of the Near East are provided by historical climatology. Firstly, there occurred a deterioration of the climate with drought and heat in the East between 8000 and 2000 B.C.,[6] which was bound to be felt with special severity in regions which, thanks

[6] See Chapter II on the climate of Italy for a brief statement on the methods and tenets of historical climatology.

to their previous favorable climate and cultural advances due to the spread of agriculture, had nurtured an ever-increasing population.[7] It must not be forgotten that the limit of the bearable density of population in an area is not only a matter of absolute numbers and fertility of the soil but depends to a great extent upon the type and degree of exploitation by human economy. The more advanced an economy and the more numerous the people and the more fertile the soil, the greater will be the catastrophe if the economic balance is upset. Secondly, and at the same time, the retreat of the ice from Central Europe had opened up virginal fertile lands of agreeable climate.[8]

In view of all these circumstances which I can only mention and not discuss in detail, the actual displacement of neolithic people from the Near East toward Europe can be assumed with a high degree of confidence.

How profoundly and in what manner the advent of the newcomers affected the ethnic composition of Europe it is of course impossible to state with any precision. With the spread of cremation as a funerary rite, especially in the Danubian lands and later in other parts of Europe, including Italy, anthropometric researches are reduced to helplessness, whether the anthropometrists admit it or not.[9]

Most scholars distinguish more than one stream of neolithic influx to Europe, but no matter how many one cares to assume the direction of their movement is mainly from east to west, the center of expansion being, as one should expect, in the general area of the Near East. There is a definite drift from Egypt, possibly having its source in the ancient Fayum cultures of the fourth millennium B.C., moving along the shores of North Africa and across the straits of Gibraltar to Spain, thence to France, Switzerland, and Britain. This current meets, it seems, on the lower Rhine and in Belgium with another which is traceable from Thessaly and across the Balkans, following the valleys of the Vardar, Morava, Danube, and Rhine. A third flow issues from the shores of the eastern Mediterranean and moves westward over the Mediterranean islands toward Spain

[7] Cf. Brooks 1922, 163.
[8] Cf. Lebon 1952, 74–75.
[9] Cf. Hooton 1946, 597.

and Western Europe. And finally one discerns a cultural movement distinguishable by the so-called corded ware (that is, pottery embellished by a design of ropes imprinted upon the wet clay before baking), by the stone battle-axes, and possibly by the domestication of the horse, a movement which takes its start in the Middle East, thence crosses the Caucasus into southern Russia, Poland, Germany, and the Alpine regions, and reaches in a northern thrust the shores of the Baltic Sea not long before 2000 B.C.[10] These highroads from the East to Europe should be kept in mind for later references.

By the year 2000 B.C. at the latest, then, all of Europe seems in some manner to have acquired neolithic cultures, which apparently flourished most vigorously in regions where the unforested fertile loess soil made agriculture easy, that is, especially in the loess lands of the Danube and its tributaries, with the mighty river itself serving as a beneficent thoroughfare. Here also arose a particularly progressive and influential culture which is generally referred to as Danubian, conspicuous by the extensive spread of a remarkably uniform equipment.

A momentous consequence of such favorable conditions and cultural change was an enormous growth in the density of population in Europe, accompanied by an ever increasing rapidity of progress. Neolithic peoples, thanks to their food-producing habits, could become sedentary and form small village communities for mutual enrichment and protection. However, despite the improved communications enhanced by trade, and attested by evidence of intense cultural borrowing, there existed many different tribes and peoples rather than one neolithic 'nation.' It is quite safe to believe that, although there prevailed what we call a neolithic culture, Europe was divided among many different subcultures and, most likely, languages and dialects, the differences being due in part to different local origins of the invaders and in part to the varying cultural and linguistic substrata. But, in speaking of dialects, I do not wish to give the impression that we have the slightest idea what dialects or what type of languages most of the neolithic inhabitants of Europe spoke. At best we get a glimmer of light, by inference,

---

[10] In this outline I am following Hencken (cf. 1946, 343) who makes the greatest and most fruitful efforts, I believe, to accommodate within his prehistoric studies the considered assumptions and postulates of Indo-European linguistics. See also Hencken 1955.

on some idioms belonging to the Indo-European family of languages, about whose origin and location more shall be said later.

As the various strains of neolithic cultures and ethnic groups spread over Europe and came in contact with one another in search of land for their increasing numbers, their meetings were not always peaceful. Perhaps they delivered the first pitched battles for *Lebensraum* that Europe witnessed. The earliest Danubians, judging from the finds of tomb furnishings with which the dead were provided to accompany them wherever they were thought to go, seem to have been peaceable folk. But later on battle-axes and flint daggers replace the hunters' tools in the graves of the males, and the excavated villages show traces of elaborate fortifications. Evidence for the violent replacement of one society by another, attested by radical, rapid cultural change, becomes more and more frequent. The Golden Age was at an end. Yet continuous warfare could not solve the problem that was inherent in the neolithic economy. The fiercely guarded independence of the small village unit made its members all the more vulnerable and defenseless in the face of any *force majeure*, human or natural, against which they had not sufficient means or foresight to protect themselves: war, drought, blight, tempest might decimate or destroy any village which could not count on help from the outside.

The solution of these problems came again from the East. Even the deterioration of the climate which had caused the neolithic migrations to Europe, had left unharmed amidst the arid steppes and the sandy desert a long belt of fertile ground, reaching from the Nile to the Euphrates and Tigris and thence to the Indus Valley (a belt whose western part from Egypt to Mesopotamia has been called the Fertile Crescent by the Egyptologist James H. Breasted). Naturally the river valleys themselves were the most productive lands, but also in between there lie smaller fertile valleys, highlands, and many an oasis. But where the land is not spontaneously flowing with milk and honey, nature is generous only if properly cajoled and propitiated. It can be coaxed by human effort and ingenuity which elsewhere are unneeded: irrigation and canalization of recurring floods are the key to life; and, to do the job adequately, man fashions for himself a geometry and a hydraulic science, watches the sky for the movement of the stars to fabricate a calendar, initiates a social organization involving division of labor and specialization of duties, a planned economy. In other words, the neolithic barbarian must civilize himself. Recognizing withal his basic impotence vis-à-vis the uncontrollable powers of nature which may inflict unforeseeable and irrevocable disaster despite all human efforts, man incorporates these powers in divine personages who inhabit the sky and the earth and the sea, and whom he seeks to conciliate with sacrifice and prayer.

Material and economic development leads man, therefore, to live in larger, tightly knit, governed, and cooperative communities, which are the beginnings of an urban civilization.

Also a new kind of 'stone' is discovered, which is malleable and can be shaped into various utensils and containers: the Copper Age has begun. And it is not long before man learns that this very peculiar stone can be smelted and poured into molds to result in more varied and intricate, more easily produced and more serviceable shapes, and that in a liquid state it can be alloyed with another metal, tin, so that the result is a harder and more useful substance. The Bronze Age is born.

It was only natural that these new material discoveries and social reorganizations should spread from their Near Eastern homelands and be eagerly accepted by neolithic Europeans to whom this new world of urban organization and metallurgy offered solutions of both their material and social problems by increasing the efficiency and yield of the individual's labor and by teaching him how to protect himself and his society against at least some of the incalculable caprices of nature.

The Copper and Bronze Age cultures, unlike the neolithic revolution, would seem to spread over Europe and the Mediterranean area without being borne by great migrations. Chief reason for this belief is that the development from the Neolithic to the Bronze Age cultures is linear and the transition gradual, and while at given moments various regions exhibit a considerable increase in the rate of change and progress, one can nowhere discern a decisive break and a sudden fundamental transformation such as a numerous horde of bringers of a new culture would doubtlessly occasion. Of course, communications of neolithic Europe with the Bronze Age East were provedly and markedly superior to those which had at one time existed between the European palaeolithic savages and the rest of the world, thus making possible importations and borrowings, and fostering a gradual process of learning not open to the isolated hunters and food gatherers of the paleolithic period. Small scale migrations and infiltrations are by no means excluded; quite the contrary. But any question concerning the race of the propagators of metal in Europe is senseless since the individuals involved, not numerous in any event, came from different areas at different periods.

The beginning of the metal ages nowhere signifies an abrupt end of the use of stone: even on the battlefield of Marathon, where in 490 B.C. the Persians fought the Athenians under Miltiades, stone arrowheads were still extensively used. In fact it is quite clear from the finds everywhere that the possession of metal implements and weapons was for a long time the prerogative of a wealthy aristocracy in the Bronze Age world. One need only to consider the manner in which, according to Homer, the Trojan War was fought. It dissolved itself mainly into duels between well-equipped chieftains who alone were able to bear the expense of acquiring bronze arms and armor, while the common troops served, as it were, as a martial chorus, keeping the camp and rowing the ships. The social consequences that can be inferred from the limited usefulness of the ordinary man as a soldier, and which are indeed described by tradition, are his political insignificance and impotence. This military criterion of a citizen's value was still current in the early Roman republic when the popular assemblies were so organized that the weight of a man's vote was determined by his wealth, in particular by his ability to provide for himself at his own expense and not through public funds, a horse and arms in case of war.

Once the process was learned through which, by means of smelting, metal could be extracted from ore-laden stone, the discovery of the most successful and useful of ores, iron, was but a question of time. The people called Hittites, living in Asia Minor, with their capital near modern Bogazköy in Turkey, seem to have been the first to produce and use iron about 1400 B.C.[11] The oldest

---

[11] Childe 1945, 38, believes that "there are many grounds for supposing that [iron] had been discovered and jealously guarded by some barbarian tribes in Armenia where rich ores exist."

known piece of iron is a dagger from Egypt, but probably manufactured by the Hittites before 1350 B.C. In Europe, iron was first
used in Greece, about 1000 B.C., a date generally taken as the beginning of the European Iron Age.

Given the advanced cultural conditions and communications
in Europe, the art of ironworking spread rapidly all over the land.
In the Danube basin and as far west as Hallstatt in Upper Austria,
an early Iron Age culture can be found by 900 B.C., and its spread
thence to northern Italy across the manageable passes of the Alps
was only a short step.

As in the preceding metal ages, the evidence for the expansion of
Iron Age cultures tends to support a hypothesis of cultural spread
through infiltration and diffusion without concomitant large migrations.

Today we are, in fact, still living in the Iron Age, unless later
generations should consider the harnessing of atomic energy to
be of sufficient cultural importance to start a new era in the history
of mankind. Possibly we stand at the threshold of something less
glamorous to be called the Plastics Age. In any event, the dreary
prediction that the metal ages "must last to the end of time" [12] is
at best pessimistic and culture-bound. I suppose that, had there
been a likeminded anthropologist among the late palaeolithic peoples, he no doubt would have come, after 500,000 long years of
Old Stone Age, to the resigned but fatuously smug conclusion that
they had gone about as far as they could go.

[12] Keane 1920, 21.

CHAPTER IX

Italy in the Stone Ages   Anthropologists believe
they have discovered the most ancient evidence of humans in Italy
in a cave called Grotta Romanelli, near Otranto on the Adriatic
coast of the Sallentine peninsula. Some have spoken of the extremely primitive finds as belonging to a protolithic culture, to be
located during the Günz-Mindel interglacial period. The great
importance of the Grotta Romanelli and another, probably the
most famous palaeolithic site in Italy, the Grimaldi caves of the
Balzi Rossi, 'Red Rocks,' rising steeply from the sea on the Franco-
Italian border on the Riviera, between Menton and Ventimiglia,
lies in that these primeval dwelling places contain a succession of
layers which represent in chronological order the condition of the
troglodytes from the earliest to the latest Palaeolithic. From these
remnants one can gather the melancholy story of how these beings, in the course of hundreds of millennia, accounting for 98
per cent of human existence on earth, made practically no material
progress at all. The improvement in tools 10,000 years old over
those 500,000 years old is distressingly insignificant.

The stone implements characteristic of palaeolithic culture in
Italy can be classified with those called, according to typical French
finds, Chellean, Acheulian, and Mousterian. They are crudely
chipped and flaked pieces of quartzite and flint. Obviously the
users of these utensils were food gatherers and hunters, ignorant
of pottery and agriculture. The only animal they may have domes-
ticated was the dog. For the most part they lived in caves, though
they may have constructed primitive shelters. The extant remains
of their dead show that they had developed no particular burial
conventions.

Yet if we classify these people, regardless of the species they
may belong to (and most of them certainly were not of the *homo
sapiens* type) as human beings, at least as anthropoids, as we must

since they possessed a human culture, shown in their ability to manufacture and use tools intelligently, we ascribe to them by definition the faculty of speech. This we can safely do, despite the complete lack of any linguistic testimony, which will forever make it impossible to determine what kind of language they spoke. However, one can confidently say that the several groups of palaeolithic inhabitants of the Grimaldi caves in Liguria, those of La Maiella in the Abruzzi, those of Matera in Lucania, and those of Villafrati near Palermo in northwestern Sicily would not have been intelligible to one another at any fixed period. The scarcity of these people and the lack of communication among them warrants this linguistic condition.[1]

To what race or races these humans belonged is a much debated question. Obviously the only results obtainable must be based on the anthropometric examination of a very small number of skeletons and bones. Considering the uncritical passion with which this game of racial classification is often played, generally *ad maiorem gloriam* of one thing or another, "it is difficult to avoid the impression that prehistoric ethnologists, whenever only fragmentary and scattered material is available, as in dealing with palaeolithic man, are only too apt to regard as racial characteristics what after all may have been nothing more than individual peculiarities." [2]

One cannot, therefore, put complete trust in the most commonly held view that the palaeolithic inhabitants of Italy, like the Grimaldi people, were negroid invaders from Africa, forming a Eurafrican race. And it is difficult to understand how anthropologists can further affirm that this race had kinky hair and was inclined to steatopygy, that is, an excessively thick layer of fat on the buttocks.[3]

However, if apart from the vaporous findings of physical anthro-

[1] Whatmough 1937, 51, Map 4, shows eleven sites for the Stone Age. Only few others have since been brought to light. Cf. Ducati 1948, 11–23.

[2] Whatmough 1937, 52 n. 1.

[3] The steatopygy of seven small female figurines found in the Barma Grande grotto of the Balzi Rossi, and of others elsewhere in Italy and in Europe, is not sufficient proof for its prevalence among living persons. The statues exaggerate also the size of the breasts. Most likely the creator of these figures expressionistically overemphasized the female characteristics. (The so-called Venus of Savignano has no head at all; in its place there rises above her huge breasts a slender cone,

pology one is willing to place the origin of the Italian palaeolithic men into the larger frame of a migration of humans from Africa into a Europe, perhaps hitherto uninhabited for reasons of climate, then a case could be made for the Eurafrican race in Italy also. Allegedly this migration took place across two then still existing land bridges between Africa and Europe, one spanning the straits between Tunisia and Sicily (of which the islands of Malta and Pantelleria would be remnants), the other connecting Gibraltar and Morocco. But the evidence for these movements is, to say the least, tenuous. And some scholars deny outright any migration from Africa to Europe at that time — although for this, it seems to me, the argument from the absence of land connections between the two continents in the quarternary epoch is not a conclusive argument, because even to prehistoric men the crossing of the straits of Gibraltar could not have been an impossible feat. What Peet said some thirty years ago still largely holds true: "The exact genetic and temporal relations of the [Italian palaeolithic] deposits to similar deposits in other parts of Europe and in north Africa is a question which it would be at present unwise to attempt to answer." [4]

In the Grotta dei Fanciulli of the Balzi Rossi human skeletons were excavated at three distinct depths: at seven feet appeared a female skeleton, at twenty-two feet another, buried in a twisted position, adorned with marine shells at chest and forehead, and at twenty-seven feet, called Stratum I, there came to light a double burial of a youth and an elderly woman. This last is the oldest testimony of interment in Italy, belonging to the Lower Palaeolithic. The two persons were identified as belonging to the aforementioned negroid Eurafrican type, which was termed Grimaldi race after the place of discovery. But the later burials, of the Upper Palaeolithic, are generally classified with a different stock, namely

---

as long as the figure's torso, like an enormously long neck without a head.) And the beauty ideal of fatness, especially steatopygy, prevalent among some African tribes of our own days, is no proof on any grounds, be it 'primitiveness' of taste, or negroid racial connection, for the physical appearance of the inhabitants of the Balzi Rossi caves and of other palaeolithic men, or at least women. Cf. Paribeni 1908. It should be noted that no male figure of equal antiquity has been found, which makes the interpretation of overrepresentation of femaleness, emphasizing fecundity, all the more plausible.

[4] Peet 1924, 563.

the Cro Magnon type which is well known from France and bears its name after a site in the Dordogne. Considering the paucity of actual evidence, these classifications are patently dubious.

Some have believed they could distinguish even a third race of the later Upper Palaeolithic, exemplified by a skeleton unearthed near Loma dei Peligni in the Maiella region of the Abruzzi To this individual, whose height was 'calculated' as 1.644 meters (note the precision to millimeters), were ascribed agility, a quick intellect, vivacity, and a fine, lean face.[5] This choice though imaginary specimen was taken to represent an alleged superior breed and was proclaimed the prototype of the so-called Mediterranean race. In this manner the Mediterranean race, which was later to take shape, at least in the works of some anthropologists, could be invested with three characteristics, all dear to Italian prehistorians with a patriotic bent: it was autochthonous to Italy, that is, of at least palaeolithic origin; it was superior to other races which it superseded; it created, thanks to its excellence and without benefit of importation of men or cultures from the outside, the subsequent neolithic culture of Italy. There is simply no factual proof for all these hypotheses compounded and piled one on top of the other. On the contrary, the Mediterranean race, if there be one, and neolithic cultures can be more plausibly accounted for otherwise than by direct derivation from the Palaeolithic, as we shall see presently.

The Mesolithic in Italy, between 8500 and 2500 B.C., presents something of a gap, more so perhaps than in the rest of Europe. The cultures of Italy of that age were identifiable with the Azilian and Tardenoisian of France, the latter extending from North Africa all over Europe to the shores of the Baltic Sea. But the progress over palaeolithic life is, as a comparison of cultures shows, inconsequential.

The decisive metamorphosis in Italy occurs in the middle of the third millennium B.C. with the advent of the Neolithic Age. It is discernible in the manufacture and shape of the stone implements, which are no longer flaked and chipped but ground or polished. More importantly, Italian neolithic man accomplishes a number of economic and social advances, amounting to a complete

[5] Ducati 1948, 20.

revolution in human institutions and ways of life, such as outlined in the chapter on the prehistory of Europe. There I also expressed the thought that the upheaval in Europe was due not to a mere import of cultures but to an actual invasion of a different, more intelligent species of men. As for Italy, the bearers of neolithic cultures seem so far advanced over their mesolithic and palaeolithic predecessors, and the change appears in the finds with such suddenness and emphasis, that here, too, the assumption of a neolithic invasion imposes itself, whereby the palaeolithic population, not numerous in any event, either was extinguished or survived sporadically for some time without leaving important traces of its existence. Whence arrived the new men with their new civilization it is difficult to state with certainty, although on cultural grounds the Near and Middle East, as we have seen, are most likely the cradle of the neolithic invaders.

Such is roughly the opinion of the older school of Italian anthropologists and archaeologists, led by Sergi and Pigorini.[6] Their theories are shared by Peet,[7] and upheld by Randall-MacIver who believes that the neolithic invaders come to Italy by two routes from Africa, either by way of Gibraltar, Spain, and the Riviera to northern Italy, where they appear as protohistoric 'Iberians' and 'Ligurians,' or through Tunisia to Sicily and southern Italy, where they are eventually called 'Siculi.'[8] They are, then, a Eurafrican race, although, it seems to me, their coming to Spain and Italy by way of North Africa does not exclude an ultimate Asian — that is, Near or Middle Eastern — origin.

Of course, an approach to northern Italy from the Danubian lands, across the Carso and the Peartree Pass, or over more westerly Alpine passes, must also be considered in accordance with the neolithic migration routes mentioned in the preceding chapter. The fact that emerges clearly enough here is that the new culture comes to Italy from the north *and* from the south, by way of the Alps *and* the Mediterranean, through a pincer movement, as it were, which has its common point of departure somewhere in the Near East.

[6] Sergi 1898, 1919, and 1934. Pigorini 1903.
[7] Peet 1909.
[8] Randall-MacIver 1928, 17–18.

But influential and loud voices have been raised against the immigration theory, especially those of Rellini and Patroni, who do not recognize a revolution which suddenly terminates the palaeolithic and brings about the neolithic cultures, but only a slow evolution, carried through locally by autochthonous forces.[9] To Lamboglia, for example, the Mesolithic seems to incorporate sufficient progress to serve as a transitional period, at least in Liguria.[10] Similarly, Patroni declines to consider the Mesolithic as some kind of cultural hiatus, but sees in it the period in which the transformation from Palaeolithic to Neolithic is accomplished on Italian soil, albeit with the aid of foreign trade and newly established maritime relations.[11]

On one crucial point, however, the defenders of migration and autochthony agree, namely, that the bearers of the neolithic cultures of Italy, as compared with the palaeolithic people, are a different, new type of race, which Sergi called Mediterranean[12] and whose direct physical descendants he thought to see in the modern physical type commonly associated with Spaniards, Italians, Greeks, and Levantines, popularly characterized by small stature, slight build, dark hair, swarthy complexion, and vivaciousness in action and speech, whom also laymen are wont to name Mediterraneans.[13] The autochthonists, as we have seen, recognize the earliest Mediterraneans already in the palaeolithic skeleton of Loma dei Peligni, whereas the immigrationists can find no trace of them in Italy before the neolithic period. Yet again both agree on the superiority of the type, that is, on its closer physical agreements with modern man, regardless of race, than with the palaeolithic species of Italy and elsewhere.

But even if one wished to accept physical as well as cultural evidence for a racial transformation, one could surely neither subscribe to the idea of the existence or emergence of a 'pure' Mediterranean race, nor hold that within such an ethnic group certain restricted physical characteristics, especially as they allegedly reveal themselves after a mere examination of skeletal remains,

---

[9] Rellini 1929 and 1934. Patroni 1927 and 1951.
[10] Lamboglia 1941, 20.
[11] Patroni 1951, 279–280.
[12] Sergi 1919.
[13] Sergi 1934, viii–ix.

should be considered sufficient evidence for a further subdivision of the stock.

Whether the palaeolithic people of Italy were actually annihilated is a difficult question to answer, again for obvious lack of evidence. Patroni, at least, believes that a Mediterranean race does not arrive from Africa (or the Near East) with the physical appearance and cultural equipment of which testimony has been unearthed in the several regions where it settled, but rather that the evidence gathered by modern physical anthropologists is in each location due to a mixture of local and immigrated ingredients, albeit amalgamated in such a way that the traits of the superior, that is, neolithic element appear dominant.[14] While this makes good sense, also in terms of linguistics, as we shall see later, it does pose the question whether, if the invaders were Mediterraneans, they should still be called Mediterraneans after considerable mixture with the natives. The new population could have been, or might have become, predominantly Mediterranean, but there can of course be no longer any question of racial unity or purity all over the Mediterranean lands, since such purity is, if it is to evolve and endure, inevitably tied to conditions of ethnic isolation and must remain untainted by mixture with different racial substrata. In this sense, then, the inhabitants of Italy in neolithic as well as modern times are in no greater degree 'Mediterraneans' than the people of England are 'Anglo-Saxons.'[15]

All in all there are sufficient grounds for the hypothesis of a neolithic revolution, in Italy exactly as in the rest of Europe, brought about by immigration in fairly large numbers of better equipped and more intelligent men who supplanted, or at least submerged, the crude, clumsy, and apparently slow-witted palaeolithic creatures.

In Italy, as elsewhere, the Neolithic Age is characterized by a

[14] Patroni 1940, 47. Cf. also Della Seta 1928, 28. But if Patroni wishes at the same time to uphold his autochthonism, his two views can only be reconciled by inferring that the later dominant immigrating element actually came to Italy in very small numbers.

[15] I agree here, except for the teleological slant, with Della Seta 1928, 30: "The neolithic culture of Italy is thus the first example of the confluence toward her from all sides of elements of the neighboring cultures and sometimes of their bearers. Henceforth there is assured to this land the task of attraction and irradiation, which is its historic mission."

considerable progress in the business and the art of living, accompanied by a great increase in population. Man becomes a tiller of the soil, a domesticator of animals (the cultivation of grain-bearing grasses was introduced from the Near East and North Africa, as was the raising of sheep for meat, wool, and milk), [16] and an enjoyer of activities beyond feeding and propagating himself. He also learns to solemnize the disposal of his deceased fellows by a ritual, attested by the existence of burials, which are in Italy ordinarily of the inhumation type, and by certain locally fixed customs concerning the shape and equipment of the grave, the position of the body, and the adornments and weapons interred with the dead. This betrays some concern with extrahuman and supernatural forces, that is, the rudiments of a religious attitude.

People also lived in larger units than before, in villages, and sought shelter in constructed huts whose foundations and various shapes and patterns of arrangement can still be perceived, especially in Emilia and along the slopes facing the Adriatic between Ancona and Bari.[17]

The neolithic cultures of southern Italy and Sicily differ in quality, though not in kind, from those of northern Italy by being generally more advanced and showing definite influences from the Aegean area and Crete, which, however, did not penetrate very far into the peninsula. This distinction will easily be accounted for by the different routes of ingress to Italy, a northern and a southern, which I mentioned before.

What can we say concerning the language or languages of the inhabitants of neolithic Italy? The preceding palaeolithic dwellers were human, hence had the faculty of speech. Whether their dialects had any influence upon those of the invaders depends on various sociological and linguistic factors (relative number of speakers, extinction or perseverance of the palaeolithic substratum, social relationship of natives and invaders, linguistic relationships of various dialects involved) which we cannot even hope to illuminate by means of the available evidence and methods of interpretation. The most reasonable guess, taking all we know into

[16] Cf. Childe 1950, 5.
[17] On their detection with the aid of aerial photography see Bradford 1946 and 1949. Cf. also Bradford 1947.

account and arguing from historic parallels, would be that the speech of the invaders prevailed, thanks chiefly to their cultural, and possibly numerical superiority.

Various attempts have been made, as we have seen, notably by Giuseppe Sergi, to establish the existence of a homogeneous Mediterranean race to which the neolithic invaders (or even autochthonous neolithic inhabitants) would belong. Many scholars, with whom I agree, either reject altogether the hypothesis of a Mediterranean race in the physical sense in which Sergi and others would have it, or at least plead agnosticism in view of insufficient evidence. No matter what the truth of the matter, neither a proved unique race nor a conglomeration of stocks and tribes is prima facie evidence for a unique language or a variety of dialects, respectively, according to our criterion that race and language are not causally connectable items. Also the existence of a relatively homogeneous neolithic culture in the eastern part of the Mediterranean basin delivers no clues as to the linguistic conditions for the same reason, namely, the noncongruence a priori of language and culture.

To learn anything about the language of neolithic Italy and some other regions of the Mediterranean basin we would have only one trustworthy resort, that is, linguistic evidence.

But since no written document of any kind is available we are forced to fall back on inferences derived from linguistic fossils in later records. Among such foreign enclaves in languages that we know from subsequent periods, like Greek, Latin, various Anatolian dialects, are sporadic items of vocabulary, characteristic suffixes, proper names, especially place and river names, which because of their foreignness in a given dialect or their manifestations in the areas of several otherwise not related dialects lend some authority to the view that they are remainders of a more ancient linguistic substratum. Some scholars think they have discerned among these items such a homogeneity that they are willing to ascribe them all to a so-called Mediterranean language. To the extent that this theory is based on the existence of a Mediterranean race it will not hold water. But, even outside of that, it seems to me that the data we have at our disposal do not permit such important linguistic conclusions, especially if, in turn, in a classical example of circular reasoning, they are advanced as proof for the existence of a single Mediterranean race. The best that can be said at the present time on the matter of the prehistoric Mediterranean idioms is that it is not impossible that they belonged to a family of related dialects, like the Indo-European or the Romanic idioms — and this is, to my mind, already a daring hypothesis.[18] According to it a connection appears established between the ancient dialects of Asia Minor and various Aegean islands, Berber, Etruscan, Basque, and so forth.[19]

It appears, then, that, while we know nothing about palaeolithic languages in Italy, we know next to nothing about the speech used by the neolithic dwellers of the peninsula, apart from a tentative name-tag denoting little substance. When I use the term 'Mediterranean dialects' in the subsequent discussion, it should always be understood with this trenchant restriction.

[18] Devoto 1940, 43–50, distinguishes in fact five great Mediterranean linguistic areas: Libyan, Iberian, Tyrrhenian, Ligurian, Picene. Some of these will be examined in detail in later chapters.

[19] For general information on the Mediterranean stratum, and varied hypotheses and opinions see Herbig 1914; Ribezzo 1920, 1950; Hrozný 1928; Krahe 1938, 1949; Trombetti 1939; Devoto 1940, 37–50. A history of the research, a bibliography, and a wordlist may be found in Devoto 1954.

CHAPTER X

Northern and Central Italy in the Metal

Ages
The next step in the development of human culture produced a knowledge of metallurgy, the working of copper, bronze, and iron. Outside of Italy it seems that the Copper and Bronze Ages were spread in Europe without the aid of large migrating bodies of men, as evidenced by the linear, albeit accelerated development of cultures. But the belief that the culturally superior newcomers arrived at least in small groups, by infiltration, is sound enough, and it is in many locations confirmed by their position as an aristocracy.

AENEOLITHIC

The same seems to be true of Italy, that is, no important invasions need be postulated for the transition from the Stone to the Metal Ages.[1] An intermediate period called Aeneolithic is attested all over Italy by finds which, though they are fundamentally alike, show decided local peculiarities.[2] On the whole, three major groupings have been distinguished: a northern, a central-southern, and a Lombardian.[3] The last is singled out because of its characteristic pile dwellings in lakes, or *palafitte*, which shall be discussed presently. Another reason why the Lombardian palafitte

[1] Cf. Peet 1909 and 1924; Patroni 1951, 467–468. Whatmough 1937, 52–53, disagrees here. He connects the importation of metal to northern Italy with an invasion by a race of Alpine men, whom Sergi called Eurasian after their alleged origin

[2] A note on terminology is necessary here. What is elsewhere, and should be also in Italy, the Copper Age, has seemed to many scholars so transitory and lacking in characteristics of its own that they chose to name it Aeneolithic, which expresses more aptly the transitional stage between Neolithic and Bronze Age. Cf. Colini 1901, 125. Elsewhere Aeneolithic might mean Late Neolithic or Danubian III, etc. The welter of terminologies in archaeology is an unfortunate but inescapable, and perplexing, inheritance.

[3] Cf. Colini 1901, 122–123.

were accorded special attention is their possible connection with Indo-European languages.

In Italy, as in the rest of Europe, copper and bronze by no means replaced stone quickly and completely. There occurred an extended period of "good cheap stone and bad expensive copper, used concurrently [in] settlements too advanced to be truly neolithic, but not advanced enough to be counted truly of the bronze age."[4]

In the Copper Age and the Early Bronze Age a peculiar phenomenon appears in the lake country of northern Italy: the palafitte erected in lakes, or, as some think, on the lake shores near the water, perhaps in the shallows.[5] These structures also exhibit an entirely new funeral rite, cremation of the dead. Both the type of settlement and the new kind of burials, especially the latter, gave rise to the belief that only migrating tribes or peoples in large numbers could be responsible for such profound innovations. Even if one is ready to concede to the autochthonists that the construction of houses on platforms erected over piles might be due merely to local exigencies and was locally developed, not imported from Switzerland and Austria where similar lake dwellings are known,[6] there still remains to be explained the cremation rite which can be in no wise due to the natural conditions of any place. And that is the reason why Peet, for example, favors immigration[7] and why others, like Antonielli, state bluntly that an observable change of funeral customs is irrefutable evidence for a change of race.[8]

It is doubtful that this case, any more than others, can be dealt with by taking absolute positions on autochthonism or migrationism. But by applying the criteria set forth in my chapter on postulates and methods, the most plausible solution seems to be that we are confronted with a numerically weak infiltration from across the Alps. The archaeological evidence, showing a gradual cultural evolution, could be explained by a mere process of borrowing and cultural transfer by diffusion. But this would be a

[4] Whatmough 1937, 61.
[5] See Vouga 1928, 404; Ducati 1948, 55.
[6] Patroni 1951, 321 ff., 560, 642 ff. This continuity theory which is outlined in Peet 1909, 496 ff., goes back to Brizio 1898.
[7] Peet 1924, 567–568.
[8] Antonielli 1927, 46, and *passim*; 1929, 39.

very difficult, indeed nearly impossible manner of accounting for the new burial rite. And the linguistic argument cinches the case. Detailed discussion of the language situation will come later, but the cumulative evidence that will accrue from here on will show that we must assume the arrival of the first speakers of Indo-European dialects during the Aeneolithic in northern Italy. And since the kind of language transfer that brings to Italy the Indo-European dialects which spread rapidly and permanently over the entire peninsula, fully replacing older linguistic strata, is, in view of its speed and thoroughness, virtually inexplicable by the inefficient process of diffusion, a transplantation of human beings must be presumed. Cultural, nonlinguistic evidence favors infiltration, as we have seen, over migration.

As for the pile dwellings themselves, I daresay that they are not the only, though perhaps the most striking and hence most debated phenomenon of the Lombard Aeneolithic, and that carriers of copper arriving from Switzerland and Austria settled also elsewhere in northern Italy, coalescing with the native population and probably teaching them their Indo-European speech. I believe with Whatmough[9] that the palafitte type of housing represents simply a transfer from Switzerland and Austria. It is, of course, associated with lakes; but when the concomitant culture spreads farther south into lakeless regions, into the Po valley and the Apennines, lake dwellings become senseless. Ducati believes that the palafitte of the Alpine fringe of Italy are not on the principal path of the Bronze Age culture and the cremation rite, which he rather derives from the eastern much lower Alpine passes, where after ascending the Danube, Drave, and Save valleys they cross the Peartree Pass and the Carso into Italy.[10] This is, as we have seen, the classical route to Italy from the east, both for migrants and merchants, and it is quite plausible that at least part of the carriers of the new metal cultures, the new burial rite, and the new idioms, took this road to the Apennine peninsula. But it is not necessary to exclude for this reason a more western approach for some of the new arrivals.

As for the race of the lake-dwelling and other northern invaders

[9] Whatmough 1937, 71.
[10] Ducati 1948, 56.

during the Aeneolithic, it will be difficult to identify them as Alpine, even if one were ready to discern such a race elsewhere.
The presence of a certain physical stock which to some anthropologists seems, or seemed, to prevail in the regions of the Alps
in Austria, Switzerland, and northern Italy, may possibly be
claimed for a later date, but certainly cannot be recognized so
early. The term Danubian, associated rather with a Central European culture and comfortably neutral as to race, might prove more
useful, though not more precise ethnically. That the invaders
were of the Mediterranean race (even in the widest sense of the
term) is more than doubtful: all criteria we possess, culture, burials,
and a reasonable linguistic hypothesis, contradict the assumption
in all important respects, and whereas singly each one would prove
little enough, jointly they render any theory of 'Northern Mediterraneans' more than gravely suspect.

I suggest, then, that the Aeneolithic culture, together with the
cremation rite and the first Indo-European languages (more about
them later), was introduced to northern Italy from Central Europe
by small incursions of invaders whose cultural and military superiority permitted them to conquer or at least infiltrate the neolithic
tribes. These, again for obvious reasons of prestige and cultural
pressure, and despite their greater number, also acquired the language of the invaders, just as, for example, the Kelts of Gaul
learned Latin after the conquest by Caesar from an assuredly
smaller number of Latin-speaking merchants, soldiers, settlers,
and administrators.[11] On the other hand, the newcomers themselves, in view of their small number (and, not unlikely, in the
absence of racial prejudices), were physically and ethnically
absorbed among the natives, as were the Romans, ethnically a
highly mixed lot in any case, in Spain and Gaul many centuries
later.

The conclusion of greatest ethnic consequence which results
from this is that in any case the immigrating 'Indo-Europeans,' if
there ever were such people (a proposition which I shall later refute

[11] Cf. Devoto 1951, 67–68: "The Indo-European migrations were certainly not
founded on numbers. . . Nor were they even founded on a technical, intellectual, or artistic superiority. . . But the fact that they diffused languages implies
a solid social organization . . ."

in detail), most certainly ceased to be ethnically 'Indo-Europeans' upon their arrival in Italy.

The foregoing events take place in the first half of the second millennium B.C. In the second half, the most remarkable phenomenon in northern Italy, mainly in the Po plain, is the so-called terramare culture, a Bronze Age civilization, characterized, briefly, by palafitte, generally erected on a common platform and united into a settlement, but on dry land, or perhaps in marshy, swampy areas subject to flooding by the Po.[12] The name is derived from a local patois expression, *terra mar(n)a*, 'fat earth,'[13] so termed because peasants found the huge heaps of decomposed refuse and offal of these settlements, within which the wooden piles were buried, a rich fertilizer for their fields. (Such rubbish heaps of prehistoric settlements were first studied in Denmark and called kitchen midden.)

In view of their peculiar habitat, the first question that occurs will be whether there is any connection between the earlier lake dwellers of the Alpine districts, the Palafitticoli, and the inhabitants of the terramare, or Terramaricoli, in the Po plain. Of course, an assumption of relationship of any kind is in no wise necessary,[14] for the local conditions of the terrain may have been such as to oblige the settlers to protect their villages by raising them on piles. People have been doing that all over the world for a long time. That the Terramaricoli constructed a common platform for a number of houses and lived together in communities is at this stage of social development no longer surprising. The consensus has been, in fact, that the construction of the terramare is simply a

[12] As usually the exact chronology is a matter of controversy. The earliest appearance of the terramare culture is fixed, for example, by Pisani 1931, 613, between 2500 and 2300 B.C., though this dating no doubt includes the lake palafitte of Lombardy; by Säflund 1938, 52, at 2100 B.C., by Montelius 1912, 176, about 1800 B.C., by Myres 1935, from 1700 B.C. on; by Hawkes 1950, 262, at 1550 B.C., and by Hermes 1935, 814, at 1250 B.C. Obviously not all these authors meant the same thing when speaking of terramare culture, and if they did, the non-expert is left to wonder what to make of these enormous discrepancies.

[13] Some use a plural *terremare* rather than *terramare*, which Devoto 1946, 293 n. 15, in dissent with Patroni, considers pedantic and linguistically unjustified. I agree.

[14] Cf. Rellini, Civiltà, 1933, 77.

response to local exigencies.[15] Since, furthermore, sites have been explored which, although culturally matching exactly the terramare civilization, show no traces of piles and platforms,[16] it can safely be assumed that there is no need to look for proto-terramare of the pile construction type outside of Italy whence this kind of architecture should have been imported.[17]

One reason for the controversy as to whether connections and relationship between Central European cultures and the terramare of Italy can be proved is, in the works of many authors, the negligence with which the terms are handled. It is not always made clear whether a given writer uses terramare in a cultural or ethnic sense, or in both meanings together; whether in speaking of immigration and importation he envisages a human movement or merely cultural borrowing; and whether, if he does explicitly speak of an invasion, he means a vast migration that obliterates the previous inhabitants of the region, or a minor transfer and infiltration of individuals and families who are physically absorbed by the natives but come to predominate culturally. The answer to any of these questions will be decisive, as we have seen, for judging the linguistic situation. And wherever none is clearly given, linguistic deductions remain specious.

It would lead too far to enter into the details of the long and complex debate on the Italian Bronze Age. Instead I shall suggest, to some degree anticipating the linguistic arguments, what seems to me a plausible view.[18]

With the terramare we are entering upon the full Bronze Age,

[15] Cf. Peet 1924, 568–570; Rellini 1929, 9–11; 1938, 10; Patroni 1932, 534, 538; Säflund 1939, 221–222; Barocelli 1942, 136–138; Cary 1949, 113–114.
[16] Cf. Säflund 1939, 236.
[17] Cf. Childe 1947, 242–244. Some archaeologists thought to have found such a place at Tószeg, on the Tisza river in Hungary. Cf. Peet 1909, 506–507; Wilke 1919, 173 ff. But this is energetically denied by Rellini 1929, 9–11, Civiltà, 1933, 77; Leopold 1929, 26. Childe 1929, 264–265, believes, quite correctly it seems, that the 'Flat Hill' of Tószeg is not the same thing as a terramara, but that it is "not impossible that Tószeg, or some more westerly station of the same type, may contain the germs from which the terramara culture of Italy sprang."
[18] I shall not give extensive and detailed references here. Consult the bibliography of Part III especially under the items Barocelli 1942; Childe 1947, 1950; Dawson 1928; Devoto 1951; Leopold 1929, 1930, 1932; Messerschmidt 1935; Myres 1935; Patroni 1930, 1932, 1943; Peet 1909, 1924; Pittioni 1938; Randall-MacIver 1924, 1928; Rellini 1929, Civiltà, 1933, 1938; Säflund 1938, 1939; Täubler 1932. Cf. also Randall-MacIver 1939 for a résumé of the entire discussion.

prepared by the preceding Copper or Aeneolithic Age. As in the rest of Europe, the advent of the Bronze Age in Italy was not revolutionary but evolutionary, which, according to a repeatedly tested criterion, implies the absence of vast migrations and ethnic turmoil.[19] However, since besides the cultural paraphernalia also a new burial rite is introduced, the assumption, as in the case of the Palafitticoli of the lakes, of a limited migration of persons from Central Europe to the Apennine peninsula recommends itself. This hypothesis is strengthened by, and in turn strengthens (and this is not a circular argument!), the belief that these newcomers brought with them new Indo-European dialects.

My words so far should not imply that I deny any connection, cultural, ethnic, and linguistic, between the lake palafitte and the terramare. Culturally, they are both the first settlements in northern Italy which exhibit a knowledge of the manufacture and use of metal, the difference between copper and bronze cultures being only a chronological one. Evidence shows that both came from Central Europe, the bronze of the terramare no doubt across the eastern end of the Alps, by way of the Danube, Drave, and Save valleys. It does not seem probable, therefore, that the lake villages, showing a stage of culture on the whole less advanced, should be derived culturally from the more advanced terramare. Nor does there seem to exist any good cause to assume that the copper-bearing invaders should have come by the way of the eastern passes of the Alps but should then have continued their march through the Po plain, without stopping, to settle in the lake district farther west. It seems more reasonable to conclude that the aeneolithic culture of the Palafitticoli of the lakes came directly from the Swiss and Austrian lakes. But the latter sites, judging by the finds, had been reached from the same general European location from which the terramare culture derived. The two are therefore related in their origins but came to Italy by different routes.

It is of course possible, as I have said, though it is not a necessary assumption, that the Terramaricoli learned the erection of villages on piles from their lake-dwelling cultural cousins, if, as seems fairly certain, the prongs of this cultural bifurcation met

[19] Cf. Kaschnitz-Weinberg 1950, 341.

somewhere in the Po plain.[20] This hypothesis in no wise contradicts, indeed it confirms, the most plausible linguistic hypothesis, namely, that the bringers of metal to Italy, of copper and bronze, in successive stages and by different roads, though always in small numbers, both carried with them Indo-European dialects.[21]

Several ramifications of the terramare theory which are of great import for future cultural, historical, and linguistic developments will be discussed at their proper places. Fundamentally they are all concerned with the extension of the terramare over other parts of Italy outside the Po plain. Again the cultural and ethnic aspects of such extensions have not been always fully distinguished from one another. Hence the unqualified assertion that there are 'terramare' along the Adriatic coast and in Apulia as far south as Taranto, albeit sporadically, has meant different things to different authors and readers, by implication and inference. As before, my position will be that the term terramare in the east and south of Italy can at best be applied to culture, although even that is questioned by some scholars.[22] All in all the evidence is such that at least cultural borrowing becomes clear beyond doubt. Migration, if it may be assumed at all, did certainly not exceed infiltration by a small number.[23] The consequences to be drawn from this view will be examined in connection with the Villanovans and the Latins.

[20] But cf. Peet 1924, 568.

[21] Cf. Devoto 1951, 75. On the linguistic point, at least, Laviosa-Zambotti 1943, 497–498, disagrees, without unfortunately making it clear who precisely did for the first time import Indo-European dialects to Italy. Of course no one, not even the most fanatic autochthonist, cares to suggest that Indo-European languages were indigenous in Italy.

[22] Cf. Randall-MacIver 1924, 95; Peet 1909, 421–424; Rellini 1929, 9–11. Leopold 1932, 37–38, believes, since not all elements distinctive of certain southern sites often referred to as terramare (Timmari, Punta del Tonno) are in fact of the terramare type, that no migration of Terramaricoli to these locations took place but only a piecemeal importation of objects. For a survey of opinions see Messerschmidt 1935, 9.

[23] On the whole, though perhaps not in all details, I agree here with Rellini 1929, 64: "The great importance [of the so-called extra-terramare sites of southern Italy] lies in the fact that in them one can see the persistence of the aeneolithic element, settled in the peninsula since remote times, into the Bronze Age, distinct from the ethnos of the Terramaricoli tribes, but whose influences it nonetheless undergoes while continuing, more or less modified in the course of the Bronze Age, the development of its culture." Cf. also Rellini 1938, 9; Childe 1950, 171–172; Säflund 1938, 22. Whether Indo-European dialects also were carried to southern Italy at that time will be discussed later.

When attempting to correlate the Terramaricoli with an ethnic name transmitted by tradition, scholars are often treading on the thin ice of nomenclature. For to suggest that the Terramaricoli were the Ananes,[24] or Proto-Italici,[25] or Euganei,[26] or Italici,[27] or Ligurians, Veneti, or Safines,[28] can result in nothing more than onomastic equations whose meaningful content will be illusory as long as each of the terms is employed in several significations by ancient authors as well as by modern scholars. I shall later attempt some sort of correlation at least in terms of linguistics.

A word should be said about the shape and construction of the terramare pile settlements because the arguments advanced have important ethnic and linguistic corollaries. Practically every book dealing with terramare reproduced the ground plan of the terramara of Castellazzo di Fontanellato as first drawn by Pigorini.[29] It is trapezoidal in outline, with the longer sides running parallel from north to south. The entire village is surrounded by a wooden rampart and a moat, and divided into four main sections by two roads which cross in the center of the platform, each section being subdivided into rectangular (except along the edges) blocks. A bridge across the moat lies at the northern end of the longer of the two principal streets, while on the eastern side there is a plot reserved for some ritual place, surrounded by smaller ditches and accessible from the platform over small bridges from the west and north. Outside the settlement there is situated a terramara for the dead, as it were, where the characteristic biconical urns, containing the ashes of the deceased and covered with a stone slab or an inverted vase, are crowded closely together, sometimes in two stories. This layout of the Castellazzo terramara was pronounced typical and then compared with the shape and plan of a Roman military camp, which contained the two main streets intersecting in the center, called *cardo* and *decumanus*, and was fortified with wooden and earthen ramparts. It was even likened to the plan of a Roman city, particularly to the ancient *Roma*

[24] Patroni 1943, 123.
[25] Randall-MacIver 1928, 35; Devoto 1951, 74.
[26] Säflund 1939, 238.
[27] Wilke 1919, 173.
[28] Conway 1926, 462.
[29] Pigorini 1892.

Quadrata, with a holy place, the *templum*, and the *mundus*, on the Palatine Hill, corresponding to the *templum* and the so-called *sulcus primigenius* on the eastern side of the terramara. These similarities seem superficial and tenuous enough, but they were transformed forthwith into a formidable theory affirming that in view of them the Terramaricoli were the physical ancestors of the Latins and Romans.[30]

We are by now familiar with this facile hybridization of ethnic, cultural, and linguistic evidence, which piles one hypothesis on the other and arrives at completely illusory results. A number of scholars did in fact reject the whole supposition of terramare ancestry for Rome.[31]

But there were more damaging arguments forthcoming, enough to annihilate practically all terramare theorizing, save the cultural aspects. As early as 1929 and 1933 Rellini said that the famous, or notorious, terramara of Castellazzo di Fontanellato was not at all typical of settlements of the terramare culture, but only one type among several, and that there could be no question of any regular or prescribed shape, size, or plan for such communities.[32] And then in 1939 Säflund showed that Pigorini's reconstructed plan of the terramara of Castellazzo was not only not typical but indeed purely conjectural and arbitrary to begin with, having no basis in any facts brought to light by the actual excavation. He then exhibited two plans of the terramara superimposed one on the other: that of Pigorini, so often reproduced in succeeding publications, and his own. There is, indeed, no similarity whatever between the two drawings, except perhaps the one main road running roughly north and south.[33]

This leaves us no more than a culture which we may continue to call, if we wish, terramare; the importance of the terramare

---

[30] Cf., for example, Täubler 1932 for this argument and further references.
[31] Patroni 1930, 428–433; Whatmough 1937, 263–264; Ducati 1938, 44–45; and especially Säflund 1939, *passim.* (See below.) In agreement with the extensive proofs marshalled by Säflund are Patroni 1940, 12 (condemning the rest of Säflund's book as not containing "a single acceptable result," which is an undeservedly harsh judgment); Barocelli 1942, 143–144; Childe 1947, 242–244. But Devoto 1951, 74–75, still does compare at least the physical appearance of the terramara and the Roman camp.
[32] Rellini 1929, 9–11; 1933, Civiltà, 78–79.
[33] Säflund 1939, Tavola 93.

village as typical for the whole Bronze Age culture had been, to say the least, highly overestimated. (Such an overestimation prevailed also, as I noted, with regard to the lake palafitte of the Aeneolithic, and the point will have to be made again below with reference to the Villanovan culture.) This peculiar way of living and constructing villages is, then, a purely local phenomenon, representing one of several kinds of construction of the Italian Bronze Age.[34]

If this is fully recognized, the problem of the so-called extra-terramare is also put into proper perspective. The only reason for calling by that name certain sites, which were not by any means pile constructions of the Pigorini or any other scheme, was the cultural agreements with the Po country villages on piles. If all these cultures are simply recognized as Bronze Age civilizations, the term extraterramare with reference to some forty stations [35] all the way down to Taranto has found its just demise.[36]

IRON

As was the case with previously described changes of culture, the first question that arises in connection with the Iron Age of Italy is whether the new culture is introduced from the outside or is the organic development of a native civilization. If the latter, it must continue the Bronze Age cultures; if the former, we must again inquire whether it is due to a mass immigration or to infiltration.

The Iron Age is very slow in taking hold in Italy. This may well be due to Italy's poverty in ores, which prevented metallurgy, especially ironworking, from becoming spontaneously popular among the natives.[37] That in itself is a fact slightly favoring the immigration theory. On the other hand the very gradualness of the transition, the absence of a violent break anywhere,

[34] Kaschnitz-Weinberg 1950, 343, distinguishes four such kinds, of which one is the terramara, another the palafitta on the lake. In the same sense Patroni, Due, 1940, wants to call the terramara simply *palafitte arginate* 'pile dwellings with ramparts.'

[35] Listed by Rellini, Civiltà, 1933, 69–71.

[36] Rellini, Civiltà, 1933, 93, proposes to call that entire 'extra-terramare' culture the Apennine culture. Säflund 1938, 21 prefers the term Adriatic culture, on the theory that it reached Italy from the Balkan peninsula by way of the Adriatic Sea, remaining untouched by the terramare culture proper.

[37] Cf. Whatmough 1937, 24.

excludes a violent incursion of great hordes of foreigners. Hence the assumption of an infiltration of nomadic groups and a slow process of learning by the natives is indicated.

There are several distinct Iron Age cultures in Italy, which, though they have much in common, may be distinguished from each other by various details. And there is a rather perceptible dissimilarity between northern sites (down to Latium and the Alban Hills) and southern sites (from the Alban Hills south and east). With the second I shall deal in the next chapter, though frequent reference will have to be made to them here.

Proceeding from north to south, the following Iron Age cultures, named after their geographic location or principal sites, should be mentioned: [38] Comacine-Golaseccan south of Lakes Maggiore and Como); Villanovan, subdivided into Villanovan proper or Northern Villanovan (of Emilia), Tuscan, and Latian; Atestine (in Venezia Euganea, called after Ateste, the modern Este); Picene (on the east coast); Apulian; Campanian; Bruttian (in Calabria, the ancient Bruttium); Sicilian. Among these I should like to discuss in some detail the Villanovan culture, not only because it has come to be regarded as the Iron Age culture of Italy par excellence (like terramare for the Bronze Age), but mainly because its origin and the course of its development will be of the greatest consequence for the linguistic history of Italy.

The name Villanovan was given to this culture by Count Giovanni Gozzadini, an archaeologist who in 1853 discovered the remains of a necropolis near the town of Villanova, a short distance from Bologna, whose finds have come to be considered typical. Since then the opinions thereon of scholars from various branches of prehistoric science have diverged greatly. Rather than discuss all views extensively and critically, I shall merely refer to them with whatever comment seems appropriate as I put down my own beliefs.[39]

[38] I am following here Whatmough 1937, 87. The division by Peet 1924, 572, is quite similar.

[39] For a concise résumé of the whole problem see Randall-MacIver 1924, 92–93. Among the scholars favoring an invasion from the north are: Brizio 1898; Piganiol 1917; von Duhn 1924; Randall-MacIver 1924, 1928; Sergi 1934; Messerschmidt 1935; Myres 1935; Whatmough 1937; Ducati 1938; Patroni 1939, 1951. For development of Villanovan from terramare pronounce themselves: Helbig 1879; Pigorini 1903; Peet 1924; Della Seta 1928; Gomme 1935; Pittioni 1938. There are

In examining the evidence together with the reports and theories based on it one cannot help noticing that conclusions depend frequently on what type of records given scholars favor in their arguments. Those who set great store by the modes of burial and seek classifications accordingly believe that we are faced with an immigration from the north, either separate from the terramare invasion or a continuation and intensification of it. The scholars who propose a separate invasion of Villanovans, following the Terramaricoli, do so on the grounds that an important innovation like the iron industry could not be a spontaneous native development but had to be imported from somewhere. The autochthonists, however, claim that the transition from the Bronze to the Iron Age was so slow, indeed hesitant, that, possibly with the aid of migrating craftsmen and traders, the indigenous population developed the art of ironworking on its own.

The infiltration theory is once more supported by linguistic considerations. While of course we know nothing of the language spoken by the Villanovans, we are inclined to think that they brought with them, again like the Terramaricoli, Indo-European dialects. But need we assume two waves of Indo-European dialects coming to Italy, first the one borne by the Terramaricoli, then the Villanovan? Could one not suppose that the Villanovan speech, if Indo-European, is the same as that of the Terramaricoli or a later form of it? It is Kaschnitz-Weinberg's opinion that indeed the Villanovans alone, and not the Terramaricoli, are invaders and that only they are responsible for the appearance of Indo-European dialects in Italy. He also believes that for the Bronze Age there is no proof whatever of a large immigration of speakers of Indo-European to Italy, and that the Terramaricoli were no new ethnos on the peninsula.[40] Also Merhart thinks of the Villanovan invasion in these terms, making the newcomers of the Iron Age responsible for the Indo-Europeanization of the Terramaricoli.[41] Patroni also suggests that the only immigration to Italy previous to the Keltic invasion of the fourth century before Christ, though still a

also some few who propose a Villanovan advance from the south; Grenier 1912; Taylor 1923; Antonielli 1927; Säflund 1938; Ducati 1948.

[40] Kaschnitz-Weinberg 1950, 365, 343–345.

[41] Merhart 1942, 66.

minor one, is represented not by the builders of palafitte of one kind or another but by Villanovans.[42] But the view, adopted by myself, which relegates the terramare culture to its true position of merely one of a number of Bronze Age cultures and which therefore obviates any discussion concerning the ethnos of the Terramaricoli, makes it inopportune to worry any longer about these ethnic relationships, especially since, as we shall see presently, also the so-called Villanovans do not in any sense constitute a closed racial or ethnic group that can be differentiated from other Iron Age peoples of Italy.

The archaeological evidence favors on the whole some kind of immigration which brought iron to northern Italy. And since the newcomers, to the best of our knowledge, came from the same cultural area as the Terramaricoli, that is, from the Danubian lands, chances are, and later corroborative evidence supports this view, that they too brought with them an Indo-European tongue.[43] But, as in preceding cases of invasion, I wish to reject the theory of a mass movement in favor of infiltration, for the usual reasons.

However, there arises in the Iron Age cultures of Italy a bothersome complication. It shows itself in the theories advanced by those who emphasized in their research the evidence of burial and language less than the record of cultural equipment. For in comparing the finds of the sites of southern Italy, Latium, and Tuscany, with those from locations north of the Apennines, the conclusion is inevitable that the former were more advanced and that the latter learned from them. (Indeed one of the most typical Villanovan relics, the biconical funerary urn, seems to have come to the Bologna area from the south.[44]) The Southern Villanovan discoveries of Latium and Tuscany are, at any given period, superior to the Northern Villanovan ones of Emilia and the Villanova site proper. This, then, poses the grave problem as to whether the 'Villanovans' did not come from the south to the north.

An affirmative answer to this question has led some prehistorians so far as to think that the so-called Villanovan culture is really no more than the Etruscan culture, originating in Etruria

[42] Patroni 1951, 565.
[43] This is also the opinion of Randall-MacIver 1924, 99; 1928, 43–50.
[44] Colini 1908, 37–39; Kaschnitz 1950, 376–377.

and thence spreading north.[45] But this extreme view is at odds with too much of what we know for certain, and has found few adherents.

Being faced with two apparently irreconcilable Iron Age movements in Italy, one from the south, the other from the north, and two corresponding migration theories, both of them founded on records which, though they are trustworthy, lead to different conclusions if they are differently weighed and emphasized, one may recall that three times before, in the discussion of the Neolithic, the Aeneolithic, and the Bronze Age, it appeared that the new cultures reached Italy on two fronts. It seems to me that the peculiar testimony of the Iron Age cultures can be interpreted in the same way.

The one feature that both the northern and the southern current have in common is iron itself. Now ironworking, as has been said, originated somewhere in the Near East, possibly among the Hittites. Thence it spread westward, like the Neolithic, Copper, and Bronze Age cultures, over a northern, Danubian, and a southern, Aegean route. In the course of this movement it became the property of various ethnic and cultural groups, so that when it crossed the Peartree Pass to Italy it was carried by people who cremated their dead and probably spoke Indo-European languages, whereas when it approached the peninsula from the south it was transmitted as the property of societies which were 'Mediterranean' in culture, inhumed their dead, and did not speak Indo-European.

It is therefore not surprising that, as I said before, scholars emphasizing different expressions of the Iron Age culture of Italy, that is, material remains, cremation rites, or linguistic conditions, should arrive at different conclusions as to its origins. What complicates matters as compared with preceding periods is that during the Iron Age the northern and the southern prongs actually met on Italian soil, intermingled thoroughly, and indeed overlapped. This accounts for the appearance of southern materials, at a late date,

[45] See Pallottino 1940, 30–31. Similarly also Clark 1952, 200. Pallottino also thinks that the Etruscans are autochthonous (a belief which the vast majority of scholars reject), hence has no difficulty with the spread of his Etruscan-Villanovan culture from Tuscany to the Emilia, regardless of dating. But Clark, who does have the Etruscans come from the Aegean area, vitiates his Villanovan theory by his own chronology, I think.

in Bologna and Este, but also for northern cremation burials and Indo-European dialects in the south.

At this point, Italian prehistory finds itself in a dilemma that cannot be solved by one's taking sides either for a north-south or a south-north migration of 'Villanovans.' If Ducati claims, for instance, that northern and southern Villanovans were one and the same 'people' (*popolo*), that both were originally 'related' (*cognato*) with the Terramaricoli, he is virtually forced by his own argument and the nature of the records to have the new-comers from the north, once they had reached Italian soil, push on rapidly across the Apennines without much pausing, establish themselves in Tuscany and Latium, and then return before long with their Southern Villanovan culture to found a Northern Villanovan culture in Emilia.[46] This is not satisfactory, nor was it so to Ducati himself, who proposed concurrently the much sounder theory, which I myself shall follow, that the north-south move-ment was both ethnic and cultural, that is, one of migration or infiltration, and the south-north movement, mostly cultural, that is, one of diffusion.[47] In other words, people who were the bearers of the Northern Villanovan culture did cross the Apennines, bring-ing with them to Etruria and Latium certain characteristics pe-culiar to their ethnos, namely, cremation burial and Indo-European speech, whereas for the Southern Villanovan culture no such mi-grating bearers can be discerned, leaving diffusion for its mode of expansion. Unlike the two traits peculiar to the northern culture, cremation and Indo-European speech, the art of ironworking itself was nothing new to the Southern Villanovans, who in fact, being in possession of a more advanced iron culture, were in a position to become the Northerners' teachers, when the meeting of cultures occurred. There is indeed considerable evidence that the northern invaders of Latium, distinguishable by their cremation graves, eventually succumbed at least in the cultural domain of the disposal of the dead to southern influences: the mixed inhumation and cre-mation graves in various parts of Latium, including the Roman Forum, show a progressive gain of inhumation over cremation as time goes by.[48] But the newly imported Indo-European dialects

[46] Ducati 1932, 68; 1938, 182. See also Merhart 1942, 54–57.
[47] Ducati 1928, 72; 1948, 88.
[48] Peet 1924, 574.

were never again superseded by a reëmergence of the older idioms.

This means, of course, that the Northern and Southern 'Villanovans' were not the same people, racially and nationally speaking, that indeed the term Villanovan should be used only to name certain Iron Age cultures in Italy, without any ethnic or political connotation.[49]

The other Iron Age cultures of Italy, not subsumed under the heading Villanovan, that is, all those practicing inhumation burials in the center and south, those south of the Alban Hills and generally those east of the crest of the Apennines, will be discussed in the next chapter. As for the remaining northern Comacine-Golaseccan and Atestine cultures, which are like the Villanovan of the cremation type, I should hold, with Whatmough, "the view . . . which sees in them units not so much gradually differentiated by special local developments and conditions as rather due to separate invasions from a common source whence they all drew their main inspiration." [50]

[49] Into this scheme fits also the description by Randall-MacIver 1924, 72, of the Northern Villanovans around Bologna as "foster children of the Danube [cultures]" and of the Southern Villanovans of Etruria as "rather backward pupils of the Aegean." Also Myres 1935, 75–176, thinks the northern different from the southern 'Villanovans.' But see also Randall-MacIver 1928, 134–140, on Northern and Southern Villanovan chronology, where he places Northern Benacci I, still of the Bronze Age, at 1050–950 B.C., whereas the earliest Southern Villanovan cultures, already of the Iron Age, appear not far north of Rome at Tolfa, in the Alban Hills, and in Rome itself around 1000 B.C. He also maintains, 1924, 79, that there was an early Villanovan population, possibly of a pre-Benacci period, in the Alban Hills as early as the twelfth and eleventh centuries. The earliest Iron Age he dates in the north, as Benacci II, between 950 and 750 or 700 B.C. Now, it is impossible that an Iron Age culture beginning around Bologna about 950 B.C. should move south and appear in Rome about 1000 B.C. (Cf. Whatmough 1937, 85.) It is also not likely that a Bronze Age culture of Bologna, Benacci I, which starts about 1050 B.C., still according to Randall-MacIver's chronolgy, should show itself in Rome as an Iron Age culture just fifty years later. An alleged cultural, and less even an ethnic movement from north to south just does not suffice to explain the southern Iron Age without cultural or chronological confusion.

Light is thrown on this problem also in Whatmough 1937, 85, by the chronology according to which "the 'Villanovans' of Latium were settled there at a date earlier than that at which the 'Villanovans' of Emilia reached their province." Whatmough's use of apostrophes here expresses the same skepticism on regarding Villanovan as an ethnic term as does my own statement in so many words above. Consequently, he finds (1937, 264–265) the infusion of Villanovan blood, that is, ethnos, to have been very slight in Rome, and considers the population of Latium, despite their Villanovan culture, to be ethnically of neolithic stock.

[50] Whatmough 1937, 87.

While Whatmough states this without specifying a number for the invaders, I should again propose their number to have been small. The western settlements of some of them, around Lakes Como and Maggiore, may possibly be considered as due to an invasion across the passes of the Alps lying immediately to the north of that region, following perhaps the same paths which some time earlier the aeneolithic lake dwellers had taken. Another, probably more numerous immigration, still from the same general Danubian area, marched across the lower eastern Alpine passes, or may have indeed come from the Balkan peninsula, and settled in Venezia Euganea to form the Atestine culture.

In conclusion, I should say that the Iron Age cultures of northern Italy are due, like their Copper and Bronze Age predecessors, to numerically weak but socially and culturally powerful infiltrations, bringing to Italy also cremation as their customary burial rite, and Indo-European dialects. In central Italy, mainly Tuscany and Latium, they encountered and overlapped other Iron Age cultures which were mainly inspired by Aegean civilizations, characterized by inhumation of the dead and non-Indo-European ('Mediterranean') speech. The meeting of these two principal strains north of the Alban Hills and west of the Apennines promoted on the one hand the northward flow of the southern type of Iron Age culture, which in the regions of Tuscany found its ultimate and most successful propagators in the non-Italian Etruscans,[51] whereas on the other hand it facilitated the spread of cremation burials from north to south, together with the linguistic Indo-Europeanization. While subsequently the incidence of cremation burials receded in both north and south, partly under the influence of the culturally powerful inhuming Etruscans, partly by the resurgence of the rites of a numerous ethnic and cultural substratum of inhumers, the establishment of Indo-European dialects was to remain permanent, except, temporarily, among the Etruscans themselves.[52]

[51] It is this aspect of apparent Southern Villanovan-Etruscan identity which no doubt led to the views of Pallottino and Clark; see n. 45 above.

[52] For a chronology of the Iron Age in the north, see Randall-MacIver 1924, 193–194; Sundwall 1928, 56–71; Hawkes 1948, 206–216; Kaschnitz-Weinberg 1950, 378.

Since the end of the Stone Ages, northern Italy had undergone important cultural developments, chiefly associated with the rise of metallurgy. This advance, together with a new type of burial rite and a new kind of dialects, leads to the assumption of immigrations which, though not strong numerically, prompted these changes. The most studied, though by no means unique cultures of these centuries are those of the palafitte on lakes, of the terramare, and the Villanovan. The question whence they came, whether they arrived together or in two or three successive waves, can perhaps best be answered in the following manner.

All the evidence we have from the Near East, Central and Eastern Europe (especially the Danube basin), and Italy points to a continuous spread of cultures from east to west. We have furthermore sufficient information to assume that this migration of cultures, certainly by the time they entered Italy, was not wholly due to trade and imitation, but was borne forward by human carriers. However, it would be unsound to propose that a certain organized group, a 'people' set out from, say, Asia Minor and finally landed in the Po valley. It is not even wise to believe that such a group commenced its journey in the plains of Hungary, or the hills of Bohemia, and arrived, as an intact group, at any location in Italy.

The movement that in my opinion took place may be compared with the ethnic or personal displacements in the settlement of the New World by European immigrants. The first arrivals were not all (as their descendants are not all now) situated on the Atlantic shores, while the succeeding migrants wandered progressively farther west: this would be a continued leap-frogging migration. Nor is it true that the first immigrants, though they landed of course on the eastern shores of the continent, were gradually pushed farther and farther inland by their European successors: this is migration by perpetual frontal pressure. Both these principal types of movement have been occurring independently, but much more often simultaneously in a bewildering variety of mixtures and complications. As a result, a given individual or group of individuals somewhere in America cannot be fitted into a period of movement or type of ethnic migration by arguing solely from his or their ultimate location.

Quite similarly, it may have happened that the direct descendant of a citizen of Homeric Troy found himself as a skilled ironworker in a Villanovan village on what was later to be the Palatine Hill of Rome. But another inhabitant of the same Roman locale, partaking of the same culture, may seek his personal antecedents no farther away than southern Austria or Villanovan Bologna. And a third may indeed be the offspring in direct line of local neolithic forebears. The fact that all three are members of the same cultural group and speak the same language at a given moment, say, in 700 B.C., is no conclusive proof, as has been repeatedly said, of their common ethnic extraction, nor is it indeed an indication that their personal ancestries should be derived from the same geographic location, and that their ultimate common dwelling place should be recognized as the final goal reached by the migration of a closed social unit. The single human particles of a unified cultural and linguistic whole need not, in their own persons or in those of their physical ancestors, have all traversed, together or successively, from beginning to end the route which their cultural equipment and their language have provedly traveled. Wherever such a Völkerwanderung actually did take place, the anthropological and archaeological record, if it be extant at all, must in fact show a continued moving together of cultural, linguistic, and ethnic characteristics borne by an advancing stream of human carriers who throughout their wandering remained a unified group in the core, whatever the defections of accretions on the fringes. No such phenomenon can be discovered in Italy during the Copper, Bronze, and Iron Ages. What we do find is a continuous flowing and infiltrating and crossing of culture boundaries and cultures, within which it is extremely difficult and hazardous to disentangle actual transfers of individuals or groups of individuals.

Colini says that "the fundamental character of the primitive Italian cultures lies in the continuity of development, in such a manner that each phase descends from the preceding one and develops under the influence of internal and external causes, and above all through the grafting on of elements derived from the more advanced peoples which flourished in the eastern countries of the Mediterranean Sea." [53] Or, as Messerschmidt puts it, one cannot argue for or against an Indo-European immigration in terms of Pigorini or Brizio, respectively, but one must rather see the truth in the "action and reaction upon one another of two basic elements: the older inhabitants of neolithic stock and the newcomers." [54]

In my own theories just stated I have sought to do justice to all the evidence which is available, archaeological, anthropological, cultural, and linguistic, without accepting hypotheses from one domain which would contradict the postulates of another.

Last but not least, my cultural and ethnic theories comply best with the manner in which linguists have come to view spread of languages and dialects and which is best schematized by Schmidt's wave theory of linguistic expansion.[55] If the metallurgists from the north actually brought Indo-European dialects to Italy, and there is scarcely any doubt that they did, then what we know about the conditions and the course of the growth and diversification of a linguistic area virtually imposes on us, in conjunction with all the nonlinguistic evidence we have, an acceptance of the ethnocultural hypothesis of the kind I proposed.

[53] Colini 1908, 35.
[54] Messerschmidt 1935, 3.
[55] Schmidt 1872. Cf. also Pulgram, On prehistoric, 1956.

CHAPTER XI

Southern Italy in the Metal Ages

A considerable body of evidence has been accumulating which points to two principal routes of importation of metal to Italy. One, a northern, comes from Asia Minor, possibly by way of Troy, the Hellespont, the Danube, and Central Europe; the other proceeds mainly by sea, from the Aegean area to Sicily and Italy, thence to Spain and Britain.[1]

It will be recalled that I mentioned Aegean connections and influences in Sicily and southern Italy during the neolithic period, which caused distinctive developments. And it is indeed affirmed that Sicily and much of the Italian peninsula were throughout the Stone, Bronze, and Iron Ages two archaeologically distinct units, one facing southeast, the other north, with relatively little cultural intercourse and exchange.[2] If that is so, then the cultures originating in the Near East approached Italy by a pincer movement, as it were.[3] The view of the existence and the non-junction of these two prongs during the Bronze Age is nicely supported by a broad belt across Italy, comprising Tuscany, Latium, Umbria, and a strip on the Adriatic coast, in which evidence of Bronze Age cultures is so meager as to be almost lacking.[4]

A double approach of metal to Italy seems quite certain. In the early Metal Ages the types of interment speak clearly: rock-

[1] To Gaul, too, the knowledge of copper came over two routes: from the south, by way of the Mediterranean, and from the east, by way of the Black Sea, Danube, and Rhine. Cf. Morgan 1924, 105.

[2] Randall-MacIver 1927, 149 ff.; Jatta 1914, 259–260, and *passim*. Krahe 1949, 32 ff. distinguishes in the same sense two pre-Indo-European regions of Italy: central and southern Italy and Sicily belonging to an Aegean-Anatolian area, northern Italy to a 'Ligurian' area.

[3] Cf. Homo 1925, 64; Peet 1909, 278–288; 1924, 568–570; Whatmough 1937, 65.

[4] Antonielli 1927, 14–23. A look at Whatmough 1937, 50–51, Map 4, confirms this impression.

cut tombs of the Aegean variety are common in Sicily but completely absent in northern Italy.[5]

As far back as the Neolithic Age one can easily distinguish the more elaborate stamped or incised and often painted pottery of Apulia and Sicily, which recalls in design and ornamentation the Aegean ware of the east, from the rougher and cruder crockery of northern Italy.[6] A similar division can be observed during the Aeneolithic, where again southern Italy and Sicily seem to lie on a cultural route which traverses the Mediterranean from east to west, whereas northern Italy derives its cultural imports from a northern current that comes by way of the Balkan peninsula, the Adriatic, and the Danube basin.[7]

Concerning the Bronze Age I have already mentioned that the so-called extraterramare of the south, which are not terramare at all but only show a corresponding culture, owe their similarity with the northern Bronze Age partly to an infiltration from the north, but mostly to an original relationship whose common source lies outside of Italy. But no extensive bodily transplantation of Terramaricoli can be claimed. On the whole, the southern Bronze Age is still easily distinguishable from the northern by its cultural peculiarities. And it has been mentioned that, apart from sporadic infiltrations and breakthroughs, the northern and southern prongs of the Bronze Age cultures of Italy did not meet, as the apparent gap of finds across central Italy shows.

Among the main cultural distinctions between north and south is the burial rite, with inhumation prevailing to the south and east, cremation prevailing to the north and west of a line running roughly from Rimini to Rome. The new cremation burials are apparently due to an importation from the north, effected by settlers, not too numerous, who also brought with them the Indo-European dialects, whereas the ancient inhumation rite was practiced by the native population of neolithic stocks. The term often applied to these southern civilizations according to their tombs is

[5] Cf. Peet 1924, 566–567. A similar bifurcal approach can also be seen in Greece where the Ionic civilization from the east and south meets the Doric invasion from the north. And, again as in Italy, the southern prong is culturally more advanced than the northern. Cf. Childe 1926, 42; Kaschnitz-Weinberg 1950, 386.

[6] Cf. Whatmough 1937, 60–61.

[7] Cf. Whatmough 1937, 65, concerning the three trade routes of the Copper Age.

Fossa Culture (*fossa* meaning 'trench'). But it must be observed that this cultural boundary was neither a sharp line nor an enduring one. For not only did cremation penetrate sporadically into the south, the chief sites being the so-called terramare of Taranto and the nearby cremation necropolis of Timmari, but also inhumation progressively regained lost ground in the north, due either to an infiltration of southern civilization, such as can be observed in the cultural paraphernalia, or to a reëmergence of the old rites, continued throughout by a numerically stronger substratum population. Most likely both factors worked together.[8]

During the Iron Age, communications between northern and southern Italy improved considerably owing to the general cultural progress and greater density of population. Indeed we have noticed that the evidence demonstrates an overlapping of Northern and Southern Villanovan cultures in the area of Tuscany and Latium. Outstanding sites testifying to this mixture are located at Terni (some fifty miles north of Rome), on the Roman Forum (in the *sepolcreto* along the *Via Sacra* near the temple of Antoninus and Faustina), and in some settlements of the Alban Hills.

The northern Italian Iron Age cultures may not have been able to penetrate along the west coast much farther south than the Monte Circeo, because the adjoining stretch of coastline was occupied from the eighth century B.C. on by Greek colonists who brought with them their own superior Hellenic civilization. The prehistoric records from Calabria are still too scanty to allow of a valid conclusion, at least up to the time when the Siculi occupied the region in spots.

About the central part of southern Italy, the Abruzzi and Lucania, little is known, and this region will attract our interest mainly in the discussion of the various Oscan-speaking tribes. The prehistoric cultures of the area, which for want of a better label may be called Apennine cultures, seem to show a mixture of elements which reach central Italy, during the early Bronze Age and thereafter, from three directions, from the north, the south, and from the Balkans.[9] This may well be the reason why a classification of the finds has proved so difficult, especially when,

[8] Cf. Säflund 1938, 26–27, 31, 54.
[9] Cf. Kaschnitz-Weinberg 1950, 355–362.

as we witnessed in other instances, the theories were based on either cultural or ethnic or linguistic evidence separately.

The Adriatic coast from Rimini all the way down to the Sallentine peninsula seems to have been continuously occupied by the same ethnic groups from neolithic times on, although undoubtedly it was exposed to cultural and limited ethnic influences from the Balkan peninsula. Some scholars think that Indo-European dialects came across the Adriatic directly, rather than by way of Venezia Giulia, and see in the bearers of these idioms tribes often identified as Illyrians. More will be said about this in later chapters.

In Apulia our knowledge shows a gap spanning about four centuries from 1100 to 700 B.C., that is, down to the Early Iron Age. Beginning with that date, the Mediterranean and Balkan influences are again unmistakable.[10]

We may now turn to a rapid survey of prehistoric Sicily. It is but obvious that, if the central and southern parts of the peninsula derive their inspiration, if not some of their peoples, from the east and south rather than the north, Sicily will partake of this development in at least equal measure.

Even to our own days, the history of Sicily has in many ways remained something quite apart, although the island is now a province of the Italian state and for centuries past has belonged to sovereigns who ruled at least a portion of the peninsula also.[11]

"The story of the islands of Sicily, Sardinia, Corsica, Malta with Gozo, and the small islands of the Maltese group, and Pantelleria, is by no means an integral part of the story of the Italian peninsula." [12] What the islands and the peninsula do have in com-

[10] For a general review see Kaschnitz-Weinberg 1950, 370–373.

[11] Separatist movements are nothing new to Sicilians, and only at the end of World War II a great deal of sincere though somewhat operatic agitation advocated Sicily's joining the United States as the forty-ninth state of the Union. The traveler who crosses the narrow straits of Messina in a few minutes time, finds himself suddenly surrounded by a civilization quite unlike that of the mainland. His impression of strangeness and insularity has been prepared by being subjected to customs procedures, and will be confirmed by finding in Sicilian cities mailboxes destined specially for 'Letters to the Continent,' that is, the Italian peninsula and beyond.

When Goethe visited Sicily he found it the quintessence of all that Italy was — or at least what he thought it should be. In his *Italienische Reise*, under the date of April 13, 1787, he noted: "Italy without Sicily leaves no picture in one's soul: only here is the key to everything."

[12] Whatmough 1937, 355.

mon is the stratum or substratum of the neolithic stock of humans. But the evidence shows unmistakably that already in neolithic times Sicily faced the Aegean area and turned its back upon Italy. The same is true during the Copper Age (in Sicilian chronology Sicel I, till about 1300 B.C., with typical site at Castelluccio in the southeast), the Bronze Age (Sicel II, till about 900 B.C., including the Early Iron Age, with sites at Plemmirio, Thapsos), and the Iron Age (Sicel III, about 900–700 B.C., and Sicel IV, the Siculo-Greek Period, about 700–500 B.C.). This does not mean, however, that Sicilian cultures were in no way dependent upon foreign imports; quite the contrary. But it is significant that from the late Copper Age on, after an era of a fairly uniform palaeolithic and neolithic cultural facies all over Sicily, the Bronze and Iron Age imports are concentrated on the east coast, pointing obviously to Aegean rather than Italian connections.

CHAPTER XII

Linguistic Inferences and Conclusions

Although in the absence of written records the harvest of linguistic facts in this section on prehistoric Italy is of necessity meager, I chose to render a detailed account because within the inferences which we can draw lie many of the roots of the remaining story.

In accordance with my postulates I had to reject throughout any a priori agreement of cultural, ethnic, and linguistic entities, particularly if based only on likeness or similarity of names. As for the cultural evidence, the archaeological record posterior to the neolithic revolution showed nowhere, at any time, a severely abrupt change. The inevitable conclusion was therefore that during the metal ages no ethnic mass migrations took place.

We are still far from the threshold of history in Italy. But eventually we shall be able to discern a variety of dialects, mostly of the Indo-European family, and we shall also learn that, apart from the Keltic invasion of the fifth century B.C., no new languages were brought to Italy in historical times until after the fall of the Roman Empire. Hence we are compelled to place the coming of the Indo-European languages into the period just covered, stretching from the Aeneolithic Age to the Iron Age. Since I had to reject mass migration, but at the same time postulated that the transplantation of an idiom in the manner observable here could occur only in conjunction with a transfer of population, no matter how weak in numbers, as long as other conditions were favorable, the explanation for the arrival and spread of the Indo-European dialects in Italy, in the course of a millennium, must be sought in a continuous process of infiltration and a series of restrained thrusts.[1] In this thesis, I hope, the principles and the visible record of anthropology, archaeology, and linguistics have

[1] Cf. Devoto 1951, 93: "The Indo-European expansion is not the result of violent events, martial enterprises, or sudden invasions, but a constant flowing, fast or slow, uninterrupted and, so to speak, improvised."

been caused to bear fruit jointly, without my violating or distorting any one of them singly.

The question as to whence the Indo-European dialects came to Italy will not be difficult to answer at this juncture. We have repeatedly observed that the cultural currents originating in the Near and Middle East, in one or the other portion of the Fertile Crescent and the neighboring regions influenced by it, reached Italy by a double, and possibly triple route: from the Mediterranean through Sicily and southern Italy; from the Danubian lands over the passes of the Alps; [2] and perhaps from the Balkan peninsula by crossing the Adriatic Sea. There is overwhelming evidence that the Aegean and Mediterranean route was, at least until the arrival of Iron Age invaders on the southern shores of the Balkan peninsula, within the domain of peoples who did not speak Indo-European languages. The recent discovery that the inscriptions of Crete in the so-called Linear B script are in Indo-European, that is, Achaean Greek, in no way disturbs this picture. [3] Indeed the historical implications are that the Achaeans from Mycenae and Pylos, whose language is also Indo-European and who use a system of writing similar to Linear B of Crete, whence they learned it (and which is a clumsy adaptation to Greek of Cretan A, itself perhaps to be derived from the syllabic script of Cyprus [4]), conquered the Minoans of Crete, bringing their language south with them, [5] and not vice versa.

In any case, the new Indo-European idioms could not have been brought to Italy, by the date at which their arrival must occur, through a southern, Aegean cultural current. There is equally overwhelming evidence (as we shall see in the next chapter) that the Indo-European languages spread westward into Europe from some eastern location or locations. Therefore, the conclusion imposes itself that speakers of Indo-European took possession of or originated the metal cultures somewhere in the Near East or in

[2] On the importance of the Danube for the beginnings of European civilization cf. Childe 1927.
[3] See Ventris, Greek, 1953; Evidence, 1953; Hrozný 1953, 198–224.
[4] Cf. Sittig 1951, but who does not recognize Cretan B as Indo-European.
[5] This antagonism between Greece and Crete finds its legendary expression in the saga of the slaying by the Athenian Theseus of the Minotaur, who was perhaps the priest-king Minos himself wearing a ritual bull's head or bull's horns, similar to the ones found on a bronze statue of a male Cretan god. Cf. Anonymous 1953.

Eastern Europe, and that henceforth the northern cultural current, by whichever way it came to Italy, carried with it at the same time the Indo-European dialects. Hence the arrival of Copper, Bronze, and Iron Age cultures in the north and northeast of Italy may rightly be associated with the coming of Indo-European languages.

The question whether the Palafitticoli or the Terramaricoli or the Villanovans were the original importers of Indo-European, whether they are descended from one another in some combination or constitute separate invasions, whether they are the 'Umbrians' or the 'Latins' or the ancestors of either, is to be resolved in the sense that the units so designated are not to be identified as ethnic but only as cultural entities, that they can have therefore under these several names no physical but only cultural successors, that any migration of persons carrying Indo-European dialects which actually took place, is ethnically and racially not identifiable, to say nothing of its being pure 'Nordic' or 'Aryan,' for the very good reason that the moving particles of this mass of humanity need not be, and probably are not, all derived from a unique location or from an unmixed race. The best that can be said is that they were probably parts of a heterogeneous stock which differed from that, perhaps slightly less hybrid because more sedentary, of the native inhabitants of the Apennine peninsula. If the latter be called, for want of a better name, and without prejudice to their racial purity and autochthony, Mediterraneans, the former could with comfortable neutrality and without claim to racial homogeneity be called Alpine-Danubians.

The linguistic Indo-Europeanization of Italy takes place, then, through the agency of a limited Alpine-Danubian immigration, in the course of the Copper, Bronze, and Iron Ages.[6] In the twilight of protohistory the process appears accomplished and speakers of Pre-Italic and Italic dialects occupy the peninsula and Sicily, with the exception of the Greek and Etruscan enclaves. But these, too, were destined to yield eventually (although, as we have seen, some scholars consider present-day sporadic islands of Greek speech in southern Italy the remnants of an unbroken continuity since the time of the colonies of Magna Graecia).

[6] Cf. Hencken 1955, 52–56.

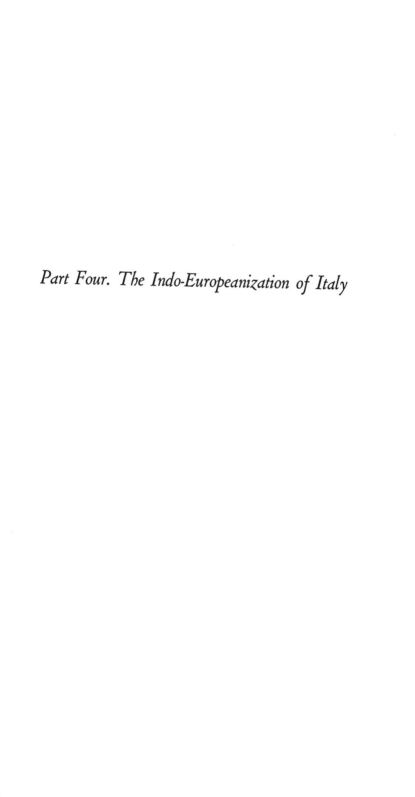

Part Four. The Indo-Europeanization of Italy

CHAPTER XIII

Indo-European and 'Indo-Europeans'

That Spanish and Italian, Polish and Czech, Dutch and English are somehow pairs of related languages is visible and audible, as it were, to the naked eye and ear. That Greek and Russian and German belong to the same Indo-European family of languages, though at a different grade of relationship, is not. Sir William Jones (1746–1794), a Supreme Court judge in Calcutta and a philologist of note, compared Sanskrit with various European languages and discovered their historic relationship, founding thereby the science of comparative Indo-European linguistics.

"By 'Indo-European' [Whatmough defines] we understand a number of languages, spoken in the Old World chiefly in India and Europe and in intervening lands (whence the name), which are connected together by the joint possession, not through borrowing but, as the expression goes, 'by inheritance,' of a common system of sounds, no matter how greatly modified by changes peculiar to the several languages in the course of their long histories, a common system of inflexion and word-formation, a common method for the expression of syntactical relationships, and a common stock of words. All these features were accompanied originally by meanings, also held in common, and all were subject to constant change by loss, addition, or other modification, so that even at the beginning of the historical period speakers of the different Indo-European languages could no longer have understood one another."[1]

---

[1] Whatmough 1937, 101. The following are the different Indo-European linguistic families, with their major ancient and modern derivatives in parentheses, but without the numerous discoverable subdialects: Tocharish, Indo-Iranian (Sanskrit, Prakrit, Pali, modern Indic dialects; Avestan, Old Persian, Modern Persian, Pashtu), Hittite, Armenian, Slavic (Old Church Slavic, Russian, Slovene, Serbo-Croatian, Bulgarian, Polish, Czech, Slovak), Baltic (Old Prussian, Lithuanian, Lettish), Hellenic (Ancient and Modern Greek), Illyrian (Albanian?), Italic

This scheme of continued inheritance presupposes some original idiom, generally called Proto-Indo-European, from which the various Indo-European tongues developed through divergences caused by increasing distance in time and space between the different varieties and by superposition upon various linguistic substrata.[2]

Yet no one who believes in the reality of a Proto-Indo-European tongue knows, or should pretend to know, when, where, how, and by whom precisely this protodialect was spoken. In fact, if one wanted to regress to the true 'beginning' of Indo-European one might possibly have to recede to the origin of language itself. For if human language and, concomitantly, man himself originated at a certain time on one point of the earth's surface and spread thence, then this point and this time also localizes the 'origin' of the Indo-European languages, together with all other language families. And if several species of man and language arose independently in several regions, and not of necessity simultaneously, then the speech of at least one such region and of one breed of man would have to correspond to primeval Proto-Indo-European. Obviously in linguistics, when we speak of Proto-Indo-European, we cannot and do not refer to such a glottogonic epoch. In other words, the parent speech we have in mind must have an arbitrarily set locus of origin in space and time which does not conceptualize any real physical beginning.[3]

(Italic dialects, Latin, Oscan, Umbrian; Italian, Rumanian, Raeto-Romanic, Sardinian, French, Provençal, Catalan, Spanish, Portuguese, Dalmatian [extinct]), Keltic (Gaulish, Welsh, Cornish, Breton, Gaelic, Manx), Germanic (Gothic, German, Frisian, Norwegian, Swedish, Danish, Dutch, English).

[2] Some scholars have thought that the assumption of an Indo-European protolanguage is unnecessary and that "the ancestors of the various branches of the Indo-European family did originally not resemble one another but became assimilated to each other to a considerable degree through constant contact, mutual influence and borrowing, yet without all of them becoming identical." (Trubetzkoy 1939, 82. Against this argues cogently Thieme 1954, 59 ff.) Cf. also Altheim, Geschichte, 1951, 4–6. For a variety of reasons, linguistic, logical, and terminological (some of them will become apparent in the subsequent discussion), I reject this formulation of linguistic development and should rather assume the existence of a real Proto-Indo-European dialect. But rapprochement of neighboring dialects is by no means an unknown phenomenon. See Pulgram 1957.

[3] This problem of where to stop on the road backwards and what to call the 'parent language' is one every compiler of an etymological dictionary must face. A Romanic dictionary gives Latin etyma and does not recede farther into Italic and Proto-Indo-European, except occasionally for special reasons; a Germanic

To illustrate this I should like to refer to the Romanic languages, whose parent language, Latin, is known. I daresay the equation that Latin is to Romanic dialects what Proto-Indo-European is to the Indo-European dialects, is not controversial. But of course, by citing Latin as the parent language of Romanic we do not imply that Latin is itself a beginning of immaculate linguistic purity and innocent of un-Latin influences, and not already the product of a long and complex and partly unknown earlier development. Even if we had full documentation it would be impossible to set any except an arbitrary boundary between some pre-Latin language and Latin, just as it is impossible to say where Latin 'ends' and a Romanic language 'begins.' Indeed our calling the various Neo-Latin languages Spanish, Italian, French, and so forth, and the Neo-Indo-European languages Sanskrit, Greek, Germanic, and so forth, is merely a convenience of nomenclature and a recognition of the fact that, since a first-century speaker of Latin would not understand, or be understood by, a twentieth-century Frenchman, and since a speaker of Proto-Indo-European of the thirtieth century B.C. could not communicate with a Roman of the fourth century B.C., we might as well give these idioms distinct names for good practical reasons. Since a language is, by definition, a system and a means of linguistic cooperation current within a social group, divergent speechways not capable of fulfilling this task are indeed best called by different names also for scientific reasons, even though they may be historically related in such a manner that no precise chronological dividing line can be drawn.

We may pursue the history of Latin back to the earliest Latin texts available, of the sixth century before Christ, to the time when only Latium was a Latin speaking area, and fix arbitrarily a beginning of Latin and its Neo-Latin or Romanic successors: geographically in Latium (we could conceivably narrow this down to Rome, or Alba Longa), chronologically in the first half of the first millennium B.C., ethnically among people very unenlighteningly called Latini, of whose race we cannot be certain — unless we call it, in

---

etymological dictionary goes as far as Proto-Germanic, a Slavic one to Old Church Slavic or Proto-Slavic, and so forth. The terminal point of each etymology is established mainly by the title of the work, and often enough by the decision of the editor alone.

its then prevailing state, the Latin race, without our falling prey, however, to any illusions or delusions concerning physical classification and racial purity. In other words, we have agreed on what to call a beginning, a proto-stage of Latin, with the full realization that back of it lies a more or less unknown previous history.

Applying the same pragmatic procedure to Indo-European we will say that we call Proto-Indo-European a type of language spoken at a given (though unknown) time, in a given (though unknown) region, by a given (though unknown) social and ethnic group or groups, without any further claim as to this idiom's virginal originality or primordial incorruption.

The only other alternative, it seems to me, would be to assume that Proto-Indo-European is an original creation, innocent of earlier history and development, sprung from the soil, or germinated in a mystic folk-soul, or created by an act of God. I do not believe anything of the sort.

Linguistic (like racial) purity is a matter of definition and depends on the criteria we choose to require for labeling an entity 'pure.' If we require of a 'pure language' no more than that it be human, then all languages are by definition pure. If mixture, no matter when it occurred in the distant past, precludes purity, then no language is pure, except possibly that of some hypothetical primeval, long isolated, endogamous clan, whose race is also (relatively) pure. Otherwise 'purity,' like 'origin,' and 'autochthony,' is, in anthropology and linguistics, at best a relative term, serviceable only in relation to a stated point of reference.

As far as Proto-Indo-European and its speakers are concerned, we have not the slightest evidence for any racial or linguistic purity as due to extended isolation and inbreeding. We simply do not know, and hardly ever shall, whether or not there existed a society which, after having somehow come into being, lived as a closed unit for long enough a time to develop a homogeneous human stock and language which, just before its dissolution or diversification, could be called pure, or at least homogeneous — albeit in a relative sense. If Proto-Indo-European represented such a stage of language and society, then we are indeed provided with the sought point of reference, with the zero-point, the beginning. But in the complete absence of evidence in all these matters, our

reconstructed Proto-Indo-European must needs remain hypothetical, a collection of formulae, without referends in any known
reality.

Having presented this view of what I mean by Proto-Indo-
European, the vexed questions concerning the *Urheimat* and the
Urvolk, the proto-home and the proto-folk (the latter often
being referred to as 'Indo-Europeans') can be answered accordingly. It must have become clear that the location and the size
of the original homeland will be determined by the date at which
we put our zero point, our basis of standard. And since we cannot
sensibly say that the date at which we set Proto-Indo-European is
6000 or 4000 or 2536 B.C. because of our ignorance on all matters
of fact necessary for a circumspect answer, and since no one took
the trouble either to define the Indo-European proto-home after
first fixing the time of which he spoke, or to fix the time of Proto-
Indo-European after first defining the area into which it fitted,
all the unending discussion by many scholars as to the race and
the society of the 'original Indo-Europeans' and the extent and
location of their 'original homeland' seems to have taken its er-
ratic course largely in a vacuum. Accordingly, the solutions were
conjectural at best, but more likely meaningless.

Not that answers have not been attempted. But their great
number and diversity alone should have been enough to make
them highly suspect and untrustworthy. And since one cannot
suppose that all who tried their hand were incompetent, one can
only conclude that the methods used were not suitable, or else
that the problem itself, or the way in which it was framed, was
specious.

All methods concerning the discovery of the proto-home and
the proto-folk must be based on linguistic inferences. I say 'linguistic' because that is the only way in which 'Indo-European'
makes sense: we are seeking nonlinguistic correlatives for it, not
vice versa. And I say 'inferences' because we have no actual recorded evidence of the Proto-Indo-European language. All we
know about it is abstracted from later-attested forms in the various
Indo-European languages by the methods of comparative linguistics. This simply means that, since we know fairly well the rules
and regularities according to which the Indo-European dialects

developed from Proto-Indo-European, we can assume the various related forms of the records to have diverged from an original (that is, we now know, relatively original) Proto-Indo-European form. The fact that this Proto-Indo-European item is not recorded is customarily indicated in print by means of the asterisk in front of it. No claim is or should be made that the Proto-Indo-European forms ever existed or were pronounced as they are written by us. (In fact many of our formulae are, and quite legitimately, unpronounceable.) This particular Proto-Indo-European is indeed not meant to represent a language but is merely a distillation of the essential features of sound and form.

Moreover, although as a rule we refer to these formulae as Proto-Indo-European, or, less aptly, Indo-European, they do not necessarily correspond to the reality of a Proto-Indo-European language we may have in mind, the one of a given zero-point, since they incorporate only what is common to the dialects in which a given word actually occurs in the records. Now if an asterisked formula is based on only three or five attested forms from that many Indo-European dialects, we have no guarantee whatever that it has an actual equivalent or parent form in what we have chosen to call Proto-Indo-European. It may well have come very early from another linguistic family and spread to only three or five Indo-European dialects, but in all of them it was so well Indo-Europeanized as to seem genuinely inherited. Just so a word that occurs, fully assimilated in sound and structure, in Italian and Spanish need not be inherited from Latin but could be of, say, Keltic origin, or it may even be an Arabic loan in Spanish, thence borrowed by Italian much later. Also if a word's cognates are attested in all Indo-European languages, there is still a chance that it is not of Proto-Indo-European origin but merely a loan that, for some reason, spread throughout the Indo-European domain. Also a common Romanic word that appears everywhere in the Romania can be of non-Latin origin, and any original 'Latin' form reconstructed from such Romanic congeners would be spurious. This means that a random number of asterisked formulae not only do not necessarily represent real Proto-Indo-European forms, but that also, if they do, the reconstructions are not all of equal age. Hence the attempt to write something in Proto-Indo-

European, though it has been made, is doomed to bring forth a profusion of linguistic forms of different degrees of authenticity and various ages, not unlike the composition by a future linguist who, for want of records, would concoct a sentence consisting of, say, Mediaeval Latin, Old French, and Modern Italian, plus a number of forms that never were pronounced at all, and call the dish Proto-Romanic.[4]

It is an elementary mistake to equate common Indo-European words with Proto-Indo-European words and to base thereon conclusions concerning the Proto-Indo-European *Urvolk* or *Urheimat*. Yet this is precisely what has often been done, indeed it seems the favorite method of inquiry.

For example, since a number of Indo-European languages have recorded cognate words for 'birch' and 'beech'[5] Proto-Indo-European must have been at home, it was said, in an area in which birches and beeches thrived. If one therefore draws the boundary of occurrence of these species of trees on a map one obtains, we are told, the boundaries of Proto-Indo-European. Linguistically this conclusion may but does not have to be valid because, as we have seen, the asterisked reconstructions of the words for birch and beech, like all others, may be no part of the particular Proto-Indo-European tongue, at a given point in time, for which we are seeking a homeland. But even if such an objection could be set aside at least for the reason that the terms in question are real Proto-Indo-European words, albeit undatable, there remain two other valid reasons for abandoning this method of linguistic palaeontology, as it has been called.

First, the existence of cognate or even identical words in various dialects and regions does not indicate that they referred in all of them and everywhere to the same things. For example, a robin in England is not the same bird at all as a robin in America. English immigrants, unable to find in the New World this bird to which they were sentimentally attached, transferred its name to the nearest likeness they could find, which happened to be a bird with a red breast. The name robin was thereby shifted

[4] Hirt 1939, 113–114, quotes Schleicher's famous fable in Indo-European *(The sheep and the horses)* and then offers a completely different version of his own. It cannot be otherwise.
[5] Buck 1949, 528–532.

from a small bird of the warbler family to one nearly twice as large of the thrush family. Future linguistic palaeontologists in search of the homeland of Proto-English might arrive at astounding results by establishing a congruence of the occurrence of the word and the thing 'robin.' Hence even if we are willing to accept the premise that Proto-Indo-European had the parent words for birch and beech, we are still far from certain that these proto-forms referred to the trees we now so call.

Second, if also the first objection could be set aside by some means (which, in the absence of linguistic evidence, I cannot imagine), it would still be impossible to agree on the boundaries of Proto-Indo-European because so far we have no knowledge what the diffusion of the test item was during the Proto-Indo-European period as compared with the present — especially since we cannot even fix any dates for such a period. Indeed what we know of climatic changes and cycles as outlined in an earlier chapter, leads us unquestionably to believe that the boundaries for all items of prehistoric flora were not the same several millennia ago as they are today.[6]

But impassioned linguistic palaeontologists have gone even farther. From the existence of certain items of vocabulary in all or a majority of the extant Indo-European languages, and blandly ignoring all the possible pitfalls just noted, they even fabricated conclusions concerning the social organization, the religion, the mores, the race of the speakers of Proto-Indo-European, whom forthwith they labeled 'Indo-Europeans.' This name cannot make sense save with the meaning 'speakers of Indo-European'; yet since for the most part it was used, explicitly and implicitly, to designate an ethnic or cultural or racial group, it had to be factually senseless, though it was expedient in the pseudoscientific pursuits of idealists, propagandists, and crackpots.

If we reconstructed Latin, says Fraser, on the evidence of the Romanic languages alone, ignoring and neglecting the existence of Greek, Keltic, Germanic and the other ancient Indo-European dialects, and if thereupon we derived from the state of the common Romanic vocabulary conclusions on the culture of the speakers

[6] For a rejection of the famous beech line from Königsberg to Odessa, to the west of which the homeland of Proto-Indo-European must allegedly be located, see Passler 1948. Cf. also Myres 1935.

of Latin (whom then we should call Latins, I suppose, and ascribe to one race or another, depending on our patriotic or political leanings), we might well arrive at the following results: Proto-Romanic *regem* and *imperatorem* shows us that the Latins lived in a monarchy under kings or emperors (but what shall we make of *rem publicam* which could presuppose a Latin republic?); since all Romanic languages contain words cognate with French *prêtre* and *évêque,* 'priest' and 'bishop,' the Latins were Christians; also words cognate with French *bière, tabac, café* are common Romanic, evoking a picture of Caesar's soldiers guzzling beer and smoking cigars in sidewalk cafés; and since all Romanic languages name a certain animal *cheval, cavallo, cal,* etc., and have words for 'war' like *guerre, guerra,* the Latins called the horse *caballum* and the war *guerram* and were no doubt warlike people with a strong cavalry.[7]

Now the more sophisticated among us could easily object here that it would take a great deal of naïveté on the part of linguistic palaeontologists to propound such views, and that the refutation can be found in a refinement of linguistic methods themselves. This is true. Yet it is equally true that in some contemporary circles such naïveté seems to enjoy the status of high acumen, as anyone can see who reads some of the numerous volumes that deal with the 'Indo-Europeans,' their lives and their mores. But if the authoring of such works is not astonishing enough, the uncritical and admiring credulity bestowed upon them by a vast number of scholars certainly is.

Especially popular, hence all the more deplorable, has been the identification of speakers of Proto-Indo-European with the Aryans, preferably of Nordic race. This mythical ethnos was further imbued with all kinds of excellent physical and mental qualities, on the assumption that by superior bravery and intelligence these people were able to conquer all those vast lands of Europe and Asia in which Indo-European languages came eventually to be employed. Thereupon one spoke not only of Aryan and Nordic Proto-Indo-Europeans, but indeed of an Indo-European, Aryan family of nations. The proof of this is, at least in verbal effusion, very simple in the opinion of some. "There is but

[7] Fraser 1926, 268.

one race whose presence can be proved within all Indo-Europeans: the Nordic. Only the leading, politically and culturally creative, intermarrying clans are the true Indo-Europeans. . . . The Indo-Europeans are originally members of the Nordic race. . . . [Thus it becomes clear] that the Indo-Europeans, as members of the Nordic race, are native to central and western Europe. . . . Nordic race and ethnic and linguistic Indo-Europeanness are fundamentally identical." [8] "The Indo-European family of nations owes its origin to the enterprising, constructive, unifying, and progressive attitude of the Nordic race." [9]

One of the most eminent Indo-Europeanists was Hermann Hirt, who through his linguistic work has fully earned the reputation and fame he now enjoys. But when he starts spinning a yarn about the Indo-Europeans his credibility sinks to zero. To make a point concerning the race of his *Indogermanen*, he adduces corroborative evidence from the United States on the survival and expansion of races as a function of climate: "In the United States of North America the Germanic element dominates decisively in the north, whereas in the southern States Italians, Frenchmen, and Spaniards come into their own. The Negro cannot get along in the north at all. There consumption decisively sets a limit to his expansion." [10] If such nonsense concerning a present and factually knowable situation is earnestly offered in support of a prehistoric theory, the reader can scarcely be reproached for viewing the result, and similar endeavors by the same author, with a measure of incredulity.

[8] Reche 1936, 312–314.

[9] Schachermeyr 1936, 229. In the same article, we are offered an equally simple (in more senses than one) explanation for the fall of the Roman Empire and ancient civilization as a whole, a problem on which the best historians disagree among themselves. (I shall not translate lest I traduce.) "So zog die übermässige politische Ausbreitung der Indogermanen nach dem Mittelmeerbereich zugleich deren kulturellen and blutmässig-rassischen Verfall nach sich. Dieser zusammen mit einer einseitigen Zivilisationsrichtung des römischen Imperiums, die Vernichtung aller Volkhaftigkeit und Bodenständigkeit zugunsten des Weltbürgertums, führten schliesslich den Untergang der antiken Welt herbei." (252)

[10] Hirt 1905, 24. It is rather disconcerting if even a scholar of Childe's stature concludes that "the Nordics' superiority in physique fitted them to be the vehicles of a superior language" (Childe 1926, 212), which is linguistic and anthropological balderdash, and affirms that "the first Aryans were Nordics" whose excellent Indo-European language generated an equally excellent mentality thanks to which they became great conquerors (*ibid.* 211), which is not much better.

If anything is certain at this point it is that there exists "no sound body of evidence — archaeological, historical, linguistic, craniological, or anthropometric — that supports the hypothesis that Nordics had any more to do with the origin and prehistoric diffusion of Aryan languages than had Alpines, or Dinarics, or even the subrace that I have called Keltic. About all that we know is that the predominantly Mediterranean types of peoples on the African shore of the Mediterranean and on the Palestinian-Syrian shore, the probably Armenoid inhabitants of Asia Minor, and all the Neolithic and earlier occupiers of the European areas bordering on the Mediterranean and in its islands certainly did not speak Aryan (Indo-European, Indo-Germanic) languages. These languages were introduced from Central Europe into Greece, Italy, and Asia Minor in the Bronze Age, probably about 1800 B.C. from Central Europe by invaders of probably mixed white subracial composition." [11]

Not only is there no reason or need to assume that the speakers of Proto-Indo-European belonged to a single race, but indeed none to believe that they were the bearers of a particular culture which in thir conquering marches they carried with them and spread together with their language.[12] In fact, we must even ask first of all, as in several instances before, as to what these alleged migrations were, who was on the move, how many persons participated, and what their cultural baggage really was.

Most theories of Indo-European expansion work with migration. The speakers of Proto-Indo-European set out, we are told, from some focal homeland (which to begin with was determined on false premises by means of specious methods, as we have seen) and thence spread the race and the language and the culture. In fact, the (Proto-) Indo-European language is often referred to as pre-ethnic Indo-European: the language prevalent before the 'ethnic division,' before the alleged Indo-European diaspora. If the thesis that a language can spread widely, not without human carriers, but certainly without a Völkerwanderung, has any merit at all, as I hope to have demonstrated, then there is good reason to assume such a process of expansion for the Indo-European

[11] Hooton 1946, 593.
[12] Laviosa-Zambotti 1947, 109, for example, by advocating the opposite thesis commits all the cardinal sins proscribed by comparative linguistics.

idioms. Unfortunately the archaeological documentation becomes progressively scantier and more difficult to interpret as we recede into prehistory. It was difficult enough to establish, by elimination, that the bringers of Indo-European to Italy were Central European metallurgists. But identification of speakers of Indo-European, previous to their appearance in Italy, with the corded-ware people, or the battle-axe people, or the tamers of the horse, or the urnfield people, has proved in each case controversial, to say the least. Moreover the necessary basic hypothesis, not easy to state in any event, of the people-culture-language equation does not increase in credibility with the decrease in evidence.

But, one may ask, did I not myself identify the speakers of Indo-European upon their arrival in Italy with a culture, that is, with metallurgy, copper, bronze, and iron, to be exact? I did say that certain persons who entered Italy introduced both metal and Indo-European speech at the same time. But I did not say that therefore metal and Indo-Europeanness were then and had previously been of necessity concomitant phenomena, least of all pertaining to one certain ethnic group; and I did not say or imply that speakers of Indo-European are the inventors, bearers, and spreaders of metallurgy everywhere and always. I merely stated that the persons coming to Italy at a certain date were metallurgists and spoke Indo-European, which does not in the least rule out the possibility that the language and metalworking may have come from different sources and locations and may merely have become joined accidentally in the persons of settlers in Central Europe, some of whom, but not all of whom, migrated to Italy. Hence the joint appearance in Italy of metallurgy and Indo-European is a locally significant but not necessarily a causally connected togetherness. The coincidence of cultural and linguistic traits at a given moment does not allow of assertions concerning a more ancient and continued unity of the two. Hence speakers of Indo-European may have acquired in prehistoric no less than in historic times, at different periods, in different places, a variety of cultures not one of which is any more typically connected with Indo-European speech than another.[13]

[13] Hermes 1935, 805, would agree with this; but she still considers the tamed horse as a safe type-phenomenon of Indo-Europeanness.

If we now sum up the foregoing discussion we must, however regretfully, concede that all attempts to establish a proto-home and a proto-folk for the Proto-Indo-European language at some prehistoric zero point have failed because of lacking evidence, a lacuna which the inappropriate and unsound conjectures of linguistic palaeontology cannot reasonably be expected to fill.

The best one can tentatively suggest in terms of geography is that, given Tocharish and Indic in the Far East, and the other Indo-European languages in the Near East and Europe, given furthermore scant but fairly circumstantial evidence that the spread occurred from a central rather than from an extreme eastern, certainly not from an extreme western or northern location, the original home of Proto-Indo-European lies somewhere between the farthest outposts, and northward rather than southward from the Caspian Sea and the Black Sea, because the south was certainly occupied by known Semitic tongues. In terms of ethnology and race nothing can be said whatever as to who the speakers of Proto-Indo-European might have been.[14]

One cannot, of course, reject out of hand the possibility that within this potential proto-home the Proto-Indo-European dialect at some remote date occupied an area not exceeding in size that of Latium, for example, the home of the earliest Latin known in Italy, though at the present time we can have no sure knowledge of this. What we do know is that, once beyond the confines of its homeland, whether we think of it as a small focal area or a large territory, a relatively unified Proto-Indo-European breaks up into dialects. We shall now examine why such dialectalization occurred, and in what manner the Indo-European languages spread.

As to the question concerning the cause of linguistic change as such, the answer is simply that change is as much in the nature of language as in the nature of all other cultural phenomena. The passage of time is itself a sufficient agent to produce differentiation and variety. If one considers furthermore that language, like the rest of culture, can be transferred in space and be superimposed

[14] It has been proposed, but without sufficient evidence, that the speakers of Proto-Indo-European were nomadic peoples who roamed the entire Eurasian area between the Danube and the Hoang-ho (Laviosa-Zambotti 1948, 12–13), and that both their language and culture were fundamentally uniform but subdivided into many smaller subcultures and dialects (Laviosa-Zambotti 1947, 111). Cf. also Fraser 1926, 270–272; Toynbee 1934, 4.392–393, 421–422.

upon different substrata, the breaking up of a unit into disparate dialectal entities can be readily understood. The manner in which this process took place with particular reference to Indo-European is another problem entirely.

To imagine that some 'Indo-Europeans' exploded out of their tight little homeland, and that the particles which then flew off in various directions were already the ethnic or racial embryo groups of Proto-Latins, Proto-Kelts, Proto-Armenians, Proto-Tocharians, and so forth, seems, after what I have said, unsound. Yet some linguists have indeed implied this by suggesting that when the Proto-Indo-European bubble burst it emitted the proto-forms of the various Indo-European dialects which migrated, carried by closed social units, to their historic locations. This is, after all, the only way in which such widely used terms as 'ethnic division,' 'pre-ethnic Indo-European,' and the references to a state of Proto-Indo-European before its break-up into dialects make sense. It has also been suggested that "all these relations [among Indo-European dialects] are best explained by assuming that they reflect the germs of dialectic variation in the parent speech, the differentiation of the later more definite divisions beginning when they were still in geographical contact and in the relative positions indicated [by a scheme on page 1], these relative positions being substantially kept in their earliest spread." [15]

Since there is of course not the slightest proof for such a hypothesis, one should think that the assumption was dictated by the knowledge of the behavior of a known language in similar known circumstances. But a language does not generally behave in this manner, certainly not of necessity. Can one perhaps pretend that the germs of French and Spanish and Rumanian were not only contained in Latin, but indeed so disposed geographically in Augustan Italy, or in prehistoric Latium, as to presage their future geographic location? The implicit or even explicit belief that Proto-Indo-European was a conglomerate of, or contained the seeds of, the future Indo-European languages is as untenable as would be the easily disproved theory that the Latin of seventh-century B.C. Latium, which not improperly one could call Proto-Romanic, already contained in embryonic form not only the modern dialects

[15] Buck 1933, 2. See also Devoto 1940, 2–3, Tav. I (facing p. 16).

of Italy but indeed the Romanic languages and possibly all their sub-dialects. That the inhabitants of protohistoric Latium were not the ancestors of present day Frenchmen, Italians, Spaniards, and Rumanians, and, yes, Argentinians and Bolivians and the rest, all of whom would have reached their historic sites as wanderers from the womb country, need scarcely be demonstrated, even though in popular parlance speakers of Romanic languages are often referred to as Latins or Latin races. Hence it is difficult to account for the respectability which analogous theories regarding Proto-Indo-European and Indo-European still enjoy in some circles.[16]

Equally naïve and incorrect would be the view of the organic growth and branching out of languages from a common stem, like branches spreading from a tree trunk. A language is no organism, it cannot literally spring from a seed or otherwise be born (save the invented artificial languages like Esperanto, Ido, or Volapük, though even they have their roots ultimately in natural languages), it cannot grow, decay, and die. If the picture of Schleicher's genealogical tree of Indo-European languages fostered this view, it has indeed done a great deal of harm.

The most reasonable theory of the spread of Indo-European languages, it seems to me, is the one already proffered, in passing, to illuminate the spread of Indo-European dialects in Italy. Namely, that a few speakers at a time move beyond the original dialect boundaries, that for some good socio-cultural reasons the natives of the receiving areas adopt the language of the newcomers, and that this process repeats itself on and on, with varying intensity and speed and extensity of spread at different periods. Migrations of vast bulks of speakers in closed social units may and do occur, but in absence of nonlinguistic evidence this must not be made a *conditio sine qua non* of linguistic expansion. The linguistic differentiation is then due, as I mentioned, to the normal divergent development of linguistic and other cultural features whose contact with the parent area weakens because of increasing distances and decreasing communication, to the passage of time itself, and, perhaps chiefly, to the diverse linguistic substrata whose speakers alter severally the original dialect or dialects which they appro-

[16] See Patroni 1940, 43; Pulgram 1957.

priate in the course of one or many generations. This theory of linguistic propagation finds its best visual representation in Schmidt's wave theory. And it is certainly no accident that its publication and its friendly acceptance by linguists coincided with the rise of scientific dialectology.[17]

Patroni, though not a linguist by profession, formulated his view of the spread of Indo-European in what seems to me eminently sensible words: "The diffusion, indeed the very formation of the Indo-European languages (and probably of all languages) occurred, as a rule, in a way quite other than the arrival of a compact tribe bringing with it its single language into the region where the language now is, or at one time was, at home. At the most one may seek a coincidence between individual cultures and languages, each of them representing an ethnos or people, which is a historic-spiritual product that has nothing to do with race in a zoological or generically biological sense (in which the word is used by physical anthropology); but it is extremely difficult to establish with certainty one single case of such a coincidence . . . But we do not wish to deny that [in the case of Indo-European] individuals and families (rather than whole peoples), at different times, and without all of them necessarily belonging to the same pure race . . . infiltrated into Europe . . . and thus introduced the ferment of those languages into Europe which came to be classified as Indo-European. But this is something altogether different from a catastrophic invasion happening all at once. . ."[18] "The only propagating power of language is imitation, put into motion either by the prestige of the giver or by the self-interest of the receiver . . . or both these causes together."[19]

If this is true, and I believe it is, then the search for an 'Indo-European culture' and an 'Indo-European race' par excellence is idle. The only *same* in Indo-European prehistory and history is the linguistic type, all concomitant *sames* are at best phenomena

[17] Cf. Pulgram 1953. But in this article I also hope to have made it clear that, by rejecting Schleicher's genealogical tree and by accepting Schmidt's wave theory for the purpose of visualizing schematically the manner of spread of the Indo-European languages, as I have done just now, I do not join those who condemn Schleicher's scheme altogether as outmoded and useless. It merely fulfills, quite adequately, another function.

[18] Patroni 1940, 27–28.

[19] Patroni 1951, 1062.

temporarily joined to it, without necessity or predictability. Hence the term 'Indo-European' must be purely linguistic, always.

One may ask, finally, what gave the impetus to the original displacement of some, however few, speakers of Proto-Indo-European, what caused the apparently minor movement which loosened a chain reaction in linguistic, though not ethnic respect, a *Sprachenwanderung*, as it were, though not a *Völkerwanderung*. Given the uncertainty of dating and placing this Proto-Indo-European, our efforts can produce very hypothetical results at best. But in general terms one might suggest that, in view of the cultural conditions in which the speakers found themselves, an ultimate natural cause which forced their removal has first place among possible theories. Foremost among such possible causes is the necessity, affecting all or some of the people, of seeking new homes in order to provide an adequate amount of food, because a climatic change for the worse (that is, since a new ice age was out of the question at that time, lack of rain) either had made their own seats unsuitable or had driven another population in whose territory the calamity occurred, to attack and dislodge them. And since we find ourselves on or not far from the steppe regions of eastern Europe and western Asia, what comes to mind are the recurrent periods of desiccation of the steppe, as conjectured, with good evidence for major climatic cycles, by the climatologists,[20] and among the historians most eminently by Toynbee.[21]

It is not impossible — though I want to make it quite clear that I am stating this as a pure conjecture without circumstantial support — that the push which set some speakers of Indo-European in motion was provided by the neolithic migration from east to west. The dates, at least, do not clash. If that is so, it is also possible that the earliest moving speakers of Indo-European, as they were swept along with or pushed ahead by the neolithic current, carried with them neolithic cultures westward. This does of course not invalidate my previously stated view, which is considerably more than a conjecture and which I am willing to defend, that the first arrivals of Indo-European speech in Italy were carriers of a metal culture.

[20] See above Chapter II.
[21] Toynbee 1933, *passim* (consult Index *ss.vv.* Indo-European, Steppe, Nomads, etc.).

Many centuries separate the two movements, and besides I have always maintained that Indo-European speech is not a priori and lastingly connected with any one culture. My view would also permit the assumption that at the time of the neolithic advance toward Europe (at least of its northern, not the Aegean, branch) speakers of Indo-European lay in its path, that is, somewhere along the route from the Middle or Near East to Europe. But this, too, I am not proposing as a thesis, but merely suggesting as a conjecture — which may or may not ever be capable of confirmation.

We shall see later that a similar eruption from the steppe, with better historic evidence and different linguistic and ethnic movement and results, has by some scholars been surmised to be the cause for the mediaeval *Völkerwanderung* which set in motion toward the boundaries of the Roman empire speakers of Germanic, Slavic, and Mongolian languages.[22]

[22] See below Chapter XXVI.

CHAPTER XIV

The Linguistic Protohistory of Italy

It would perhaps be well to sum up a few conclusions established so far in this book.

(1) While one cannot commit oneself either on a precise date or, consequently, on a circumscribed homeland for Proto-Indo-European, it is at least clear that this type of language was spoken outside of Italy earlier than the second millennium B.C.

(2) It is therefore impossible to ascribe to the speakers of Proto-Indo-European any single culture. But one can conclude from the evidence that Indo-European dialects reached northern Italy together with the knowledge of metallurgy by a transalpine (and possibly Adriatic) route, originating roughly in the Danubian area. (The southern approach of metal cultures by way of the Mediterranean did not have any Indo-Europeanizing consequences.)

(3) Although one can distinguish three innovating cultural thrusts (copper, bronze, and iron), typically exemplified in the palafitte, the terramare, and at Villanova, respectively, there is no proof that either these material cultures, or the new dialects, were borne into Italy by vast migrations; rather does it seem more appropriate to assume infiltration by a moderate number of carriers.

(4) It is therefore plausible and probable, and not contradicted by any evidence available so far, that the civilizations to which we owe the palafitte, terramare, and Northern Villanovan cultures (and whose bearers are called Palafitticoli, Terramaricoli, and Villanovans, without implication concerning their racial individualities), are also the ones among which Indo-European dialects first were spoken in Italy. But this does not mean that *all* persons in possession of these cultures were speakers of Indo-European. One can therefore not assert that *all* archaeologically recognizable Palafitticoli, Terramaricoli, and Villanovans of Italy were invaders of Indo-

European speech, to say nothing of their being 'Indo-Europeans.'

(5) Since therefore it makes no sense to speak of invading Indo-European tribes or nations, any ethnic identification of speakers of Indo-European between the arrival of the dialects and their first appearance in writing calls for most careful review. Such scrutiny is the task of the present chapter.

The Italian chronologies constructed by anthropologists and archaeologists diverge widely, as I had occasion to note, but on the whole one may accept the early second millennium before Christ as the period into which the beginning of the Indo-Europeanization of Italy falls. The linguist can add no records to ease the work of the prehistorian because he is utterly bereft of evidence until he gets something readable. But in view of the ultimate known linguistic situation he can posit certain requirements, which the prehistorian should do his best to heed before committing himself to a theory.

By the time Indo-European linguistic records become available in Italy a thousand years or more have passed since the arrival of the dialects, and we have reached the middle of the first millennium B.C. Only then do we also obtain historical evidence for a number of ethnic and linguistic names, preserved not by the as yet barbarian Italici but generally by Greek authors who extended their interest in the Apennine peninsula beyond the confines of their own Magna Graecia. Unfortunately their testimony is not always trustworthy, and it should not be, though often it has been, taken at face value. Such identifications by name as we are thus apprised of, in addition to being factually disputable, also fit an ethnic and linguistic situation anywhere from five hundred to one thousand years posterior to the arrival of Indo-European speech in Italy. Consequently, if the earliest sources we possess mention, say, the Umbrians as situated where inscriptional evidence of a yet later date may show us an Indo-European dialect which we choose to call Umbrian, it would be audacious and foolhardy indeed to skip blithely a half or a whole millennium for which we have neither ethnoonomastic nor linguistic information, and identify the Iron Age Villanovans, in whose area we happen to find our later Umbrian texts, as 'Umbrians,' or even as speakers of 'Umbrian.'

Similarly, linguists often speak, or spoke, albeit with some risk of being misunderstood, of Proto-Latins, whereby they mean a hypothetical group of persons who were the first to speak the (unattested) dialect or dialects of Latium which we later discern in Old Latin and, in part, in Faliscan. Obviously this is, or should be, a purely linguistic denomination, signifying no more than speakers of Proto-Latin. Now if the linguist interested in some kind of cultural or ethnic correlation turns to the palaeoethnologists for help, he will find that they are operating with an ethnic group called Proto-Latins, which migrates from the north, about the middle of the second millennium, in a body toward Latium. This seems like useful information, until on closer examination the linguist discovers that these Proto-Latins are nothing else but his own linguistic Proto-Latins, by the palaeoethnologists now guilelessly but wrongly invested with an ethnic or racial individuality and reality on no greater authority than the facile assumption that speakers of Proto-Latin must be Proto-Latins by race or ethnos, and that therefore such a race or ethnos must exist. In addition, since Latin is attested in Latium, and since Latin is Indo-European, and since Indo-European comes from the north, the so-called Proto-Latins of Latium of 600 B.C. were equated ethnically with some apocryphal prehistoric Proto-Latins in the Po valley of a thousand years before. This is obviously a wholly specious onomastic operation, it is not cooperation between sciences, and it explains nothing. Hence the 'Proto-Latins' are, except in the linguistic sense alone, as factitious an entity as are the Indo-Europeans. Playing with names and words provides no true knowledge.[1]

Unfortunately, for the centuries between the arrival of Indo-European dialects in Italy and their documented appearance, no linguistic clues are available, and none are likely to be discovered

---

[1] See Pulgram, Names, 1956. I am reminded of what Mephistopheles, robed in Faust's cloak, says sarcastically to the naïve young student who timidly suggests that there should be a concept, a thought, what we might call a referend to go with each word one uses in intelligent discourse (in Goethe, *Faust*, Part I, in Faust's study, trl. by Bayard Taylor, Boston 1898, vol. 1, p. 80):

> Of course! But only shun too over-sharp a tension,
> For just where fails the comprehension,
> A word steps promptly in as deputy.
> With words 't is excellent disputing;
> Systems to words 't is easy suiting;
> On words 't is excellent believing;
> No word can ever lose a jot from thieving.

because the inhabitants of Italy speaking Pre-Italic and Italic dialects learned the art of writing only from the Etruscans in Italy, the pivotal date of whose arrival is so relatively near our earliest evidence in Italic that, allowing for a certain lapse of time for the learning process, a very small part at best of the gap could be bridged by new discoveries. But since rash conclusions without sufficient factual proof have been propounded and have found acceptance, I shall attempt to clear the air of what seem to me misconceptions arising from them.

In some regions prehistoric and protohistoric cultures and civilizations have left at least some sort of precipitation in mythology, in sagas, in legends, and in folklore. The hypercritical school of historiography which rejects everything that is not plainly recorded and documented has been progressively giving way to a more conciliatory approach that is willing to do some sleuthing, with the aid of prehistoric sciences, among the not strictly historical sources — but, of course, with great care and a healthy dose of skepticism. Thanks to this modicum of confidence in the legendary tradition, coupled with the perseverance of a Schlieman, for example, Homer's Troy was actually discovered and the Trojan War is now considered a real event.

But while we can and shall avail ourselves of such testimony for the protohistory of Rome and the Romans, no similar clues are to be ferreted out for the era of pre-Roman Italy as a whole, outside of Magna Graecia, between 1500 and 500 B.C. This in itself is significant. The insouciance of the non-Roman Italics with their country's dim past as confronted with the frantic search of the Romans to discover, indeed to invent for themselves, a heroic, legendary age; the lack of a genuine mythical story of ancient Italy and the subsequent fabrication of one by the Romans, but always from a Roman point of view; all this confirms the archaeologically perceivable cultural and social fragmentation of pre-Roman Italy, and testifies to the absence of any notion or consciousness of *Schicksalsgemeinschaft* among the tribes. In that age of Italy's history, it is impossible to discern in the archaeological record any racial, cultural,[2] linguistic, political, religious, or eco-

---

[2] Altheim, Römische, 1951, 160, thinks otherwise: even the Terramaricoli had allegedly given all of Italy, north, center, and south, an Italic unity.

nomic unity; hence we can in fact write no prehistory of Italy as a whole for the period.[3] We cannot find even legendary clues for one.

Two ethnic names which occur in a number of ancient authors,[4] the *Aborigines* and the *Oenotrians*, have been used by old and, alas, modern writers with so many meanings that it is as hopeless as it would be useless to try to unravel the skein of confusion. The Aborigines, whose name has been etymologized for (at best doubtful) enlightenment, have been called autochthonous inhabitants of Italy (from *origo*, 'origin'), or nomadic wanderers (Aberrigines, from *errare*, 'to wander'), or mountain people (from Βορείγονοι). But the only fixed significance which the name in the end attains is that of 'very ancient, autochthonous,' in short, 'aboriginal.' Archaeologically and, of course, linguistically, this tribe or nation is wholly unidentifiable, hence operating with it is suspect. The Oenotrians are an item of similar obscurity. By tradition they are invaders from the Balkans, arriving allegedly at the beginning of the seventh century before Christ. (Does this make them Illyrians? See below.) Eventually they were called Itali, we are told, after their king Italus, who was followed by Morgis, after whom they were then named Morgetes (which is another legendary ethnicon); part of the kingdom then falls to Siculus, after whom the Siculi are named. This labored parturition of eponymous heroes renders the whole series of tales highly improbable. In other words, we do not know who or what the Aborigines and the Oenotrians were, let alone what language they spoke.

Not much better are we informed concerning the *Pelasgians*. There seems to be general agreement in the ancient sources that they were a pre-Hellenic tribe originally inhabiting northern Greece.[5] Archaeologically they too are intangible. Linguistically they have been fitted into what some (for example, Schachermeyr, Kretschmer, Georgiev) have come to claim as a pre-Hellenic Indo-European layer in the Aegean area. Quite apart from the controversial nature of this linguistic hypothesis which has little to recommend itself, the reasons wherefore the nebulous Pelasgians, supplied by means of etymology and linguistic palaeontology with a civiliza-

[3] Whatmough 1937, 400–401.
[4] For references consult PW, the *Enciclopedia Italiana*, Nissen 1883, PID, and others, *ss.vv.*
[5] Bérard 1941, 492–503.

tion and even a religion, were made the carriers of this language are curious. They are, we are told with naïve candor, "purely practical, for all one knows about the Pelasgians, which term shall serve here to designate the people who spoke this Indo-European language, is that they inhabited pre-Hellenic Greece and some other regions in the south of Europe." [6] Indeed, this is precisely what one does not know about the Pelasgians, and what should be the result, not the fundament, of an inquiry about them. If we furthermore credulously accept also Herodotus' report about Pelasgians speaking a non-Greek unintelligible idiom at Cortona in Tuscany, near Arezzo (these 'Pelasgians' probably being Etruscans who indeed held Cortona), then we shall have discovered a pre-pre-Italic Indo-European stratum of race and language in Italy.

The *Ausones* are said to have occupied the west coast of Italy between the Volturno and the Liri rivers. In the tradition they appear as a powerful, warlike, autochthonous people, known to the Greeks as early (or, from our point of view, as late) as the fifth century B.C. Their name, some say, is the Grecized earlier (unrhotacized) form of the Italic Aurunci, which eventually comes to be extended to cover various tribes of central and even other parts of Italy. But by some it was claimed that the Ausones are part of the Oscans,[7] whereas on the other hand we are told that on the contrary the Oscans are part of the Ausones who are Indo-European invaders to Campania from the north and who are subdivided into Itali, Oenotrians, and Morgetes (whose acquaintance we have just made in entirely different connections) in the south and Oscans in the north of the river Liri.[8] Since the Oscans known to us several centuries later speak an Indo-European language, it seems to have followed, thanks to the customary overextension of terms, that the Ausones too would have to speak such a dialect, or simply, by a further onomastic legerdemain, be Indo-Europeans. From that to their being Nordics by race it is only a small step. Their name then is derived from the color of their gold-blond hair (Ausones from *ausum*, later *aurum*, 'gold'), just as is that of the Rutuli (which really should be Rufuli, we are assured, from a root

---

[6] van Windekens 1952, 158. Cf. also the reviews of this book by Messing 1954 and Schick 1953.

[7] Nissen 1883, 1.531.

[8] Heurgon 1942, 50.

rudh-, 'red') who are part of the Ausones. Also the Latini are a portion of the Ausones, the argument goes on, and indeed all Ausones speak Latin.[9] The speciousness of all this reasoning is palpable. In truth, all we know of the Ausones is, as usually, that somebody used this label to name some group, we do not know which. The rest is gratuitous.[10]

The land of the Ausones was conquered by people called 'Οπικοί, we are told, and all, the conquerors and the conquered, are henceforth called 'Οπικοί, whom in the mountains of Samnium, that is, in the Abruzzi, we know as Samnites since the fourth century B.C.[11] Since the Samnites, according to the rules of this onomastic *divertissement* are Oscans (whereas in reality all we know is that in the second half of the first millennium B.C. we get from the area of Samnium a number of inscriptions in an Indo-European dialect which we have named Oscan), it seems to follow that the 'Οπικοί were Indo-Europeans, or invaders from Central Europe. This type of deduction, if transferred to another and better known time and place, would go like this: The members of an ethnic or tribal unit called Franks appear from the fifth century of the Christian era on in Gaul and become known eventually, some centuries later, under the name *Français*, at which point they speak a neo-Latin language; hence the Franks were Latins, or Romans.

From the Adriatic seaboard south of the Po delta we have a number of inscriptions which have not been deciphered. Archaeologically, the culture of the area shows, up to the Iron Age, certain conservative features, including burial by inhumation while neighboring regions had changed over to incineration of the bodies (the boundary between the two types running roughly along a line from Rimini to Rome). This led many scholars (Brizio, Peet, Randall-MacIver) to think of its bearers as direct descendants from the neolithic inhabitants undisturbed by foreign influx or influence.[12] The protracted isolation of these tribes is ascribed by some to their

---

[9] Ribezzo 1950, 62–64.

[10] It is unfortunate, and merely conducive to further confusion and pyramiding of hypotheses, if recently a phase of an Italian Bronze Age culture was named 'Ausonian,' with the illusory result that we now have 'Ausones' who are 'identified' by a culture of their own. Cf. Bernabò Brea 1952.

[11] Wikén 1937, 119–120.

[12] Randall-MacIver 1927, 145; Dumitrescu 1932, 325.

fierce, warlike nature which shows itself in the preponderance of weapons among their tomb furnishings and in other finds.[13]

The inscriptions of the area, which so far have not been translated, are divided into a northern and a southern group and, for want of a better name, are called East Italic. However, they are not all in the same language, as far as one can tell. The inscriptions of the northern group, from Novilara, Fano, Pesaro, "are as distinct in language as they certainly are in alphabet from the Southern 'East Italic' or so-called 'Old Sabellic' inscriptions." [14] Apparently they are not Indo-European. But the southern group, on the other hand, seem to be in an Illyrian type of language, or this is at least the consensus at this point. In any event, "it is difficult not to believe that [their langauge] is Indo-European." [15]

Next to the two oldest inscriptions of Italy of the eighth century, both Etruscan, hence non-Indo-European (from Vetulonia, found in the Tomba del Guerriero and the Tomba del Duce), the East-Italic inscriptions seem to be the most ancient forms of continuous writing discovered until now, going back as far as the sixth or seventh century B.C. This being so, the so-called *Picenes*, or *Picentes*, archaeologically identified by many ancient and modern authorities as a very ancient ethnos directly descended from the non-Indo-European neolithic 'Mediterraneans,' should not be regarded, under the same name, as the authors of both the Indo-European and the non-Indo-European among the East Italic inscriptions. Again we are faced with a terminological dilemma. Perhaps a solution would be to distinguish the neolithic 'Picenes' from the historic 'Picenes,' the former being the native, possibly Mediterranean stock (some call it 'Ligurian'; see below), whose undecipherable language may then be represented in the Northern East Italic inscriptions, the latter, of undetermined race, mixed or unmixed, being the manufacturers of the southern inscriptions which have at least tentatively been read but on whose interpretation scholars do not agree, except to the extent that they are probably Indo-European.[16]

---

[13] Randall-MacIver, Forerunners, 1928, 143–144; Italy, 1928, 46–47, 104–107.

[14] PID 2.209.

[15] Whatmough 1937, 256.

[16] Kaschnitz-Weinberg 1950, 393. *Ibid.*, 391–392, the Picentes, together with the Iapodes, are transadriatic invaders. So also Norden 1934, 249. Cf. Dumitrescu 1929, 166–181.

This interpretation would, by the way, explain that the northern inscriptions appeared to some scholars as Etruscoid or even Etruscan, provided that we accept the hypothesis that Etruscan may be a Mediterranean type of language hence related to that of the Northern East Italic 'Mediterranean' inscriptions.[17]

One of the most recently found inscriptions classed as Southern East Italic is on an interesting though ungainly statue named after its site the Warrior of Capestrano (at the foot of the Gran Sasso), which has provoked also certain interesting ethnic cogitations. On the evidence of the alphabet it was dated as older than the fifth century.[18] The enormous helmet or hat which the figure is wearing (a very strange item of apparel, vaguely reminiscent only of the headgear worn by some men on the Etruscan bucket from Certosa near Bologna, the so-called Certosa Situla) has occasioned the lame theory that the man represented is an Illyrian and that with him all the 'Picenes,' as speakers of Indo-European Southern East Italic, are Illyrians also.[19] But the same hat has equally inspired the thought that the Warrior of Capestrano, and the 'Picenes,' and their language, are Germanic and must be accounted for by an early Germanic invasion of Italy.[20]

So we are again driven to the conclusion that the name Picenes, or Picentes, is inoperative because it means different things to different people and because "any term which requires definition on every occasion it is used . . . is already discredited and better discarded altogether." [21] Maybe it can be explained etymologically from Illyrian,[22] or Italic,[23] or perhaps it is related to Latin *picus*,

[17] The latest opinion of Pisani 1954, 49, is that Northern East Italic is indeed non-Indo-European without clear connection with other non-Indo-European languages, whereas Southern East Italic has at least some Indo-European traits.

[18] Carpenter 1945, 461. For an attempted translation see Vetter 1943.

[19] For details see Altheim 1950, 48; Borgeaud 1943, 143–144. In both a reference to Plautus *Trin.* 851–852 plays a major role, where a big mushroom-shaped hat is associated typically with the Illyrians. No one seems to worry, if about nothing else in this tale, then at least about the matter of four hundred years intervening between the Warrior and Plautus.

[20] Kretschmer 1948, 19–21; the queer big helmet is worn, we are tipped off, because the Germans cannot take the hot Italian sun. The most reasonable explanation is, to my knowledge, that of Holland 1956: the statue represents a *deuotus* who did not find, as he was expected to, death in battle and whose effigy had to be buried instead. See Liv. 8.10.12. See also Boëthius 1956.

[21] PID 2.226.

[22] Norden 1934, 229–231.

[23] Rix 1951, 247.

'woodpecker,' which would be the totemic animal of the tribe (compare the Hirpini from *hirpus*, 'wolf,' Bouianum from *boues*, 'oxen,' etc.), possibly first connected with a Sacred Spring (see below) migratory group.[24] But, whatever the truth of the matter, this term refers unambiguously only to a cultural or social unit known by that name not before the second half of the first millennium B.C.. and it should therefore not be used for anything that falls into preceding centuries. Furthermore, to identify ethnically the 'Picenes' because of certain hypotheses concerning their language as either Mediterraneans,[25] or Indo-Europeans,[26] is equally illicit because we do not know such races or nations.

We can be sure of two things. First, between 1000 and 500 B.C. the area coinciding roughly with the later Picenum and adjacent regions shows archaeologically a conservative, warlike culture in which inhumation was practiced; linguistically (provided the inscriptions are old enough) there may be discernible toward the end of the period in the southern portion of the area an Indo-European type of speech, although some scholars disagree on that. Second, after 500 B.C. the tribes are referred to as Picenes, or Picentes, but otherwise not much light is thrown on them until they enter the orbit of Roman history and become Romanized culturally and linguistically. Hence we cannot speak of prehistoric Picenes or Picentes, nor assign to them a culture and a language.

The Euganean Hills between Padua and Este, an extinct volcanic elevation, owe their name to an alleged prehistoric people which historically is presented to us under the name *Euganeans*. Practically nothing is known of them. Livy (1.1) calls them an autochthonous population originally occupying all the land between the Adriatic and the Alps, but later pushed out by invading Illyrians. If anyone wishes to identify them archaeologically as part of the Terramaricoli,[27] no harm is done as long as no deductions are pyramided on top of this purely onomastic equation.

Yet precisely this was done, with the aid of a number of interesting inscriptions from the Val Camonica, the valley of the Oglio river north of the Lago d'Iseo, so called after the ancient tribe

[24] Altheim 1941, 1.46; Kretschmer 1925, 85–86.
[25] Ribezzo 1950, 205–206.
[26] Rix 1951, 247.
[27] Altheim — Trautmann 1937, 101–103.

of the *Camuni*. To Cato we owe the information that the Camuni and the Trumplini (whose name is remembered nearby in the Val Trompia, east of the Lago d'Iseo) are part of the Euganean people.[28] The language of the Val Camonica inscription was recognized as Italic, of a kind more closely related to the Latin-Faliscan than to the Osco-Umbrian type.[29]

Now, it was argued, since the Val Camonica inscriptions (all of a date much after 500 B.C.) are of the Latin-Faliscan group, and since the Camuni according to ancient testimony are Euganeans, and since the Euganeans are Terramaricoli, the Latin-Faliscans too are by ethnos Terramaricoli or descendants of them. Consequently, the Euganeans themselves are also speakers of the Latin-Faliscan type of Italic, so that at least those portions of the Terramaricoli which appear as Euganeans and as Latin-Faliscans, if not all of them, spoke that kind of dialect. Therefore, the Terramaricoli are invading 'Indo-Europeans' of Latin-Faliscan speech.

This would be a wonderful way of finding out what language the Terramaricoli spoke. But this frail chain of syllogisms has a specially weak link in its very center, namely, where the Euganeans are identified with the Camuni of our inscriptions on one side and with the Terramaricoli on the other. By definition of the terms, either *can* be true, but not both *need* be true, and neither is *proved* to be true: for the equation Camuni = Euganei = Terramaricoli equates only onomastically but without the slightest factual justification, over the treacherous, merely onomastic bridge of the Euganeans, the linguistically identified Camuni of the inscriptions of *post*-500 B.C. with the archaeologically identified Terramaricoli of a certain culture of *ante*-1000 B.C. It would be difficult to commit more blunders in one operation.

All we really know is that inscriptions from an area occupied by the historical Camuni, who are possibly, if the tradition is right, members of a nonhistorical not further identifiable group called Euganeans, are written in a language which seems to be closely related to the Latin-Faliscan type of Italic. It is further possible,

[28] Cato ap. Plin. *N.H.* 3.134. But Strabo 4.206 thinks they are Raetic. Nissen 1883, 1.486 f. indeed makes all Euganeans Raetic.

[29] Altheim — Trautmann 1940, 17–19; Altheim 1941, 1.49–51; Altheim, Römische, 1951, 15–18; Altheim, Geschichte, 1951, 92–123, with bibliography. For a mild protest see Devoto 1951, 50.

though not proven, that the speakers of Latin-Faliscan and the Camuni were divided from one another by a wedge which an apparently later group of newcomers drove between them. If the people of this wedge spoke Illyrian, then the recent opinion that Venetic is not Illyrian but rather related to Latin-Faliscan [30] would be further strengthened, or it would at least become apparent why many scholars had hitherto thought on linguistic grounds (supported in any event by ancient tradition according to which the Veneti are Illyrians) Venetic to be Illyrian: Venetic, attested mainly in the very center of the Euganean land, would have been in some degree Illyrianized by Illyrian-speaking invaders but remained fundamentally Italic.

The *Illyrians* have repeatedly figured in the preceding discussion. There can be no doubt that the name corresponds to a social and linguistic reality in historical times, although we know little about it. But what about the prehistoric 'Illyrians'? Who were they, what did they speak, and how can we materialize them? The problem in this instance is all the more vexed because of late there has been fashionable a trend that one may call Panillyrianism, or less flatteringly Illyriomania.[31]

The linguistic evidence we have should be divided into two kinds: the direct, representing through at least allegedly related idioms the language of the historical Illyrians, and the indirect, concerning the prehistoric 'Illyrians.' Of the first, there is little enough: one inscription of three words from the Balkan peninsula, and from Italy about two hundred Messapic inscriptions (*if* they are in any sense Illyrian) of Apulia, plus whatever portion of Illyrian material may be contained in some one hundred and fifty Venetic inscriptions just alluded to, plus a few glosses and loan words. Of the second, there is of course even less: only local, personal, and divine names, whose Illyrianness is often contested. The combined evidence has been sufficient for most scholars to declare Illyrian an Indo-European language, although its exact classification within the Indo-European dialects is still doubtful.[32]

[30] Beeler 1949.
[31] Cf. the critique by Pisani 1937, 277; Devoto 1937, *passim*; Laviosa-Zambotti 1947, 145–148.
[32] For example, there is no agreement on whether Illyrian is a so-called *kentum*

For the moment, it is only the second category of records which interests us, together with any theories that have been propounded to account culturally and ethnically for the prehistoric Illyrians. The question which immediately arises is: Can we isolate any unit which for good reasons we may connect with the historical Illyrians and therefore call by the same name?

So-called Illyrian proper names have been discovered by impassioned Illyrianists over an immense area, almost the whole classical world: in Asia Minor, on the Balkan peninsula, practically all over Italy, in the Alpine regions (Raetia, Noricum), in the Danube basin (Pannonia), even in western Poland, Switzerland, Germany, France, Spain, and the British Isles.[33] It is not unnatural that this extraordinary *embarras de richesses* aroused skepticism, both of a specific and a general nature. Specifically, it was pointed out by several scholars that the widespread linguistic traits of similar name formation in stem and suffix may well be due not to 'Illyrian' but to a common vast substratum, for which the name Illyrian, because of its historical connotation, is inappropriate, but for which instead the Mediterranean or some other group of related dialects might be adduced.[34] Generally, it was convincingly proposed that local names despite any deceptively uniform appearance may belong to more than one linguistic family, hence are no sure proof of ethnic extension and migration;[35] more bluntly it was said that "etymologically untransparent, impervious to the regular phonetic changes, and nearly always surviving a long series of invasions, local names are the least suitable material to prove no matter what concerning the relationship of two peoples. . . . Correlating the enigmatic names of peoples and cities of the ancient Mediterranean is not ethnography."[36] In fact, one of the most zealous champions of Illyrianism, Krahe, has in his latest work embraced a much more modest and critical theory and has somewhat narrowed down the concept of 'Illyrian,' but still does not, to my mind, sufficiently

---

or *satem* language. Cf. Devoto 1937. See now also Krahe 1955, reviewed unfavorably by Pisani 1956.

[33] Kretschmer 1925, 87; Krahe 1929, 143–148; 1937, 125–132; 1940, 64–68; 1949, 44; Pokorny 1935; Altheim, Geschichte, 1951, 60.

[34] Pisani 1937, 285–289; Devoto 1938; 1951, 53–54; Laviosa-Zambotti 1947, 145–148; Ribezzo 1950, 191–192.

[35] Braun 1933, 1007–1015; see also Palmer 1954, 55.

[36] Dumézil 1944, 141–142.

take into practical account at least the more moderate of the grave objections raised against the onomastic-ethnic method.[37] Whatever one's personal convictions on the urgency of rejecting arguments from toponymy, it is surely true, at least, that "in this type of research, with more than a thousand years not infrequently separating the earliest scanty records available from the presumable dates of coinage or borrowing, and with [ancient as well as] mediaeval scribes, copyists, and translators almost doomed to garble those place names whose actual meaning even the cleverest among them were unable to grasp (to say nothing of disguises brought about by folk etymology), the margin of error of interpretation remains singularly broad." [38]

Once the entire map of Europe had been enthusiastically and generously sprinkled with 'Illyrian' names, it was to be expected that vast Illyrian migrations would be conjured to explain their ubiquitousness. Consequently, the fabulous Illyrians became the most widely traveled denizens of prehistoric Europe. After the middle of the second millennium B.C. they are identified with the bearers of the Lausitz culture and as the practitioners of the crowded cremation burials in so-called urnfield cemeteries, and are forthwith set in motion on their trek starting from Bohemia, or maybe western Poland, or eastern Germany, or the Baltic shores. Thereafter they are everywhere; they provide the label which everyone sticks onto something: they are the Villanovans,[39] they are, somehow, responsible for the Doric migration into Greece [40] and for the coming of the Latins to Rome,[41] they are even the Palestinian Philistines.[42] In short, the Illyrians fairly swarm all over Europe and Asia Minor.[43] All that seems like a great mass of im-

[37] Krahe 1954, 98–104, and *passim*.
[38] Malkiel 1954, 590.
[39] Sergi 1934, 67–68.
[40] Altheim, Geschichte, 1951, 50.
[41] Krahe 1949, 14: "Without the Illyrians no Rome . . . , without the Illyrians no Sparta. . ."
[42] Krahe 1938, 4, thinks it possible, and seems more certain of it in 1949, 12–13; Bonfante 1946, is sure of it; Altheim, Geschichte 1951, 59, rather believes that the "Illyrian portions of the Philistines" (what is that?) are the Veneti rather than the Illyrians themselves. The confusion is scarcely alleviated if we are earnestly assured, by Borgeaud 1943, 10, that, in reality, "the Illyrians are a variety of the Veneti" and not vice versa as everyone had thought.
[43] Krahe 1938, 4; 1940, 69–71; 1949, 10–13; Pokorny 1935; Pittioni 1938, 204,

portant conclusions on the basis of a number of local names, ascribed to a language which ceased to be spoken in antiquity and of which we know pitifully little.[44]

Last but not least we must return to the question why these alleged prehistoric wanderers and purveyors of so many local names should be called Illyrians in the first place. By what rights, even accepting the onomastic evidence at face value and unskeptically, can we extend the name under which the ancients knew a Balkan tribe, to this remarkable ethno-socio-cultural entity avowedly existing a millennium earlier? By that token, to a future ethnolinguist who lacks all linguistic records except local names in the British Isles, but who is somewhat though not much better provided with American evidence, including the national designation 'American' attested in, say, a Japanese historian, King Arthur and his knights would be Americans! In other words, we know nothing of prehistoric Illyrians.

When linguists speak of *Umbrians* they mean the speakers of a dialect represented chiefly by a set of inscriptions on bronze tablets concerning a religious festival which took place in ancient Iguuium (now Gubbio) in the province of Umbria, the earliest of which date probably from the third century B.C., but all of which render most likely an older form of speech (in the manner of ritual texts and ritual language of all ages and lands). When ethnologists and ethnolinguists use the term, Umbrian refers to a variety of things between 2000 and 300 B.C. According to a remark by a classical author,[45] the Umbrians are the most ancient people in Italy. One wonders how he knew and, indeed, what he meant. But the same statement is reverently repeated in modern authors, also without further explanation or definition of terms.[46] At Bologna we find

---

according to whom the Illyrians are responsible for the Iron Age in Europe; Altheim, Geschichte, 1951, 32–33.

[44] If modern Albanian is the latest stage in the development of this ancient Illyrian language, and if also ancient Messapic is at least partly Illyrian (see below), it is strange indeed that no connection can be established between Messapic and Albanian. Whatmough PID 2. 264, prefers to separate Albanian from Illyrian and Messapic because, he believes, Messapic is almost certainly not a *satem* dialect of Indo-European and Illyrian is probably not one either, whereas Albanian is. On the other hand, Devoto 1937, 266, attempts to prove that Messapic is a *satem* idiom. See also Hamp 1957.

[45] Plin. *N.H.* 3.19.112.

[46] Pais 1933, 1.51.

these Umbrians as the forerunners of the Etruscans, by whom they were vanquished, losing three hundred cities to their conquerors.[47] According to another source,[48] not the Etruscans but the Pelasgians beat the Umbrians. (We have already seen that, at least in Cortona, the Pelasgians may have been none other than the Etruscans.) But once we have got Umbrians as forerunners of the Etruscans in the Bologna area, it becomes irresistibly tempting to identify them with the Villanovans, which was done.[49] These Umbrian Villanovans allegedly move from the south (Etruria) toward the north (Bologna) and bring with them the knowledge of iron.[50]

Patroni, while conceding that the prehistoric Umbrians were Villanovans, insists nonetheless that racially they were not Indo-Europeans but Mediterraneans (which leads to a corollary theory on the ethnos of the historic Umbrians which I am unable to understand).[51]

And finally we are served the thought that the Umbrians are really the Germanic Ambrones who enter Italy in three stages: in the second millennium B.C., as the last wave of the Italic invasion; at an uncertain date, but not later than the sixth century B.C., producing the "Ueberschichtung[?] der Ligurer[?]"; and in 102 B.C., together with the Cimbri and Teutones.[52] For a tribe of which the world on the whole has taken little notice the Ambrones would show wondrous durability and strength.

What do we actually know? We have inscriptions, which we can read and understand, in a dialect which has been named Umbrian. If we want to retain that name, and there is no reason why we should not, then we have no call to apply it equally to any

---

[47] Plin. *N.H.* 3.19.112; cf. also Grenier 1912, 2–3, 506–507.

[48] Dion. Hal. 1.20.4–1.26.1.

[49] Notably by Grenier 1912, 2–3, 7–8, 505–508, and *passim*; but note this contradictory passage, 479: "It is an arbitrary hypothesis to attribute to the Umbrians . . . the so-called Villanovan culture." For a review of this book refuting the Villanovan-Umbrian equation see von Duhn 1913.

[50] Grenier 1912, 13, 506–507. This cannot please the Illyrianists according to whom the Illyrians were the bringers of iron to Central Europe, importing it to Italy from the north or east.

[51] Patroni 1940, 31; 1951, 784–790.

[52] Kretschmer 1932. (Note that for Kretschmer also the big-hatted warrior from Capestrano is a German.) Against this view writes Lamboglia 1941, 96, who wants to reserve the Ambrones for the Indo-European element among the Ligurians. To Bottiglioni 1954, 2, the Ambrones, whose name appears as that of the Umbrians after their Indo-Europeanization, are Ligurians.

prehistoric cultural or ethnic or racial group, real or surmised, for reasons which by now should be abundantly clear. If we prefer to follow Pliny and Dionysius of Halicarnassus and assign the name Umbrian to a prehistoric entity, if we further are satisfied with viewing this entity as bearing the Villanovan culture, then it becomes mandatory to eschew this name with reference to the inscriptions authored by the historic inhabitants of Iguuium, and to call the dialect, say, Iguvine instead, so as to avoid all confusion and any suggestion of connectedness.[53] Would that Grenier, when writing about the Umbrians and Villanovans, had known what he knew three decades later with reference to the Ligurians: "The use of an historical name outside of the time and outside of the space for which it is historically attested, can produce only confusion. It contributes nothing but an illusory clarity." [54]

Along with the Umbrians, sometimes equated with them, the *Ligurians* [55] are often honored by being called the, or among the, most ancient nations of Italy, their original domain, again like that of the Umbrians, far exceeding the confines of the Roman and modern province bearing their name.

The craniometrists send us off to an, even for them, extraordinarily unpropitious start. One says that the Ligurians are dolicocephalic and of the Mediterranean race,[56] the other that they are brachycephalic and of the Mongolian race.[57] Either these anthropologists do not talk about the same skulls, or they do not know what they are talking about. In this instance possibly both.

An historian seems to be nearly clairvoyant: "The Ligurians are the most ancient nation of western Europe, rough, robust, tenacious people. Their somatic characteristics are: a slim and spare build, brown complexion, dark hair and eyes, dolicocephalic skull." [58] How does one arrive at this intelligence concerning perishable and otherwise unattested physical and mental characteristics? Methodologically, by putting the cart before the horse,

---

[53] Cf. Whatmough 1937, 193–195. Devoto 1951, 113: "It is one thing to affirm that the Umbrians are the oldest people, and another thing to affirm the antiquity of the term 'Umbrian.'"
[54] Grenier 1940, 159.
[55] For a résumé of the entire Ligurian controversy see Grenier 1940.
[56] Sergi 1885 and 1898.
[57] Nicolucci 1863.
[58] Pais 1933, 143.

which is expressed verbally by inserting the little word 'still,' thus: "In our times, a large portion of the inhabitants of the Provence and of the maritime Alps are *still* of Ligurian stock." [59] (Italics mine.)

The Ligurians were described as Indo-Europeans, Non-Indo-Europeans, Iberians, Tyrrhenians, Mediterraneans, Hellenes, Africans, Basques, Kelts, Nordics.[60] In view of such profusion, it is as usually a good bet that the term Ligurian was not defined, or not defined in the same way, before the persons so called were classified within a larger ethnic or racial group, to say nothing of the fact that also the larger classes whose names I just cited, especially when applied to prehistory, are themselves in urgent need of an unequivocal and universally acceptable racial *or* cultural *or* linguistic definition. Consequently, 'Ligurian' is no more enlightening or precise an appellation than 'Indian' is for all pre-Columbian inhabitants of the Americas.

What evidence do we possess? What do we know? As with the Umbrians, the Illyrians, etc., we need to distinguish first of all the Ligurians known to the Romans and Greeks as a nation or tribe in the province of Liguria from some ancient real or fictitious people to whom the same name can be given only through an illicit terminological extension. Conversely, if we agreed to call a prehistoric group Ligurians, then we should refrain from using this title in historic times since we lack all proof of connection. But the latter would be an awkward solution because we should have to disallow a name widespread among the contemporaries of the historic Ligurians. Accordingly, it is preferable not to name the prehistoric evidence from Liguria 'Ligurian' except in a strictly geographic sense. But if in the historic period we find the term used by ancient authors with not only a geographic but also a linguistic and even ethnic meaning, we must not therefore blandly speak of the historic Ligurians as the most ancient people of Italy and direct descendants of neolithic or even older forebears whom we choose to call, for no compelling reason, by the same name, nor must we conclude from it that the language of which we have desperately scanty and inconclusive records is therefore pre-Indo-European, that is, non-

---

[59] Pais 1933, 1.43.
[60] Instead of giving a full bibliography here I refer to Curotto 1940, 11–27, where a general review may be found.

Indo-European. If the linguistic evidence were not so extraordinarily meager (mainly local names, a few words, and no connected text) due to the early extinction of 'Ligurian' speech, we should be able to answer the linguistic question easily enough. But since the records are insufficient, terminological juggling with 'Ligurian,' tempting though it may be, brings us no nearer to an illuminating answer.[61] If, then, we call Ligurians the speakers of the however badly known Ligurian dialect of historical times, we must not refer to anything prehistoric as Ligurian, unless it were a related language; but such a one, of course, we do not know. And the prehistoric dwellers of Liguria of palaeolithic, neolithic and (prehistoric) metal age cultures, whoever they were and wherever they came from,[62] were 'Ligurians' no more than the prehistoric inhabitants of Umbria were 'Umbrians,' or the Anglo-Saxons were Englishmen.

With the prehistoric denizens of Liguria, under the name Ligurians, are often connected, in one way or another, the *Sicels*, or *Siculi*. As their name shows, they are primarily known in Sicily, but their presence there, together with or because of their Indo-European dialect, is frequently explained by immigration from a northern location. The pattern of my subsequent argument and its conclusion can by now be foreseen: the linguistic evidence, which is poor but better for Siculan than for Illyrian or Ligurian, shows us an undoubtedly Indo-European language, which must have come to Sicily from somewhere else, some time, somehow. Prelinguistically, that is, archaeologically we may discern, aided possibly, but only corroboratively, by prehistoric toponomastic vestiges, certain cultural groupings and transfers, not to all of which we may for good reasons apply the term Siculan.

The palaeoethnological situation in Sicily is complicated by the fact that ancient tradition knows besides the Siculi two other ethnica, the Elymi and the Sicani. On the authority of this almost unanimous tradition, the Elymi are Trojans who migrated to Sicily

---

[61] As in the case of Illyrian, much has again been made of local names (cf., among others, Dottin 1916, 183–184; Conway 1926, 433; Pokorny 1938, 59–71), with the same uncertain results, and followed by the same objections: cf., among others, Ettmayer 1926, 26, 31–34; Berthelot 1933, 288–301; Gamillscheg 1934, 2.203; Whatmough 1937, 127–128; Bertoldi 1952, 80.

[62] See PID 2.147–158, and Whatmough 1937, 126–129, for the most reasonable and authoritative discussion of this problem.

at the end of the Trojan War.[63] The proper names that are known are said to point to Anatolian provenance.[64] While it is possible to identify Homer's Troy archaeologically, it is not possible to prove in the same manner the migration of the Elymi because, as we have seen, Sicily was throughout the neolithic and metal ages culturally oriented toward the Aegean,[65] hence an invasion from Troy would not necessarily leave sufficiently distinctive traces on the island. However, an ethnic movement from this direction is by no means out of the question, as the Etruscan arrival in Italy will show.[66] Other scholars think that the Elymi are autochthonous Mediterraneans who differentiated themselves from the Sicani, with whom they had been identical at one time, only under the impact of other unknown influences and immigrations.[67] Tradition ascribes to the Elymi homes in the western corner of Sicily, centering at Segesta and Eryx.[68]

The Sicani are also generally considered as (relatively) autochthonous inhabitants of Sicily. Whence they came originally, if from anywhere, whether from Spain as 'Iberians,' or from Africa, need not concern us here since they left no linguistic records and none are ascribed to them.

If the palaeoethnologists and archaeologists are satisfied that such people as the Elymi and the Sicani existed, and if they wish to call them by these names, as a linguist I have no authority or reason to quarrel with that as long as neither such ethnic groups nor their names interfere and conflict in any way with the linguistic evidence and history, and nomenclature, as best I see it. But the Siculi, to whom ancient inscriptional records are indeed attributed, and after whom a dialect is called, are a different matter.

Scarce as the linguistic evidence for the dialect called Siculan, or Sicel, is (consisting of three inscriptions), it suffices nonetheless

[63] Wikén 1937, 66.
[64] Schulze 1904, 596.
[65] Colini 1904, 156–159; Conway 1926, 437–438.
[66] In fact there exists a view which connects the migrations of the Etruscans and the Elymi with one another; see Schulten 1930, 418–420. Whether the Elymi were originally 'Illyrians' who, prior to their voyage to Italy, had reached Asia Minor from a Balkan location (so Malten 1931, 58–59) is a question which we may pass over in silence in view of what has just been said about the Illyrians.
[67] Pace 1935, 1.113, 163, 167.
[68] Cf. Kahrstedt 1947.

to classify the dialect as Indo-European.[69] However, about the ethnic classification and prehistory of the persons to whom we owe these records and who are called Siculi there exist a number of violently clashing theories. I shall simply cite a few, retaining the ethnic and linguistic terminology of the originals, without comment.[70]

The Ligurians occupy not only Liguria proper but also Latium and, under the name Siculi, the island of Sicily.[71]

There is no proof for the ethnic relation of Siculi and Latini. The burials of the Siculi correspond to those of the Ligurians, not to those of the Italici; they stem from the end of the Neolithic Age, whereas the first Aryan tombs in Italy, due to the Terramaricoli, are of the Bronze Age. But the Siculi do come from Italy and are not the same as the Sicani who originate from Africa.[72]

The very ancient Ligurians come to Sicily in two groups, called Siculi and Sicani, respectively, though each probably does overlay a different substratum on the island and thus develops its own characteristics.[73]

The Sicani and the Siculi are not the same. The Sicani are originally African settlers in Sicily who are squeezed out by the Illyrian Siculi about 1270 B.C. (according to Hellanicus) or 1050 B.C. (according to Thucydides).[74]

The Siculi, being one of the two main groups of prehistoric populations, come from Africa and settle mainly on the islands (except Corsica). The other group are continental Europeans, the so-called Ligurians, who occupy the north and the center of Italy.[75]

[69] Translation is another matter. I shall cite two translations of the inscription on the famous Centuripa Vase (PID 2.444–449), the first by Pisani 1931, 611, the second by Pagliaro 1935, 153.

"This offering is a gift to [the goddess] Nana by A. Nonus St. and Imarus Sta. As this gift is offered with gladness, let not the heirs use it for profane drinking bouts."

"No drunkard tends me the bottle. Taking it from me is difficult. O barrel, since taking from me is difficult, put only pure wine into this container."

[70] For references to and discussion of ancient testimony, see Conway 1926, 438; PID 2.431–438.

[71] Sergi 1901, 163–164.

[72] Modestov 1907, 129–132, 137.

[73] PW *s.v.* Siculi, by Philipp, 1923.

[74] PW *s.v.* Sikaner, by Schulten, 1923.

[75] von Duhn 1924, 1.114–115.

The Siculi are the only true great ethnic reality of prehistory in central and southern Italy. All other names are merely tribal or geographic.[76]

The Latini and the Siculi are not of diverse race.[77]

There is both nonlinguistic and linguistic evidence that the Siculi are northern invaders. They, together with the Latini, form the oldest Indo-European invasion of Italy, preceding the arrival of the Italici proper.[78]

The Sicani and Siculi may be the same, the different suffixes in their names being comparable to those of Romani and Romulus.[79]

The Siculi are invaders of Indo-European speech who conquer and extinguish the native speakers of a Mediterranean idiom.[80]

The Siculi are closely related (*strettamente affini*) to the Latini, and so [that is, it seems, as both consequence and cause] are the dialects of the two peoples. But Siculan is established upon an ancient Ligurian substratum, the Ligurians having previously inhabited Sicily.[81]

The concordances between Latin and Siculan are undeniable; Siculan is a pre-Latin dialect. But there is no archaeological evidence of a migration from Italy to Sicily.[82]

There is a strong relationship between Latin and Siculan, both belonging, together with Ligurian, to the western Indo-European languages, whereas Oscan and Umbrian are of the eastern type, to whose influence Ligurian later owes a number of secondary changes.[83]

Both Siculi and Sicani are Mediterraneans. In Etruria, the Siculi appear as Etruscans who are, therefore, autochthonous in Italy. The Picenes are of the same stratum.[84]

The Siculi are the oldest Indo-Europeans on Italian soil; their

---

[76] Patroni 1934, 353.

[77] Pais 1933, 1.228.

[78] Pace 1935, 1.105–109, 163. But on pp. 163 and 167 the Siculi are also referred to as Italici: obviously in one instance this name is restricted to Oscans and Umbrians, and in the other it covers all speakers of Indo-European (or all 'Indo-Europeans,' or 'Aryans') of Italy.

[79] Wikén 1937, 62. So also Pace 1935, 1.108.

[80] Bertoldi 1937, 169.

[81] Pagliaro 1938, 367–368.

[82] Devoto 1940, 55–56.

[83] Pisani 1941, 395.

[84] Ribezzo 1950, 200.

move southward, occurring at the end of the third millennium B.C., precedes that of other Indo-Europeans by a thousand years. They are, together with Euganeans and Faliscans, the nearest relatives (*die nächsten Verwandten*) of the Latini. The Sicani are a pre-Indo-European population of Sicily, of North African origins.[85]

The Siculi are part of a vast Siculo-Ligurian population which ever has been and still is the only truly fundamental ethno-anthropological element of the peninsula. The migration of the Siculi to Sicily occurs in the Bronze Age, as is evidenced archaeologically, prehistorically, linguistically, and by tradition, although the Siculan dialect as we know it is only of the Iron Age.[86]

Siculan shows no connection whatever with Latin.[87]

My setting side by side a number of typical views of the past fifty years concerning the Siculi was to shed light upon and expose the typical besetting vice of all such ethno-linguistic researches, namely, that ethnologists and linguists and ethnolinguists either do not use their terms and names in the same sense or, worse even, use them without sense and without precise referends as items in a prehistoric crossword puzzle. This alone, together with the inadequacy of the evidence, can explain the enormously divergent theories of serious scholars.

Ethnic names and names of dialects belong properly to history because, by definition, they remain hidden from us in prehistory except possibly for a relatively brief period of protohistoric twilight. Prehistory is the province of the archaeologist, the palaeoethnologist, who should properly deal with cultures, not with nations, least of all with nations bearing historical names. If ever a transfer of historical nomenclature to prehistory is attempted, a *conditio sine qua non* for this procedure is a fairly undisturbed, linear development of an ethnos in one place, without racial or cultural interference from the outside, so that it is fairly plausible that no harm can come from extending a known name backwards over some allowable time. Such a situation of rest and equilibrium did certainly not prevail anywhere in Italy between 1500 and 500 B.C., as pre-

[85] Altheim, Römische, 1951, 1.51–55; Geschichte, 1951, 17–19.
[86] Patroni 1951, 431, 470–471; cf. also 334–336, 432–433.
[87] Pisani 954, 50. Cf. Pisani's previous contrary opinion, above fn. 83.

historic evidence of all types fully shows (except during part of this period for the people called Etruscans). Hence the names Siculan, Umbrian, Illyrian, Ligurian, etc. cannot be meaningfully employed *in the same sense, with the same ethnic and cultural referends, for historic and prehistoric items*, not even in the same geographic area. What Pallottino says with reference to Ligurian applies to virtually all such names as are treated in this chapter: "The concept of 'Ligurian people' is far from being defined in space and time; but it oscillates ever between the mobile onomastic mirages of Greco-Roman ethnography, the attempts of a real reconstruction and linguistic classification by modern linguists, and the silent, often ambiguous testimonies of prehistoric and protohistoric archaeology." [88]

Exactly the same is true for the transfer of names of languages, even more peremptorily so, because here not even a proven continuity of culture, or race, or nationality, is in the slightest indicative of linguistic continuity. "Clearly it is not only unnecessary but actually misleading, to *force* the classification of the dialects to match the classification of earlier civilizations." [89] (Italics mine.)

Much of the reasoning that strings together not only the Ligurians but also the Ligurian language with some prehistoric nation or nations is of two types: either it relies on local names, or it etymologizes vocables. Of the first I have already spoken. As for the second, its weaknesses are fully known and the treachery of the etymological method has finally been recognized by all, especially, in the prehistory of Italy, because of its signal failure to interpret Etruscan. (See the next chapter.) This is only to be expected where a few single items of an otherwise unknown language are related, purely on the basis of ancient spellings of which we do not even always know the phonetic equivalences, to a known tongue. By that method, French *feu* and German *Feuer*, both standing for 'fire,' English *bad* and Modern Persian *bad*, both meaning the same, Greek ποταμός and American Indian *potomac*, 'river,' Greek θεός and Mexican *teotl*, 'god,' could father pretty

---

[88] Pallottino 1952, 83. For a long overdue clean-up of Sicilian archaeology as regards prehistoric and historic cultural entities and their ethnic names see Bernabò Brea 1953.

[89] Whatmough 1937, 245.

linguistic and ethnic theories of migration, if we knew about any of these languages and the fate of its speakers as little as we do in fact know about Illyrian, Ligurian, and the rest.[90] The comparison of single items of vocabulary and onomastic items, culled from largely unknown idioms, with their alleged prehistoric predecessors is a travesty upon honest comparative linguistics and should be abandoned forthwith.[91]

[90] It has been done, however; cf. Santangelo 1949 and 1955, who seriously offers both the ποταμός — *potomac* and the θεός — *teotl* examples, and thousands of others of the same stripe, and arrives at the conclusion that all languages of the world have an identical lexicon owing to the monogenesis of language.

[91] But let me not be misunderstood. I do of course not propose to nullify with a facile stroke of the pen the enormous and valuable work of men like Krahe, for example, on ancient European hydronomastics. (In Krahe 1954, and serially in *BzN*.) Etymological though the method may be, if employed in rigid conjunction with nonlinguistic evidence a good argument can be made that the river-names of large tracts of Europe may be due to tongues that are more closely related to one another than are the Indo-European dialects now occupying the corresponding areas. But otherwise ethnic and linguistic names make strange river-bedfellows. Hence, I should reject labeling the speakers of these pre-Indo-European idioms with cultural, ethnic, or linguistic names prevalent centuries later in the same places.

CHAPTER XV

The Etruscan Problem   Unlike some of the ethno-linguistic names of the preceding chapter, the term Etruscan
is archaeologically and linguistically safely localized in Tuscany
(and temporarily also north of the Apennines and in Campania),
and fully identifiable through cultural and linguistic evidence.
But the interpretation of the records is another matter entirely
and has produced the most heated and lasting disputes. There can
be no question of offering in this chapter anything more than a
brief discussion in general terms, emphasizing those aspects of the
problem which concern the argument of the present book as a
whole.[1]

As usually, there are two basic questions to be asked: Who
were the Etruscans?[2] What kind of language did they speak?[3]
For better or for worse, the answers will be intertwined and will
have to be treated in the same manner in my own exposition.

To the first question three answers, each with a number of
variations and permutations, have been given: (1) the Etruscans
are autochthonous in Italy,[4] (2) they are invaders from original
locations north of the Alps,[5] (3) they are immigrants from the
Anatolian-Aegean regions.[6] It may be worthwhile to deal with

[1] The most recent extensive and detailed work on Etruscology is Pallottino
1955, to which I shall have to refer frequently. (Also available in English translation in a paperbound edition.)

[2] For an extensive listing of ancient testimony on the identity of the Etruscans,
especially on their origins, see Mühlestein 1929, 1–7.

[3] A readable and lucid résumé of the entire linguistic problem may be found
in Renard 1943. See also Johnstone 1930, 185–207; Messerschmidt 1935, 38–39;
Pallottino 1955, 55–91.

[4] Dionysius of Halicarnassus; Antonielli, Devoto, Pallottino, Pisani, Ribezzo,
Schuchhardt, etc.

[5] Livy; Beloch, Helbig, Kretschmer (1940), Ed. Meyer, Mommsen, Müller,
Niebuhr, Nissen, Nogara, Pareti, Pigorini, de Sanctis, Trombetti, etc.

[6] Herodotus; Åberg, Altheim, Brandenstein, Brizio, Conway, Della Seta,
Ducati, von Duhn, Fabretti, Gammurini, Herbig, Hrozný, Körte, Kretschmer
(1932), Patroni, Piganiol, Randall-MacIver, Rose, Schachermeyr, Sergi, Whatmough, etc.

some of the reasoning behind these divergent opinions and to allude to possible shadings within them.[7]

The argument of the autochthonists takes its inception generally from a certain view of the archaeological record. But if, as they argue, no invasion from anywhere took place, then why speak in the area in question of an Etruscan rather than (Southern) Villanovan culture in the first place? If there is no archaeological reason for a change in terminology the autochthonists of the strictest, most uncompromising stripe should have rejected it, regardless of whether or not they thereby collided with the traditional ethnic name or the exigencies of accounting for the Etruscan language, since they should have known that, as we have seen repeatedly, traditional names are not sacrosanct and correlation between culture and language is in any event not a necessity. But if also archaeologically something Etruscan, or in any event non-Italic can be discerned, then the case of the autochthonists is in danger of collapsing of itself. This non-Italic feature is generally seen as an orientalizing trait in the remains of Etruria from the eighth (some say seventh) century on.[8] Now it is easy to say that this new trait is a purely indigenous development which took place without the intervention of foreign invaders, but this does not suffice to explain, first, why and how precisely oriental, that is to say, mainly Aegean features should make their appearance, and second, why exactly in this particular region of Italy a *sudden and momentous* flourishing of civilization should manifest itself.

Here some scholars attempt conciliatory explanations. These may be rather naïve, like blandly claiming that the Etruscans are "relatively autochthonous,"[9] which explains nothing because autochthonous has no meaning in an absolute sense anyhow, least of all in Italy. But it can be a sophisticated position, like Pallottino's, to the effect that, while "the Etruscan people is not . . . a 'primitive people of Italy'" it is, as a nation, formed out of "the meeting and the mixture of independent elements which tend

[7] Because of the existence of such nuances the simplified tripartition of opinions may not have done full justice to some authors whose names I cited under one of the three categories. The reader may be forewarned that I belong to the third — but with important modifications which reconcile me with some of the views of the autochthonists of the Pallottino school, as will be seen presently.
[8] For the dating see Ducati 1932, 59–60.
[9] Trombetti 1927, 237.

progressively to shape themselves into a new, unified historical experience."[10] This is further refined by Devoto who sees in the Etruscan culture a fusion of native Apennine elements which he calls Tyrrhenian, with Etruscan culture proper, from the Villanovan period on.[11] To him the Tyrrhenians are, like the Picenes, pre-Indo-European inhabitants of the peninsula,[12] that is, autochthonous in relation to the Italici who are immigrants. However, apart from Tyrrhenian being a strange name as applied to an indigenous Apennine culture, this cultural change of the Tyrrhenians which leads to their Etruscanization, while it allows the resulting Etruscans to be autochthonous and while it might even account for the Mediterranean type of language which Etruscan may be, still does not explain, any more than Pallottino's theory of "meeting and mixture of independent elements," why this culture should exhibit precisely orientalizing traits, nor whence, nor how they came to Italy. Moreover, this view does not really disprove the participation of an Anatolian element in the fusion whose result is Etruscan; it merely denies it. It has been said that the orientalizing features were "borrowed" (from whom? by whom? how?) not "imported" by newcomers.[13] However, according to the criteria established in Chapter VII above, the speed with which Etruscan type of evidence accrues, its quantity, and its pervasiveness, and above all its essential strangeness within the Bronze and Iron Ages of Italy, cannot be accounted for by mere diffusion, borrowings, and influences.

I should agree with the autochthonists, and I have made precisely this point several times in the present book in other connections, that the 'Etruscans' known to us by that name from historic sources are probably not the Etruscans of the orientalizing culture. Nonetheless, I do not think the name Etruscan in reference to all of them inappropriate because for them, unlike for the 'Siculans' and the 'Ligurians,' we can indeed establish a continuous chronol-

---

[10] Pallottino 1947, 150, 151. Similarly Pisani 1953, 290: "The Etruscan people originated in Italy out of the confluence of various tribes and various cultures."

[11] Devoto 1951, 87–88.

[12] Devoto 1951, 57–58.

[13] Schuchhardt 1925, 121–122. *Ibid.*, 123, the Etruscans are classified as members of the Alpine race (they are *pingues et obesi*, 'fat and obese'), their type being still (N.B.) discernible in the present population of Tuscany.

ogy that is held together by more than a mere national or tribal name,[14] and we have an unbroken series of linguistic monuments (beginning with the oldest inscriptions from Vetulonia, contemporaneous with the beginnings of the orientalizing art), from the same locations, which, though largely untranslatable, are unmistakably all written in the same language, with due allowance for normal linguistic change over several centuries. (If it were illicit to use the name Etruscan under such circumstances over a long period, we could also not use Roman and Latin with reference to persons and a language of both 300 B.C. and A.D. 300. Surely there is, for Roman and Latin as well as for Etruscan, sufficient and proven linguistic, political, and cultural continuity to justify this terminology no matter what the changes of detail wrought by time. On the other hand, for modern inhabitants of Rome to think and speak of themselves as Romans or Latins in the Augustan sense, is certainly stretching a point unbearably.) And since Whatmough has brilliantly demonstrated that the Etruscan language was in fact introduced in Italy by no others but the bearers of the orientalizing culture,[15] it is legitimate to connect the two. Hence whatever the constituting elements of everything 'Etruscan' in Italy, whatever the indigenous cultural and linguistic substratum, I have no quarrel with the name, although of course I should never claim that the persons of the orientalizing period necessarily so called themselves, or that the later known Etruscans were their racially unmixed descendants. I reject therefore the autochthonous theory in all its guises and disguises as being wholly inadequate to explain all the non-Italic peculiarities we encounter under the name Etruscan.

Among the scholars who, after Livy, advocate a northern origin of the Etruscans, only two, Nogara and Kretschmer, fall within the past two decades, and Kretschmer held a different opinion before. That the Etruscans were, though not brothers, at least cousins of the 'Indo-Europeans';[16] that they were Nordics;[17] that they

[14] Cf., for example, Fiesel 1931, 52–53 (based on Randall-MacIver's works); Akerström 1934, 196; Renard 1943, 57–58.

[15] Whatmough 1937, 224–230.

[16] Kretschmer 1940, 86, 215.

[17] Kretschmer 1943, 84–87, 244–245. This is 'proven' by the fact that the Etruscan racial psychology ("Rassenpsychologie") is purely Nordic. One regrets that Kretschmer came to operate with such peculiar anthropological theories.

were racially the same as the Palafitticoli, Terramaricoli, and Villanovans, and that as Villanovans of Emilia they come to Etruria and appear there as Etruscans;[18] that there was no break in the cultural facies of Tuscany from the beginning of the Iron Age until the full classical age[19] — all this, even if it were true, which in my opinion it is not, does not make northern invasion palatable. For it does not alter the fact that in Tuscany the arrival and at least the beginings of an orientalizing art,[20] of an orientalizing religion,[21] of orientalizing tombs and burial rite (chiefly inhumation),[22] of an oriental alphabet and an oriental language (see below), cannot be explained by northern imports at any time (any more than by local developments, or by Greek influence which does not precede 650 B.C.).[23]

Moreover, there is simply no evidence whatever of anything Etruscan in the Po country prior to the date of colonization of this area by Etruscans from the south, beginning with the city of Felsina (Bologna) in the last quarter of the sixth century.[24]

[18] Pareti, Origini, 1926, 212, 324–327, 331–332.

[19] Pareti, Come, 1926, 44.

[20] It is no doubt correct to maintain that the so-called orientalizing art is not something wholly imported and imposed as such but rather a development of Italic art albeit under the impulse and influence of the art of the invading Etruscans. Cf. Bosch-Gimpera 1929, 39. Richter 1955, 7, says that "Italic influence shows itself only occasionally, for instance, in the early tomb structures — the pit and trench graves (*tombe a pozzo e tombe a fossa*), which, however, are soon succeeded by the Eastern corridor and chamber tombs (*tombe a corridoio* and *a camera*), and, above all, in the pottery." Perhaps it would be better here to speak of 'persistence' rather than 'influence.' Persistence of Italic burials is to be expected, after what I said earlier, because it involves a religious attitude which is not so quickly superseded by new fashions; and persistence of Italic pottery in Etruscan lands is no doubt due to the numerical Italic majority in population who naturally retain their household implements. But art is of course the property of the more highly civilized Etruscan minority.

[21] Consider, for example, the Etruscan bronze liver of Piacenza and the Babylonian clay liver, both destined for divining purposes. They are so much alike that incidental similarity must be excluded. See Conway 1933, 57; Brandenstein 1937, figs. 3, 4, pp. 28, 29; Randall-MacIver 1943, 93; Grenier 1948, 76–81; Hrozný 1953, figs. 44, 45, pp. 91, 92.

[22] Åkerström 1934, 183–184; Cultrera 1937, 74; Whatmough 1937, 215–224. To say, as does Piganiol 1917, 53–59, that the orientalizing tombs of Tuscany are due, not to the Etruscans but to the Pelasgians, is not saying much of consequence, as we have seen.

[23] Whatmough 1937, 214.

[24] Grenier 1912, 8–9; Renard 1943, 11–14. Randall-MacIver 1924, 257–259, thinks that the Villanovans were at Bologna fully five hundred years before the Etruscans crossed the Apennines from the south.

Surely Etruscans invading from the north would have left some traces of their passage before settling in Etruria. For all these reasons, it seems to me that the theory of a northern invasion must be rejected.

The thesis of an Anatolian provenance of the Etruscans begins with Herodotus.[25] Their arrival in Italy has been set by modern authors at various dates, among which the end of the ninth or the beginning of the eighth century B.C. seems the most agreeable.[26] All the evidence indicates that they did not come in considerable force but by infiltration, in several detachments, possibly in piratic raiding parties to begin with.[27] This sparsity would also account for the comparative tenacity and continuity of the Villanovan Iron Age, which remained for a long time the real backbone of the rising Etruscan culture and nation,[28] a fact which probably led some scholars, as we have seen, to deny on archaeological grounds an invasion altogether. But if I say nation, the word should not be understood in the modern sense. At best, the Etruscans throughout their history formed a number of federated city-states, first along the Tyrrhenian coast (Vetulonia, Populonia, Tarquinia, Caere, Rusellae, Vulci), later on farther inland (Orvieto, Volaterrae, Volsinii, Felsina, Cortona, Arretium, Clusium, Perusia, Veii).[29]

Their settling at first along the coast north rather than south of the mouth of the Tiber need not be interpreted to mean that they arrived at a time when the Greeks were already in possession of the Campanian and other southern sites, that is, after 750 B.C. For the Etruscans were probably in search of iron and other

[25] Her. 1.94. For a different and unusual interpretation of this passage and, instead, reliance on Her. 1.57, advancing an allegedly autochthonous hypothesis for the Etruscans, see Pallottino 1948.
[26] For a considerably earlier dating and two distinct invasions, the first at the beginning of the tenth century, see Schachermeyr 1929, 199, 304–307. Gagé 1950, 30, however, argues for as late a date as the beginning of the seventh century.
[27] Randall-MacIver compares their coming with that of the Normans to Sicily and England in the eleventh century after Christ.
[28] Peet 1924, 573; Åberg 1930, 213; Bérard 1941, 512–516.
[29] The Etruscan Twelve Cities (cf. Liv. 4.23.5, 5.33.9; Dion. Hal. 6.75.3), whose number is reminiscent of the Ionian Dodekapolis around the sanctum of the Artemis of Ephesus, or the federation of the twelve cities of Miletos, are thought to be legendary, like the later thirty members of the Latin League (Dion. Hal. 5.61); cf. Beloch 1880, 160–161; Altheim 1950, 66–67.

minerals,[30] possibly to supply the eastern Mediterranean area, which they found in Etruria, on the nearby island of Elba, and also on Corsica. Their interest, and that of the Greeks, in maritime trade actually opened Italy, hitherto in possession of landlocked barbarians, to the civilizing influences of the East.

Their relatively small number, together with their loose internal alliance which often turned into open disunity, prevented the Etruscans from becoming anything more in Italy than colonial overlords, over several restricted areas, of subject peoples.[31] But this role they filled efficiently and during a long period. Their greatest power they attained about the middle of the sixth century, and their decline began shortly thereafter, toward the end of the same century, when they failed in an attack on Greek Cumae and when an Etruscan chieftain, or 'king,' was driven from Rome.[32] But it was not until the middle of the third century B.C. that all Etruscan independence ceased under the relentless blows of the Roman legions.

Whereas the terramare and Villanovan settlements had been fairly primitive villages, the Etruscans brought with them an urban civilization and created real cities, which also points to an eastern origin.[33] We shall see later how the Etruscans merged several disparate settlements into the city of Rome.

On the whole, then, the evidence overwhelmingly favors an immigration of some persons from the Aegean area, who fertilized and changed the native Italic culture of Tuscany profoundly and sufficiently so as to warrant giving it a new name. But who were these Aegean immigrants ethnically or racially? By calling them Tyrrhenians we avoid, as I said before, the equation of prehistoric Anatolian invaders with protohistoric and historic Etruscans,[34] but we have merely assigned a name to some

[30] Bosch-Gimpera 1929, 33. Åkerström 1943, 158.

[31] Whatmough 1937, 235–236.

[32] See Renard 1943, 18 ff., for a chronology of their rise and decline, conquests and losses.

[33] Toutain 1930, 210–216.

[34] Toynbee 1934, 2.86 so equates the two and he concludes therefore that unlike their migrating brethren "the Etruscans who stayed at home never did anything worth recording." But who exactly were the 'Etruscans' who stayed at home? Altheim 1950, 31–35, thinks that the identification of the (Aegean) Tyrrhenians with the (Italian) Etruscans is monstrous ("*ein Unding*"). True, but who were the 'Tyrrhenians?'

entity without otherwise defining it or giving it a reality. We cannot possibly support the fantastic identification of the Etruscans with descendants of Proto-Illyrian, that is, Indo-European-speaking Trojans.[35] Nor does the classification of the Etruscan language as being of an Uralian type (*uralisch-artig*), even if it were true, allow the conclusion that the Aegean forebears of the Etruscans came originally from southern Russia.[36] Pelasgian connections are of course not enlightening.[37] And Tyrsenoi and Rasenna are mere names, unless the former are the Tursha of Egyptian monuments, who together with the Lukki and Akaiwasha, that is, the Lykians and the Achaeans, raided Egypt in the thirteenth century B.C.[38]

At the present state of our knowledge it is best to concede that we cannot really know the ethnic and racial classification of these immigrants to Italy who in later records appear under the name of the Etruscans. But this technical admission, too, does not justify the denial of the factual existence of foreign newcomers. Hence Devoto is only partly right when he says this: "Just as at the beginnings of the history of France one does not quarrel over the problem of a southeastern (Latin), autochthonous (Ligurian or Gaulish), or northeastern (Frankish) origin of the French [N.B.] people, so one must now undramatize Etruscan history, and in the place of the mirage of the origins and provenience of the Etruscans which has caused scholars to be divided into the three exclusive and stereotyped schools of orientalists, autochthonists, and nordists, one must put the problem of the formation of the Etruscan nation and culture and of the elements which concurred therein." [39] This is true enough as far as the Etruscan problem of Italy and within Italy is concerned. Yet if one does not quarrel about the

[35] Georgiev 1943, 15; 1948; 1950, 409. This view permits the Trojan fugitive Aeneas to enter the legend as a proto-Etruscan.

[36] Stoltenberg 1950, 407.

[37] Sergi 1901, 165–166; 1934, 71–73; Mühlestein 1929, 12–20.

[38] About the Tyrsenoi of Lemnos see below. For a derivation of the words Tusci and Etrusci from Τυρσηνοί see Krahe 1954, 153–154; cf. also Schachermeyr 1929, 222–224. But to connect these names etymologically with the name Troia, as does Georgiev 1948, seems rather adventurous. Rasenna is what according to Dion. Hal. 1.30 the Etruscans of Italy called themselves; cf. Schachermeyr 1929, 224–225. At least one person, Quispel 1940, has found both Tyrsenoi and Rasenna in the Old Testament, the first in *Gen.* 10.2 as the sons of Japhet, called Tiras, the second in *Ezech.* 38.2 as a people called Rôš!

[39] Devoto 1946, 285. In the same spirit Pallottino 1955, 86, replaces the concept of Etruscan 'origins' by that of 'formation.'

questions Devoto lists in regard to France, the reason is that everyone knows that the questions as they stand are specious. Nonetheless there are comparable problems for Gallo-Roman France
also. For example, was there or was there not a migration to
France and subsequent ethnic mixture? (Answer: Yes, on several
known occasions, by Germanic tribes, beginning with the Franks.)
Was there an importation of a non-Latin language? (Answer: Yes,
several Germanic dialects.) Was there a pre-Latin substratum in
France? (Answer: Yes, Keltic.) Was this substratum related to
the newly imported language? (Answer: Not closely, but both
are Indo-European.) Our knowing these answers is only due to
better evidence, not to a difference in the type of problem. So
despite our relative ignorance of such matters in Italy around 800
B.C., we still may conclude that some non-Italic people, possibly
few persons to begin with, must somehow be responsible for the
indisputably and integrally non-Italic Etruscanness of the cultural
and linguistic phenomena which appear in Tuscany, and less
densely elsewhere in Italy, from about 800 B.C. on.

I find myself therefore up to a point in agreement with Pallottino, namely, that what in the historic period we call 'Etruscan' is indeed a product of Italy and that we cannot, if we wish
to be precise, speak of an 'Etruscan' invasion in the same sense
of the word,[40] any more than we can speak of a 'French' invasion
of Gaul after Caesar's conquest. Pallottino rejects all three hypotheses of origin because he denies the very concepts of origin and
provenience: the Etruscans, their nation, their language, their
culture, neither came from anywhere nor were they autochthonous in Italy; but "there exist, in the formation of the Etruscan
nation, oriental, European, Italian elements which must be studied,
circumscribed, evaluated, and placed into relationship with one
another." [41] That is so. But I am asking just exactly what these
various elements are and whence and how they came to make up
'Etruscan,' and I have come to the conclusion that those features
which put the most characteristic stamp upon the Etruscan culture
of Italy, in art, in language, and in other aspects, are the oriental
ones which, since all scholars, including Pallottino, call them thus,

[40] Pallottino, in various writings, most recently 1955, 55–91.
[41] Pallottino 1955, 87.

are imported by definition.[42] Hence I say once more that I do not see 'Etruscan' invaders in the same sense in which I see 'Etruscan' soldiers fighting the Romans at Veii, but I see some invaders from the east whom I cannot provide, prior to their arrival in Italy, with an ethnic or national label because I do not know it. (However, I have explained above why the continued use of the term Etruscan is less objectionable and more meaningful than a similar extension for 'Ligurian' or 'Illyrian.')

Consequently, even if one agrees that the Etruscan problem is mainly a linguistic one and that its archaeological importance is overrated,[43] and even if one agrees that the "formative process of the nation [and of the language] can have taken place only in Etruria itself," [44] certain questions on the provenance of some of the constitutive factors are still legitimate and must still be answered.

It has by some been suggested that the Etruscans are 'Mediterraneans.' But these students have often not borne in mind, as we are committed to do, that, as far as is known at the present time, this term is not ethnic but either merely geographic, or tentatively linguistic, referring to non-Indo-European dialects possibly spoken around the entire Mediterranean basin and to which we owe some alleged widespread onomastic and lexical relics in known languages. And this brings us to the second of the two questions asked at the beginning of this chapter, concerning the classification of the Etruscan language. A sizable portion of the discussion and of my argument has been of necessity anticipated in the preceding pages, yet a few more remarks are indicated.

If the Etruscans are linguistically part of the ancient population of Mediterranean speech, then the fact that their language is undoubtedly non-Indo-European is thereby explained, whereas whatever Indo-European traits and items it does contain can be ascribed to the influence of its Indo-European surroundings in Italy,[45]

---

[42] Pallottino 1955, 31, describes the Etruscan language as "substantially a non-Indo-European language with Aegean and Asian affinities." And whence and how did these affinities get to Italy?

[43] Kaschnitz-Weinberg 1950, 380.

[44] Pallottino 1955, 87.

[45] Hrozný 1928, 171–175; 1929, 190; Devoto 1930; Sergi 1934, 72–73; Altheim, *Geschichte*, 1951, 214–215.

just as we have accounted for Italic aspects of the Etruscan culture in this way.

But even as this partly Italic character of the culture has prompted some to declare Etruscan civilization as wholly native, so the overemphasis on undoubtedly recognizable Indo-European features in the language, together with certain Indo-European and 'Aryan' propensities in a number of writers, have caused some to make Etruscan a wholly Indo-European dialect.[46]

In recognition of the obvious strangeness of Etruscan with reference to Indo-European, but withal unwilling to accept an Anatolian, non-Indo-European theory, some hypotheses relegate Etruscan to a pre-Indo-European stratum, called *Protindogermanisch*, in English Pre-Proto-Indo-European,[47] or, in other not dissimilar theories, peri-Indo-European.[48] Kretschmer sets up a *protindogermanisch* parent language from which are derived two major families, the Indo-European, and the Raeto-Tyrrhenian. To the first belong the conventional Indo-European dialects, to the second Raetic, Tyrrhenian, Pelasgian, and Etruscan.[49] This view permits the existence of something 'Indo-European,' which however is not very similar, except insofar as it is *urverwandt*, to anything generally called Indo-European; but it requires also a rather early thrust of at least some speakers of Pre-Proto-Indo-

[46] Buonamici 1927, 253 (Etruscan belongs to a very ancient Thraco-Phrygo-Illyrian family); Goldmann 1929; Hempl 1932, 15, 146 (it is closely akin to Latin, it is *qu*-Indo-European); Meriggi 1936 (Etruscan as well as Lydian and Lykian are Indo-European); Georgiev 1943; 1950, 409 (it is not merely *"Indogermanoid"* but genuine Indo-European); Pei 1945 (it is basically Indo-European with large non-Indo-European admixture); Coli 1947, xi (it is closely related to Greek); Margani 1951, ix (it is an "older sister" of Greek and Latin). Interesting is the case of Wilhelm Deecke who in 1875 demolished in 39 pages the thesis of Corssen, 1874, propounded in 1,700 pages, that Etruscan was Indo-European, but who in 1882 (cf. Deecke — Pauli 1881) and again in 1896 recanted and sided with the Indo-European faction. Kretschmer held until 1925 that Etruscan was non-Indo-European but then sought an Indo-European compromise (see below).

[47] Kretschmer 1925; 1940; 1943. Since Proto-Indo-European already means something else in English, corresponding to German *Indogermanisch*, Kretschmer's *Protindogermanisch* would have to be translated as Pre-Proto-Indo-European.

[48] Devoto 1944; 1951.

[49] Kretschmer 1943, 214. Note that, of the second group, Raetic is the only one of the four languages of which we have sure, albeit scarce knowledge; Tyrrhenian, if we want to call it thus, is possibly known from an inscription from Lemnos, hitherto untranslated (although attempts have been made, but with questionable results); Etruscan is untranslated; and Pelasgian, whatever it is, if anything, is unattested.

European into southern Europe, resulting in a Pre-Proto-Indo-European layer inserted between the older non-Indo-European and the later Indo-European strata.[50] Etruscan of Italy is thus due to a "compenetration" of the languages of the Pre-Proto-Indo-European-speaking Proto-Etruscan ('Tyrrhenian') inhabitants of Italy and that of the later Indo-European-speaking newcomers, whereby the autochthony of the 'Etruscans' is salvaged and at the same time their foreign-sounding language accounted for.[51]

The evidence of such a Pre-Proto-Indo-European stratum or linguistic type is so volatile, and its employment for the explanation of the Indo-Europeanness of the Etruscan language has such an *ad hoc* flavor that I cannot persuade myself to accept it at this moment without a great deal of further substantial proof, which has yet to be forthcoming.[52]

Of course, a mysterious item like the Etruscan language always calls forth mistaken theories and attracts pseudo-scholars and crackpots. It is not necessary to deal with this subnormal fringe in any detail.[53] What one learns from these unhappy but

[50] Kretschmer 1925, 317–319; 1940, 267, 276.

[51] Devoto 1944, 190–191; 1951, 57–58, 60–62. (I do not, of course, mean to equate Devoto's *peri-indo-europeo* and Kretschmer's *Protindogermanisch*, but in our context they may be discussed together since both attempt to explain the Indo-European features of Etruscan, the one through a *protindogermanisch* substratum, the other through a *peri-indo-europeo*, that is, not yet wholly Indo-Europeanized stratum.)

[52] Whatmough 1956, 67, counsels to keep an open mind: "The hypothesis of a [Pre-] proto-Indo-European stratum of languages, to which various Anatolian tongues, and, more distinctly, Iberian . . . , Eteocretic, Vannic . . . , and perhaps Lemnian and Etruscan, are to be related, has never been completely established, for want of sufficient and convincing evidence. But neither has it been put out of court. . . ." Without giving it a name of its own, Carnoy 1952, 328, also operates with a "first wave of Indo-European invasions into the Mediterranean regions" which brings Etruscan and Pelasgian upon the stage. Could Sturtevant's hypothesis of Hittite being a sister rather than a daughter language of Proto-Indo-European fit in here, inasmuch as, in keeping with the genealogical tree simile here employed, both Proto-Indo-European and Hittite would then be descended from a Pre-Proto-Indo-European parent language? (Cf. Sturtevant 1951.)

[53] According to some of them, Etruscan is, for example, "intermediate" (not mixed) between Indo-European and Caucasian (Trombetti 1909, unfavorably criticized by Herbig 1909, 362–364 and Sergi 1922, 7–8; Trombetti 1927; 1928, v-vi and *passim*, fully discredited by Cortsen 1932, 43 ff.); it is of the Finno-Ugric family (Martha 1913); it is Ural-Altaic (Hrkal 1947); it is of an Uralian type ("*uralartig*," Stoltenberg 1950); it is Egyptian (down to the word *urbs*, the city of Rome having been founded by the Egyptians: Wanscher 1951).

vociferous failures is at least that the undiluted etymological method which compares isolated words and often establishes its own soundlaws according to need as it goes along, is completely unsatisfactory.

The best procedure which has produced convincing results in the hands of a skilled Etruscologist is that employed by Pallottino and which he calls the method of storico-cultural comparison.[54] He has come to the conclusion, as have many others independent of him, that "Etruscan is basically, in phonology, morphology, and lexicon a Mediterranean language, more or less closely related with Lemnian, the idioms of Asia Minor, and perhaps of the Pre-Hellenes, the pre-Indo-European substratum of Italy, etc." [55] Accordingly, Etruscan, while not autochthonous in Italy, may well have been superimposed there upon a non-Indo-European Mediterranean dialect with which it was not entirely unrelated,[56] unless at the time of the Etruscan arrival on the scene all inhabitants of Etruria already spoke Indo-European — but on this the present state of our knowledge gives no information.

Weighing all the evidence, linguistic and nonlinguistic together, it becomes quite certain that, little though we know how to interpret Etruscan texts, which are not exactly rare, but unenlightening because they consist largely of names and stereotyped phrases,[57] Etruscan is not an Indo-European language.[58] Hence all attempts to solve the riddle by Indo-European means, including the gratuitous assumption of Indo-European grammatical categories such as the parts of speech, conjugation, declension, can lead only to illusory insights.

Another difficulty that is often ignored [59] is that our Etruscan

[54] Pallottino 1950, 159–164; 1955, 299–366.
[55] Pallottino 1936, 15. If, therefore, Schulten 1930, finds traces of Etruscan occupation not only everywhere in Italy but also in Spain on the evidence of local names, he may well be facing Mediterranean and not properly Etruscan toponymy.
[56] Cultrera 1937; Whatmough 1937, 232.
[57] For an inventory of our sources, see Pallottino, Etruschi, 1940, 5 ff. The ten longest inscriptions, of which the last seven have fewer than a hundred words together, are described by Renard 1943, 34–35.
[58] For a full development of the argument see Whatmough 1937, 224–232.
[59] Though it was stressed by Fiesel 1929, 188, and reëmphasized by Pallottino, Studi, 1940, 10.

records stretch over a period of more than six centuries [60] and that we have to count therefore upon linguistic change which inevitably attends the passing of time. If one contemplates the appearance of Latin in 200 B.C. and A.D. 400, or that of English in A.D. 1300 and 1900, one cannot but view with misgivings a method that analyzes Etruscan texts of 700 and 100 B.C. as though they were contemporaneous and represented same stages of the language, even if one might be willing to surmise that Etruscan changed less than other languages over a comparable period of time, for which belief, however, it will be difficult to marshall proofs.

Also dialectal variations in a speech area extending from Campania to the Po river should be expected.[61]

Although this book is not the place for an extended disquisition on all matters concerning the Etruscans, I shall at least briefly mention two more items of importance. One is the famous stele of Lemnos, showing an inscription whose language is without doubt related to Etruscan.[62] Regardless of whether it was written by the actual forebears of the Italian Etruscans, or by the Tyrsenoi, or by the Pelasgians, or by people of whatever name one may care to choose, it does demonstrate that on a location geographically intermediate between Asia Minor and Italy a language very similar to Etruscan was employed by some persons. This inevitable conclusion allows of course of no extension concerning the ethnic classification of the Lemnians of that epoch, nor does it imply that all Lemnians of that time spoke the language of the stele.

One of the criteria which helped in establishing the linguistic

[60] A passage of Amm. Marc. 23.5.10–15 may even imply that there were still 'Etruscan' soothsayers plying their trade, in the Etruscan language, as late as A.D. 363, at the time of the emperor Julian the Apostate. But did they speak genuine Etruscan, any more than fortune-telling gypsies speak genuine Romany?

[61] Pallottino 1936, 16; Altheim 1950, 35–36.

[62] Conway 1926, 408; Fiesel 1931, 63–64; Pallottino 1947, 9–11; 1955, 73–74 and Tavola iv; Falkner 1948, 108–109; Gagé 1950, 15–28. To Kretschmer 1943, 213–214, the idiom of the Lemnos stele is Tyrrhenian, the dialect of the Tyrsenoi, a sister language of Etruscan, as also of Pelasgian and Raetic, all derived through a Raeto-Tyrrhenian ancestor from Pre-Proto-Indo-European. See fn. 49 above. There is at least one dissenter, who most unconvincingly argues that Lemnian is to be connected not with Etruscan but with Sanskrit, Greek, Latin, and 'Lusitanian': Margani 1954.

identity of the Lemnos inscription was the alphabet which shows
clear relationships with that of the Etruscans, the second item I
wish to note briefly. The Proto-Etruscans, whoever they were,
brought with them a writing of a very ancient Greek type.[63] It
seems that their ancestors learned it on the way to Italy; at least
there is no evidence of its use east of Lemnos. If previously the
Proto-Etruscans wrote at all, they must have used a different
script.[64] This is one more reason why we cannot actually find any
'Etruscans' outside of Italy.[65] The presence in the Etruscan alphabet of the letter 8 for [ʃ] which otherwise occurs only in Lydia,
has by the way been an argument for the Anatolian extraction
of the Etruscan language and even of the Etruscans.[66] In Italy
this ancient alphabet developed certain local varieties which became the actual bases for Italic writing of different areas.[67]

Whatever the disputed details on the spread and development
of these Italic scripts,[68] the fact remains that the speakers of Indo-
European dialects in Italy acquired the art of writing from the
Etruscans. It is therefore the Etruscans to whose civilizing influence we owe our earliest records in Italy, sparse and late though
they are in comparison with those of the more eastern Mediterranean regions, to say nothing of Egyptian and Babylonian. No
doubt if the Etruscans had not been literate, the people of Italy
would nonetheless have learned eventually the use of an alphabet
from the Greeks of Magna Graecia. But since the Greeks were
notoriously reluctant to leave the coast and to penetrate inland,
and since they were in the manner of true colonial masters interested in nothing but the efficient exploitation of the colonies, it

[63] For a detailed chronology of alphabets starting with Proto-Semitic, see
Moorhouse 1953, 150. *Ibid.* 129 fig. 36 is a very illuminating table juxtaposing the
Phoenician, archaic, eastern and western Greek, Etruscan, and archaic and
classical Latin alphabets. Cf. Gelb 1952.

[64] Whatmough 1937, 230.

[65] Hoenigswald 1952 and 1953 suggests that the punct marks, such as appear
in Southern Etruscan, Campanian Etruscan, and Venetic writing, are meaningless in an alphabetic script and point to an older state of syllabic writing among
the Etruscans, perhaps similar to the one found on Cyprus.

[66] But there is a difficulty because this rare character does not appear on the
oldest but only on later Etruscan inscriptions. For attempts to explain this see
Kretschmer 1927, 108; Moorhouse 1953, 132.

[67] A comparative table of early Italic alphabets is in PID 2.502, together with
a detailed description of them, 501–543.

[68] Carpenter 1945.

would have taken a very long time for Greek writing to reach the heart of the Abruzzi, Umbria, the Po valley, and the Alps. In addition to the material progress which the Etruscans brought to Italy, and by far outweighing it in importance for the subsequent history of Italy, we have then the linguistic contribution of the Etruscans which, however, does not involve the spread and imposition of their language among the Italians but rather the purveyance of the means whereby Italy entered upon the stage of history.

THE DIALECTS OF ANCIENT ITALY

ca. 5th. Ct. B.C.

CHAPTER XVI

The Pre-Italic Dialects

First I must state how I propose to employ the terms Pre-Italic, Italic, and Latinian. From an Indo-Europeanist's point of view Italic signifies all those Indo-European dialects which, regardless of type, time, and place, he finds in ancient Italy; in other words, he speaks of an Italic branch of Indo-European, which is then further subdivided in the manner of the genealogical tree scheme. Until now I have used the term Italic generically in this sense. Also archaeologists and prehistorians, when speaking of Italic peoples, usually mean thereby the speakers of all these idioms. (If they mean anything more, like ethnic homogeneity, they are of course wrong.)

Often, however, Italic refers merely to the dialects of all non-Latin-speaking Italici. There is no reason why this should not be permissible, not only because we are free to choose our own terminological conventions, but also because Italici is sanctioned by tradition in the sense of non-Latin-speaking inhabitants of Italy in general, and the non-Latin confederated nations of the Social War (91-88 B.C.) in particular.[1]

But some scholars, like Devoto in the title of his book, mean by Italici only the tribes of Oscan and Umbrian speech.[2] If this convention is followed, then the other non-Latin Italic idioms of Italy should be designated by another term, which is generally Pre-Italic.[3] This is the distinction I shall henceforth adhere to. It is not a fortunate one, because it could give rise to the erroneous idea, as indeed it has, that a chronological sequence is involved. But rather than indulge in coining new names, I shall let the old ones stand.

[1] Whatmough 1937, 108–109. On p. 114 he includes also Latinian among the Italic dialects.

[2] Devoto 1951, 5.

[3] Whatmough 1937, 114, includes here also Keltic of Italy, that is, he uses Pre-Italic in a geographic sense (but without Oscan, Umbrian, Latinian, which are Italic).

The term Latinian seems more appropriate than Latin because it includes a variety of Latian dialects besides the urban Latin of Rome, though our evidence of them is meager enough.

The division in Pre-Italic, Italic, and Latinian dialects of Italy is, therefore, one of convenience, and nothing should be inferred from it concerning either the chronology or the ethnic, racial composition of the population of Italy. But both these errors have been committed, and, as usually, by making arbitrary terminological distinctions the starting point for ethnic and linguistic theories or hypotheses, writers confounded the issues instead of elucidating them.

In the course of the previous chapters the prehistory and proto-history of Italy have been told as far as the middle of the first millennium. From this point on, the names of tribes and dialects take on more definite shapes and meanings. The evidence will remain scanty enough for a while yet, and the dating of the linguistic records very difficult and unsure, but on the whole we shall be on safer ground, and the alleged ethnic and linguistic entities of the preceding centuries which we had to regard with considerable skepticism can now more confidently be placed in their respective domains and associated with definite records. I shall describe one unit after the other, starting in the northwest, but seeing to it that the linguistic history of Italy as a whole becomes discernible through the parts.[4]

The Ligurians are known to us linguistically through a small number of glosses and local names in the *Ligurian* dialect.[5] As so often pointed out, also here the traditional tribal or national name is not in harmony with historical facts, and in matters of linguistics it is good advice that "rather than to ask ourselves what 'Ligurian' is, it is necessary to ask ourselves every time what languages given populations spoke whom the ancients called 'Ligurians.' "[6]

Since I believe that the term Ligurian, being historical, should be applied, not to the ubiquitous 'Ligurians' of probably Mediterranean relations in language and of unknown ethnos [7] which were

---

[4] For the location of the tribes and dialects see Whatmough 1937, maps 5, 6, pp. 99, 119, respectively. Cf. also Staehelin 1948, 4–10, with a good bibliography.

[5] PID 2.147–165; Whatmough 1937, 129–132.

[6] Terracini 1926, 123.

[7] Though this correlation is suggested by Krahe 1936, 255: "Ligurian proper

discussed in Chapter XIV, but rather to the evidence we possess, I must speak of Ligurian as an Indo-European dialect, for the records, however deficient, seem unambiguous enough on that score.[8] But it is also certain that the Ligurian region, no less than the rest of Italy, belonged once to a non-Indo-European, perhaps Mediterranean, speech,[9] unless it is thought that there was no language there at all, which is impossible by definition of the word language because we possess, particularly from Liguria (in the Grimaldi caves), human remains dating as far back as the Palaeolithic Age.

To account, then, for both the pre-Indo-European stratum and the Indo-European Ligurian stratum, both very poorly attested only by glosses and names and not by inscriptions, we should ask ourselves, and answer, if possible, four fundamental questions.[10] (1) What evidence is there, if any, to prove, what is a perfectly valid assumption, namely the existence, in Liguria, of a non-Indo-European language spoken there before the adoption of Indo-European? (2) What is the correct classification of the Indo-European but pre-Latin speech that we find spoken there — Keltic, Italic, or neither? (3) By what names should these pre-Indo-European and Indo-European languages be designated? (4) By whom, and at what date, was the Indo-European language introduced? [11] Whatmough gives the following answers. (1) The evidence we have is mainly toponymic. (But the suffix — *asca*, so often claimed as the pre-Indo-European *Leitfossil* of the area, could be also Indo-European.) Otherwise our evidence is

---

(*das eigentliche ligurisch*) is probably pre-Indo-European." *Id.* 1954, 164. Accordingly, to Krahe 'Ligurian' is non-Indo-European, contrary to general opinion, not as a matter of fact but only as a matter of names.
[8] Whatmough 1937, 129–130.
[9] Pisani 1941, 387–388. Patroni 1951, 974: "Primitive Ligurian is non-Aryan and Mediterranean. . . . In prehistoric times Ligurian manifestly underwent Indo-Europeanization." The kernel of this is true, but the terminology is murky and conducive to continued obfuscation; if "primitive Ligurian" is hypothesized as non-Indo-European, then the Indo-European dialect of the records should not be called Ligurian, and vice versa. Patroni's statement is tantamount to saying: Primitive French was non-Romanic and Keltic. . . . In the period of Roman domination French manifestly underwent Romanization.
[10] After Whatmough 1944, 77–80.
[11] Note that the same questions could profitably be asked with regard to Umbrian, Siculan, etc. I trust that my exposition in Chapter XIV and in the present chapter can be read so as to provide adequate replies.

inferential (as stated at the end of the preceding paragraph), but obviously sound. (2) It is neither Keltic nor Italic, but stands midway between the two. (3) The pre-Indo-European stratum cannot be more definitely named (except as we choose to insert it in the catch-all category of Mediterranean). For the dimly discernible Indo-European language, Ligurian is an appropriate and distinctive term. (4) By an Indo-European-speaking people who had a dialect intermediate between Keltic and Italic and whom one may well call, for want of anything better, Ligurians; they arrived at a very remote date, but after the splitting up of the Italic-Keltic unity since there is no evidence of mixture of Italic and Keltic in Ligurian.[12]

To all this I should make only one correction, pertaining to answer (4). I take my usual stand, namely, that we have no evidence for assuming the migration of a people, certainly not one whom we may call Ligurians (though of course Whatmough attributed to them this name because they imported the Indo-European dialect so-called to the region in question). Again, because of the unbroken continuity of the archaeological evidence which presents itself without a major break or upheaval, I suggest that very few speakers of Indo-European penetrated into the Ligurian region and, like their fellow Indo-European speakers elsewhere, imposed their language upon the natives who probably were not too numerous themselves. Again it is only the result which, being linguistically and ethnically neither wholly that of the newcomers nor of the indigenes, we may term Ligurian. And if I may venture a guess as to the more remote identity of the Indo-European speakers who came to Liguria, I should derive them from the Palafitticoli and the owners of the Comacine culture of the western lake area, Bronze and Iron Age people, respectively, to whom I ascribed, as to the later Terramaricoli, an Indo-European language. Hence Ligurian, in our sense of the term, may well have been the oldest type of Indo-European spoken in Italy, which may in part account for the paucity of its records. Moreover it was early superseded by Keltic, which was to occupy

[12] What to Whatmough is an intermediate position between Keltic and Italic seemed to some a mixture, or a predivisional Italo-Keltic unity of the two, and Jullian 1916, 269–270, claimed the Ligurians as the speakers of this predivisional Italo-Keltic.

eventually most of the Po country.[13] Strabo's famous Κελτολίγυες [14] would then be Kelticized Ligurians, the 'Kelticized' to be understood in a national and eventually in a linguistic sense. If the tribe of the Taurini (from whom the city of Turin [Torino] took its name) have been referred to either as Ligurians [15] or as Kelts,[16] their national and linguistic situation may have been similar to that, say, of the originally German-speaking, at present largely bilingual (German and Italian) inhabitants of the former Austrian South Tirol (Alto Adige), now annexed to Italy, whom foreign observers could well call Italians or Germans or Austrians, depending on what kind of impressions predominate or what records are emphasized. As for the scarcity of ancient Ligurian linguistic evidence, it should be noted also that Liguria was far removed from the Etruscan and Greek hubs of civilization whence other tribes of Italy acquired their alphabets, that indeed the Etruscans who penetrated north of the Apennines into the eastern Po valley found in the Kelts of the west implacable foes to whom they were before long to succumb. And the Kelts of Italy, being themselves largely illiterate (we have only three isolated Keltic inscriptions from Italy[17] of which only one comes from Gallia Cisalpina proper, to testify to several centuries of Keltic domination: the Kelts were completely and permanently subjugated only in the reign of Augustus), could scarcely teach the subject Ligurians how to record their language.

As the preceding paragraphs have already intimated, the history of *Keltic* in Italy can be told quickly. If it were not for safe inferences and certain knowledge from nonlinguistic sources, we should scarcely know of its existence. Its importance in the linguistic development of Italy is extremely slight,[18] being restricted chiefly to its influence on Ligurian and other northern dialects which

[13] The date of the earliest Keltic incursions is unknown, but some scholars would set them as early as the sixth century, others in the fifth. The Kelts were, in any event, numerous and strong enough to drive the Etruscans out of Felsina (Bologna) at the end of the fifth century, and to sack Rome early in the fourth.

[14] Strabo 4.6.3. § 203C.

[15] Strabo 4.6.6. § 204C; Plin. *N.H.* 3.123.

[16] Polyb. 3.60.8–11.

[17] PID 2.170–178.

[18] Whatmough 1944, 28. However, there is a report, of doubtful authenticity, in Sulp. Sev. *Dial.* 1.27.1, that among the country people Keltic was still spoken in the fifth century of the Christian era.

are yet to be mentioned, and showing itself perhaps as a sub-stratum influence in those modern Italian dialects which are called Gallo-Italian. (I need hardly note here that Gallic, or Gaulish, is simply a local geographic term applied to Keltic in the Gauls.) There are furthermore a number of borrowings of Keltic in Latin, and Keltic names in the inscription of Cisalpine Gaul. It is not doubtful in the least that we may for once equate the historic *Celtae* with the speakers of Keltic dialects and identify them prehistorically as the bearers of the Iron Age La Tène culture.[19] However, according to our criteria (see Chapter VII) all this is still not sufficient to postulate a Keltic race.[20]

But there exists sufficient archaeological and historic information that the Kelts actually migrated in large bands: obviously a few stragglers could not have overcome by force of arms an Etruscan city like Felsina, or Rome. On the other hand, they seem to have lacked altogether unity of purpose, a national or ethnic conscience, with the consequence that all their fulminating conquests south of the Apennines were ephemeral. Had they behaved, not like the Etruscans before them but rather like the Romans after them, they might have risen to the opportunity of becoming the masters of Italy and of altering the history of the entire world. Instead, it seems that they quickly lost their identity by merging with the more purposeful, better organized, and surely more numerous other tribes of Italy.[21]

I shall briefly deal with the vexed problem of an Italo-Keltic linguistic unity in the next chapter.

The inscriptions called *Lepontic*, found in the regions around the western lakes (Orta, Maggiore, Lugano, Como) of northern

---

[19] On the evidence of La Tène in Italy, which does not precede 400 B.C., is based the argument of a rather late date for the Keltic immigration; Whatmough 1937, 149.

[20] Grenier 1945, 13. There is surely no sense in a statement like the following by an otherwise trustworthy scholar like Lot 1948, 26: "If, then, we want to represent the Gauls such as they were at the time when Caesar made them subjects of Rome, let us look at our compatriots [in France] around us, and let us look at ourselves in the mirror." And little Arab schoolboys in North Africa would open their patriotic textbooks and earnestly read: "*Nos ancêtres, les Gaulois* . . . ," 'Our ancestors, the Gauls . . .'

[21] Hence Polyb. 2.35.4 may be right when he says that already in his time, about the middle of the second century B.C., the Kelts of northern Italy were either absorbed by the indigenes or extinct.

Italy and in the valleys leading up to them, can be classed linguistically with Ligurian,[22] that is, they too are Kelto-Ligurian, neither fully Keltic nor Italic.[23]

Since I ventured to connect Ligurian with the speakers of Indo-European whom I saw in the Palafitticoli and in the owners of the Comacine culture of the lake district, and since Lepontic is so closely related to Ligurian, it is virtually inevitable to seek the Palafitticoli also in the early speakers of Lepontic.[24] (Needless to say, I do not thereby mean that all the Palafitticoli spoke Lepontic, or were the historic Lepontii who, through mere convenience, lent their name to the dialect we now discuss.) Although much research has been done on this matter, the archaeological-linguistic connections are still largely guesswork.[25] As for the separation of Ligurian from Lepontic, it may well be due to the invading Kelts who forced the speakers of Lepontic back into the valleys of the southern Alpine slopes.

It is also illicit to say, on linguistic grounds, that the Lepontii are Ligurians,[26] because these two ethnic terms, as the dialects which go by the same names, make sense only each in its own location, as a result of the interplay of a number of specific local forces, among which the only factor they provedly have fully in common is Indo-Europeanness of speech.

The alphabet of the Lepontic inscriptions is, of course, fundamentally Etruscan, of the so-called North Etruscan or Subalpine variety. Its use in this region falls between the fourth and the second century B.C., which gives also a *terminus post quem* for the inscriptions. In the later records, the Latin alphabet encroaches upon the native and finally replaces it, as the Latin language in the first century after Christ supplanted the Lepontic dialect.

[22] So think Pedersen, Kretschmer, Dottin, Pisani, Whatmough; Danielsson, Krahe, Rhys call them Keltic, possibly persuaded in part by the identity of the alphabets; others, like Pauli, Sommer, Herbig, vacillate between the two. A summary of the discussion is in Whatmough 1927, 13–14. For an extensive bibliography see PID 2.65–73.

[23] PID 2.65–146; the reasons for the name Lepontic *ibid.* 66–70.

[24] So also Whatmough 1937, 105–106, 136–137.

[25] But see Randall-MacIver 1927, 93–99.

[26] So Merlo 1946, 76 (who habitually and steadfastly refuses to distinguish between ethnic and linguistic data). This is like saying, two thousand years hence, that the 'Swiss' of the Canton Ticino were 'Italians,' or that the 'Americans' were 'Indians.'

The *Raetic* dialect has given rise to more lively disagreements although, or possibly because the linguistic evidence is somewhat richer. But the same cannot be said of the archaeological record, whence arises the controversy on the ethnos and the origin of the Raeti, which has thrown its shadow also on the classification of their dialect. As usually, it will be erroneous to use Raeti with reference to both the authors of the inscriptions and some alleged prehistoric predecessors, because no doubt the Raeti whom we know, and Raetic as we know it, are bound to the place where, and the time when we know them, with no guarantee that the people and the language migrated together from some other place or have a long, completely unified history. On the contrary, the sites from which we draw our records, north and south of the Brenner Pass in the valley of the Adige and neighboring regions, have lain on what from time immemorial has been and still is one of the most important thoroughfares of Europe. And if ancient authors tell us of the Etruscan origins of the Raeti [27] they are likely not to take account of this important geopolitical circumstance (as even some scholars of our days do not), and besides they do not really have a more trustworthy knowledge of the facts than we do.[28] For archaeology tells us today what no ancient author could know, namely that the cultural evidence of Etruscans in the area of Raetic is practically nil, consisting merely of strays due to trade.[29] As for olders finds which would allow us to connect the Raeti or their ancestors with any of the Bronze or Iron Age cultures we know, the situation has remained until now hopeless, although certain reflexes of Comacine and even terramare have been unearthed, but nothing in sufficient quantity to permit even guesses. Also our last and in any case most precarious resort, local names, does not in this area support an Etruscan hypothesis.[30]

[27] Liv. 5.33.11: "The Alpine tribes have also, no doubt, the same [Etruscan] origin, especially the Raetians; who have been rendered so savage by the very nature of the country as to retain nothing of their ancient character save the sound of their speech, and even that is corrupted" (LCL, trl. by B. O. Foster).

Plin *N.H.* 3.133: "It is believed that the Raeti are of Tuscan progeny."

[28] Whatmough, Tusca, 1937, 181, says the passage of Livy amounts to nothing at all: "Livy says that the Raeti were of Etruscan origin. I say that they were not."

[29] Whatmough 1937, 166; Tusca, 1937, 182 ff.

[30] Whatmough 1934, 28.

Apart from the ancient tradition, two items contributed to the modern theories on the 'Etruscan origin of the Raeti.' (Be it noted that I retain what I should ordinarily reject as unclear terminology, because clarity is lacking in some authors' discussion, much to the detriment of their credibility).[31] First, the alphabet and the language, the former of necessity of Etruscan origin, the latter apparently containing a number of Etruscan features, especially in proper names; and, second, the theory of the arrival of the Etruscans from the north (see the names of the scholars proposing it with those in the footnote above). Since I have dealt with the second, it remains only to have a look at the dialect itself.

At the outset it must be said, as many times before, that, even if the Raeti were physically related to or descended from the Etruscans, this in itself could prove nothing for their language, and vice versa. And since any trustworthy evidence on the racial descent of the Raeti is completely lacking (also their possibly being Italici cut off from their brethren by the Keltic invasion, has no racial implications, the Italici themselves not being racially homogeneous), I can speak of nothing but their dialect. Once the support derived from a northern Etruscan invasion is withdrawn, once the argument from the alphabet is put in its proper place (what other than the Etruscan alphabet was there for writers of Raetic to choose?), and once the evidence of Etruscan names in Raetic[32] is explained by borrowing rather than inheritance, the case for the Etruscanness of the dialect would have to be made purely from the linguistic evidence. And an examination of the inscriptions does not add up to any sustainable theory. Circumspect authors like Vetter and Whatmough, who do not have an Etruscan axe to grind, have convincingly concluded that Raetic is in fact Indo-European,[33] possibly a "frontier dialect in which Keltic, Germanic, and Illyrian elements meet," though this judgment may have to be modified as, and if, documents from north of the Brenner Pass come to light.[34]

[31] Advocated among others by Battisti, Buonamici, Cortsen, Herbig, Nogara, Pedersen, Ribezzo, Thurneysen, Trombetti.
[32] Kretschmer 1943, 178.
[33] Whatmough 1923; 1937, 166–171.
[34] Whatmough 1937, 104. At least Bonfante 1935, declares Raetic an Illyrian

But just as we have noted Kretschmer's and Devoto's conciliatory attempts with regard to a classification of Etruscan by assigning it to a Peri-Indo-European or Pre-Proto-Indo-European stratum, so we now find Kretschmer endeavoring a similar solution for Raetic,[35] placing it, as I had occasion to mention before, as a sister language on a level with Etruscan, Tyrrhenian, and Pelasgian, all descended from Raetotyrrhenian, which is, as is its sister Proto-Indo-European itself, a derivative of ancient Pre-Proto-Indo-European. Accordingly, Raetic is then the language of the indigenous Rasenna, who are a mixture of the Italian *Urbevölkerung*, or autochthonous population, with the Indo-Europeans.[36] As in the discussion of Pelasgian and Etruscan, I believe again that there is not enough evidence for any such daring hypothesis. But, according to it, Raetic is not Indo-European with Etruscan admixtures, not Etruscan,[37] but 'Etruscoid' (does this mean by the way, that French being a sister language of Italian, is 'Italoid'?) with Indo-European influences, albeit on its way to complete Indo-Europeanization, a process which was interrupted by the Romanization of the region.[38]

Similarly, Pisani justifies his classification of Raetic as non-Indo-European on the basis that it is fundamentally a pre-Indo-European language, connected with the pre-Indo-European substratum that lies under Ligurian (which he considers Indo-European) and Venetic.[39] All these superseded pre-Indo-European strata, and Etruscan, are parts of a general Mediterranean substratum that reaches all the way from the Caucasus to Spain. That part of Raetic which conceivably to some might seem Etruscan is, then,

---

dialect outright. Note that Whatmough 1937, 166 believes that the name Raeti is derived from a stem Grai-, as in *Alpes Graiae*, which is Illyrian. But this would of course prove Illyrian origins neither for the people themselves, nor for the language, any more than the name Français, derived from the Franks, proves Germanic origins for Frenchmen or for the French language.

[35] Kretschmer 1943, 182–184, 213–214, and elsewhere.

[36] Kretschmer 1932, 135. It should be remembered that in 1932, unlike in 1940 and thereafter, Kretschmer still believed in an Aegean immigration of the Etruscans.

[37] Kretschmer 1943, 178–180.

[38] Kretschmer 1943, 182–183. I daresay that much of the burden of this to me unconvincing argumentation must be laid to a literal, biological view of the genealogical tree scheme of linguistic relationships.

[39] Pisani 1935, 103; 1954, 48.

due to the common Mediterranean heritage and not to imports from Etruscan, and Raetic is neither Etruscan nor an Etruscan dialect. As in Kretschmer's theory, the speakers of this Raetic are the Rasenna, who are, according to Pisani, (note the switch again) Mediterraneans, as are the Etruscans.[40] Aside from the ethnic portions of the argument, which seem to me unwarranted, the linguistic records appear to Pisani, as to Kretschmer, more non-Indo-European than Indo-European, whereas Whatmough and Vetter would, cautiously, take the opposite view. It is obviously difficult to decide definitely the full truth of the matter without firmer support than the scant evidence which Raetic offers. It is sometimes irksome enough a task to classify a language that is much better attested. However, just as English, despite its 50 per cent Romanic vocabulary, will not appear to sensible future linguists any more than it does to us as a Romanic language, because its structure is wholly Germanic, so the argument from the Raetic lexicon, to say nothing of the onomasticon, strikes me as none too convincing: does it not rest upon the same etymological method which in Etruscan, and elsewhere, has deceived us so blatantly, often ridiculously?[41]

I prefer to see, then, in Raetic an Indo-European dialect whose peculiarities are not due to a 'Raetic' migration and the importation of a 'Raetic' language, but rather to a development *in situ* and to the interplay of many local factors of which we can discern clearly only the Indo-European portion, and somewhat nebulously a Mediterranean substratum. But who the 'Raeti' were by race we do not know.

The eastern neighbor of Raetic was a language called *Venetic*, covering roughly the region between the Adige River and the head of the Adriatic, but with the most important and richest finds coming from the district of Este, the ancient Ateste, and Padua. We have now reached a language whose records are suf-

[40] Pisani 1935, 107.
[41] But see Kretschmer 1943, 176–178, for a discussion of Etruscan, or rather Etruscoid, morphological features in Raetic; cf. also Pisani 1953, 303–313. Etruscan interpretation of Raetic morphemes leads, needless to say, to translations of the inscriptions quite different from those of Vetter 1953 and Whatmough PID 2, who operate with Raetic morphology on the assumption that it is largely Indo-European.

ficiently transparent and numerous to allow its categorical classification among Indo-European dialects, without doubts and without dissents, though its precise relationship within them is a thornier problem.

But the origin of its speakers, generally called Veneti, is again another matter. As usually, we start with a negative statement, namely, that the Veneti of the inscriptions cannot be catapulted into prehistory and there be made the exponents, under the name Veneti, of a certain culture. Nor does the widespread use of the name (see *Lacus Venetus,* 'Lake Constance,' the *Veneti* of Gaulish Armorica, the *Venetulani* of Latium, the Slavonic *Venedi,* in German *Wenden*; the 'Ενετοί of Paphlagonia are doubtful [42]) allow us to see in them a once far-flung people or race.[43]

Archaeologically, the area of the later Veneti largely coincides with that of the Iron Age culture called Atestine, whose unbroken development we can follow chiefly at Ateste, from 900 B.C. on, and which reached its height in the first half of the fifth century before Christ, when Villanovan Bologna had already begun its decline.[44] Though there are many points of agreement in the Atestine and Villanovan cultures, especially during the Benacci II period, the two can be readily distinguished.[45] Este acquired its extraordinary metallurgical skills from the inhabitants of the Danube basin, whence also, ultimately, its Indo-European dialect must have come. But as usually we must not conclude from this coincidence upon an immigration of Venetic 'Indo-Europeans' at the beginning or in the course of the Iron Age. In fact, the archaeological record speaks against this here as it does in other places. And also during the period of its artistic decline, when Este exported mass-produced wares to the northern barbarians (nobody wanted them in the south, where Greeks and Etruscans supplied the market with merchandise of higher quality), the archaeological evidence shows an undisturbed development and "a singular ten-

[42] Krahe 1941, 137–139.

[43] Krahe 1941, 137, thought them all 'Illyrians,' but reached other conclusions in 1954, 114–115.

[44] Este, now nine miles north of the Adige and in a rather isolated spot, once was actually situated on the banks of this river, which only in A.D. 589, in consequence of a gigantic flood, sought a new bed.

[45] Randall-MacIver, Italy, 1928, 83–86; Forerunners, 1928, 140–142.

acity even in its decadence." [46] For this reason one could almost speak of an Atestine nationality, which according to the inscriptions appears to have been of Venetic speech,[47] as existing from the Iron Age down to its peaceful conquest by the Romans in 184 B.C. It was spared both Etruscan and Keltic domination to which so many other northern Italian tribes had fallen prey, and preserved its national peculiarities in customs and dress and language down to the beginning of the Christian era. We do not know when the Atestines started to speak Venetic, and when it became their national tongue. But it is not impossible that the first speakers of Indo-European were the same wanderers from the Danube basin or from the northern Balkans, again few in number according to the archaeology of Venetia, who brought with them the advanced metallurgy of their homeland. We also do not know whether these immigrants were the same racially or ethnically as those who in a similar fashion had a hand in the foundation of the Villanovan culture; it is possible, though not necessarily true.

But the historic Veneti and their language appear again as the local fusion of a variety of cultural, ethnic, and linguistic factors which could not have been present elsewhere in the same mixture and proportions and therefore could not have produced the same results.

Some scholars claim that the Illyrians had a part in the origin (the word begins to seem a little odd in this context, as it should) of the Veneti.[48] Now that is again a matter of nomenclature,

[46] Randall-MacIver, Italy, 1928, 92.

[47] The oldest inscription is on a vase from Padua, of the sixth century B.C., according to Conway 1926, 441; cf. PID 1.139–141.

[48] This view is ultimately due to Herod. 1.196, who speaks of Ἰλλυριῶν Ἐνετοί, by whom he means, however, not the Veneti of Italy but a tribe in the northern Balkan peninsula; cf. Krahe 1954, 114–115. According to Pokorny 1935, 346, the Veneti are the bearers of the Lausitz culture of Bohemia, which moves south, reaching Italy about 1000 B.C. The goddess Reitia, whose name occurs on numerous Venetic votive inscriptions, also was used to argue for Illyrian origins of the Veneti by connecting her with the Spartan Orthia (cf. PID 1.90–93; Kretschmer 1943, 155–156; Altheim-Trautmann 1941, 360–361, 366–368; Altheim, Geschichte, 1951, 47–50; Borgeaud 1943, 84; against this view Beeler 1949, criticized unfavorably by Pellegrini 1951) through the hypothesis that some Illyrians came to Greece and Sparta as part of the Doric migration (Altheim-Trautmann 1941, 368). But another opinion, without having recourse to Illyrians, finds the cult of a goddess who is concerned, like Reitia, with mothers and their health, and to

with which I have dealt in several connections. For if we name Illyrians not some prehistoric tribe but, as we must, the people who spoke Illyrian, a language about which we know pitifully little in any case, then they cannot have had any share in the 'origin' of the 'Veneti,' insofar as this event refers to prehistory. But if anyone wants to indicate thereby, albeit awkwardly, his belief that the Indo-European dialect which the Atestines learned was of an Illyrian type, then the argument is legitimate enough, provided that Illyrian affinities can actually be found in Venetic.

Until quite recently Venetic was in fact thought to be an Illyrian kind of dialect, like Messapic of Apulia. But the present consensus to which I subscribe is that it is not, that rather it appears more closely connected with Latinian.[49] This unobjectionable verdict was enthusiastically but erroneously taken as the signal for declaring that the Veneti were after all not 'Illyrians' but that instead they were related to the 'Proto-Latins,' a modification of ethnic theory which, of course, cannot possibly follow from a revised linguistic opinion in the first place. Krahe, who at one time (1941) still thought, as I mentioned before, that all tribes with names related to that of the Veneti were Illyrians, came later to the conclusion that they were not, and that their language also was not Illyrian, although the name Veneti[50] itself and many local names of their land are of Illyrian origin, whereas personal names are more Venetic.[51] Hence the Illyrian layer seems to be older than the Venetic layer. If that is so, then Venetic has both a Mediterranean and an Illyrian substratum, which may well have in some measure entitled earlier scholars to see in it an Illyrian dialect — if, of course, they knew exactly what they meant by Illyrian to begin with.

Also a Latinian substratum is claimed by some for Venetic, caused by the fact that the 'Veneti' upon their arrival in Italy supplanted the 'Proto-Latins,' some of whom moved south to

---

whom votive pins like the ones of the Veneti are dedicated, spread over large parts of Europe (Barb 1952, 164-166).

[49] Pisani 1937, 281-282, 290; Kretschmer 1943, 135-149; Beeler 1949, 48-57; Lejeune 1952; Krahe 1954, 119-121; Hamp 1954.

[50] Connected with a root *uen-* 'to love,' as in Latin *Venus*, Skt. *vanetah* 'desired,' by Krahe 1941, 140, and Borgeaud 1943, 114-115.

[51] Krahe 1954, 115-118.

Latium, and some of whom were squeezed into the Alpine valleys where we meet them as 'Euganei' and as authors of the inscriptions of the Val Camonica.[52]

The Venetic inscriptions are recorded in a characteristic Italic alphabet which is fundamentally Etruscan but has certain peculiarities, among others the use of puncts (as in Etruscan itself), which are actually meaningless in a letter alphabet and were therefore connected, as I mentioned before, with syllabaric types of script of the Aegean area.[53]

The dialects of central Italy have in part already been dealt with (Etruscan in Chapter XV and East Italic in Chapter XIV), and, in part, being Italic dialects (Oscan, Umbrian, and related minor idioms), they will be discussed in the next chapter; the Latinian dialects will be treated separately in Part V of this book. The languages of Sicily were also examined in Chapter XIV.

This leaves only one major dialect to be mentioned here, *Messapic*, spoken in ancient Apulia and Calabria (all of which is now called Apulia). The Greeks named all the tribes of Apulia (there are Daunii, Peucetii, Calabri, Messapii, Sallentini) Iapyges or Messapii (as French *Allemands*, derived from the single tribe of the Alemani, does service for all Germans), and consequently the language of all pre-Latin inscriptions of the area is called Messapic. This is all the more legitimate since all records exhibit a fairly uniform dialect. Of course, we know nothing about prehistoric Messapii who 'originally' spoke Messapic. In fact, in matters of Apulian prehistory we are still very much in the dark, chiefly because archaeological exploration has treated the province in a rather stepmotherly fashion. Except for the wholly uncharacteristic finds of Timmari, which, as I mentioned, are by some linked to the terramare culture,[54] there is a broad gap in our knowledge between the neolithic Molfetta and Matera period and the appearance of the Apulian pottery in the middle of the

[52] Altheim, in various publications; so also Krahe 1949, 53. This is denied by von Merhart 1942, 67–68, who does not find enough evidence. See above Chapter XIV, on the Euganeans. For alleged Germanic traits in Venetic and their explanation see Altheim-Trautmann 1940, 21–29; Altheim, Geschichte, 1951, 124–130.

[53] Vetter 1936; Beeler 1949, 2–13; Kretschmer 1951, 10–14; a survey of the problem in Hoenigswald 1953.

[54] For a view that connects it with a southern, maritime thrust of Iron Age invaders practicing cremation, see Pallottino 1955, 46, and below.

seventh century. Strangely enough, most of our Iron Age information must be derived from crockery. But I have spoken before of the orientation of all of southern Italy and Sicily toward the Aegean area rather than the north of Italy, hence it would not be surprising if forthcoming evidence of the cultural facies of the Apulian Iron Age turned out to be fundamentally different from anything that has come to light farther north. In the meantime, however, it is impossible even to make a guess as to who were the ancestors of the people who eventually spoke Messapic.

But, as so often, the Illyrians crop up. Descent of the Messapians (or Iapygians) from invading Illyrians was propounded in a paper by Helbig, whose conclusions have been in vogue now for eighty years.[55]

Apart from the traditional sources, the theory is based chiefly, as it had to be, on the evidence of names, local and personal, about whose limited worth in general and in relation to Illyrian in particular I have already spoken. It may be rash to dismiss offhand Helbig's argument, but unless it is coordinated, which it cannot be as of now, with nonlinguistic and nonphilological information its conclusiveness is more than questionable.

It has been said that also the language of the Messapic inscriptions, the oldest of which date from the fifth century before Christ [56] shows affinities with Illyrian — which is, be it noted again, a language of which we know very little besides names, except in so far as we claim to recognize it in Messapic (and formerly in Venetic). The reasoning here seems circular. But more about the language below. At the moment let us see who those alleged Illyrian ancestors of the Messapii could have been. The term Messapii becomes attributable to a tribal unit not before the sixth century B.C., whereas the 'Illyrians' are supposed to have migrated to Italy, according to a cautious estimate, between the tenth and the eighth centuries.[57] Now, even if, for the moment, we accept a large ethnic migration of Illyrians from the Balkan peninsula across the Adriatic Sea to Apulia, we are still left with a gap of from two to four centuries between the 'Illyrians' and the 'Mes-

[55] Helbig 1876. (Three years later, Helbig 1879 proposed the northern invasion of the Etruscans.) So still, Kaschnitz-Weinberg, 1950, 394.

[56] PID 2.533, dated on the evidence of the alphabet.

[57] PID 2.262.

sapii.' It is said that these "Illyrian Messapians" could not have come by the long land route around the head of the Adriatic without "disrupting their national unity and without destroying their national character." [58] But what do we actually know about a national unity and national character, or indeed about a cultural unity of the 'Illyrian Messapians' between the tenth and fifth centuries? And even afterward the only unity we have evidence for is the linguistic one attested to by the inscriptions; and that still does not guarantee that *all* the inhabitants of the region spoke this dialect, to say nothing of a common physical ancestry. Hence it is injudicious to speak of the Messapii as descendants of Illyrian invaders. In fact, we do not even possess nonlinguistic evidence of an Illyrian invasion in force because, as we have seen, Apulia is more than other places a closed book for the late Bronze and the early Iron Age.

The Messapic language is no doubt Indo-European, and we may also accept the judgment that it is of an Illyrian type as long as we are cognizant of the uncertain and limited real content of the term 'Illyrian.' I do not mean to inject exaggerated skepticism into this classification of Messapic by pointing to Venetic whose Illyrianness has finally been rejected, but such a thing could happen also to Messapic, especially since Illyrian is so little known a quantity in the equation.[59]

Whereas in the northern dialect areas we could at least determine, in given districts, Bronze and Iron Age cultures which preceded the appearance of linguistic records, albeit over a long gap which we dared not bridge by means of a name alone, in Apulia the archaeological evidence fails us for anything later than the Neolithic Age. Hence the gap between the neolithic cultures and Messapic is even wider, and the Illyrians are notoriously too indeterminate an item to operate with safely. All we can say, then, with certainty is that an Indo-European speech was introduced by someone, maybe again by a mere handful of stragglers,

[58] PID 2.261–262.

[59] It is significant that Krahe 1937, 21–29, although one of the most ardent supporters of Illyrianism, finds that the name Messapii itself is not Illyrian but Mediterranean. However, he considers the Messapians nonetheless ethnically as 'Illyrians,' with a Cretan admixture (there is a river Messapos in Crete), the latter providing the Mediterranean element also in the local archaeology (cf. Mayer 1914).

although it must be admitted that the absence of all evidence so far is due to the small amount of archaeological work done in Apulia and can therefore not be grounds for categorically excluding a larger migration. If Messapic is to be definitely established as an Illyrian type of Indo-European dialect,[60] then the propagators of the new language were indeed Illyrians, in this narrow sense of the word. Upon what linguistic substratum this imported Illyrian produced Messapic it is impossible to say;[61] it may have been again the local brand of Mediterranean alone, or a combination of it and a superimposed Italic stratum, but one cannot be certain of this.[62] In any case, Messapic was not the first language spoken in Apulia since the Messapii were not the first human beings there. On this, at least, the archaeological record is unequivocal.

[60] I must note once more, however, that in modern Albanian, generally considered as descended from Illyrian, no affinities whatever with Messapic can be discovered.

[61] Devoto 1951, 51, thinks it is Proto-Latin, arrived with the migration of the Protolatini (which preceded that of the Osco-Umbrians).

[62] PID 2.261.

CHAPTER XVII

The Italic and Latinian Dialects Concerning the Italic dialects (Oscan, Umbrian, and minor dialects like Paelignian, Aequian, Marsian, Marrucinian, Vestinian, and Volscian) several linguistic facts have been safely established. All are Indo-European. They are more closely related to Latin than to other Indo-European languages; they are more closely related to one another than each is to Latin. Umbrian was spoken in some parts of modern Umbria, but we do not know exactly where or in what form since virtually all the records we have come from one place, Iguuium (modern Gubbio), and may or may not be typical of the speech of the whole region.[1] Oscan dialects were spoken on either side of the spinal ridge of the Apennines in their southern half, in Campania, and in Calabria.

Concerning the Latinian dialects we are equally sure that they are Indo-European, that they were spoken in Latium and in the Alban Hills, and that one of them was Latin of the city of Rome.

I need scarcely say that Umbrian here means the dialect of which we have records, and the Umbrians are the people who spoke it. Oscan and Oscans I use in the same sense, although we do know that the name Oscan goes back to Ὀπικοί, persons who did not speak an Indo-European language but who eventually learned the Italic language of the tribes of Samnium, whom we know as Samnites, and to whom they gave their name; ". . . the *Osca lingua* was properly Samnite, though the Oscans were not, in the main, Sabelli or Samnites; and . . . although the Samnites are said to have spoken Oscan, they were not, in any sense or degree, Oscans. . . . 'Oscan' is the name given to the dialect which the Sabellians [or Samnites] introduced into Campania, the land of the Osci or Ὀπικοί, but clearly it was not the original speech of

[1] Whatmough 1937, 186.

that tribe. . . ."[2] The Oscans occupy, with reference to the Samnite idiom called Oscan by the Romans *after them*, the same position as the Alemani with reference to the Germanic idiom called *Allemand* by the French.

Latin and Latinian are called by the same name as the tribes who spoke these dialects and whom we meet as Latini in Latium. About their predecessors we know nothing.[3]

The small Sabellian tribes are those in the hills north and east of Rome who later also appear as speakers of Italic (either nearer to Oscan or nearer to Umbrian) dialects. Sabellian as a linguistic name is therefore a generic term, meaning Italic of a certain kind and location.

For the Indo-European dialects of the north (Ligurian, Lepontic, Raetic, Venetic) it was plausible enough to assume, with the support of archaeology, that the persons who long ago brought the Indo-European element into the historic locations of these dialects, came across the Alps, at various points and over different passes. I have mentioned that to the traveler from the north, once he has reached by slow ascent the upper course of the rivers belonging to the Danube's tributary system, the scaling of the last heights is not a formidable enterprise, and that especially the Peartree Pass is so easy a route into the plains of northern Italy that it has been since time immemorial a gateway for friend and foe.

The Messapians of Apulia, on the other hand, seem to owe their Indo-European speech to import from across the Adriatic Sea. The possible Illyrian connections of Messapic, the absence of any archaeological, cultural traces along a presumed route of 'Proto-Messapians' marching south in Italy, and the lack of agree-

---

[2] Whatmough 1937, 284. For an etymology of *Osci* as either 'agriculturists' or 'worshipers of Ops,' see Devoto 1951, 112. For the meaning and etymology of Samnite, Sabelli, Sabini, etc., see Devoto 1951, 113–115. The Samnites called themselves *Safinim*, while to the Romans the Samnites north and east of Rome were *Sabelli*; the *Sabini* are only the inhabitants of Sabinum.

Mommsen 1850, 293, connects etymologically Sabini and Safini with *sapinus* 'pine,' and Peucetii with πεύκη 'pine,' which makes these people 'the inhabitants of pine forests.' The Osci (Opsci) and Ὀπικοί are derived from the same root as *operari* 'to labor (in the fields),' (cf. German *Bauer*, that is, *Anbauer* 'planter, peasant') which makes them agricultural workers.

[3] Concerning the use and meaning of 'Umbrians,' 'Oscans,' and 'Proto-Latins' in a prehistoric sense, see the preceding chapters.

ment between the northern and southern cultures on the whole, make the transadriatic thesis of the Indo-Europeanization of Apulia very likely, if not indispensable.

But now we are dealing with Indo-European dialects which are certainly not linguistically connected to Illyria, and with cultures which we cannot easily and obviously derive through either a northern or an eastern provenance, and with locations equally easy or difficult of access whether from the north or from the east. It is therefore not surprising that both a northern and an eastern origin for the Italic and Latinian dialects have been proposed. If I say origin, I mean here of course only their location immediately preceding their appearance in Italy; previous to that we are carried once more into a general Danubian area, and ultimately into the famous original Indo-European homeland. The whole question, then, comes really to this: Did Italic and Latinian, after their departure from the Danube lands, come to Italy by way of Switzerland, Austria, and northern Yugoslavia, like the northern Indo-European dialects of Italy, or by way of southern Yugoslavia, Albania, and perhaps Greece, like Messapian?

It so happens that Umbrian and Latinian lie mainly to the west of the Rimini-Rome line that separates inhumation from cremation grave areas, and Oscan to the east of it. It was therefore inevitable that one would try to establish a combined ethnic-cultural-linguistic boundary along the same line. The most egregious and most persuasive attempt to do just that is von Duhn's theory of cremating and inhuming Italici.[4]

When von Duhn speaks of Italici he means persons not only united by their linguistic heritages but also ethnically or racially related, people who came to Italy in two distinct migrations, but as fully formed units, from locations north of the Alps. The older of these invasions brings the cremating, the younger the inhuming Italici, who appear situated west and east, respectively, of the Rome-Rimini line, who are, in other words, the Umbrians and Latins, on the one hand, and the various Sabellian tribes, the Picenes, and the Oscans on the other.

In discussing the 'Picenes' and the East Italic inscriptions (Chapter XIV), I adopted Randall-MacIver's view that the people re-

[4] von Duhn 1924. For a critique see Whatmough 1937, 243-245.

sponsible for the culture of this region were probably descendants of the older neolithic stock who had remained undisturbed culturally and linguistically (with the exception of the originators of the Southern East Italic inscriptions — *if* these are in any measure Illyrian or Indo-European). But even if, for lack of racial evidence, they cannot be proved to be the physical descendants of older population strata, the material evidence makes it imperative to separate them clearly from other Iron Ages peoples of Italy, both cremating and inhuming. The Picenes are therefore not Italici, either in a linguistic or a cultural sense; and if they are not, one of the pillars upholding von Duhn's theory collapses.

Moreover, the correlation of linguistic and funerary evidence raises grave difficulties and doubts. Both Latin and Umbrian lie in cremating, the Oscan dialects, introduced according to von Duhn by the inhuming Italici, in inhuming territory; yet Oscan is more closely related to Umbrian than it is to Latin, and Latin and Umbrian are quite different from one another.

On their way south, the inhuming Italici, especially since the theory requires them to have moved in large hordes, should have left some traces of their march. They did not, however, and no evidence of their passing can be found west and north of the Rome-Rimini boundary.[5]

The theory of two types of Italici who reached Italian soil in two major thrusts is intimately tied up with the hypothesis of mass migrations from the north. If one can dispense, as I have attempted to do throughout this book wherever the evidence counsels it, with vast invasions, then the theory of cremating and inhuming Italici becomes unnecessary. There are then, in fact, no cremating and inhuming Italici, indeed no 'Italici' — except in the sense of speakers of Italic dialects. And this linguistic situation can be and will be accounted for, as usually, by infiltration and not by movements of definite, circumscribed social or ethnic units.

It is probably correct that in Italy cremation was imported by speakers of Indo-European whom we may first recognize in the palafitte, terramare, and the Villanovan settlements, that is,

[5] Whatmough 1937, 244; Ducati 1928, 56–57; 1938, 179–180; von Merhart 1942, 68.

in an area where, later, Venetic, Umbrian, and Latin will be spoken. But that does not mean that all speakers of Indo-European everywhere were cremators (the Kelts, for example, were not), or that cremation is a sign of Indo-Europeanness. All we can legitimately conclude from this coincidence is that some of the speakers of Indo-European, who came to Italy, belonged to a culture or cultures which practiced cremation.[6]

Indeed we do not even know whether cremation and the corresponding graves became universal in what we call cremating districts, or when they did. If we imagine, as we must, that the spread of the Indo-European languages among original speakers of non-Indo-European dialects was a gradual one, although we have no sure evidence for the manner and the speed of the transition (except to say that it was too pervasive and too rapid to be due to mere diffusion), we may assume that the propagation of a new funerary rite takes its course probably in the same manner, especially if there is involved in burial rites something which one may call a religious attitude.[7] Furthermore, distinctiveness in funerary rites is of and by itself no more an indication of racial conditions than any other cultural features, including linguistic ones.[8] Only when and if there occurs a sudden and radical change in funerary customs, affecting a large area and an entire culture, can we assume also some ethnic change, through infiltration or migration.

But in Iron Age Italy we cannot even be sure, I daresay, that the tombs that have actually been unearthed are so characteristic for the region and its inhabitants as to permit generalizations on the cultures. It was noted, for example, that those ancient tombs of neolithic and later Europe which were provided with furnishings, never contain any agricultural implements although agriculture was without any doubt practiced by then; it is, in fact, the most important cultural feature distinguishing later from palaeolithic conditions. The only tools one finds are knives, and they are,

[6] Devoto 1951, 71–72.
[7] In mentioning this I have no intention of suggesting that the inhumers left the body intact because they believed in a life after death, whereas the cremators did not. To transfer such a Judeo-Christian philosophy to Iron Age people is unwarranted. But it was done: Schuchhardt 1933, 316–318.
[8] Dumézil 1944, 134–137, deals with this in detail.

like axes, weapons at the same time.[9] Could it be that all the burial places we know, excepting perhaps the vast popular urn-field cemeteries in which every burial takes so little space and where some 'democratic' idea seems to have prevailed, are those of well-to-do persons, of warriors, of aristocrats, whereas the bodies of the poor, the peasants, were left to rot on some pre-historic potters field that can no longer be found and explored? Let us remember that even republican Rome deposited the corpses of its proletariat not in opulent, inscribed sarcophagi like those of the Scipios, or in tombs like those along the Via Appia, but threw them into the stinking *puticuli* on the Esquiline Hill, where but a handful of dirt was strewn over them. Obviously funerary customs of this type are likely to remain unknown to archaeology, because no tomb furnishings were piously provided for heaps of decaying corpses.[10] How can we know, therefore, on the basis of the evidence we have, that either cremation or inhumation were somewhere, during the Iron Age, characteristic, common, popular modes of disposing of the dead? Devoto argues, as I have done, that not a sporadic occurrence of a new funerary rite but the coherent replacement of the old by the new custom indicates cultural change.[11] But in view of what I just said, can we be so sure that there is any coherence, or thoroughness in the apparent alternation of the two burial types of Italy?

Perhaps this is so skeptical a view of the whole matter that on pragmatic grounds it would not be well to adopt it wholly, although theoretically it is hardly objectionable. I stated it in order to place the evidence of burial rites in its due perspective and, putting it bluntly, to cut it down to proper size.

One more thing must be said. If the burials by both inhumation and cremation were imported from outside, by Italici or by whatever tribes or nations whom we pretend to recognize according to one or the other mode of disposing of dead bodies, what, then, was the rite of the natives before this twofold immi-

---

[9] Childe 1945, 84.

[10] In attempting an etymology for *puticuli*, Varr. *L.L.* 525 suggests either a derivation from *puteus* 'well, pit,' or from *putescere* 'to rot,' because, he says, the corpses were left to decompose practically in the open air. Romans complained about the stench.

[11] Devoto 1951, 71–72.

gration? They must have done something to corpses, and we ought to have found some evidence of it, unless they threw dead bodies in the water or devoured them. Since it could scarcely be anything but inhumation or cremation, either *some* of the inhuming graves, or *some* of the cremating graves that have been unearthed, must be not characteristic of the invaders.

Last but not least, there is again the matter of chronology. When we talk about cremation versus inhumation burials, about the Rome-Rimini line, we are around the year 1000 B.C.; but when we talk about Italic dialects we are at a point five hundred years later. Hence the inhuming and cremating Italici, even if they had existed in von Duhn's sense, would furnish no parallel argument concerning the dialects.

I must reject also Pallottino's theory which, though it refutes von Duhn's, sets up a new linguistic distinction based on the Rome-Rimini burial line.[12] According to Pallottino, the area of inhumation corresponds to the Indo-European languages, that of cremation to the non-Indo-European languages. This completely reverses earlier views of dialectal and funerary correlations. His premise is: "If already at the beginning of the period of the spread of Iron Age cultures the Italic peoples may be considered as situated in their historic homes and on the whole ethnically formed — as is proved by epigraphic documents of only slightly later date — then it is clear that the Indo-Europeanization of Italy belongs to a very remote period." [13]

But against this view grave chronological objections must be raised. If one accepts the "beginning of the period of the spread of Iron Age cultures" as the tenth century B.C., and there can scarcely be any serious quarrel about that, and if one dates furthermore the earliest epigraphic documents, excepting Etruscan, which is non-Indo-European in any event, as of the sixth or, more likely, of the fifth century before Christ, and there can scarcely be any quarrel about that either, these documents do not prove, as Pallottino holds they do, that we may consider the Italic tribes "as situated in their historic home and on the whole ethnically formed" at the beginning of the Iron Age, because the

[12] Pallottino 1955, maps on pp. 33, 45.
[13] Pallottino 1955, 51–52.

set of linguistic records is not of "slightly later date" but fully five hundred years younger than the set of archaeological records involving evidence of burials. Hence, the juxtaposition, or the superposition of Pallottino's linguistic and ethnic maps is wholly unjustified because each presents a series of data entirely non-correlatable with, and irrelevant to, those of the other. Instead of Pallottino's I rather accept here Whatmough's view (not as concerns implied mass migration of peoples but as concerns chronology). "The fact must never be lost sight of that our dialect evidence, apart from proper names, begins at a date considerably later than the movement of these peoples into and within Italy, later even than their permanent settlements and, so to speak, their 'naturalization' in Italy." [14] It is true, of course, that our earliest texts are of Iron Age cultures which we may trace back for some time, but we must not correlate the beginning of these Iron Age cultures with the arrival of certain dialects in central Italy, especially since in fact our documentation of these dialects commences five centuries after the beginning of the cultures.

Although, therefore, we can accept neither large, successive migrations of 'Italici' nor a correlation of these hosts of newcomers with archaeologically identifiable Iron Age cultures, we still have to account somehow for the Indo-Europeanness of the speech of the later, historic Italici, that is, we must determine in some way the derivation of the new dialects, even though only relatively few persons seem to be involved in its importation. (We are approximately in the same position as we were in regard to the Etruscans. Somebody must be answerable for the typical Italicness as for the typical Etruscanness of certain phenomena which become manifest from a given point of time on.) Since we have abandoned racial identification as impractical we shall not attempt to equate the Italic speakers with a new race; and we shall not endeavor to equate Italic speakers with one or more Iron Age cultures (except to the extent that some Indo-European languages come to Italy together with metallurgical skills) since we also rejected cultural identification because of chronological difficulties, namely, the lag of five centuries. The only permissible

[14] Whatmough 1937, 195.

argument that might lead to further enlightenment is, therefore, a linguistic one.

Pallottino says that the Indo-European languages came to Italy by importation from the east rather than the north, and he cites as proof their relative location. He places what he considers non-Indo-European or not-wholly-Indo-European languages generally in the north and west of Italy (Ligurian, Raetic, Etruscan), and the fully Indo-European languages in the east and south (Venetic, Umbrian, Sabellian, Latin, Oscan, Messapic, Sicel). The dividing line is, roughly, the course of the Tiber or, again, the Rome-Rimini line.[15] Now, without following Pallottino any further in correlating or equating the dialect boundary of 500 B.C. with the cultural (funerary rites) boundary of 1000 B.C. (see above), we are indeed left with a tripartite layer of Indo-European across the boot of Italy from west to east: Latinian; Oscan-Umbrian; Venetic, perhaps East Italic, Messapic. Accordingly, Pallottino argues for three waves of migration, moving from east to west, that is, across the Adriatic and Italy; the first (Latin) penetrated farthest west, the second (Oscan-Umbrian) remained in the center of the peninsula, and the last (perhaps 'Illyrian') went no farther than the east coast.[16] Pallottino deals here indeed with vast invasions of speakers of Indo-European, which is surprising in one who so steadfastly resists invasion theories for so much stranger and perceptibly distinct an entity in Italy as are the Etruscans. But his argument and his own wording leave no doubt: ". . . the Umbro-Sabellian *wave* drove back these [proto-Latin] *people* . . .", and ". . . the arrival of the Indo-European languages from the east no doubt *pushed* toward the western margins of Italy the older idioms. . ."[17] (Italics mine.) How can a language be pushed except through movement of speakers? And what is a wave which drives before itself a whole people but one of mass migration?

I wish to reject the migrations, whether they are alleged to have

[15] Pallottino 1955, 32–34.
[16] Pallottino 1955, 34–37.
[17] Pallottino 1955, 36, 39. On this migration of people and languages by continued frontal pressure, see my remarks concerning the expansion of Indo-European in Chapter XIII above.

taken place in three waves, or in two waves of Italici, or even in one wave of Indo-European immigrants, since there is simply no evidence for them at this point, and also since both the locations and the relationships of the Italic and Latinian dialects can be explained exactly in the same manner as those of the other Indo-European dialects of Italy, and of Europe, that is, by local formation, as the fusion of native dialects with a superimposed Indo-European dialect or Indo-European dialects.

The resultant speeches in Italy were generally Indo-European rather than non-Indo-European, whence we speak of a non-Indo-European substratum and not of an Indo-European superstratum.[18] In this process there occurred no doubt at different dates infiltrations of Indo-European-speaking persons whose languages the natives adopted; and it is safe to conjecture that the variations developing on Italian soil are due to a variety of substrata as well as to dialectal differences among the Indo-European-speaking newcomers.

We need invading 'Italici' of one or two or three types no more to explain the dialects of ancient Italy than we need invading Proto-Spaniards of one or three or fifty kinds to explain the modern dialects of Spain. Whatever sort of Latin was spoken by the Roman legions and colonials who occupied Gaul, and Spain, and Dacia, it is certain that they did not speak what would even remotely be called Proto-French, or Proto-Spanish, or Proto-Rumanian, except in the large sense that Latin is Proto-Romanic; just so, whatever kind of Italic the invaders of the Bronze Age and Iron Age Italy talked, our best and most intelligent guess is that they did not come as speakers of Proto-Latin, or Proto-Oscan, or Proto-Umbrian, except in the sense that they spoke a brand of Indo-European which, because of its later varied development in Italy, we may call Italic. Once this is understood, the relegation of ethnic Proto-Latins, Proto-Umbrians, and Proto-Oscans to the realm of myths becomes as inevitable as a similar fate for the Proto-Indo-Europeans. The term 'Proto-Italic,' if it is worth salvaging at all, would then signify merely the recognition that a number of otherwise wholly unidentifiable persons spoke an unattested type or types of Italic,

---

[18] Cf. Chapter XXIV, n. 16.

just as the 'Proto-Indo-Europeans' spoke an unattested 'Proto-Indo-European.'[19]

In some instances we were able to identify the cultural substratum of a district in which we later find Indo-European dialects: Venetic appears upon Atestine, Lepontic upon Golaseccan, Umbrian perhaps upon Northern Villanovan, Latin on Latian (a mere onomastic equation here, unless Latian is of the Southern Villanovan variety); for Messapic we do not know the Iron Age culture upon which it grew, nor for Siculan, except that they were probably of an Aegean type. As for the Italic dialects, there is no certainty either; however, in recent years Italian archaeologists[20] believed to have discovered what they call an Apennine culture which is fairly widespread in the central mountainous strip of the peninsula, and which may well be the soil upon which the Italic dialects came into being. I only hope that what I have said so far in this book may at least deter future linguists and ethnologists from seeking, and discovering, Proto-Apenninici talking Oscan and Umbrian dialects, who migrated from somewhere into Italy.

The prehistoric spread of the Italic dialects, especially Oscan, the language of the Samnites, through central and southern Italy, and with it perhaps that of the prehistoric Apennine culture, has often been explained through a phenomenon known from historic times, the *uer sacrum*, or 'Sacred Spring.' According to this custom, the young men of a tribe or a locality, once the native soil could no longer support the increasing population, were periodically sent forth during springtime to search for new land and new homes. This testifies, it seems, to two things: the prolificness of the tribes, due ultimately to higher civilization and a better life; and the relative sparsity of population and easy availability of land which permitted the *uer sacrum* migrants to find living space elsewhere

[19] Patroni 1951, 989–990, recognizes that there is no immigration discernible in the records to explain the origin of the Italic (that is, Osco-Umbrian) dialects in Italy, but that they are local products grown on the soil of the native pre-Indo-European speeches, their seeds being introduced by infiltration of speakers of Indo-European. But he claims, on the other hand, that Latin was brought to Italy through the Villanovan migration. This is no more necessary than is an Osco-Umbrian immigration: in fact, Villanovan is a culture, and there is no evidence of any large-scale migration connected with it; while its originators probably spoke Indo-European, they did not come from outside of Italy as speakers of Latin, or Proto-Latin, or any one dialect known to us.

[20] Rellini 1933; Patroni, in various sources.

without too much trouble. And all this again may well betray some deeper lying facts, namely, that a thin native population, inferior in civilization, would oppose but weak obstacles to the spread of the civilization of the newcomers; and that these thinly sown natives, who had little intertribal communication, would probably speak, if they spoke related Mediterranean idioms at all, very different dialects which functioned as linguistic substrata, with local variations probably much more trenchant than those of the present day in Italy, which are founded upon them. In other words, the arriving Indo-European dialect or dialects were superimposed on strongly divergent substrata, hence naturally came to diverge from one another greatly. Consequently, there is good reason to favor the theory propounded by some,[21] that the agreements in many details among the historic Italic dialects and Latin are due not so much to ancient relationships as to a convergence caused by the lasting vicinity and the improving communications of the tribes in Italy, and are more recent than the disagreements between them. This opinion provides grammatical support for the theory that there was no pre-divisional Italic-Latin unity, a view which I have just refuted on other grounds.[22]

I have already mentioned that some of the attested tribal and local names of speakers of Italic may be connected with *uer sacrum* migrations, if we accept the idea that the seceding groups dedicated themselves to a god or called themselves after a totemic animal. Thus we get not only the Hirpini from *hirpus*, 'wolf,' the Picentes from *picus*, 'wood pecker,' but also the Vestini from Vesta, Marsi from Mars, Mamertini from Mamers, Volsci from Volcanus, Osci from Ops, Bouianum from *bouem*, 'ox,' and so forth.[23] If this is true,

[21] For example, Devoto 1951, 45–47.

[22] Beeler 1952, also denies a Proto-Italic unity and explains the agreements of Latin with Oscan-Umbrian by their existing in close vicinity over several pre-documentary centuries. But he believes that, previous to that, they underwent a thousand years of independent development after Latin had split off from a still essentially unified Western Indo-European speech community, in which Pre-Latin and Pre-Oscan-Umbrian dialects occupied adjoining areas. There is of course no real, *archaeological* evidence of an essentially unified 'Western-Indo-European speech community' (what does this mean?) or of a splitting off of Pre-Latin before Oscan-Umbrian, or of their rejoining on the soil of Italy a thousand years later. And the linguistic evidence need not necessarily be interpreted in this manner.

[23] Myres 1914; von Blumenthal 1938, 31–33; Rix 1954, finds evidence of Illyrian

it supports in turn the theory of cultural and linguistic spread through *uer sacrum* secessions which I just proposed. Furthermore, if for once the *uer sacrum* migrations furnish trustworthy evidence concerning the manner of the spread of Italic in Italy at a late date, we may possibly surmise that this type of linguistic propagation of Italic dialects might also apply to more remote times for which we do not have any *uer sacrum* reports. In this case, we are further encouraged to abandon invasions and migrations by masses of speakers of Indo-European, but may start the spread of Oscan and Umbrian from one or several focal points somewhere north of Rome, possibly from Umbria, between the mutually hostile regions of Venetic, East Italic, and Etruscan idioms. This would account also for the fact that the Italic dialects expand initially southward along the center of the peninsula and reach the coasts only where politically and culturally powerful speakers of other languages do not bar the way, that is, in Bruttium and Lucania.

Since I do not believe in the existence of Umbrian, Oscan, and Latinian types of dialects outside of Italy which were imported by two or three or more migrating national or racial groups, since I do not even believe in an Italic dialect as a branch of Indo-European outside of Italy which was imported by one migrating nation and then broke up in Italy, my answer to the question whether there was or was not an earlier Italo-Keltic unity of language is implicitly "No, there was not." [24] It, too, existed only in the sense that there was an Indo-European unity, which by definition included all Indo-European dialects, but which did in no way 'contain' Keltic or Italic any more than Latin 'contained' French or Spanish; which did not give birth to an Italo-Keltic unity that later

---

tribal names of this type in southern Italy and Dalmatia. Cf. also Rauhut 1946, 139; Merkelbach, 1956.

[24] For a refutation on grammatical grounds, see Devoto 1951, 44–47. Unfortunately the exposition is marred by a *non sequitur* to the effect that "the prehistory of the Italici does not begin therefore with a hypothetic breaking up of the Italico-Latini after they had been for a long time far from their original seats, but in the heart of the still united Indo-European nation." (47) Nation? What nation? What united Indo-European nation?

I have noted above, Chapter XVI, n. 12, that claims to have discovered in the record a predivisional Italo-Keltic unity may be due to a dialect, like Ligurian, in which Italic and Keltic elements are merely mixed. For a general and programmatic statement on linguistic expansion and diversification in time and place, see Pulgram 1957; on Italic and Keltic in particular, 246–247.

split up into Italic and Keltic any more than Latin gave birth to a Hispano-Portuguese unity that later split up into Spanish and Portuguese. This sort of thinking is derived, as I said before, from a biological view of the genealogical tree simile of linguistic relationships, a scheme that must not be understood in the sense of physical descent, whether its originator so intended it or not, but only as indicating relative chronology, namely, to give an example, that Italic was spoken earlier than Italian. All terms of family relationship (descent, mother language, daughter languages, inheritance) are purely metaphorical. It will be recalled that I said with reference to Proto-Indo-European (Chapter XIII) that the various Indo-European tongues developed from Proto-Indo-European through divergences caused by increasing distance in time and space between the different varieties, that is, are phenomena bound to, and caused by, their peculiar position in time and space, and that I rejected the theory that Proto-Indo-European contained severally the germs of the later Indo-European languages. If this principle has been accepted by the reader, then my theories concerning the differentiation and the differences of the ancient dialects of Italy must be equally unexceptionable because they constitute merely an extension of the same principle.

If one asked, therefore, whether the Italic and Latinian [25] dialects, and other dialects of ancient Italy constitute two or more different languages, or whether they are only dialects of the same language, we can truthfully answer that this is a "dispute about terms which have no precise scientific definition," [26] at least not in a synchronic sense. One might as well ask whether Russian and English and Dutch are dialects of the same language or different languages. Diachronically, historically viewed, all Indo-European languages are in fact dialects of the same proto-language, though I daresay that the diachronic use of the term dialect is somewhat unusual, and if an author chooses to employ it thus, the reader should be specifically forewarned.

[25] If I seem to have dealt with Latinian too briefly, the reason is that a fuller treatment follows in Chapter XIX.
[26] Palmer 1954, 6.

CHAPTER XVIII

Conclusions On the matter of the so-called Indo-European migrations I have in the preceding chapters propounded a very cautious, almost agnostic view, restricting myself to stating that speakers of Indo-European came to Italy, neither in closed migratory groups nor in large numbers, but through infiltration over a long period. At least this is the opinion which an unbiased consideration of the evidence recommends. "The complex solutions which derive from this must not frighten us. Once the mass migrations are eliminated and the process of Indo-Europeanization entrusted to small nuclei, no danger need be feared from the multiplicity of these nuclei." [1]

I have further rejected the theory that such infiltrations are due to the physical ancestors of ethnic or linguistic groups which can be recognized as such only much later.

A review and résumé of the possibilities suggested by various scholars might be instructive. Since these writers are not all incompetent, and since the records on which they build their theses are much the same, their differing conclusions are due either to varying emphasis on single features of the evidence, or to such shortcomings of the records themselves as must inevitably engender divergent interpretations.

The questions as to whether Indo-European speech was introduced in Italy by the Bronze Age Terramaricoli (Pigorini, Colini, Peet), or by the Iron Age Villanovans (Randall-MacIver, von Duhn), whether the Terramaricoli are autochthonous and the Villanovans 'Indoeuropeans' (Brizio), or whether both are Indo-European invaders (Pigorini, Helbig, Peet, Modestov, von Duhn), I have answered in the sense that neither of these cultural units seems to correspond wholly to a linguistic type, but that rather the cultures of the Terramaricoli and the Villanovans are due to the

[1] Devoto 1950, 184.

amalgamation of the 'autochthonous' with the imported cultural features, among the latter probably being Indo-European speech. This does not mean that *all* Terramaricoli and *all* Villanovans spoke Indo-European, and even less that they were 'Indo-Europeans,' just as it would be nonsense to claim that the inhabitants of Gaul after the Roman conquest all at once started speaking Latin or became 'Latins,' though their culture certainly became pervaded with Latinisms, as it were.

Therefore, I cannot persuade myself that the Terramaricoli were Protolatins, or the ancestors of the Latins (note the confusion of linguistic and cultural nomenclature), or that the Villanovans were the physical and linguistic forebears of the (Osco-)Umbrians.[2] Nor can I see much virtue in the hypothesis of two distinct mass invasions with the ancestors of the Latins arriving first (disregarding the problem whether they are Terramaricoli or Villanovans, or both, or neither), followed by the ancestors of the Osco-Umbrians[3] with the linguistic diversification taking place prior to their arrival, outside of Italy.[4]

The chronologies suggested for all these invasions are hopelessly discordant and irreconcilable, going as low as 2500 B.C. for the Latins (and Siculans) and 2300 B.C. for the Osco-Umbrians,[5] and as high as the end of the second millennium for the first, and the tenth century B.C. for the second.[6] Because of my own opinion I find least disagreeable the single invasion theory, which has Italici

---

[2] Modestov 1907, 235; Ducati 1928, 75; 1942, 27; Krahe 1937, 119–120.

[3] Modestov 1907, 236; Ducati 1928, 75; 1942, 27; Randall-MacIver, Forerunners, 1928, 27–34, but with this important difference: the first wave of invaders were Terramaricoli, or Proto-Italici, at the end of the thirteenth century B.C., the second were the "western cremators," that is, the Comacines, Villanovans, Atestines. Pisani 1931, 613 n. 2, 647; Krahe 1937, 119–120; Lejeune 1943, 15–16, with an excellent bibliography on the history of Italic theories; Laviosa-Zambotti 1948, 16–17; Altheim, Geschichte, 1951, 138–139; Römische, 1951, 150–154; Palmer 1954, 58.

[4] For an extreme and wholly improbable, and improvable, view see Bonfante 1937, 70: "The Latins separated in very ancient times from the other Indo-Europeans and passed many centuries, perhaps millennia, of autonomous life before presenting themselves, at the time of the tumults of the Gaulish invasion, in the light of history." See also Altheim, Geschichte, 1951, 150–154.

[5] Pisani 1931, 647. *Ibid.*, 613, he says that the following peoples *(N.B.)* are in Italy "not long after 2000 B.C.": Ligurians, Veneti, Umbrians, Oscan tribes, Latins, Messapians, Siculi. I should not commit myself to any such classification, in *these terms*, earlier than the fifth century B.C.

[6] Ducati 1928, 75.

(in the Indo-European sense, generally distinct from Illyrians) reach Italy in one migration, although scholars do not always agree on the time and the route. There may be northern invaders starting at the beginning of the Bronze Age,[7] or at the end of the Bronze Age,[8] or between 1200 and 1000 B.C.,[9] or toward the end of the second millennium B.C.,[10] or during the Iron Age;[11] or they may come across the Peartree Pass not before the turn of the millennium.[12]

However, the theory of slow, protracted infiltration like my own is also represented, and is most vigorously and persistently advocated by Patroni, except that, unfortunately and, to my mind, wrongly, Patroni's bringers of Indo-European speech all infiltrate across the Adriatic Sea, as early as the end of the Neolithic Age, and are by race 'Mediterraneans.'[13] Apart from this, I find most attractive in Patroni's view of the problem the thought that the later Italic peoples, culturally and linguistically, are local formations, that is to say, the result of the symbiosis of the original inhabitants (whom Patroni chooses to call Liguro-Siculan, and for whom I myself should have no ethnic name but only a nomenclature based on a variety of cultures) and the infiltrating foreigners.[14] In this mixture the native element possibly predominated physically, but the culture of the more advanced foreigners played a large part, thanks mainly to their metallurgical skills and a more integrated social organization, and the language of the newcomers superseded entirely the earlier dialects. Devoto makes much of this sociological point: even though the newcomers may be few, and poor, and even though they would not even need to be intellectually or technically advanced, "the fact that they have spread languages implies a solidity of social organization, a compactness of family nuclei, which cannot be explained by uncertain 'ferments' [Patroni's term] but by the effective presense of men who must be, though

---

[7] Piganiol 1917, 36–37.
[8] Randall-MacIver, Forerunners, 1928, 30–33: his Proto-Italici (see above).
[9] Altheim, in various places.
[10] Matz 1938.
[11] Lamboglia 1941, 76.
[12] Altheim 1941, I, chapter 1.
[13] Patroni 1940, 30–31; 1951, *passim.*
[14] Patroni 1940, 30–31; 1951, 472, and *passim.*

they be poor and few, organized." [15] But Devoto's requiring on this basis a mass migration not only contravenes the dictum that they may be "poor and few," but is also unnecessary. For the correctly postulated solidity and compactness was certainly a characteristic also of the original small groups like those of the *uer sacrum*, living among foreigners into whose districts they have come, and penetrating farther and farther among the aboriginal inhabitants; but no mass migration need be the precondition of such social solidarity. There is nothing strange in all this; it is exactly the way in which Gaul and Spain and Rumania and indeed Italy itself were eventually Latinized and Romanized.

I should therefore prefer not to see in the variety of the pre-Italic and Italic dialects a testimony of repeated invasions of closed units of speakers of Indo-European whose dialects had already become differentiated before they reached Italian soil, or of one single invasion which broke up in Italy because of a number of obstacles and varying traveling routes, thus giving rise to linguistic variegation, but to account for the diversity only as the natural and normal result of the gradual superimposition, in the course of centuries, of the same language, that is, Indo-European(it may be called Proto-Italic if that is convenient although 'same' here must be taken in a historical and not synchronic sense and does not exclude dialectal variations, about which of course we can know nothing) upon a variety of earlier dialects of Italy, many of which possibly, but not surely, belonged to another large linguistic family which some call Mediterranean.[16] There is nothing strange in all this either; to take again Gaul after Caesar's conquest for comparison, the Latin language (it may be called Proto-French if that is convenient though it was probably not a strictly uniform dialect but at best a koinë which may have varied according to the provenance of the imigrants) was superimposed upon a variety of local dialects, of which there were certainly more than one for each of Caesar's *partes tres*,[17] but all of which belonged, not possibly but surely, to the Keltic family; and out of those numerous linguistic combina-

---

[15] Devoto 1951, 67–68.
[16] For an opposition of Indo-European and Mediterranean culture, though with the use of a tribal and ethnic nomenclature I have rejected, see Piganiol 1917, 211–214, and *passim*.
[17] Whatmough 1949.

tions grew the dialects of Romanized Gaul and indeed ultimately, though of course after many shifts and variations, the modern dialects of France.

Although I have disagreed with Devoto and Pallottino in a number of details, I should in conclusion like to quote two general statements of theirs concerning the Indo-Europeanization of Italy, with which I wholly agree.

"The Indo-European expansion is not the result of violent episodes, warring enterprises, or sudden invasions, which would have left a memory in some epics; [18] rather is it a flow, at times fast, at other times slow, but uninterrupted and, one may say, unperceived. We remember of it only the crystallized and static phases, which we can distinguish from one another but not put in relation to one another in an unequivocal manner." [19]

"We have reproached the ancients so much for having invented founding heroes, like Romulus and Remus, or for having imagined the existence of fantastic peoples, like the Aborigines and the Pelasgians. But what should we say of a modern science which has created the 'Villanovan people' simply out of the fact that certain primitive tribes of Italy had in common a type of cinerary urn which was discovered for the first time at Villanova in Emilia? Or a science which, on the basis of resemblances of Latin with Oscan and Umbrian believed for a long time in the existence of an original 'Italic language,' whereas in truth the Italic unity is realized only by the coexistence of Indo-European peoples in Italy and by the spread of Latin? Or a science which invented, literally invented, an 'Indo-European culture' in Italy, while in truth the concept of Indo-European is a purely linguistic one and, as we know now, in no wise connected with the appearance and change of culture? *All these reconstructions, though they may seem more or less schematic and absurd in the face of the most recent advances of our studies, have nonetheless dominated our science for several decades, with a dogmatism which often verges on intolerance, leaving so deep an imprint in the procedures of research that even today, while we place against them new concepts, we are still subconsciously*

[18] Concerning other reasons for the absence of an Italic legendary epic, see above p. 160. (My footnote.)

[19] Devoto 1951, 93.

induced to use terms and expressions which were born of them and are derived from them." (Italics mine.) [20]

I may have wielded the pruning shears rather inexorably in order to lop off the wild growths of prehistoric reconstruction and onomastic charades, but not, I hope, too ruthlessly. Unfortunately, I have in many instances nothing to put in the place of the severed shoots of fancy; indeed I refrained from grafting my own imaginings upon branches just restored to health. Much of what some of us thought healthy sprouts of knowledge concerning the linguistic prehistory and protohistory of Italy were in many instances weeds pullulating chiefly upon premises which modern linguistic science vigorously rejects, namely, the arbitrary equation and correlation of race, culture, and language. The results of this method do not arise from a knowledge of facts but, conversely and perversely, they spawn imaginary facts. The procedure is further contaminated by the improper and specious dilatation of historically known quantities, cultural, linguistic, and onomastic, to cover prehistoric domains.

After this necessary pruning operation, our knowledge of the linguistic history of pre-Roman Italy, especially for the crucial period of the five centuries between 1000 and 500 B.C. may seem disappointingly meager. But this is due to an honest instead of a fanciful appraisal of the records as best I know how to perform it today. At what future date discoveries of unequivocal evidence, or a considerable refinement in methodology, or a yet closer collaboration and deeper interpenetration of the sciences of the anthropologist, ethnologist, sociologist, and linguist will lead us to new and greater insights it is impossible to foresee.

[20] Pallottino 1955, 21–22. See also Pallottino, Origini, 1955, with whom I agree fully on general statements concerning Italian prehistory and proto-history, especially as regards premises and methods, but not on all particulars. (I saw this work only after the completion of my manuscript, too late to refer to it and deal with it in detail.)

BOOK THREE
ROMAN ITALY

Part Five. The Latinization of Italy

CHAPTER XIX

The Proto-Latin Period   Among the various Iron
Age cultures we distinguished also the Villanovan culture, which
was divided conveniently into a Northern, a Tuscan, and a Latian
branch, the last two being often, though not quite correctly, combined under the name Southern Villanovan, with the Arno River
separating it from the Northern.[1] It was noted especially that we
cannot and must not speak of any 'Villanovans' in an ethnic sense,
or of a large-scale Villanovan immigration, although no doubt the
knowledge of ironworking, particularly in its Villanovan form,
was due to the influence of some foreigners who had penetrated
into Italy. It was further brought out that there are discernible
two prongs of Iron Age cultures on their way to Italy, one by the
continental route and from the north, the other by sea across the
Aegean, and that the two currents meet and overlap in the Tuscan-
Latian area. (It should also be noted that, judging by the small
quantity of Southern Villanovan finds in Latium, the bearers of
this culture were probably not numerous. It is more than unlikely
that supposed sites of the Aeneas legend in the Roman Campagna,
like Ardea and Lavinium, were actually occupied as early as the
time of the Trojan War, about 1200 B.C.[2] In fact, pre-Iron Age
finds are only sporadic in Latium, hence the population may have
been very sparse before about 1000 B.C.,[3] its subsequent increase
and prosperity being no doubt due, as usually in human societies,
to a general cultural improvement.) What language was the
property of the southern prong we do not know: most likely it

[1] While Randall-MacIver 1928, 68–70, retains the habitual division in Northern
and Southern Villanovan, he carefully distinguishes within the latter the con-
trasting areas of Etruria, between the Arno and Tiber rivers, and of Latium,
south of the Tiber.
[2] Laviosa-Zambotti 1947, 144, speaks of Latium as a melting pot. But her
identifying northern invaders as Ligurians, and southern as Sicani is, as we have
seen, meaningless.
[3] Whatmough 1937, 262–263.

was not Indo-European, but rather of the Mediterranean type; at least, if it was Indo-European, we have no records of it. As for the northern prong, we have concluded from a variety of what I trust are plausible reasons, that the language of the newcomers was Indo-European.

The earliest settlements of the Southern Villanovan culture must probably be dated in the eleventh century before Christ,[4] or not much later. We find them at Tolfa, a site in the hills of southern Etruria, and in various locations of the Alban Hills southeast of Rome. When the 'Etruscans' arrived from Asia Minor, they brought with them, as has been shown, an orientalizing type of Iron Age culture, which spread from Tuscany as its center. It also constituted a convenient bridge across which the Northern and Southern Villanovan cultures could further interact and fuse. At stations like Vetulonia or Tarquinia one can distinguish a pre-Etruscan Southern Villanovan culture which then is transformed, that is, raised in tone, by the Etruscan influx. We noted before that this state of affairs has indeed tempted some scholars, especially the autochthonists among the Etruscologists, to declare Villanovan and Etruscan identical. True enough, from the seventh century on it becomes impossible to discriminate clearly between the Etruscan and Villanovan cultures in Etruria; yet this it not so because originally they were the same or because the latter was obliterated by the former, but rather because of their fusion.

In Latium and in the Emilia, that is, at the outermost locations where the leveling Etruscan influence penetrates later, the difference between Northern and Southern Villanovan is more palpable. For example, as concerns burial modes, the stereotyped and immensely frequent biconical Emilian ossuary of handmade pottery was never used in Latium. There in its place we find various kinds of hut-shaped urns, the oldest round, the later, under Etruscan influence, oblong, manufactured of terracotta or bronze, which represent dwelling places for the deceased and are no doubt miniature reproductions of the homes of the living, with the round representing a style of house which persisted for several centuries.[5] Thus, the

---

[4] According to Randall-MacIver 1928, 66. Åberg 1930, 211–217, fixes the date a little before 750 B.C., which seems rather late.

[5] Randall-MacIver 1928, 67. According to Lake 1937, the later Roman house is a direct descendant of these Italic huts known to us from cinerary urns.

typical Aegean rite of inhuming the dead in funerary houses, which in Italy is most elaborately consummated in the grand chamber tombs, either hewn into the rock or accommodated in the man-made tumuli of the Etruscans at Tarquinia, Vulci, Caere, and other necropoles, is carried over and adapted to the cremating rite, by which, instead of the whole corpse, only its ashes are placed in a house of reduced size.

Also the tomb furniture is quite different south and north of the Apennines, the pottery in particular. Latian Iron Age pottery has an indigenous, conservative, Mediterranean character, whereas that of Northern Villanovan Bologna is more innovative. The reason for this may again be sought in the fact that Italy south and east of the Tiber had always been oriented toward the east. Aegean imports, therefore, even though their appearance in quantity heralds a new civilization — that of the Iron Age — are not as foreign and novel to the area as are transalpine Iron Age imports in the north.

In Latium, on the very spot which was later to become the Roman Forum, we not only find the amalgamation of the northern and southern Iron Age, but we also discover in the inhumation burials older traces of the pre-Iron Age civilization. About the turn of our century, on the Forum, near the temple of Antoninus and Faustina, along the *Via Sacra*, a number of graves were un-earthed of both the inhuming and cremating type, that is, so-called *fossa* 'trench,' and *pozzo* 'pit' tombs, respectively.[6] Since I rejected the theory of inhuming and cremating Italici, I shall not propose that the two kinds of tombs are witnesses to two types of invasions: first the cremating then the inhuming Italici, that is, in Rome; first the 'Protolatini,' then the 'Protoitalici.' (The nomenclature is confusing: it reflects, and contributes to, the uncertainty of the whole set of theories.) I rather believe that the inhumation burials of Latium, including those of Rome, are the continuation of an older culture, just as is the inhumation practiced in southern Italy and along the Adriatic (Picene) coast. I say this without any ethnic or racial prejudice as to who was buried in any of these tombs. Of course, it is not impossible that the inhumation burials of the Roman Forum may be ascribed to the ancestors of the people who later appear as 'Sabines' or 'Sabellians,' and the cremating graves to those

[6] Boni 1902 ff.

of the later '(Proto-)Latins.' In fact, it appears that Roman families of Sabine antecedents clung for a long time to inhumation. The legendary second king of Rome, Numa Pompilius (traditionally 717–673 B.C.), a citizen of Cures, hence a Sabine, (the *p*- of his name, as in *Pompeius, popina* 'kitchen,' in distinction from latin *c* or *qu*, as in *Quintus, coquina*, is also a clue to his, or at least his name's, non-Latin origin) allegedly wished to be buried after his death, not cremated like his predecessor Romulus, a Latian. The members of the famous noble families of the Valerii, Claudii, and Cornelii (among whom the Scipios), all of Sabine origin according to tradition, were buried. (The inscriptions on the sarcophagi of the Scipios are historically and linguistically important documents.) Sulla was the first Cornelius to be cremated. Cicero[7] and Pliny[8] are not wrong, as von Duhn says they are,[9] when they claim that the oldest Roman burial rite is inhumation, as long as 'Roman' is used in a geographic and not political or linguistic sense. Nor does the belief of some, that the inhumation *fosse* of the Forum cemetery seem younger than the cremation *pozzi*, alter the picture. The area of Rome, like the rest of Latium and Italy, *was* an inhuming district and eventually became a mixed or cremating one. That we do not know with certainty how to classify these early inhumers ethnically or linguistically, has nothing to do with the archaeological facts.

The peaceful meeting of the two rites on the soil of Rome is further attested by a provision of the ancient law code of the Twelve Tables, of the fifth century B.C., which prescribes that both inhumation and cremation are prohibited within the city.[10] The Romans of the Republic also practiced both cults.

But, although with the cremation and inhumation tombs of Latium and the Sabine Hills we have come very close to the threshold of history (in particular, the sites in the area of the city of Rome are no older than the eighth century), and, although the historical evidence is fairly clear in ascribing the first kind of burials to the Latians and the second to the Sabines, I believe we should even in this case refrain from speaking of prehistoric in-

[7] Cic. *de leg.* 2.22–23.
[8] Plin. *N.H.* 7.187.
[9] von Duhn 1924, 427–430.
[10] Quoted by Cic. *de leg.* 2.22–23.

huming Sabines and cremating Latians, or Latins, especially if this view leads us back to a hypothesis of two kinds of invading Italici, inhuming and cremating. It is altogether possible, indeed the evidence renders it probable, that speakers of Indo-European observed two different burial rites in neighboring regions, without their coming in two different ethnic thrusts, each speaking a different dialect. If inhuming was, as it appears to have been, the rite of pre-Indo-European Italy, then some speakers of Indo-European, regardless of when they came and what dialect they spoke, appropriated this rite for themselves, for a variety of possible and easily imaginable though unknown cultural reasons. On the other hand, other speakers of the same or other Indo-European dialects managed, again for a number of equal cultural reasons, to impose not only their dialect but also their funerary custom upon the older stratum of population. We do not really know, because we do not and cannot have the complete evidence, to what degree in the first instance the newcomers and in the second instance the natives gave up their original practice, but we do note a cultural mixing in this respect. Since the inhuming area will be before long identifiable as the home of non-Latinian Sabine or Sabellian, and the cremating area as that of Latinian dialects, it is indeed tempting, in view of the briefness of the chronological gap, to equate for once the earlier cultural with the later linguistic evidence. I shall not do this, as a matter of principle, although I may be overly cautious.[11]

We have, then, in the melting pot of the Latian plain and its surrounding hills a meeting and mingling of various Iron Age

[11] Antonielli 1929, 37, and Scott 1929, 29, assert that most inhumation graves are on the Esquiline Hill, which undoubtedly was a location of Sabine, that is, Italic, non-Latinian speech. But it seems that even here there is room for the contrary interpretation of the record. Pallottino 1940, 291, for example, suggests that the Proto-Latini (among whom, by the way, he then included the Ausonians, Opici, Oenotrians, and Siculi, but some of whom, I am certain, he would call fantastic today), who were speakers of Latin, were the bearers of the inhuming or *fossa* culture. If he uses Proto-Latin merely in a linguistic sense then he is probably correct to the extent that surely some speakers of Proto-Latin inhumed their dead, notably those who had retained this as their native rite although they had accepted an Indo-European tongue. But if he implies, as I think that he does, that the Proto-Latini were an ethnic invading group, one of whose characteristics was inhumation, then he is wrong, I believe, for no such group can be identified from the records at our disposal, hence no known culture can be its peculiar property.

cultures and of native (Mediterranean) dialects with Indo-European imports.

What is true, to my mind, of the formation of other ancient dialects of Italy applies also to Latinian. It is a dialect, or a group of related dialects, which was not imported ready-made by hordes of migrating 'Villanovans' or 'Terramaricoli,' nor was it the movable and moved property of Latins, or Protolatins, who came as a ready-made unit from the Proto-Indo-European *Urheimat* to occupy their historic seats in Latium.[12] Latinian is an idiom which grew peculiarly and uniquely in Latium, out of the Indo-European seeds carried south by relatively few invaders of Iron Age civilization but of unknown race, and implanted upon a native linguistic substratum of which we know little except that it possibly was 'Mediterranean.' Latins, or Protolatins, can therefore be found, as speakers of Latin or Protolatin, not in the Indo-European homeland, not at intermediate points in Emilia and elsewhere, but only in Latium.[13] In the same way, Frenchmen, as speakers of French, or of Protofrench, can be found at home between 500 B.C. and A.D. 1900 not in Latium, not at intermediate spots between Rome and Paris, in the Piedmont or elsewhere in Italy, but only in France. (And in recent French colonies and overseas possessions.)

We find, then, in Latium and southern Etruria an Iron Age culture which, according to its appearance, may be classified as Villanovan, or rather a mixture of what is commonly called Northern and Southern Villanovan. We also conclude, on the strength of the circumstantial evidence available, that after the turn of the millennium Indo-European types of speech were brought to the region, carried by the persons who represent the Northern Villanovan civilization. Out of this fusion grew the typical Latian Iron Age

[12] Bonfante 1939, 86, thinks so, and even relates a date and circumstances: "The Latins detached themselves from the central kernel *before* the other Indo-European peoples (we now can fix the date: some centuries before the year 2000): they conserve an archaic language and culture." See also Bonfante 1934, 300. Bonfante, being an areal linguist, must see in Latin, because of its marginal position in relation to the Proto-Indo-European *Urheimat*, a conservative and archaic dialect and can explain what he considers the conservative and archaic features of Latin as due to its marginal position. I have said elsewhere (Pulgram 1956, 414–415) why I consider the tenets of areal linguistics inapplicable in this instance.

[13] And not before the tenth or ninth century B.C., so that, if and when Aeneas landed after his flight from Troy, according to Virgil, near the mouth of the Tiber, his scouts could not have reported that the land belonged to the 'Latins.'

culture and the typical Latian kinds of Indo-European dialects which we call Latinian. Of the latter we have, needless to say, no records from this early stage.

One of the preferred locations of this civilization seems to have been that of the Alban Hills region. It offered numerous good defensive positions, the volcanic soil on the slopes and in the lowlands was fertile, water was plentiful (apart from springs and creeks there were also Lake Albano and Lake Nemi, filling the craters of extinct volcanoes), and the sea was not too far (though the Latians of the Iron Age do not seem to have been great seafarers). Other good sites in Latium were those later known as Tibur, Praeneste, Ardea, Gabii, Satricum, Lavinium, all south of the Tiber, and Veii, Caere, Tarquinia, Vulci, north of the river in later Etruscan territory. All of them stand a few miles inland, because the coastline was probably swampy, and all chose an easily defensible spot on a height between streams, or on a wedge of high ground between two confluent streams. Different from this topographic pattern (see Chapter XX) was a hilly site at the Tiber, near a place where the river could be traversed more easily because an island divided it into two narrow branches. Tradition has it that the powerful Latian city of Alba Longa, situated on the narrow ridge above the Alban Lake, possibly where today the town of Castel Gandolfo stands, sent colonists, perhaps one of the customary *uer sacrum* contingents, to occupy that inviting and strategically important station down by the river, only fourteen miles away. And the archaeological evidence not only does not contradict tradition but indeed supports it: the oldest Latian finds at the Tiber location can easily be derived from the Alban Hills.[14] There, on the hills by the Tiber, was to be Rome.

[14] Scott 1929, 24–29.

CHAPTER XX

The Origins of Rome   It is odd to find some scholars arguing that the origin and the history of Rome owe nothing to the natural advantages of the site.[1] The contrary is so obvious, as a glance at good physical maps of Italy and Latium will show.[2] The city came to lie partly on isolated hence easily defended hills (Aventine, Capitoline, Palatine), partly on mountain spurs (Quirinal, Viminal, Esquiline, Caelius) enclosing on three sides the low area of the Forum. The spurs are really continuations of the high-lying Sabine hinterland, an important fact that should be borne in mind. The entire area is situated close by the Tiber, the most important river of peninsular Italy, at a spot where an island divides the broad stream. Since the depth of the stream so near its mouth and the rapidity of the current make fording impossible, bridges are necessary for crossing it, and it is an easier engineering problem to build two short bridges connecting either bank with the island instead of one long one. Traffic between the regions north and south of the middle and lower course of the Tiber was therefore naturally funneled toward the island crossing. It may also be assumed that, because of different conditions of the watershed and the heavier forestation along the length of the Tiber and its tributaries, the river was in antiquity a less changeable water course, navigable for ships of moderate size over a longer stretch than it is today, hence an important waterway. But land traffic from the east to the west of the Italian boot also must willingly have followed the valley of the Tiber from its origins in the mountains of Umbria down to the sea. This was, perhaps, the line of the very ancient Via Salaria, along which salt from the beds in the neighborhood of Ostia (a city of later foundation, not archae-

[1] So Strabo 5.3.2, 7.
[2] Fraccaro 1926.

ologically discernible before the end of the fourth century B.C.[3]) was carried upstream and inland. Thus, Rome grew at the crossing of two most important roads. This fortunate situation even made up for the handicap of considerable distance from the sea and the lack of a good harbor. (In fact, to this day, despite the valiant efforts of the emperors Claudius and Trajan, Rome does not have a port. Just as modern liners anchor at Naples, so ancient shipping sought shelter in the nearby bay of Puteoli, modern Pozzuoli. The west coast of Italy from La Spezia to Gaeta is singularly devoid of harbors, and even the most important landing places of the seafaring Etruscans, Graviscae and Pyrgi, the ports of Tarquinia and Caere, respectively, could have been little more than convenient stretches of shore on which boats of modest proportions could be beached.)

I mentioned that the site of Rome was different from that of other places which may have borne Iron Age and later proto-historic settlements.[4] In fact, in comparison with Ardea, Alba Longa, Veii, and Tarquinia, the location may well be considered inferior (it certainly is a nightmare for the modern city planner). Perhaps it is for this reason that some recent historians have disclaimed all natural advantages: the place is all buttes and a pell-mell of low hills (the highest rises less than 300 feet), surrounding one swampy flat (the later Forum), and bordered by others along the river (the later vegetable and meat markets). But this picture corresponds to an unfavorable urbanistic reality only if we contemplate the site as occupied by *one* city — Rome. Instead of this, however, we had better imagine that the isolated hills and the spurs were in prehistory occupied by a number of settlements, that each height was crowned by its own village. And, seen in this manner, singly and not connected within a larger whole, each settlement becomes again an example of the normal Latian and Etruscan type of hilltop town. It so happened that on this particular site near the Tiber, which was so valuable for traffic and trade and communications, a number of elevations were available in close propinquity,

[3] Tilly 1947, 14–15.
[4] Cf. Cary 1949, 130–133. I am adopting in the following description of the site of Rome and its development, to some extent the views and ideas expressed by Frank E. Brown, in two lectures, which I heard at the University of Michigan (in the spring of 1954) and at the American Academy in Rome (in the fall of 1954). See also the comparison of Rome and Ardea in Van Buren 1936, 43–44.

and a number of communities chose severally such convenient and pleasant situations.

The subsequent history of the locality is one of consolidation, of unification of the modest villages around the swampy hollow into a city; it was not, as tradition has it, the rise and spread of one single, founded city.[5]

According to the archaeological record available thus far, all the small villages begin somewhere around the eighth century, but all stop functioning and growing as individual settlements in the sixth century: this is the date at which they are incorporated into a single town. It is then that the Forum cemetery ceases to be used; it is covered up, the whole marshy area is drained, and stone buildings are constructed in what had hitherto been unusable no man's land.[6] Thus the Forum was begun, not accidentally but deliberately and designedly, as the commercial and administrative and religious center of something — which could only be the united villages of the surrounding hills. The date of this historical event of the first order would fall into the period of the Etruscan kings, possibly of Servius Tullius (578–535 B.C.), to whom tradition assigns other reforms of extraordinary importance also.[7] It is only fitting that the event should take place under the aegis of an Etruscan ruler, during the Etruscan domination of the district, if one considers that the evolution of the organized city and of urban life in Italy was due to the Etruscans, who came, as most scholars believe, from a part of the ancient world — the Near East — in which a highly integrated urbanism had been instituted long since, whereas in Italy this type of social organization remained unknown until their arrival and that of the Greeks. Only from that date on, then, in the early or middle sixth century B.C., a single name for the entire locality is justified. We might call it Rome, but without prejudice

[5] I shall not compare and match in detail the tradition and the real history of earliest Rome; this may be learned from various books mentioned in the bibliography, and it can be conveniently found in Showerman 1924, Part II, chapters 2, 3 (though it must be noted that discoveries of the past three decades have altered some details). For a résumé of legends concerning the foundations of Rome, see Cardinali 1949, 7–17 (the remainder of the book may be ignored).

[6] It is significant that Lugli 1937, finds the oldest centers of 'Rome' to have been, not the later Forum Romanum site, but the Forum Boarium and the Forum Holitorium, the later meat and vegetable markets, respectively, situated also at the foot of the Capitoline hill, but to the west, on the Tiber.

[7] Gjerstad 1952, 63.

as to its real name at the time. And before that date one should not speak of Romans, except in the vague and noncommittal sense of dwellers in an area which eventually was to become Rome. The legendary date of 753 B.C. can therefore not refer to the 'foundation' of Rome but at best, if it has any meaning at all, to the origin of the Latian, or Latin village upon the Palatine. That the Latin speech of these settlers should come to predominate over all the others may possibly be grounds for seeing in them the earliest 'Romans.' But this name does not permit any conclusions on the ethnic composition of the Romans whom we know in history.

I have emphasized the convergence toward the Latian plain of two major types of Iron Age cultures (Northern and Southern Villanovan), the meeting of two funeral rites in the region, and the occupation of the hills of Rome by speakers of two major kinds of Indo-European speech, Italic (in the narrower sense) and Latinian. But I want to stress again that these various phenomena should not be paired off against one another in such a way that the Italici are inhuming Northern Villanovans, speaking Osco-Umbrian, and the Latins cremating Southern Villanovans, speaking Latin, or in any other manner which, to suit someone's idea of orderliness, exceeds the present limits of our knowledge, or contradicts the evidence.

About the race of the Iron Age inhabitants of Latium and the Roman hills nearly all that is known has already been said in the preceding chapters. At best one can assume, though not distinguish in the physical remains, a native stock and newcomers. The native race may have been 'pure' in the sense that it had inhabited the region sufficiently long and in sufficient isolation to develop a somatic type, though we have no proof of this. As for the new arrivals, they could not have been 'Italici' (of one or two or more racial varieties), nor 'Indo-Europeans,' nor 'Nordics,' because the first two of these terms are meaningful only with reference to language, the third certainly makes no sense in Italy, if it does anywhere. We shall have to return to the matter of these alleged Latian races in the discussion of patricians and plebeians of republican Rome.

The languages spoken in Latium may have been to begin with dialects of the Mediterranean variety, and if this term is not evocative of precisely identifiable idioms and grammars the fault lies with the complete unavailability of records. If it is true, as it appears to be, that Latium, perhaps all of Italy, was rather thinly settled before the Iron Age, and that communications were poor, then we may also believe that these local Mediterranean dialects were rather different from one another, even within a small area. And if this is so, then one can easily understand why the Indo-European speech, which was superimposed on them, and which, owing to different local origins (from many successive hearths of *uer sacrum* movements?) and diverse dates of arrival in new locations, was not uniform at the time of its acceptance by various groups of natives, should appear in such divergent shapes, even in the records of a relatively late period, after the local idioms had already undergone a few centuries of convergent development. On the whole, the Italic dialects (not tribes!) move southward along the center of the peninsula, either from old Umbrian centers or, less probably, after import across the Adriatic, whereas the Latinian dialects must have reached Latium earlier and were practically encircled there by Italic and, later, Etruscan. On the site of Rome, this duality shows itself in that the highland spurs reaching out toward the Forum (Quirinal, Viminal, Esquiline) were most likely occupied by speakers of Italic, whereas the Palatine and the Capitoline, perhaps also the Aventine, all on the other side of the Forum, were in the hands of speakers of Latinian who had reached the Tiber from the Alban Hills.

The people who appear in the records as Sabines, occupying the tongues of high plain and the hinterland north of the Forum, are next to the Etruscans the most important non-Latin element in Rome's protohistory. According to what I have said, the Sabines are of Italic speech, and there are in the Latin language a number of words whose phonetic shape can only be explained by Italic, that is, in the case of Rome, Sabine provenance, since they follow Italic rather than Latin soundlaws in their development from Proto-Indo-European. They are very common, ordinary words (*lupus* 'wolf,' *popina* 'kitchen,' *bos* 'ox,' *lacruma* 'tear,' *consul*, *infernus* 'lowest,' *scrofa* 'sow,' and many others [8]), which shows

---

[8] On the rare occasions when I quote linguistic forms I shall not bother to give specific references: the story can be found easily in all handbooks and historical grammars, of which I cite some in the bibliography.

that we must be dealing with a thorough and everyday social mixture of the speakers of the two dialects.[9] Perhaps the ancient formulae *populus Romanus Quiritium* and *populus Romanus Quiritesque* are also an indication of the close synoikismus of Sabines and Romans, if Paulus (ex Festus 47) is correct, as I believe he is, in equating *quiritibus* with *Curensibus*, the latter being the inhabitants of the most powerful Sabine city, Cures.[10]

However, there is no unanimity as to what hills were occupied by the speakers of Latin and what hills by the speakers of Sabine Italic. My own proposal above took into account the geographic location (and others add also the type of burials). But it has also been suggested that the Palatine should be paired with the neighboring Esquiline as Latin possession, the Capitoline with the neighboring Quirinal as Sabine possession. The Capitoline and the Palatine, being solitary hills, accordingly represented the acropolises of the two settlements where people would take refuge in times of attack, whereas upon their adjunct spurs of the highlands, the Quirinal and the Esquiline, respectively, arose the cities proper.[11] This arrangement of acropolis, or *arx*, on an elevation of smaller surface or at the tip of a spur, and of the city in a more commodious area is indeed the plan according to which many ancient Latian cities (Veii, Vulci, Ardea, Lanuvium, Praeneste, Tibur, Gabii, Signia, and others) were laid out. (At other places, where the natural configuration of the terrain does not permit this plan, the acropolis is merely the highest point within the city, as at Setia, Norba, Antium, Ferentinum.) Whatever the truth, in Rome we must almost certainly look for the earliest Latin settlement on the Palatine.[12]

[9] Goidanich 1929, *passim*, ascribes to the Sabine elements of ancient Rome so much political power that they imposed a condominium, but such a small number that they did not replace the Latin language with their own.

[10] Ribezzo 1930, 62. Could the ancient *S P Q R* then stand for *Senatus Populus Quiritium Romanorum* or the like? For a complete but not altogether convincing rejection of such Sabine theories see Dumézil 1944, 151–165.

[11] Scott 1929, 18–19; Lugli 1937, 380–381.

[12] Puglisi 1951. Tradition seems correct here again, for it reports that Romulus founded Rome upon the Palatine. Indeed on the slope facing the valley of the Circus Maximus, away from the Forum, the foundations of an Iron Age hut (holes dug into the rock to hold the upright poles that supported the walls, and a drainage ditch around the hut) are known, romantically but spuriously, as the 'House of Romulus.' I shall omit a discussion of the traditional four stages in the development of old Rome: Roma quadrata, the Septimontium, the City of the Four Regions, and the Servian City. The legendary has not yet been fully win-

This is of some importance for the linguistic history of Rome because it allows us to consider the Palatine Hill as the center from which Latin spread over the other Roman hills. It was this Palatine Latin which, mixed with Sabine elements, became the speech of the city of Rome, which in turn superseded the other Latin dialects of Latium (not without, in the rural districts, assuming a particular local coloring, a *rusticitas* which the Romans of the capital soon decried as uncouth) and eventually all the Italic and non-Italic dialects of Italy. I emphasize that the standard Latin of Italy during the Republic and the Empire was, in its written form, the Latin of Rome, and not that of Praeneste, or Falerii, or any other less prominent town. Roman was the model for Latin as, centuries later, Florentine became the model for Italian.

Of the various non-Roman Latinian dialects we have but scant records: a handful of inscriptions (indeed the earliest known Latinian inscription, on the so-called Fibula Praenestina, comes from Praeneste, modern Palestrina), provincialisms due to non-Roman scribes or stonemasons which might be noticeable in early Roman and Latian documents, and the more durable borrowings (like the Sabine) that are still alive in Classical Latin but so much assimilated that they yield the secret of their non-Roman origin only to the comparative linguist.

But we are better informed in regard to Faliscan. Of course we do not possess Faliscan evidence of sufficient antiquity to teach us anything about the oldest form of the dialect. But the extant remains show clearly at least that Faliscan was a Latinian dialect,[13] though this does of course not allow us to infer, as some writers did,[14] that the 'Latins' and the 'Faliscans' are ethnically related. (The predominant funeral rite in Faliscan country in the seventh

---

nowed from the factual, and besides, little is to be learned from the problem as concerns the linguistic history. But I should like to call attention to Holland 1953, where a good case is made for Septimontium as having nothing to do with *septem montes* 'seven hills' but being derived from *saepti montes* 'the fenced in hills.' (On the other hand, just one year earlier, Gjerstad 1952, 63, had declared the Septimontium an historic reality. See also Bloch 1946, 56–58.) In fact, the number of Roman hills can be seven as well as five, or nine, or eleven, depending on how one counts: is the Velia a hill? does the Esquiline consist of three heights (Oppius, Fagutal, Cespius) or is it one? should the isolated Aventine be counted among or omitted from the hills of Rome? (See Beloch 1926, 203).

[13] Pisani 1953, 332.
[14] Deecke 1888, 20–22.

and sixth centuries B.C. was, by the way, inhumation and not cremation.[15]) The Romans conquered the Faliscan capital, Falerii, as early
as 241 B.C. and dealt severely with it by removing it from its nearly
impregnable position (where stands high on a towering cliff, the
modern Civita Castellana) to a site in the plain, a few miles away,
of which the somnolent remnants and the mighty walls can still be
seen. The Romans thought this inclemency necessary because
the Faliscans had in the course of centuries become altogether too
profoundly assimilated, in culture and to some extent in language,
by the Etruscans, whom the Romans considered the ever-menacing
archenemy of their state. Being political realists, the Romans
worried little about their 'blood brothers' to the north who spoke
nearly the same language, but ruthlessly proceeded to crush what
threatened to become an Etruscanized enemy not far from Rome
in a position to sever the important Via Flaminia and to block the
Tiber.

What was, then, the relationship of the Latians to the Etruscans
in the earliest times? The Etruscans must have established themselves as the lords of Etruria not long after the Iron Age settlements
on the hills of Rome had started their primitive lives, and they
surely brought with them, as we have seen, a civilization far superior
to the one that existed in the crude round cottages of wattle and
daub, of wood and reeds, that speckled the heights above the Tiber.
It was inevitable that the Etruscans and the Italians should in some
way, peacefully or otherwise, come to grips.[16]

It has been established that Campania, with Capua as its capital,
was Etruscanized from the late seventh and early sixth century on
more thoroughly than Latium, and that the Etruscans maintained
until the beginning of the sixth century communications between
their Etrurian and later acquired Campanian possessions by a road
which led, not over the shortest and easiest distance through Latium,
crossing the Tiber at Rome, but along the slopes of the Apennines
bordering the plain, by way of Fidenae, Gabii, and Praeneste.[17]

Geographically this is a paradox which can historically best
be explained by the fact that even in those early days the Latinian

[15] Holland 1925, 129.
[16] For a detailed history of the Etruscans in Italy see Pallottino 1955.
[17] Frank 1927, 22.

tribes were strong and united enough to oppose a foreign enemy. Even if they were not politically allied in a modern sense they were in some measure made aware of their relatedness by a common Latian religious festival of the *Iuppiter Latiaris* which, as I mentioned, took place annually on the summit of the Alban Mount (now Monte Cavo) and in which, according to tradition, as many as forty-seven Latinian towns participated by the end of the sixth century. And of course their unity of language above all must have instilled in them a sense of community and concord.

In Rome, this is the age of the kings (from Romulus, 753 B.C., to the expulsion of Tarquinius Superbus in 509 B.C.). Their names (Romulus, Numa Pompilius, Tullus Hostilius, Ancus Martius, Lucius Tarquinius Priscus, Servius Tullius, Tarquinius Superbus) may be legendary, and so may the dates of their reigns (each would have occupied the throne an average of nearly thirty-five years, which is incredibly long), but there is no doubt in the minds of modern historians that there is a core of truth in the sagas of their regime. Of the last three kings, the Tarquinii were certainly Etruscans, Servius Tullius was probably also. Now, since there are several Etruscan kings in Rome from the sixth century on, one should suppose that the site of Rome, and with it perhaps tracts of Latium, had been conquered by the Etruscans and were under their domination. But if by conquest and domination one were to understand an invasion by Etruscans and a subsequent, at least temporary Etruscanization, one would get the wrong picture entirely. For the record of realia, archaeological and linguistic, does in no wise warrant the conclusion that any part of Latium became truly and fully Etruscan in any sense of the word. While it is perhaps exaggerated to claim that Rome remained, despite the reign of the Tarquins, a purely Latin city in language, religion, and customs,[18] it is also easy to magnify disproportionately the weight and the strength of the Etruscan element. Nonetheless, and this seems an even greater paradox, it is not wrong to say that Rome owes to the Etruscans possibly its name, and probably its existence. How is this to be understood?

When speaking of the earlier kings we should not be misled by

[18] Beloch 1926, 227. For a catalogue of Etruscana in Rome see Whatmough 1937, 274–275.

the regal sound of the title; it was hardly appropriate for the rulers of the primitive hamlets populated by shepherds and peasants of which I have spoken. Moreover, the name Rome was inappropriate before the beginning of the sixth century, since until then the villages on the various heights were largely autonomous settlements. Hence the earliest 'kings of Rome,' Romulus and his two followers (I am employing here the traditional names *in lieu* of whatever they stand for in reality), were most likely no more than the chieftains of the burg on the Palatine.

When I spoke of the association of the villages I mentioned that their coalescence probably was due to Etruscan influence, occurring possibly under Servius Tullius, the next to the last king, whose reigning period is traditionally given as 578–535 B.C. He and his Etruscan predecessor and successor, the Tarquinii, seem to have been, not generals of an invading army, but rather condottieri, freebooters, who settled among the backward hill folk on the Tiber and made themselves their lords and masters. To accomplish this and to attain the coveted prize in such a semi-peaceful manner was perhaps easier than to gain it by force of arms alone. Indeed tradition relates that Tarquinius Priscus was elected by the people, and it does not seem impossible that a strong-willed rich man, representing a superior culture, should win great honors among the simple Latian homesteaders even though he was a foreigner.

Servius Tullius is often described as the father of the Roman constitution. To him are due, as the story reports, the division of the people in five classes according to wealth for purposes of the census and voting, which in fact initiated the plutocratic republican order that is the key to the history of the early Roman republic. (But the names of the previous three tribes of nobles, each including ten *curiae*, which survived as the names of cavalry units of the Roman army, were certainly also Etruscan: *Ramnes, Tities, Luceres.*[19]) Servius Tullius allegedly built the strong Servian wall which bears his name and which, since it encloses in its circuit Palatine, Capitoline, Quirinal, Viminal, Esquiline, Caelius, and Aventine, would testify to the unification of the entire site into a city, a social organization hitherto unknown in Italy. Now

[19] A discussion of these tribes, with further references, in Piganiol 1917, 244–252.

the Forum occupies the center of the new large town, and it is forthwith drained by the last king, Tarquinius Superbus, and made usable by means of a vast canal, the *cloaca maxima*, tracts of which are still visible and in use, and which is obviously of Etruscan workmanship. A temple is built on the Capitoline hill to *Iuppiter Optimus Maximus*, in which the divine triad of Jupiter, Juno, and Minerva was worshiped by all Romans of all the hills.

The archaeological evidence therefore supports the tradition of a regal period of Rome, but in addition it makes it plausible that Rome was founded, not by Romulus, but in a sense, by an Etruscan ruler.

But there is also linguistic support for this theory. The name of the city, though difficult to explain, seems best derived from some Etruscan word. Several choices have been proposed, for example, *rumon* 'river' (attested as the ancient name of the Tiber[20]); an Etruscan family named *Ruma* (compare the *gens Romilia, Romulia* of Rome).[21] A fair number of Latin words have their etyma in Etruscan, and some features of Latin phonology and sound change are due to Etruscan influence.

It is not surprising that the Etruscans of Rome formed something of an aristocracy among the Latin and Sabine population. Etruscan lords ruled in the manner in which the great families of the Medici, Gonzaga, Este, and others governed their Italian Renaissance towns as uncrowned monarchs and with all the appurtenances of sovereign dynasties. And I have argued elsewhere that the Roman institution of family names, which is an onomastic device otherwise unknown in Indo-European languages up to that time, is an imitation by Romans of an originally Etruscan institution whereby social rank and class were expressed: those who had a family name had also a family worth mentioning, that is, they were of noble descent.[22]

[20] Serv. *ad Verg. Aen.* 8.63, 90; Lugli 1943, 12.

[21] Schulze 1904, 579–582. Migliorini 1929, 430, rejects the Etruscan etymon on the grounds that Rome is an Italic foundation. In a certain sense, as we have seen, Rome is an Etruscan foundation and could therefore well bear an Etruscan name.

[22] Pulgram 1948. Dion. Hal. 2.7.4 tells us that during the regal period, when the kings called the people to a meeting, only the members of the (implicitly noble) *gentes* were called by their own and their fathers' names, that is, by a *nomen gentile*; ordinary folk had no family name. Perhaps also the increasing complexity of civil administration of the growing city and the state necessitated the indication of family relationships by means of a fixed hereditary nomenclature.

There is sufficient and convincing evidence, then, that at the beginning or toward the middle of the sixth century the hill villages were consolidated, under the aegis of Etruscan rulers, into the city of Rome, which, however, never became an Etruscan city, despite the strong Etruscanizing influences to which it was exposed. By the end of the sixth century, Rome was larger than other cities of Latium and Etruria, excepting possibly Veii, and it surely had become as important a city as the legends claim. It is also not surprising that its inhabitants, who were overwhelmingly non-Etruscan in speech and allegiance, should in the end become conscious of their national character and expel a foreign ruler, especially one who had made himself a hated tyrant. And even if it were not true that his son violated the chaste Lucretia, who killed herself, which according to tradition was the spark that exploded the latent resentment, the legend is nonetheless indicative of the antagonism between the town and its master. So Tarquinius was allegedly driven into exile by Lucius Iunius Brutus, and Rome became a city-state with a republican form of government, presided over by two consuls, of whom the first were Collatinus, the husband of the abused Lucretia, and Brutus, the revolutionary, the ancestor of the Brutus who four and a half centuries later struck down Caesar, another tyrant accused of wishing to strangle that republic.

Since we have no direct evidence on the linguistic conditions during the monarchic age of Rome, we can only draw certain not too precise conclusions on it from whatever scraps of social and economic history we know. The outstanding feature of early Roman society was the unconciliatory and severe split into two classes: the patricians and the plebeians, the aristocrats and the commoners, the virtual rulers of the state and the followers. This political and social cleavage was not characteristic of Rome alone but appeared as well in other Italian cities and also in Greek city-states at a comparable stage of development.

The patricians (*patricii*, since they were themselves *patres* 'senators' or descendants of senators) owed their power to their wealth, chiefly in landholdings, their ability to equip themselves better than the plebeians for war (each citizen had to arm himself at his own expense without subvention by the state, until the war against Etruscan Veii, early in the fifth century, when payment to soldiers was first made because of the length of the siege) and thereby to render the state greater service, and their social organization into powerful clans (*gentes*). They also profited greatly from their clients (*clientes*) who owed them services on their lands, support in politics, and aid in battle, for which the patricians in turn guarded the interests and protected the lives of the clients. The clients themselves, whose position was, like that of their lords, hereditary and immutable (the origins of this rigid relationship are unknown, but it reappears independently in mediaeval feudalism between the lord and the villains), formed a considerable portion of the plebeians.

The plebeians, however, were not all poor and unfree. Yet, although they may have possessed some land, or be prosperous craftsmen, shopkeepers, and laborers, they were not allowed to be members of the senate or participate directly in the burdens and privileges of the city's administration; that is to say, they could not hold magistracies and elective offices. They were permitted as voting members of the *Comitia Curiata*, the assemblies of all men able to bear arms (there were thirty *curiae*, ten for each of the old *tribus*, or electoral wards), dealing with matters of interest to the community (granting of citizenship, testaments, adoptions, declarations of war, even the appointment of a new king) but without legislative power. The plebeians were also permitted to participate in the later *Comitia Centuriata*, which were legislative assemblies of all citizens, but whose membership and manner of balloting were so rigged that the propertied classes could not lose a vote. Moreover, the decisions of either type of assembly remained, until 339 B.C. (Lex Publilia) and 287 B.C. (Lex Maenia), respectively, merely advisory since the Senate retained the power of the veto. Needless to add, intermarrying of patricians and plebeians was forbidden (until the Lex Canuleia of 445 B.C.).

There is no evidence that this social and political dualism in the state rested upon a racial or ethnic, and with it linguistic cleavage, although there are numerous, albeit wholly irreconcilable hypotheses to propound such a case.[23] None of the arguments is really convincing, and many are born of the prejudices of their

---

[23] Listed by Piganiol 1917, 247–252.

authors and times. The principal racial protagonists are supposedly the Sabines and the Latins, whose fancied racial parallel to their real linguistic heterogeneity is exploited to explain the patrician and plebeian opposition. One author may claim that the Sabines are the patricians and the Latins the plebeians;[24] another that the patricians are an amalgamation of Romans, Sabines, and Etruscans, whereas the plebeians are the autochthonous Ligurians;[25] a third that patriciate, patriarchy and Indo-Europeanism go together against plebeianism, matriarchy, and Mediterraneanism;[26] a fourth that the patricians are descendants of the northern invaders, cremating Indo-Europeans, pastoral nomads, worshipers of the sky-god, and wearers of wool clothing, and that the plebeians are autochthonous Mediterraneans, inhumers, worshipers of earth and fertility spirits, clad in linen.[27] In proper Nazi garb this theorizing could not but culminate in the view, as base as it is baseless, that the founders of Rome, the future patricians, were a sturdy peasant people of superior Nordic race, whereas the plebeians are descended from an inferior non-Nordic slave population.[28] It seems to be much saner, as long as trustworthy evidence for a different answer is lacking, to seek the dualism of classes not in racial heterogeneity but in a deeply ingrained social inequality.[29] True enough, this explanation merely begs the question. But the precise and ultimate causes of this situation have remained hidden from us until now, and none should be invented to fill the gap.

As concerns the part of the Etruscans in this society, it is a safe assumption that, as an upper-class minority of high civilization, they would be found among, or at least be the social equals of, the patricians rather than the plebeians, despite their essential foreignness, just as, for example, the British administrators and civilian residents of India enjoyed a high rather than a low social status within the rigid caste system of the natives. And there is no record that the expulsion of the last Etruscan tyrant led to

[24] Ridgeway 1907, 19.
[25] Husband 1910, 63–64.
[26] Piganiol 1917, 145–170.
[27] Gomme 1935, 14.
[28] Günther 1936, 328.
[29] Altheim 1941, 217; Dumézil 1944, 139.

a general persecution of the Etruscan element among the population of Rome. On the contrary, it is unlikely that the city of
Rome, in which flourished many arts and crafts learned from the
Etruscans, whose inhabitants lived a way of life which in its social
and economic aspects rested to a great extent upon Etruscan institutions, and which through its governing aristocracy perpetuated
a constitution largely framed under an Etruscan king, should have
turned against the citizens of Etruscan ancestry, especially since
the ruling class itself harbored most such persons, who would
scarcely favor their own destruction or banishment. There is no
record and no legend of a de-Etruscanizing of Rome beyond the
chasing out of an Etruscan chief.

In a sternly stratified society like that of early Rome, the
members of whose upper and lower layers were separated by a
rift far wider than that between Judy O'Grady and the colonel's
lady, regardless of whether they were or were not all brothers
and sisters under their skins, there can be no question but that with
the crass differences in culture and civilization must have gone
hand in hand gross divergences in speech. Unfortunately records
are totally lacking until the third century B.C. But we know from
later days of Latin linguistic history, even though the evidence
for the spoken language remains scanty and is always overpowered by the observance of the canons of literary niceties and conventions, that in ancient Rome as much as, and rather more than,
in contemporary societies a person's manner of speech was determined not only by his local origin but also by his socio-economic
place. Unless one is willing to contend, as I am not, that the
socio-economic hierarchy of the city corresponded to a linguistic
split in such a way that 'Latins' belonged to the higher and 'Sabines'
to the lower classes, or vice versa, we must content ourselves,
apart from the general statement on social dialectalization that
I have made, with agnosticism. We also have no idea just how
long the speakers of Sabine and Etruscan, who were incorporated
in the city at the time of the coalescing of the villages, may have
retained their non-Latin speech. But the extraordinary scarcity
of Etruscan and Sabine (that is, so-called Oscan) inscriptions in
the area of protohistoric Latin Rome and in the immediate surroundings cannot but lead one to think that the non-Latin-speak-

ing inhabitants of the new town soon gave up their native tongues in favor of Latin.

At the time of the origin of the Roman republic, in 509 B.C., we have then a city of fair size which, regardless of the ethnic elements it may enclose, is Latin in speech, but so profoundly cleft by social, political, and economic fissures that we may assume deeply divergent social dialects among its population. This cardinal fact of Roman linguistic history should be borne in mind until we come to a discussion of the development of a literary language, and of spoken and written Latin.

The following two centuries of Roman history, the fifth and the fourth B.C., are filled to a large extent with the story of the attempts of the plebeian state within the state to obtain civil rights commensurate with its civic obligations. Eventually these internal causes of upheaval and discord are, at least formally, removed with the plebeians carrying off successively what seemed splendid social advances and great democratic gains. In reality, however, the aristocrats, the patricians, and the old authorities retain to a large degree the substance of their power, by the simple device of preserving, or arrogating, for themselves the privilege of deciding as to what matters should be brought to a vote in the council of the plebs, and who should run for what elective office. In any event, among public offices hitherto closed to plebeians they attain the following: quaestorship in 409 B.C.; consulate (with at least one consul a plebeian each year since 319 B.C.), curule aedileship, and dictatorship in 366 B.C. (but the last was held by only seven plebeians as against thirty-two patricians until 300 B.C.); censorship in 351 B.C. (with one of the two censors regularly a plebeian from 332 B.C. on); praetorship in 377 B.C.; office of *magister equitum*, the chief of the cavalry, in 315 B.C.; priesthood and augurship in 300 B.C. (but with the Colleges of the *Flamines, Salii,* and the office of the *Rex sacrorum*, the High Priest, permanently remaining reserved for patricians).

Not long after 509 B.C. the *Lex Valeria de prouocatione* was passed, giving each citizen the right to appeal to the assembly before being put to death by the courts.

To protect the poor man's personal liberty, and after the legendary secession of the protesting plebs to the Sacred Mount

in 495 (or 471) B.C., the office of the *tribunus plebis*, the tribune
of the people, was instituted, whose powers quickly grew in extent
and importance. The codification of customary law in the Twelve
Tables (451 B.C.?), drawn up by a committee of *decemuiri* 'ten
men' who for two successive years replaced the consuls, aided
considerably in strengthening plebeian legal rights. A law of 449
B.C. enforced public recognition by the state of plebiscites originating in the legislative assembly. In 449 the office of *quaestor*, best
translated as 'treasurer of the state,' was made elective instead of
appointive. The famous *Lex Canuleia* of 445 legalized marriages
between plebeians and patricians. After the conquest of Veii,
during the siege of which payment for military service was first
introduced, territory taken from the vanquished city was distributed among Roman citizens, whereby an old Latin custom was
revived and Roman colonization inaugurated. From the censorship of Appius Claudius in 312 B.C. on, the wealth and civic standing of a citizen was no longer determined, as hitherto, by his
possession of land and real estate alone, but also his movable property, particularly money, was counted. In this way, many plebeians
who had managed to enrich themselves through trade and business,
formed a new 'nobility' of wealth and position — which must
not be confused, however, with the old aristocracy. In the manner
of parvenus, they hastened to dissociate themselves from the class
of which they sprang. In 287 B.C. equal manhood suffrage was
established by compelling the legislative assemblies (*Comitia centuriata*), which voted by classes based on property and heavily
favored the wealthy, especially the patricians, to recognize the
equal standing of the tribal assemblies (*Comitia tributa*), which
voted by wards and heavily favored the peasants of the thinly
settled country (if they only bothered to come to Rome to cast
their ballots) over the thickly settled city dwellers. But it is
more than doubtful whether two competing assemblies, neither
of them democratically representative, did the state and the people
much good in the end.

This progress was due, not to the benevolence of the patricians,
but rather to the realization that the awakening and expanding
state had need, in peace and war, of its masses of citizens, who
accordingly had to be at least moderately satisfied with their lot.

Yet, despite all advances in this direction, many of which were illusory in any event, Rome was not anywhere near to being or becoming a democratic state.

But once the body politic of Rome had learned to function with reasonable efficiency and had grown sufficiently strong, it turned to ventures and adventures beyond its confining boundaries. Thanks to a variety of factors, not least the sturdiness and doggedness of the peasant citizens, this increasing strength and self-confidence of the community, seconded by the usual human desire for aggrandizement and success, personal and national, will lead in good time to the subjugation of all Italy.

CHAPTER XXI

The Spread of Latin in Italy

While my subject is linguistic history, it is impossible to view the spread of Latin apart from the conquest of territory by Roman arms. Since I cannot review Roman history, I must refer to the various handbooks for the information needed to comprehend the following exposition.[1] But *Appendix I* to this chapter, lists some of the pertinent dates of Roman history during Rome's occupation of the entire peninsula, and the dates of territorial accretions in particular.

It does not concern us much whether Rome entered upon her conquests for the sake of defending herself and her allies and to repair wrongs committed against the state, or whether she was driven by an imperial lust for power. Whoever starts with the first is virtually bound to succumb to the second. Boak puts the problem succinctly: "In the ancient Roman formula employed in declaring war, that uttered by the representatives of the priestly college called the Fetiales, war appears as the last means employed to obtain reparation for wrongs that had been suffered at the hands of the enemy. Yet, although the Roman attitude in such matters was doubtless at one time sincere, we may well question how long this sincerity continued and whether the injuries complained of were not sometimes the result of Roman provocation. Such attempts to place the moral responsibility for a war upon the enemy are common to all ages and are not always convincing. If, however, we may not convict the Romans of conscious imperialism prior to 265 [B.C.], at any rate the methods which they pursued in their relations with the other peoples of Italy made their domination inevitable in view of the Roman national character and their political and military organization." [2]

[1] For authoritative, concise, and pleasant reading I recommend Boak 1955.
[2] Boak 1955, 59.

What is decisive for the linguistic history of Rome is the fact that, in pursuance of her policy, whether defensive or imperialistic, Rome extended her influence in widening circles from Latium outward, and that she progressively converted independent allies into dependent satellites who were not allowed to leave this involuntary commonwealth lest their move be considered an act of hostility and severely punished. It is inevitable that this method of enveloping one tribe and one nation of Italy after the other in a spreading web of entangling alliances should produce a progressive Romanization of the peninsula not only politically but also linguistically. For soon "there came about beside a national state of mind also a linguistic state of mind in consequence of which the penetration of the Latin language in the [conquered territory] found a favorable basis. And when this aspiration was joined with one aiming toward equality of political rights, that is, when the dominant sentiment [among the non-Romans] was no longer self-defense, the reclusion within their own borders, but aimed toward an ever more intimate union with the organism of the Roman state, then also the fate of the diffusion of Latin was decided in a favorable sense." [3]

Unlike some modern conquerors the Romans did not impose upon their allies and subjects any policy of linguistic assimilation, in part surely because they rightly feared that attempted suppression of a local language would only enhance its importance as a possible sentimental rallying point for anti-Roman discontent, but also because the policy of *diuide et impera* 'divide and conquer' made it seem more opportune to withhold from the peoples of Italy such an effective instrument of unification as a common language with all its inherent dangers of facilitating a common understanding against the Roman rulers.[4] Being hardheaded political realists

---

[3] Devoto 1940, 187.

[4] The notion of St. Augustine, *Ciu. Dei* 19.7, that "the victorious [Roman] nation imposed upon the vanquished peoples not only the political yoke but also its own language for the sake of peace" seems a misinterpretation of the facts. Göhler 1939, 29, finds this a modern point of view, not pertinent to Roman politics, and indeed one held by a non-Roman. Liv. 40.42 relates that in 180 B.C. the citizens of Cumae, once a Greek colony overrun by Samnites, made application and received permission to use Latin as their official language. This, if true, may well be an indication that the Romans actually did not favor unconditional, rapid Latinization of the tribes.

the Romans did not engage, as far as is known, in minor and un-promising schemes of psychological warfare, such as enforced Latinization, so as to show their satellites who was master. In fact, it seems that the Romans did not much care whether their sub-jects were actually ever fully conscious, in terms of diplomatic treaties and political theory, as to who ruled them — as long as in practical reality the question was not asked, nor anti-Roman answers assayed. One must indeed say that the Romans on the whole treated their subject peoples, once the actual fighting was over and the brutal sale of slaves accomplished, mildly and not unjustly, although they exploited them and made them work and live for the benefit of Rome, and they led them by stages, with or without consent of the subjects, into full citizenship. Of course, the prime objective in this procedure was the advantage of the Roman state and only coincidentally that of the allies.

The Romanization, nationally and linguistically, progressed with astounding thoroughness, though it is clear that the cultural, including the linguistic, aspects lagged behind the political. If, therefore, we can fix the dates and the process of conquests by Roman arms and of the subsequent peaceful penetration by admin-istrators and colonizers, we have not established thereby dates or even a sequence of the Latinization of the towns and districts in question, beyond establishing the *terminus post quem*.

It must be kept in mind that, in dealing with the republican and the early imperial epoch of Rome, Italian history was made in and exported from Rome, that Italy was not a state in the sense in which it is one today, but that the state was the city, that for all practical purposes the government of Rome, its assem-blies and its senate, conducted Italian affairs through Rome, in Roman terms, through Roman eyes, and for Roman interests, as though all the vast peninsula and the islands, to say nothing of the provinces, were mere appendages. True, as Roman territory grew the accretions were either incorporated into existing *tribus*, that is, electoral wards or tribes, or else new *tribus* were founded. But any member of a tribe who wished actually to cast his vote in a Tribal Assembly could do so only in Rome and not in his own precinct. Given the slowness and discomfort of transporta-tion facilities, the expenses of travel, and the inconveniences arising from an occasional but necessarily protracted absence from home of persons able and willing to vote on vital issues, it must have been considerably more bothersome for Roman citizens resident outside of Rome to fulfill their civic obligations and to take advantage of their rights than it would be, say, for Americans living at comparable distances from Washington to travel to the capital for this purpose. Moreover, the tribes, which reached their maximum number of thirty-five by 242 B.C. (from an original twenty-one, four urban and seventeen rustic), were constantly but unevenly enlarged by new citizens and therefore came to be very unequal in membership. This invested the votes of some individuals with much greater weight than those of others and could but lead to what is now called gerrymandering of districts and wards. Regions and citizens belonging to the same tribe did not even have to be situated in geographical contiguity. The censor also had the right, easily abused (though on the whole censors seem to have been honorable men), to put a new citizen in any tribe he wished, and also to switch citizens from one tribe to another. Freedmen are all attached to urban (that is, Roman) tribes (since 169 B.C. all are in one tribe), which becomes of great importance with the rapid increase of their number. And when, in the middle of the first century B.C., all residents of Italy become citizens, they are all assigned to no more than eight of the old tribes, whereby the value of the individual's vote was on purpose diminished to insignificant proportions. It is no wonder, therefore, that Rome and the inhabitants of the city, favored by a constitution growing ever more inequitable in this respect,[5] impressed the stamp of their desires and advantages upon all the actions of the state: officials who were to function as representatives of the whole state were in fact elected in and by Rome, hence inevit-

[5] Polybius (in the middle of the second century B.C.), an ardent and sincere admirer of the Roman constitution, its checks and balances and its calm wisdom, was himself a Greek, a citizen of a newly conquered land whose statutes were notoriously inept as instruments of a common national purpose, and he therefore perhaps overemphasized the value of the Roman constitution in foreign policy, where it indeed allowed the state to face the foe with the support of a united and strong citizenry. But its internal efficiency was another matter and presented less admirable features. See Gomme 1935, 49: "No one would expect such a constitution ever to work; it says volumes for the sanity of the Romans, though nothing for their sense of logic, that, for a time, it did."

ably, to a greater or lesser degree, for Rome. This, too, could but have profound influences upon the linguistic situation of Italy, for it automatically relegated the local speech, just as it did local political initiative and concerns, to a secondary, subordinate, and ever retreating position.[6]

What were the technical means whereby Italy became gradually Roman after the dust of each battle had settled and the swords were sheathed? I should say that there are two principal devices: the colonies and, intimately connected with them, the Roman roads. It will surprise no one that the colonies are planned in and executed from Rome and must emanate from an act of state performed in Rome, and that all roads lead to Rome. To obtain a realistic picture of the spread of the language of Rome in Italy it will be well to examine the sociological and cultural impact of these two instruments of Roman expansion.

THE COLONIES

It is necessary to distinguish carefully two types of colonies, the Latin and the Roman. The first took their inception and their name from the boundary fortresses which Rome founded in alliance with her friends of the Latin League from the late sixth century B.C. on [7]: Cora, Pometia (503), Signia (495), Velitrae (494), Norba (492 B.C.) — all five as bulwarks against the ever threatening and dangerous Volsci. The inhabitants of these fortresses were recruited from various Latin cities, of which Rome was one, and the political standing of the new towns within the League was equal to that of the older ones. Ardea in the land of the Rutuli was then colonized in 442 B.C., and Circei (393) and Satricum (385) again were intended to protect the Volscian border. Nepet and Sutrium (383) were established to fortify the frontier against the Etruscans after the fall of nearby Veii; Setia (382) and Fregellae (328) were once more defenses against

---

[6] Buck 1906, 100–104, lists the non-Latin-speaking tribes of Italy and the dates of their conquest.

[7] Salmon 1953, argues that the Latin colonies deduced before 338 B.C., the date of the dissolution of the Latin League, were wholly Latin foundations, with the Latin League rather than Rome deciding when and where to plant such colonies. Linguistically this could scarcely be of consequence since the Latins and the Romans spoke much the same language, although dialectal differences most likely did exist.

the irrepressible Volsci. From that time on, however, owing to the dissolution of the Latin League in 338 and the concomitant rise of Rome's hegemony, the so-called Latin colonies became in reality purely Roman enterprises and sprang up not just for the protection of the Latin tribes but as outer bulwarks, in more distant parts of Italy, to strengthen and expand the spheres of influence which Rome alone was creating for herself: Cales in Campania (334), Luceria in Apulia (314), Suessa Aurunca in the land of the Aurunci in northern Campania (313), and so forth, in all regions of Italy where Roman and Latin arms had conquered. Part of the colonials, who either actually founded a new town or moved into an existing one, were of course Roman citizens of Rome; but Romans who went to live in them actually forfeited the right of citizenship, since Latin colonies, regardless of their dates of establishment, that is, regardless of whether they were true Latin foundations or merely Roman fortresses set up to watch Rome's interests after the fading away of Latin strength, were not given such rights. From 338 on one speaks of Latin colonies of Roman deduction. Of these, the nineteen founded between 338 and 273 all were still granted the so-called 'better law' or *ius Latinum uetus* including *connubium* and *commercium*, that is, free trade and intermarriage with Roman citizens. Those founded between 268 and 181, totaling twelve and ending with Aquileia, which was the last Latin colony of Italy (apart from the colonies of Gallia Transpadana founded by the *Lex Pompeia* of 89 B.C.), were given only the 'lesser law' *ius Latinum nouum*, that is, *commercium* only, in order to safeguard some degree of Roman supremacy. Each Latin colony was legally self-governing, passed its own laws, elected magistrates, issued coin, and controlled its own census. Unlike other allies of Rome in Italy, the citizens of Latin towns were part of the *nomen Latinum*; but since they did not serve in the Roman legions proper, they were bound to provide separate contingents of infantry and cavalry.

   Although, as I implied, the name Latin colony was legally correct but factually something of a misnomer after 338 B.C., it is nonetheless improper to speak of these cities simply as of Roman colonies, because this term was reserved for the second and entirely different type of colonial expansion. In a Roman colony the settlers remained full Roman citizens with the same rights and duties as the inhabitants of Rome. If one disregards Ostia, which may have become a 'colony,' in a looser sense of the word, at the time of the king Ancus Martius, the oldest Roman colony is Antium, of 338 B.C., a date at which precisely the character, though not the constitution of the Latin colonies changed in consequence of the dissolution of the Latin League. The twenty-six Roman colonies deduced between 338 and 157 B.C. were mainly *coloniae maritimae*, designed to protect the coasts. From 157 till 122, colonization remained at a standstill, engineered chiefly by the aristocratic families who looked with misgivings upon the increase in the number of citizens, and the reduction of their own power; by the rising class of capitalistic entrepreneurs (*equites* 'knights' — the title has nothing to do with their function or position) who preferred extension of the provincial type of administration which is more lucrative; and also by the plebeians who as citizens were exempted from paying taxes and wanted to make sure that there remained enough noncitizens in the land to shoulder in perpetuity that unpleasant burden.

But when, subsequent to the Gracchan social reforms, the founding of Roman colonies is resumed, those arising until 31 B.C., the beginning of Augustus' reign, are no longer of a strategic and occupational character, garrisons among hostile or at least not fully friendly allies, but they are instead destined to alleviate the poverty of the proletariat by providing land for settlers, to break up large and inefficiently exploited estates, and they are turned over to civilians and discharged soldiers who need to be provided with a source of income. From Augustus on, Roman colonies, which came to be founded by the hundreds in all parts of the empire outside of Italy, were turned over almost exclusively to veterans.

Appendix II (pages 285–287) lists the Latin and Roman colonies in chronological order of their deduction, adding also the district in which, or the people among whom, each colony was established.[8]

An intermediate and, as regards citizenship, often transitory

[8] For detailed information see Kornemann 1900.

position between the Roman and the Latin colonies was held by the *municipia* of Etruria, Latium, and Campania. The inhabitants of these towns enjoyed what one might somewhat euphemistically call partial citizenship, amounting in fact to carrying the burdens but not enjoying the privileges, in particular that of suffrage, of being citizens. But in the end this situation generally evolved for each municipality into full citizenship, and during the intermediate stage and afterward the town was allowed to retain to a degree its own officials and civic organization, although in its external relations it was subject to the control of Roman authorities. Hence the advantage gained by the inhabitants was the continuity of local autonomy (though much curtailed by Roman interference), and by Rome that of being able ultimately to incorporate among its citizenry persons who had already been assimiliated and could be counted upon to alleviate the increased demands of manpower imposed upon the state through continued wars and expansion. The institution of municipia was a peculiarly Roman invention and achievement, born of the realization that the enormously growing burdens of government, administration, and further conquests could in the long run not be sustained by the Romans or Rome alone. In our present context, however, the municipia are of lesser weight since, unlike the colonies, they do not accomplish a diffusion of Romans and of the Latin language, but merely the extension of Roman citizenship to non-Romans.

Finally one must not overlook the fact that much land where military fortifications were unnecessary was assigned *uiritim* 'individually' (notably the territory of Veii), and that wherever occurred some concentration of such holdings, so-called *fora* and *conciliabula* sprang up, which were trading centers and small villages without municipal or colonial statutes. It is evident that such townships exerted a linguistic influence upon the surrounding countryside. But if I shall shortly have to concede that we possess little linguistically useful knowledge concerning even the colonies, especially as regards the spread of the Latin language, it will astonish no one that illuminating evidence from these relatively insignificant markets is totally lacking, no matter how important some of them may have been as centers of linguistic diffusion.

When it became clear, during the latter part of the second century, that the responsibilities imposed upon both Latin and non-Latin allies were growing so unbearably burdensome as to outweigh all possible gains which a peaceful alliance with Rome had to offer, when the 'allies' realized, in other words, that they had to become mere satellites of a great power,[9] they sought Roman citizenship. Their attempts were rebuffed in Rome in 125, in 122, and again in 91 B.C. The Latin allies took advantage of a privilege not shared by their non-Latin fellows, which granted them Roman citizenship if they actually settled in Rome, and they started an exodus to the city which seriously depopulated Latin towns. To forestall economic and demographic consequences which threatened disaster to both Rome and the countryside, the Roman Senate could not help revoking this privilege, in 95 B.C., an action, necessary though it was, which was hardly apt to allay the mounting discontent. The result was the taking up of arms by the allies in the Social War of 91–89 B.C. It is strange yet significant for the irreversible progress of the Latin language in Italy, that this anti-Roman confederacy, which under the leadership of the Oscans made Corfinium its rival capital and issued its own money, minted coins inscribed in Latin. Nonetheless it seems a fair guess that, had the Italian allies been victorious on the battlefield, and not only half-victorious in their struggle for civil rights, Italy would have acquired a (North) Oscan dialect, and the 'Romanic' languages, provided there were to be any, would have been descendants of Oscan rather than Latin.

The Romans were forced to give in to the demands of the allies, and by a series of laws of 90, 89, and 49 B.C., full Roman citizenship was granted to all inhabitants of Italy, including Cisalpine Gaul. With this universal dispensation, by the way, the Latin colonies of noncitizens in Italy came automatically to an end, as did communities of allies, and municipia without suffrage.

It is not exaggerated to claim that "the history of Roman col-

[9] Liv. 27.9.13 reports that, for example, in the first year of the Hannibalic war, the allies provided 40,000 infantry and 4,400 cavalry, as contrasted with 24,000 and 1,800, respectively, put up by the Romans. While these numbers were in keeping with the relative sizes of population, they were out of proportion to the interest which the Romans and the allies respectively had in ridding Italy of Hannibal, and to the advantages to be thus obtained by either.

onization is the history of the Roman state"; [10] in the same sense
it is also the history of the diffusion of Roman speech, of Latin.
But, while from evidence available we can easily learn when
a certain district of Italy came under Roman political domination,
be it as either type of colony or as an allied state, the record unfortunately gives us no information on details from which we
could reconstruct the impact of each conquest and colonization
upon the linguistic fate of the district and its inhabitants. We should
need precise data to tell that story in meaningful and enlightening
form, in terms of evolution rather than of results. How many
speakers of Latin were deduced into the colonies? (It seems that
no more than three hundred families were sent into the earlier
colonies, but about the later ones we know next to nothing; and
while we are engaged in wishing we might as well want to know
their exact provenance — from Rome, Praeneste, Tibur, or what
other.) How many natives were the newcomers obliged to live
with if the colony was not a new foundation? (We know that it
was customary for the Romans to appropriate as public land one-
third of the area belonging to beaten enemies, and to distribute
this, or part of it, among the colonials. Yet, not knowing either
the size of this *ager publicus* 'public land' or what portion of it
was distributed and what portion retained by the state, ethno-
graphic clues are scarcely obtainable from this evidence; it is
certain that in such colonies the Romans formed the upper classes
of society, that the local Senate was selected from among them,
that, in other words, they set the tone socially, and *ipso facto*
linguistically.) What were the local provisions, which must have
varied, concerning the use of the indigenous and the Latin language, and local popular usage — does there persist a social and a
concomitant linguistic cleavage, and for how long? To what extent
does intermarriage take place? Do the natives of the town and
the district become bilingual after the first, second, or a later
generation? Does the Latin language conquer easily and quickly?
We do not know how many Roman and Latin colonists and
their descendants actually remained in their new homes after
the original deduction and land distribution and for how long a
time. There is good reason to believe that many, especially the

[10] Kornemann 1900, 560.

veterans and the Roman city people who were not expert farmers, soon sold their alloted holdings to the great landholders and returned to the big city to enjoy life and to live on the dole with which a nervously vigilant and apprehensive government sought to pacify the unruly mob.

All these things remain largely unknown because the ancients were not in the habit of keeping statistics. We are certain only of the result — the ultimate Latinization of Italy. The records in the native language, where such are available at all, simply cease and Latin takes over. Even a sporadic non-Latin inscription of a relatively late date after the Roman conquest is really of no great use in determining the degree of Latinization in the people's speech habits since it gives no indication whatever whether its existence is due to the caprice or the stubbornness of an individual, or to the persistence of a widespread oral, though not literate and literary, use of the pre-Latin dialect. We can merely say that at least someone still knew it, though not even that can be gleaned with certainty from some types of records, such as ritual texts or funerary inscriptions, the wording of which may well be a stereotyped or traditional repetition of older formulae whose semantic content is of no importance to the reader and may without damage remain hidden from him, as it may well have remained unknown to the writer himself. (Compare Latin or Hebrew inscriptions in modern churches and synagogues, and on tombstones.) And, vice versa, the use of the Latin language in documents and monuments that have come down to us is not necessarily proof for the penetration of Rome's idiom among the people, but may be due only to the fact that anything important enough to be written down at all would be written in the prestige language of the capital — Latin. This was virtually inevitable where the local dialect had not at all or very rarely been reduced to writing, so that there was no weighty precedent or tradition, nor even the technical proficiency, for using it otherwise than orally: writing meant writing in Latin.

On the number of colonists we have every now and then ancient testimony; but it is uncertain whether this information rests on precise knowledge. Modern authors have attempted to assemble and, sometimes, supplement these facts, and have succeeded in proposing figures for a number of colonies.[11] Yet, even if we are willing to accept these sporadic numbers at face value, which I do not think we can, we still are not nearer to answering all the questions I listed and which would constitute the cultural skeleton for the history of Italy's Latinization. The ancients, as I said, provide us with no statistics (we do not even know for sure how many inhabitants the city of Rome had at any given moment, except by inference and guess), least of all with statistics on an item so unimportant within the framework of Roman political thinking and statecraft as the linguistic habits of citizens, let alone allies. Our full and precise knowledge of the spread of Latin is therefore circumscribed by our knowledge of the expansion of the Roman state and on the establishment of the colonies, and by the phenomenon of accomplished Latinization, that is to say, by causes and result. We remain ignorant of the manner of progress.

Perhaps the distinction between earlier and later colonies on one hand, and Latin and Roman colonies on the other, contains the basis of some linguistic differentiation, which, however, remains unverifiable. Until the time of the Gracchan social reforms, colonies served a prevalently military purpose and were established as garrisons in newly conquered lands or at the borders of enemy nations. The lots were given to Roman citizens who had to apply for the privilege and who could be rejected if they were persons of bad character — though we are not told what 'bad character' was. (Rarely it happened that colonizers actually had to be 'invited' to avail themselves of the opportunity to become landholders, in which case the invitation took the form of very involuntary recruitment.) But from the end of the second century B.C. on, the colonies were used mainly to alleviate economic suffering in Rome, and the colonials came from among the city mob and discharged soldiers. (It should be noted that from the time of Marius, from about 100 B.C. on, the veterans themselves changed in social type. Before Marius, only citizens of a certain income, that is, social position, could afford to serve the state as soldiers — except in times of national peril when everybody served. Under Marius and after him, all citizens, including those without wealth who were only *capite censi* 'counted by head', and not by wealth,

[11] Beloch 1880, 116–117, 149–150; Frank 1927, 32–33, 40 ff.

called proletarians because they were rich only in *proles* 'children,' were subject to service and entitled to severance benefits when discharged.) These persons, who hardly cared for the bucolic joys of country life, or its hardships, would often resell their holdings to landholders who wanted to round out their growing, slave-worked latifundia. But even if they remained in their colonies they surely constituted on the whole a lower type of colonate in terms of motivation, industry, and skill than their earlier counterparts. They came no doubt from a lower social order than earlier colonials. Transferring these characteristics onto the linguistic plane, we may assume that they probably spoke, and taught the natives, a more popular, slangy type of Latin, possibly one also richer in foreign expressions and borrowing which they had either acquired in military service or inherited from foreign-born parents if they were freedmen, as many were. Moreover, with the progressively increasing masses of non-Latin subjects and allies in the armies of Rome, the number of veterans who were themselves not native speakers of Latin grew apace. In one way, this furthered the expansion of Latin among original non-speakers, and favored the rise of a standard spoken koinë, but it also contributed to the number of those who spoke Latin with a foreign accent and who passed it on in this not wholly Roman form to new learners, who, in other words, did not speak the 'good' Latin of Rome. However, our factual information from and about the various colonies is so bland and perfunctory that the import of all this upon linguistic conditions must remain pure surmise.

Comparing Latin and Roman colonies, we can at least say that the Latin colonies were more populous and therefore may have exerted a deeper and faster Latinizing influence. On the other hand, they were likely to include, especially in the earlier periods, a number of non-Roman Latin speakers, so that the Latin current in them may have been of a more rustic rather than urban type. Again the records tell us nothing about this, and all such reasoning must be wholly speculative.

THE ROADS

Even if the Romans had not been such skilled politicians and administrators, the exigencies of civilian travel and trade would have necessitated the network of roads which in the course of time came to cover Italy and the provinces.[12] Ancient Latium, which as early as the Iron Age was fairly thickly settled and which in the protohistoric centuries of Rome probably nourished a denser population than ever since (excepting of course the city of Rome itself), must have been traversed by roads and paths now forgotten and nameless. But, as soon as the Romans and other Latins together, and later the Romans alone, planted their colonial fortresses, it became necessary to connect these outposts with Rome if they were to have durability and strength. The great roads which we know by the names of their builders, generally the censors in office, were doubtless the final formalization and official recognition of a long evolution. The oldest of them all, at least in its most ancient portion, is the *Via Latina*. (Does the fact that it is not called after a sponsoring censor indicate that it is older than that office, which originated in 444 B.C.?) We know that by 334 B.C. it had reached Cales in Campania, which in the same year became the first Latin colony outside of Latium and southern Etruria: the connection is obvious. It was later continued to Casilinum, where at a distance of 135 miles from Rome it merged with the most famous of all Roman roads, the *Via Appia*, built under the censorate of Appius Claudius Caecus in 312 B.C. Upon issuing from Rome the Via Appia took a more westerly course than the Via Latina, traversed the Pontine marshes, and ended for the time being at Capua after a course of 132 miles. Together the Appia and the Latina served the numerous colonies, Latin and Roman, which had by then sprung up in Latium and northern Campania, mostly with the purpose of containing the various mountain tribes of the western Apennines, above all the unruly Volscians. By 244 B.C., the Via Appia had been extended eastward, crossing the Apennines by way of Beneventum and Venusia, continuing southward through Apulia to Tarentum and ending at Brundisium, the most important harbor for all communications with Greece and the east. (A shorter route from Beneventum to Brundisium by way of Canusium and Barium was the later *Via Traiana* along which Horace once traveled, a journey which he describes in one of his

[12] For a good description of the roads of the empire see Lemosse 1950.

poems).[13] This extension took care of the tribes of Samnium and Apulia and the colonies established in their territories, but it also laid the necessary tactical and logistic groundwork for the future conquest of Greece.

Directly toward the east Rome sent out the very ancient *Via Tiburtina* (note the name) to Tibur, which about 300 B.C. was lengthened to Carsioli, Alba Fucens, and Cerfennia, servicing the colonies established in the country of the Sabines, the Aequi, and the Marsi, and which, when it was paved under the censor M. Valerius Messalla, in 154 B.C., got its official name of *Via Valeria*. Finally the emperor Claudius (41–54 after Christ) extended it to Alerum on the Adriatic, and it was named *Via Claudia Valeria*. Its total length across the breadth of Italy was 136 miles.

In the meantime, after having to satisfy herself for a while with the fringes of Etruria, Rome penetrated deeper and deeper among the Etruscans, founding the colonies of Nepet, Sutrium, Cosa, Alsium, Fregenae in Etruria, and of Narnia, Spoletium, Hadria, Ariminum, Firmum, Sena Gallica, and Aesis as far north as Umbria and Picenum. Hence under the censor C. Flaminius of 220 B.C. the *Via Flaminia* was opened, running 209 miles from Rome through Narnia, Nuceria, Fanum Fortunae and Pisaurum on the Adriatic Coast, to Ariminum. (An alternate road from Narnia to Nuceria by way of Interamnia, Spoletium, and Fulginium was built after A.D. 69. From Nuceria a branch leads also to Ancona, not quite correctly called Via Flaminia.) In this manner Etruria, Umbria, and Picenum became pacified and Romanized.

Not long afterward, in 187 B.C. under the consulate of M. Aemilius Lepidus, the *Via Aemilia* continued the Via Flaminia from Ariminum to Placentia, over a total of 176 miles, touching many of the important places and colonies of the newly conquered Gallia Cisalpina (Cispadana), like Placentia, Bononia, Mutina, Parma (but not Ravenna).

Soon, perhaps around 170 B.C., the *Via Cassia* crossed the very heart of the Etruscan land, running from Rome through Volsinii and Clusium to Arretium.

This left only the Tyrrhenian coast without a major road, a want which was soon remedied by the opening of the *Via Aurelia*,

[13] Hor. *Sat.* 1.5.

between Rome and Vada Volterrana, 175 miles long. The date is not ascertained, but it must have been before 109 B.C., at which date an extension sponsored by M. Aemilius Scaurus (hence sometimes called *Via Aemilia Scauri*; it was paved by Augustus and renamed *Via Iulia Augusta*) continued the Aurelia as far as Arelate (north of Marseilles) and Vada Sabatia. In this manner the Etruscan coast and Liguria (Saturnia, Graviscae, Luna, Dertona, Narbo) were secured and the way paved — literally — for the expansion of Rome into Spain.

And, finally, again in Gallia Cisalpina, the *Via Postumia*, built by Spurius Postumius Albinus, consul in 148 B.C., cut through the country north of the Po River, connecting Genoa and Dertona with Cremona, Mantua, and Aquileia (near the Istrian peninsula at the head of the Adriatic Sea). This stretch of road often appears incorrectly as Via Aemilia in the itineraries.

The South — Calabria, Lucania, and Sicily — was not neglected, and in 132 the *Via Popillia* branched off the Via Appia a short distance beyond Capua and ran the entire length of Calabria, not along the coast but approximately where the modern inland road lies, to Rhegium. It was often called Via Appia. It continued in Sicily, leading from Messina through Panormus (Palermo) to Eryx at the western tip of the triangular island.

It need not be added that these ancient highways formed only the principal lines of a dense network of smaller roads along which, as through the minor blood vessels of the human body, the flow of life of Italy was pumped to and from the main arteries. The heart of this pulsating, living organism was always Rome. But Rome was also, unhappily for my metaphor and for Italy, its head.

By the end of the second century B.C., then, the Romans had conquered and colonized all of Italy, they had established an admirable system of uniform administration, and they had constructed an efficient system of communication throughout the land. It is only natural that upon these premises the linguistic Romanization, which had already commenced and progressed according to the history of each area, should be inevitably completed and that Italy should become a country of Latin speech.

One more remark, conjectural but eminently credible, on the

diffusion of Latin may be apposite here. The system of colonization and roadbuilding which I have described does not expand Roman domain in such a manner that its contiguous area increases, but it rather allows the Romans to leap into the very midst of a new region and to establish there a center of political influence and conquest and of linguistic diffusion. Hence, previous to the Social War, Roman territory did not constitute a compact block from whose confines Romanization pushed forward, eating progressively into new territory, but it is made up outside of Latium of a number of islands from which the military and civil Romanization radiates in all directions until its circles of influence meet and overlap. I should compare this type of expansion with the spreading of waves in a pool: by throwing in one rock, the waves will emanate from this center and slowly and with decreasing strength spread over the entire surface; but by throwing in several rocks in succession at strategic spots, the movement of the waves will more quickly and efficiently cover a wider area. Since linguistic spread is often likened to such wave formations, the simile illustrates how the Latinization of Italy could be more rapid and profound by issuing from a number of foci rather than from one. Of course, Rome's aims were not linguistic but military and political, but there is no doubt that the strategy is eminently sound for this purpose, too. (It was, by the way, employed in the Second World War in the occupation by the United States of the immense area of the Pacific Ocean and was commonly known as 'island hopping.')

I have already said that we can see the Latinization of Italy mainly in its result rather than its progress, although one may describe the conditions and vehicles through which the result was achieved. There is, however, a way of discerning in some small degree, though far from accurately, the persistence of local speech. I do not mean sporadic inscriptional remnants of it, whose inadequacy I have already discussed, but the amount of non-Latin items in phonology, morphology, and syntax which the Latin of a given area retained. But here, too, the obstacles in the path toward sure knowledge are great. While it is true that older inscriptions render genuine speech habits more faithfully and allow us to perceive dialectal, local features, this becomes less true in the measure in which written Latin itself develops into a rigidly codified, highly artificial, artful, classical language — a *Schriftsprache*, in which local and social peculiarities are by definition suppressed. If we therefore manage to discover in the written documents from one given area a greater preponderance of dialectal features than in those from another, this difference may in fact not be due to the greater resistance of native speech in the first as compared with the second, but only to a later acceptance of the usage of the emerging codes and rules for written Latin. From this difference, then, we may not conclude on local speech habits but only on local literacy, or literateness, that is, on the degree to which those who knew Latin at all had learned 'good' Latin. And again no certain knowledge emerges concerning the speed and thoroughness of the Latinization of all the people.

Finally, some think (and I myself am among them) that in modern Italian dialects the Italic linguistic substratum, which in writing though not in speech was wholly overwhelmed by the Latin of Rome, is still discernible and gives a measure of the endurance of pre-Latin speech. Yet even if this is so, it offers nothing that could be added to this chapter, in which I have sought to describe the progress rather than the result of the diffusion of Latin in Italy. Remnants and fossils that have lasted more than two thousand years are themselves results and not yardsticks on which any computing of progress can be performed.

I now must make the unpleasant yet inevitable admission that we cannot describe in any socio-cultural terms the diffusion of a language, which is in fact a socio-cultural event, with as little information on such matter as we have at our disposal from ancient Italy. The Romans kept no records on such demographic aspects of their polity. Nor had they any interest in the linguistic history of the dialect geography of their country. Happy the linguist of the future who is writing a linguistic history of the United States and has discovered the decennial census, and the Linguistic Atlas of the United States!

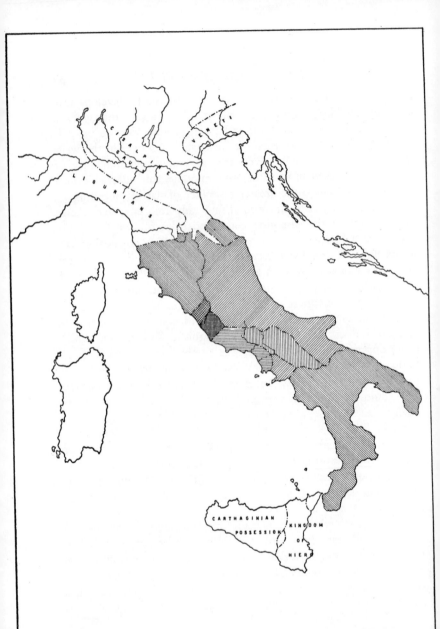

THE ROMAN CONQUEST OF ITALY TO 265 B.C.

TERRITORY OF ROME AND ROMAN ALLIES 487 B.C.	ADDITIONS TO 300 B.C.
ADDITIONS TO 387 "	ADDITIONS TO 290 "
ADDITIONS TO 334 "	ADDITIONS TO 265 "

APPENDIX I

(Territorial accretions are set off in italics.)

505 B.C.   Etruscans defeated at Aricia and driven from *Latium.*

492   Alliance of Romans and other Latins, the Latin League, with right of mutual *commercium* (free trade) and *connubium* (intermarriage).

5th century Wars with *Aequi* and *Volsci.*

(The latter part of the fifth century is characterized by a continuous pressure exerted by the mountain tribes of the interior upon the inhabitants of the more favored lowlands by the sea. This pattern of rushes toward the better land in the warm plain becomes a regular feature of early Italian history, and the struggles of Rome and the city's ultimate supremacy owing to their favorable outcome, are in a sense due to the more desirable geographic position of the city and the plain of Latium. Especially the Volsci in the mountains southeast of Rome proved an implacable and obstinate enemy.)

392   Conquest of *Veii.*

390   Gauls sack Rome.

(How insignificant Rome still was to the rest of the world at that time is shown by a report of Heracleides Ponticus, ap. Plut. *Cam.* 22.2, who, in a 'Treatise on the Soul' tells the story of how an army of Hyperboreans had captured "a Greek city called Rome, situated somewhere on the shores of the Great Sea.")

390–338 Renewed revolts of *Aequi, Volsci*, and Southern *Etruscans*, who are finally subdued.

340–338 Latin War against revolting Latin allies who had joined with Campanian cities against Rome. Roman treaty with the latter, Roman territory extended *to the Bay of Naples.*

326–304 Samnite wars, first phase. Samnites are beaten but retain territory. Roman alliances with *Apulia, southern Campania, Lucanians, Marsi, Marrucini, Frentani, Paeligni*, who become, in modern terminology, 'satellites.' Annexation of *Hernici* and *Aequi.*

298–290 Samnite wars, second phase. Alliance of Samnites, Gauls, Etruscans, Sabines. Subjugation of *Samnium.*

285   Defeat of Gauls and Etruscans. Occupation of *Ager Gallicus*. New alliance with Etruscan cities.

281–272 War against Tarentum and Pyrrhus.

272   Fall of *Tarentum*. Rome allied with cities of *Southern Italy.*

(By 265 B.C. Rome owns outright or controls through alliances and colonization the Apennine peninsula approximately from the river Arno and the springs of the Tiber to the straits of Messina, the Ionian Sea, and the straits of Otranto.)

264–241 First Punic War.

241   Carthage cedes *Sicily* (except the independent territory of Syracuse) and the *islands* between Sicily and Italy.

238   Romans take *Corsica* and *Sardinia* from Carthage.

233   Colonization of *Ager Gallicus* (Roman since 285 B.C.).

225–222 Wars with Gauls of North Italy; conquest of *lower and middle Po valley.*

221–219 Occupation of the head of the Adriatic Sea as far east as Istria.

(By 218 B.C. Rome's sphere of influence extends over all of Italy, except the upper Po valley and Liguria, Sicily, except Syracuse, and the islands of the Tyrrhenian Sea.)

218–202 Second Punic War. Loss of Cisalpine Gaul.

212   Fall of *Syracuse.*

201   Rome occupies *Carthage* and surrounding territory.

201   Annexation of *Carthaginian Spain* (organized as Roman provinces 197 B.C.)

198–191 Reconquest of *Cisalpine Gaul.*

191–172 Subjugation of *Liguria.*

(After the conquest of Liguria two whole tribes of coastal Ligurians, numbering 40,000 persons, were bodily transplanted to Samnium, to a place not far from Beneventum.)

(By 172 B.C. Rome controls all of Italy from the Alps to the bottom of the heel, Sicily, Sardinia, and Corsica, and has begun to conquer and colonize the Mediterranean basin. For statistics on the increasing surface area see Beloch 1880, 67–77.)

APPENDIX II

THE COLONIES

Latin

Before 500	Fidenae–Latium		290–286	Hadria — Picenum
503	Cora — Volsci		273	Cosa — Etruria
503	(Suessa) Ponetia — Volsci		273	Paestum — Lucania
495	Signia — Volsci		268	Ariminum — Aemilia
494	Velitrae — Volsci		268	Beneuentum — Samnium
492	Norba — Volsci		264	Firmum — Picenum
467	Antium — Volsci		263	Aesernia — Samnium
442	Ardea — Rutuli		246	Brundisium — Calabria
418	Labicum — Latium		241	Spoletium — Umbria
393	Circeii — Volsci		218	Cremona — Gallia Cisalpina
385	Satricum — Volsci		218	Placentia — Gallia Cisalpina
383	Nepet — Etruria		193	Copia (Thurii) — Bruttium
383	Sutrium — Etruria		192	Vibo Valentia — Bruttium
382	Setia — Volsci		189	Bononia — Gallia Cisalpina
334	Cales — Campania		181	Aquileia — Gallia Cisalpina
328	Fregellae — Volsci			
314	Luceria — Apulia			Bergomum
313	Suessa Aurunca — Aurunci			Brixia
313	Pontiae — Volscian islands			Comum
313	Saticula — Samnium			Laus Pompeia
312	Interamna Lirinas — Volsci			Mantua
303	Sora — Volsci			Mediolanum
303	Alba — Marsi			Nouaria
299	Narnia — Umbria			Vercellae
298	Carsioli — Aequi			Verona
291	Venusia — Apulia			

Bergomum, Brixia, Comum, Laus Pompeia, Mantua, Mediolanum, Nouaria, Vercellae, Verona — all created through the Lex Pompeia, 89 B.C., in Gallia Transpadana

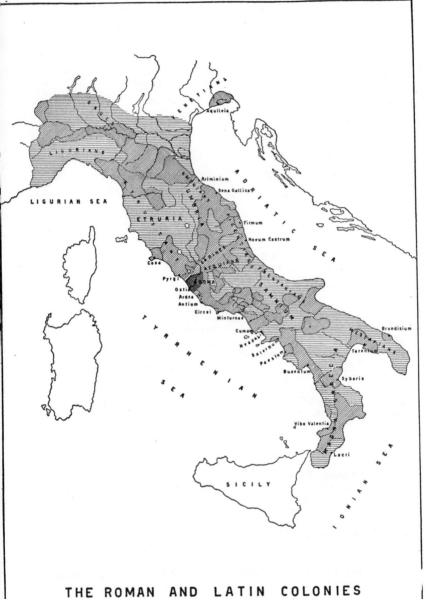

THE ROMAN AND LATIN COLONIES
OF ITALY   ca. 100 B.C.

ROMAN TERRITORY
AND ADDITIONS UNTIL 396

ROMAN TERRITORY
AND ROMAN COLONIES

LATIN COLONIES

ROMAN ALLIES

Roman

338	Antium — Volsci	194	Sipontum — Apulia
329	Tarracina — Volsci	194	Tempsa — Bruttium
296	Minturnae — Aurunci	194	Croton — Bruttium
296	Sinuessa — Aurunci	191	Pyrgi — Etruria
290–286	Castrum nouum — Picenum or Etruria	184	Potentia — Lucania
		184	Pisaurum — Umbria
283	Sena Gallica — Umbria	183	Mutina — Aemilia
247	Aesis — Umbria	183	Parma — Aemilia
247	Alsium — Etruria	183	Saturnia — Etruria
245	Fregenae — Etruria	181	Grauiscae — Etruria
194	Volturnum — Campania	177	Luna — Etruria
194	Liternum — Campania	157	Auximum — Picenum
194	Puteoli — Campania	122	Tarentum — Apulia
194	Salernum — Campania	122	Scolacium — Bruttium
194	Buxentum — Lucania	?	Dertona — Liguria

(I am terminating the list here; subsequent colonies in Italy must have had small importance for the spread of Latin since the colonies deduced by Sulla, Caesar, and the Triumvirate, for which no more free state land — *ager publicus* — was available for distribution, were founded upon land purchased or confiscated outright, hence subjected to previous Latinization. It may further be assumed that by the end of the Republic all of Italy had at least been exposed to Latinization, albeit to an unknown degree.)

Part Six. The History of Latin

CHAPTER XXII

Historic Background (200 B.C.–A.D. 300) From

the preceding chapters it should have become clear that the Roman state contained from its inception a stark socio-cultural cleavage separating patricians and plebeians, rich and poor, senators and equestrians, Optimates and Populares. It would be an error to believe that there existed simply a two-class society and to derive this scission from two otherwise unidentifiable prehistoric primary races. Yet one cannot escape the impression that, while the society of the Roman state was, like any complex social body, constructed of manifold layers according to physical means and intellectual accomplishments, there prevailed a basic division into two principal groups, separated by a gap so wide that only few persons could hope to traverse it, and that those who did so cut all ties with the past. It lies in the nature of such a social construction that a small number of aristocrats of birth or office or wealth (most frequently these three factors were combined) faced a vast proletariat, and while the class struggle may not often have reached acute Marxian stages, the bisection of society was characterized by the continued desire of the 'haves' to retain their position and to bolster it by removing themselves even farther from the masses, and the perennial struggle of the 'have-nots' at least to emulate, if not to eliminate, their more favored fellows. Since language is but one of the cultural planes on which the battlelines are drawn, a consideration of the dialects may usefully start with a brief sketch of some pertinent features of socio-economic and cultural history.[1]

---

[1] See also Chapters XXI and XXII. Dividing the present chapter into two historical periods, on the Republic from 200 B.C. (the earlier part was dealt with in Chapter XXI) and on the Empire, seems convenient also from a linguistic point of view since the greatest flowering and the beginning of the decline of the highest social dialect, the classical literary language, coincide with the end of the republic and the beginning of the monarchy.

It may be well to begin with an ingenious and pithy epitome of the rise and fall of Rome. "During the *first three centuries of the Republic*, the wholesome life of an agricultural people bred a virile race of free men little concerned in economic questions outside of their immediate work. *After the Punic War* there followed a period of capitalistic farming with slave labor and of the exploitation of the provinces. The citizen body changed seriously because of the rapid merging into it of freed slaves. The consequence of imperialism and slavery was the monarchy. *During the first century of the Empire* the monarchy became ever more autocratic and encouraged the private exploitation of the resources of the provinces under the *pax Romana*. Individual initiative disappeared in government and industry. *The third century* was a period of anarchy which ended in a totalitarian government with an economic system centering about the emperor and his army that saved the state for the final dry rot. In a word, the decline of Rome may in the last analysis be attributed to the failure of vision on the part of the landed gentry: their willingness during the Republic to betray the free yeomanry for the sake of profitable estates worked by slaves; and their readiness during the Empire to accept a totalitarian regime for the sake of the prospect of personal safety."[2] (Italics mine.)

The great plebeian victories in the social struggle of the fourth century B.C. are apt to give the appearance of progress toward a more democratic form of government. But no equalizing development worthy of that name occurred in the domain of politics, and the governmental powers remained largely in the hands of the aristocracy. The important change that did take place was that, from the early third century on, not only patricians of the ancient nobility but also plebeians of sufficient property formed together a mixed ruling class of birth and wealth, with the latter bearing some of the burdens and enjoying the advantages of public office and senatorial rank. But plebeians thus advanced in the social scale promptly forgot and denied their antecedents. Hence in the course of the third century B.C., with the concurrence of all, the senatorial order became a *de facto*, though not *de iure* closed caste which

[2] Frank 1940, 304.

monopolized public office and actually ruled the state, virtually superseding the constitutional powers of the popular assemblies. Between 200 and 146 B.C., of one hundred and eight consuls in office only eight came of families in which no one had held this exalted post before. Such extraordinary persons, upstarts in the eyes of their colleagues, were called *homines noui* 'parvenus.' Cato the Elder, and, later, Marius and Cicero are the outstanding examples of this small group.

The second century also witnesses the rise of a large class of rich businessmen and financiers, many of whom belonged to the equestrian order, and who, standing socially outside the governing aristocracy, can take upon themselves all the business denied by law [3] and custom to the senatorial orders: large commercial enterprises, state contracts for public works, collecting of taxes and harbor dues, operation of mines, and, for a time, banking and moneylending. They form stock companies of limited responsibility and become exploiters of the provinces. Thanks to the legislation of the Gracchi, who wished to strengthen this class in order to keep a morally declining and greedy senate in check, their powers increased continuously. A good part of the last century of the Republic is filled with the arguments and open warfare between these two factions, always to the detriment of the state as a whole. As far as the lower classes and the provincials were concerned, anti-senatorial legislation had merely caused the cudgel to pass into other hands. Since the equestrians managed to pack the juries, it became virtually impossible to obtain restraining court orders against abuses perpetrated by one of their number in the provinces, to say nothing of redress for wrongs. (Honest provincial officials were disheartened by the fate that befell one of them, Rutilius Rufus, who was tried in 92 B.C. on trumped-up charges of extortion precisely because he had tried to check the blatant rapacity of the *publicani*, the state-licensed tax collectors, in the province of Asia. Rufus retired to live peacefully in the same province, enjoying the esteem of the inhabitants for whose alleged welfare calumniators had wrecked his career.)

[3] In particular the *Lex Claudia*, of 218 B.C., which limited the capacity of ships which could be owned by senators to the trifling size of 300 amphorae, or 225 bushels, thus virtually excluding senators from trade and commerce.

Lending money at crushing rates of interest, from 12 per cent to 48 per cent per year, became a not dishonorable source of income which eventually also the noble senators, who for a while had held aloof from what was considered a dirty business, ceased to reject. Thus, they further damaged their reputation and their integrity. Gone were the days when Cato likened moneylending to homicide.[4] Far away must have seemed the time when, in 280 B.C., Cineas, sent as ambassador to Rome by his king Pyrrhus of Epirus, could report to his master that the Roman senate was an assembly of many kings.

When Cincinnatus was called from his plough to become dictator and lead Rome's army in 458 B.C., he left, we are told, an estate of four iugera (about two and one-half acres) on the Vatican Hill, and returned to his fields when the war was ended. He is the prototype and the ideal of the Roman peasant-soldier who lived frugally on a small piece of land which he owned and tilled. Each citizen of old Rome lived thus, like Cincinnatus, as a soldier and peasant, and only those who could equip themselves with arms and horses were privileged to lay down their lives for the state. And there were enough such men to protect and vastly enlarge their country. But, four centuries later, Cicero quotes, with disbelief but without disproof, a man's saying that "there are no two-thousand men in the republic who own land." [5] A few decades thereafter an author says that " a man considers himself cramped for space if his house takes as much room as did Cincinnatus' whole farm." [6] What had happened?

Appian tells the story with great perspicacity and succinctness from the begininngs of Roman expansion to the end of the Republic. "The Romans, as they subdued the Italian peoples in war, used to seize a part of their lands and build towns there, or enrol colonists of their own to occupy those already existing, and their idea was to use these as outposts; but of the land acquired by war they assigned the cultivated part forthwith to the colonists, or sold or leased it. Since they had no leisure as yet to allot the part which then lay desolated by war (this was generally the greater part), they made

[4] Cf. n. 9 below.
[5] Cic. *de off.* 2.26.
[6] Val. Max. 4.7.

proclamation that in the meantime those who were willing to work it might do so for a toll of the yearly crops, a tenth of the grain and a fifth of the fruit. From those who kept flocks was required a toll of the animals, both oxen and small cattle. They did these things in order to multiply the Italian race, which they considered the most laborious of peoples, so that they might have plenty of allies at home. But the very opposite thing happened; for the rich, getting possession of the greater part of the undistributed lands, and being emboldened by the lapse of time to believe that they would never be dispossessed, absorbing any adjacent strips and their poor neighbors' allotments, partly by purchase under persuasion and partly by force, came to cultivate vast tracts instead of single estates, using slaves as laborers and herdsmen, lest free laborers should be drawn from agriculture into the army. At the same time the owner-ship of slaves brought them great gain from the multitude of their progeny, who increased because they were exempt from military service. Thus certain powerful men became extremely rich and the race of slaves multiplied throughout the country, while the Italian people dwindled in numbers and strength, being oppressed by penury, taxes, and military service. If they had any respite from these evils they passed their time in idleness, because the land was held by the rich, who employed slaves instead of freemen as culti-vators." [7]

According to this opinion the main causes for the disappearance of the Roman peasant-soldier and his virtues were: the acquisition of land by a few rich at the expense of the small farmer and the formation of so-called *latifundia*; the replacement of the free workers by slaves who came to Italy as a consequence of Rome's new imperialistic conquests outside of the peninsula; the shrinkage of the free Italian population owing to their continued engagement in wars, whereas, ironically, the slaves who were exempt from military service multiplied all over the land, and as freedmen and their descendants gave the demography of Italy a wholly new aspect.

When Rome was an agricultural village like so many others of Latium and Italy, its peasant inhabitants were self-sufficient, as was the town itself. But as Rome grew into a city and absorbed more

[7] App. *B.C.* 1.1.7 (LCL, trl. by Horace White).

people, its economic life had to be organized on a more complex scale, and not all its inhabitants could be farmers; trade and commerce and specialized crafts were needed to keep the city alive. Yet the ancient ideal of the peasant-farmer, who as a citizen also takes interest in and guides the course of the state, persisted with typical Roman conservatism. Hence those who owned land, the patricians, the senators, continued to be the persons of the greatest prestige, though they were socially and economically no nearer to the ideal of the citizen-farmer than today a Prince Torlonia is to a Calabrian peasant.

But, as they bought up property from small farmers who moved to the city, and occupied the common land, the so-called *ager publicus*, formally as a leaseholding, practically as private property, they soon acquired landed estate of such proportions that they could only become absentee owners whose property was administered by employees while they themselves were gentlemen of the city. "Of the territory which the Romans won in war from their neighbors, a part they sold, and a part they made common land, and assigned it for occupation for the poor and indigent among the citizens, on payment of a small rent into the public treasury. And when the rich began to offer larger rents and drove out the poor, a law was enacted [in 367 B.C.] forbidding the holding by one person of more than five-hundred iugera [330 acres] of land. For a short time this enactment gave a check to the rapacity of the rich, and was of assistance to the poor, who remained in their places on the land which they had rented and occupied the allotment which each had held from the outset. But later on, the neighboring rich men, by means of fictitious personages, transferred these rentals to themselves, and finally held most of the land openly in their own names. Then the poor, who had been ejected from their land, no longer showed themselves eager for military service, and neglected the bringing up of children, so that soon all Italy was conscious of a dearth of freemen, and was filled with gangs of foreign slaves, by whose aid the rich cultivated their estates, from which they had driven away the free citizens." [8] But even though many persons were worried by the growth of landed property in the hands of few with the consequent impoverishment of many,

[8] Plut. *Tib. Gracchus* 8.1–3 (LCL, trl. by Bernadotte Perrin).

and remedial laws were passed, the situation was not improved: indeed those who would have the power to institute effective reforms were the very ones who were most interested in retaining the *status quo*.

We find no indication in pre-Roman days, or even during the early Republic, that Italy's earth did not sufficiently provide for all the people. But in the period during and after the Second Punic War (218–201 B.C.) occurs the first historical evidence that food had to be imported into Italy because much of the peninsula was either actually in the hands of the Carthaginians or was so ravaged and pillaged by incessant warfare that agricultural pursuits could not be maintained. (In 210, Rome was forced to appeal to King Ptolemy Philopator of Egypt for grain, and had to pay three times the regular market price.)

After the war, it turned out that imported grain, especially from Sicily and later from Egypt, was and remained cheaper than the native crop. In order to stay in business Italian landowners even more ruthlessly increased their landholdings at the expense of the small farmers, and large *latifundia* devoured ever more of the family farms. To produce crops at competitive prices the landowners employed more and more slaves, driving the free man, who in addition was burdened by the inexorable duties of military service, from the land and into the city where he became part of a growing, restive, unruly mob. And most importantly, many latifundists changed over from grain to now more lucrative orchards, vineyards, market garden crops, and especially cattle and sheep raising.[9] The sheep were allowed to overgraze the progressively deforested countryside and, being notoriously close croppers, they turned good agricul-

[9] Treatises written during the Empire on agriculture and cattle breeding accord the first a very insignificant place. Of Columella's thirteen books *De re rustica* not one is entirely devoted to grain, but two and one-half to viticulture, one and one-half to olive and other orchards, four to livestock, poultry, bees, and one, composed in verse, to gardening. But even long before that it is attributed to Cato that "when he was asked what was the most profitable feature of an estate, he replied: 'Raising cattle successfully.' What next to that? 'Raising cattle with fair success,' And next? 'Raising cattle with but slight success.' And when his questioner said: 'How about money-lending?', Cato replied: 'How about murder?'" (Cic. *de off.* 2.25; LCL, trl. by Walter Miller). Vineyards spread with such rapidity throughout Italy and the provinces as to cause an economic problem. The emperor Domitian (81–96) forbade the planting of new ones in Italy and ordered the conversion of half of those in the provinces into agricultural land. But his decrees seem not to have been enforced.

tural land into dustbowls whence the topsoil was blown and washed away forever.

In 218 B.C. the *Lex Claudia* (see p. 293) was passed, forbidding senators and their sons to own and operate ships holding more than three hundred amphorae (225 bushels). The purpose of this was to exclude the leaders of the state from speculative business and to tie them down, according to the *mos maiorum*, to ownership of real estate. Since in our Western civilization, ancient and modern, it is customary for a man to want to become rich, and for a rich man to become richer, the senators sought to circumvent the law by subterfuge, thus damaging their reputation and with it that of the state. They were also driven into buying up more and more land, since this was now the only legal way open to them to enrich themselves, and furthered thereby the rise of latifundia and made that kind of pernicious land ownership respectable. In 200 B.C. the words which Manius Curius had uttered only ninety years earlier must have sounded hollow and odd; he had said, "after celebrating triumphs and making a vast addition of territory to the empire, . . . that a man not satisfied with seven iugera [4½ acres] must be deemed a dangerous citizen; for that was the acreage assigned for commoners after the expulsion of the kings." [10]

By the last third of the second century the situation was desperate. Tiberius Gracchus describes it in a speech perhaps not altogether objectively and unemotionally, but the core of truth cannot be denied: "The wild beasts that roam over Italy have everyone of them a cave or lair to lurk in; but the men who fight and die for Italy enjoy the common air and light, indeed, but nothing else; houseless and homeless they wander about with their wives and children. And it is with lying lips that their imperators exhort the soldiers in their battles to defend sepulchres and shrines from the enemy; for not a man of them has a hereditary altar, not one of all those many Romans an ancestral tomb, but they fight and die to support others in wealth and luxury, and though they are styled masters of the world, they have not a single clod of earth that is their own." [11]

In 140 B.C. Gaius Laelius sponsored a new law designed to

[10] Plin. *N.H.* 18.1 (LCL, trl. by H. Rackham).
[11] Plut. *Tib. Gracchus* 9.5. (LCL, trl. by Bernadotte Perrin).

limit the growth of large estates. But the senators, more faithful to the interests of their own class than to the welfare of the commonwealth, dropped it. Subsequently, Tiberius and Gaius Gracchus sought agrarian reforms, mainly by restriction of acreage per family and distribution to colonists of public land habitually but illegally held by private owners. Some of these corrections were reluctantly instituted, but presently sabotaged. Tiberius Gracchus was murdered amidst a carnage of his followers in 132; his brother Gaius had himself stabbed to death, in 122, by a faithful servant when capture and death at the hands of the vengeful senate appeared imminent. With the violent deaths of these two men began nearly a century of internecine bloodshed and strife in which the vaunted Roman virtues of old, civic conscience, frugality, honesty were completely submerged and virtually rooted out.

A law of 121 (or 120) permitted the Gracchan colonists to sell their allotments, which meant that the great landholders could resume not only their buying up of land, but also their practice of driving small holders into forced sales. Between 118 and 112 the Gracchan land commission for the redistribution of land was abolished. In 111, in a partial reversal of the annulment of Gracchan land policies, all lands previously assigned by the land commission became private property, as did former holdings of public lands up to 500 iugera (330 acres), all of them rent-free. This was a considerable blow to the latifundists, who it is estimated lost some 1,000,000 acres through this action. Some further recovery of the Italian farmer was brought about by Caesar's law requiring that one-third of the labor force employed on plantations consist of free men.

Pliny says that "the latifundia ruined Italy." [12] In a way this is true. But the deeper truth probably is that "the latifundia and corruption are but different aspects of the same social phenomenon. If the moral disintegration was due to the disappearance of the self-supporting, self-respecting farmer class, and the inordinate wealth and fantastic luxury of the small upper class, the latifundia were but a real-estate expression of the same phenomenon." [13]

Men will always debate as to which comes first, the moral or the material disintegration of a society. But it is certain that, during

[12] Plin. *N.H.* 18.7.
[13] Simkhovich 1916, 203.

the first century B.C. in Italy, both the moral and the material level of the Romans were sinking to pitiful depths.

The costly Punic Wars, the numerous wars of the second century, and the bloody civil strife from the Gracchi to the establishment of the monarchy under Augustus wrought serious damage also upon the population and brought about intermittent manpower shortages, particularly in the country. Especially the south was grievously damaged by the havoc of the Hannibalic wars, and an improvident government failed to restore it to health. In 210 B.C. twelve Latin colonies refused to furnish the quotas of soldiers demanded of them: they simply had no men. The years between 164 and 136 B.C. saw a decline in the census from 337,000 to 317,000, indicating a loss of nearly 6 per cent of male citizens of military age who were subject to military service — either through actual decline in the numbers of the living, or through their impoverishment below the quota requisite for the draft. During Sulla's brutal regime, 2,600 members of the equestrian order were killed and 200 senators; the peasants of Samnium and Etruria who had taken the side of the Populares against Sulla and his Optimates were practically eradicated. Ten years of raging civil war had cost the lives of 150,000 persons, mainly Italians.

The countryside was further depopulated by the ruin of the small farmers and their migration to Rome or emigration to the provinces. The vast numbers of Italians who perished in the defense of Cirta in North Africa during the war against Jugurtha (113 B.C.) and the 80,000 Italian residents in Asia Minor who were massacred on the order of Mithradates (88 B.C.), show how many had fled the peninsula in search of a better life elsewhere.

During the first three centuries of the Republic, the Latin farmer was required regularly to serve in the citizen militia in the defense of the state. But when, from the Second Punic War on, the government, now bent on an offensive and imperialist policy of aggrandizement, called the farmer to arms too often and for too long periods, he was forced to neglect his home and his fields, and fell into debt. Since he received no war booty, he could not afford to employ labor, nor to pay taxes, nor to borrow capital. He was bought out by the latifundists, and moved to Rome, sometimes even before extreme necessity forced this step, in order to escape the military draft. The truth was that, just as the Roman constitution, designed to govern a city, was inadequate for running a great state, so the Roman peasant militia, sufficient to protect an agricultural area of the size of Latium, became more and more unsuited for the military adventures of empire.

The place of the citizen in the army was taken over by mercenaries. As early as the Second Punic War, after the disastrous blood bath of Cannae (216) when a Roman army of 50,000 to 80,000 men (tradition gives the latter figure) was virtually annihilated by the numerically inferior but superbly led forces of Hannibal, 8,000 slaves were enrolled in the Roman legions and promised freedom as a reward for faithful service. Although Rome was not often obliged to rely upon slave soldiers, foreign mercenaries did find a place in increasing numbers in the armed forces. Among the troops which the senate sent against Gaius Gracchus, barricaded on the Aventine Hill shortly before his death (122 B.C.), were Cretan archers: thus the bald political murder of a Roman was made even more reprehensible. From the time of Marius (consul six times between 104 and 99 B.C.), who could not find enough free men to fill the ranks of his armies, a paid soldiery, among whom were many non-Italians, came into being. To these 'Roman' legionnaires the fate of the state in whose service they fought could be only indifferent. They were employed for sixteen, then twenty years, and received pay, booty, and a discharge allowance. As they had no other career open to them, they were willing to sell their services to generals who could maintain them or at least make the most enticing promises, and to pledge their loyalty to their military leaders rather than to the state government. Thus the army was proletarized and the proletariat militarized, and the generals became dictators.[14] The result of this was civil war.

From Marius on, citizenship could be bestowed upon soldiers and veterans for their service. Hence Roman citizenship was put up for sale as part of the soldiers' wages by generals in need of men for their private ambitions, and many undesirable foreigners availed themselves of this opportunity. "Nothing had contributed more directly to the failure of the republican form of government

---

[14] Kornemann 1948, 1.370.

than the growth of the professional army and the inability of the senate to control its commanders." [15]

The place of the free peasant population in Italy was taken largely by slaves who were cheaply imported by the landowners and kept in inhuman squalor and degradation on the plantations. (The directions on how to deal with slaves, how to squeeze the last drop of blood out of them and then to discard them, stem from none other than the honest, sturdy, puritanical Roman patriot Cato, who, one must believe, in this respect also represented a most Roman trait: moneylending was worse than murder, but butchering slaves by working them to death was merely good farm management.) The ever-advancing Roman legions provided the slave market with an unending flow of merchandise from virtually the whole known world; this was part of the booty of war.[16] Some of them, or of their notoriously numerous progeny, were set free and populated Italy with rapidly increasing numbers of fully or only partly assimilated foreigners. In 88 B.C. Sulla freed 10,000 slaves of proscribed Romans. Between 73 and 71 there raged a revolt in which no fewer than 70,000 slaves rose desperately in arms against their masters. The Gauls and Germans among them followed Crixus as their leader, the Thracians the famous Spartacus. The uprising was with difficulty and bloodily suppressed, and 6,000 of Spartacus' men were crucified. Augustus, in order to stem the tide and to forestall the swamping of the Italian element in the nation, instituted two laws, in 2 B.C. and A.D. 5, the first imposing a limit upon the number of slaves a single master was allowed to set free in his testament, the

---

[15] Boak 1955, 264.

[16] To indicate the variety of sources whence slaves were imported I shall list the Roman possessions outside of Italy, with the date of conquest: Sicily 241 B.C., Corsica, Sardinia 238, Syracuse 212, Gallia Cisalpina 225–210, Spain 197, Dalmatia 167, Epirus 165, Macedonia 148, Achaea 146, Carthage 146, (Province of) Asia 129, Balearic Islands 122, Gallia Narbonensis 121, Cilicia 101, Bythinia 75, Cyrenaica 74, Crete 67, Syria (western) 64, Pontus 64, Gaul 58–51, Cyprus 58, Massilia 49, Numidia 46, Egypt 30, Phrygia, Galatia, Pisidia, Lycaonia 25, Galicia (Spain) 19, Raetia, Noricum 15, Illyricum 15, Pannonia, Upper Germany 9 (the latter lost again in A.D. 9), Moesia A.D. 3–4, Palestine (western) 6, Cappadocia 17, Mauretania 40, Britain 43, Thracia 46, Lycia 48, Lesser Armenia 72, Lower Germany 73–155, Syria (eastern) 75, Palestine (eastern) 93, Arabia Petraea 105, Dacia 106, Armenia 114, Assyria, Mesopotamia 115 (the last three all lost again in 117), Osrhoëne 195, Sophene 296. The personal names of slaves (which were generally not their native names but often are derived from their country of origin, for example, Thracius) also give us a picture of their varied provenience.

second imposing a similar restriction upon the number which could be manumitted during the owner's lifetime. The enactment of such countermeasures suffices, even without quantifying statistics on original conditions and results, to indicate the gravity of the situation.

In addition to the slaves, the city of Rome contained vast numbers of free foreigners, who had flocked to Rome, the growing capital of the world, as teachers, traders, craftsmen, merchants, physicians, artists, or just as idle mob. The senate and the office seekers supported these crowds with a dole and largesses. Thus, the Roman assemblies in fact ceased to be 'Roman.'

Mention should also be made of the gaining fashion of childlessness among the upper classes, who, at least theoretically, were most apt and capable to continue old Roman culture and traditions. This phenomenon seems to be characteristic in the ruling classes of many civilized, perhaps overcivilized, societies, and often accompanies and enhances cultural and national transformation. The pity of this is not that the 'good' stock commits 'race suicide' and lets the 'bad' stock flood the country, but that it implies the diminution of that social class which, given the nature of Western money culture and the class structure of most nations, certainly of ancient Rome, can afford to attain and maintain certain civic and civilized ideals in a realm and on a plane not accessible to those who spend most of their efforts in acquiring their daily bread. The Julian Laws of 19 and 18 B.C., enacted by Augustus, attempted to restore the soundness of family life, to encourage marriage, to discountenance childlessness by imposing certain legal disabilities on unmarried and childless citizens, and in general to remedy the laxity of morals. (The poet Ovid, 43 B.C.–A.D. 17, probably owes his banishment to bleak Tomi on the Black Sea to the more slippery and sensual of his writings which clashed with the moral crusade undertaken by Augustus.) Despite the opposition which this legislation generated, it was further strengthened by the Papian Poppaean law of A.D. 9 which discriminated against childless candidates for office, favoring their competitors who had children. Again, as in the case of legislation concerning the manumission of slaves, Augustus' intervention indicates the urgency of such measures.

It has often been said by modern historians that it was this foreign 'blood' which ruined the Italian stock and its great virtues, and led to luxury, sumptuousness, vice, and debauchery in social and cultural life, and ultimately to the prostration of the Republic. It is true that ethnic or racial mixture occurred; but it was not the biological transformation which caused the corruption of the mores and the culture of the Roman nation. If, nonetheless, it can be justly maintained that the influence of the foreigners is to a great degree responsibile for the deterioration of the state, the guilt is not theirs, or that of any racial inferiority, so much as that of the Romans who failed to educate the new citizens in the ways and virtues of a republican form of government. But how could the Romans of the second and first century B.C. fulfill such a task since they themselves had ceased to practice these ways and virtues which alone could have saved the republic, what with the Senate and the aristocracy themselves setting the tone in conspicuous extravagance, unscrupulous business dealings, and political irresponsibility? (In 28 B.C. Augustus eliminated no fewer than two hundred iniquitous holders of the senatorial office, or every fifth man, from the rolls of the Senate.) The truth of the matter is that the Roman state could not absorb and did not provide for the acculturation of its new citizens and noncitizen inhabitants. (Naturally, this failure will also extend to the domain of language.)

The end of the Republic was imminent, and Caesar dealt the death blow. Cicero who had desired, wisely and honestly, the continuity of the republican form of government, tragically was obliged to seek its realization through a governing body which had become both unworthy and incapable of its noble responsibility. Caesar being aware, as Sulla had not been some forty years earlier, of the political and moral decadence of the Senate, and also of the utter impossibility of constructing a true popular republic upon the shoulders of the mob of Rome (and it is more than doubtful that he would have chosen this course even if it had been possible), consciously proceeded to deliver the republic a *coup de grâce.* "The Republic which Caesar had overthrown was no system of popular government but one whereby a small group of Roman nobles and capitalists exploited for their own personal ends and for the satisfaction of an idle city mob millions of subjects in the provinces. The republican organs of government had ceased to voice the opinion even of the whole Roman citizen body. The governing circles had proven themselves incapable of bringing about any improvement in the situation and had completely lost the power of preserving peace in the state." [17]

THE PRINCIPATE

"The transformation which society underwent during the Empire may be aptly described as the transition from a regime of individual initiative to a regime of status, that is, from one in which the position of an individual in society was mainly determined by his own volition to one in which this was fixed by the accident of his birth. The population of the Empire was divided into a number of sharply defined castes, each of which was compelled to play a definite role in the life of the state. The sons of senators, soldiers, *curiales* ['municipal councillors'], *corporati* ['members of business, trade, and crafts associations'], and *coloni* ['tenant farmers and agricultural workers'] had to follow in their fathers' walks of life, and each sought to escape from the tasks to which he was born. In the eyes of the government *collegiati* [or *corporati*], *curiales*, and *coloni* existed solely to work or to pay taxes for the support of the bureaucracy and the army. The consequence was the attempted flight of the population to the army, civil service, the church, or the wilderness. Private industry languished, commerce declined, the fields lay untilled; a general feeling of hopelessness paralyzed all initiative. And when the barbarians began to occupy the provinces they encountered no national resistance; rather were they looked upon as deliverers from the burdensome yoke of Rome." [18]

One of the great and not by any means atypical success stories of the first century after Christ (reported with tongue in cheek by Petronius in a novel entitled *Satyricon*) is that of the freedman Trimalchio, told by the hero himself at a blatantly sumptuous dinner party, the famous *Cena Trimalchionis*. He was freed by his master and went into the wine transport business. On his first voyage he lost all of his five ships by shipwreck, but he tried again with bigger and better ships and made a million on his first successful trip. He bought the farm of his former master and converted

[17] Boak 1955, 239–240.
[18] Boak 1955, 468.

it from agriculture to livestock raising; he dismissed the free laborers, bought slaves to work the farm, and hired freedmen agents to run it. Then he retired to Rome and engaged in successful banking enterprises, growing richer by the day.

The Emperor Tiberius (14–37), Augustus' successor, writes this to the Senate about luxury and corruption of morals among the wealthy class: "On what am I to make my first effort at prohibition and retrenchment to the ancient standard? On the infinite expanse of our villas? The number — the nations — of our slaves? The weight of our silver and gold? The miracles of bronze and canvas? The promiscuous dress of male and female — and the specially female extravagance by which, for the sake of jewels, our wealth is transported to alien or hostile countries? I am aware that at dinner-parties and social gatherings these things are condemned, and the call is for restriction; but let anyone pass a law and prescribe a penalty, and the same voices will be uplifted against 'this subversion of the state, this death-blow to all magnificence, this charge of which not a man is guiltless . . .' Why was frugality once the rule? Because every man controlled himself; because we were burghers of a single town; nor were there even the same temptations while our empire was confined to Italy." [19]

But the prosperity necessary for this extravagance did not seep down into the poorer classes, and the Augustan renaissance and the *pax Romana* profited the proletariat little. Hence, the profound rift in Roman society is perpetuated through a period of affluence which, theoretically, offered the best promises for bridging it.

In agriculture there continued the trend already observed during the late Republic and which brings ever greater calamities to the free peasant population of Italy. To stimulate agriculture, Trajan (97–117) makes available loans by the state to the farmer at low rates of interest. Fortunately, the second century is one of good government and internal peace throughout the empire, which has its temporary beneficial effect at least upon the small landowners of Italy. Slave labor declines, owing to the manumission of great numbers of slaves, and since no important foreign conquests are

[19] Tac. *Ann.* 3.53–54. Frank 1940, 29, says that "the generation that came to maturity under the Julio-Claudian emperors provides one of the best examples known to history of an upstart aristocracy that abused the benefits of prosperity."

made the supply of slaves is reduced and their price increased. But toward the end of the century, due to renewed warfare on the borders of the Empire and increased expenses for the growing machinery of the state, the taxes gathered by merciless collectors, who are liable to the state with their personal fortunes, become so oppressive as to make small farming again unlucrative, and once more a flight from the land sets in. The third century is fully catastrophic: wars, civil disorders, pestilence, barbarian invasions, all conspire to shake the state to its foundations. The counter-measures are ever greater repression, a wholly inept attempt at price-fixing (under Diocletian in 301), raising of taxes to support a court and a bureaucracy of oriental sumptuousness and pomp, and the institution of virtual serfdom for the farmer by allowing neither him nor his heirs to leave the land which they work with less and less reward. In addition, agriculture makes no technical advances whatever, and neither the fertility of the soil nor the efficiency of human labor is augmented. Although there is no evidence of soil exhaustion, and although erosion, already grave enough a problem, does not seem to make important progress, by the end of the fourth century agriculture is nonetheless prostrate, and farmers, excepting the latifundists, are utterly ruined.

The government, the population, and the army, continuing the trend observed in the late republic, become progressively less Roman and Italian. Vespasian (69–79), an Italian from Reate, the son of an equestrian, is the first emperor not of the Roman nobility. Trajan (97–117) is the first prince of provincial origin, a native of Italica in Farther Spain.[20] Hadrian (117–138) is also a Spaniard, Antoninus Pius (138–180) comes from Gaul. Since these last four emperors are worthy men and praised by all as good, honest rulers, any reluctance to raise a non-Italian to the principate which may have hitherto prevailed is stilled by these fortunate precedents. From that time on, all emperors of Rome with very few exceptions are non-Italians or of non-Italian descent: Africans (Septimius Severus, Macrinus), Syrians (Elagabalus, Severus Alexander), Thracians (Maximinus), Illyrians (Aurelianus and his dynasty, Constantine), Pannonians (Valerius Maximianus, Valentinian I and

[20] On the gradual de-Italianizing of the Senate between Vespasian and Trajan, see Stech 1912.

his dynasty), and so forth. Hadrian spends more than half of his reign on tours of inspection and campaigns outside of Italy. Septimius Severus (193–211), of Punic stock and married to a Syrian woman, is completely unappreciative of Roman tradition. He carries the scheme (commenced by Trajan) of substituting an imperial for the Roman-Italian policy to its logical conclusion: he deprives the Roman Senate of all governmental functions; he admits to high positions in government, in civil service, and in the army a great number of provincials, especially from Africa and Syria, his and his wife's home, respectively; he abolishes the privileges Italy enjoys among the provinces; he bars Italians from the Praetorian Guard, his personal bodyguard and the house regiment of Rome; he excludes Italians also from holding the centuriate, that is, junior officership, in any legion and thereby de-Romanizes the army also in the higher enlisted ranks. His son and successor, Caracalla (211–217), one of the most worthless men to occupy the principate, extends Roman citizenship to all inhabitants of the Empire (212).[21]

Macrinus (217–218), made emperor by the army, is the first monarch not of the senatorial order, and also the first never to set foot in the city of Rome.

It cannot be said that fundamentally these acts of depriving Italy of its favored position *vis à vis* the Empire were harmful or illogical, although of course the senators of Rome were loath to see their exalted position diminished. Tacitus, a strong supporter of the senatorial against the equestrian order, complained already in the time of Nero, in the middle of the first century after Christ, of the *noua prouincialium superbia* 'the novel arrogance of the provincials.'[22] But, after all, there existed now a Roman Empire which comprised a big portion of the world, and it may as well be governed as one, and not as a mere appendage to Italy whence Italians derived their wealth. What was wrong with the new policy was that it did not enable the Empire to coalesce its various units into an organic whole, either by making all of it Italian in culture, or by establishing a large area of mixed culture but with identical interests and aims. The mere conferring of citizenship, important though it

[21] It has been suggested that Caracalla, son of a Punic father and a Syrian mother, used this as his "method of telling the Romans that he was as good as they." (Frank 1923, 535.)

[22] Tac. *Ann.* 15.20.

was for the eventual Romanization of some areas, especially the Latin West, was not an efficient instrument for creating a cohesive empire out of an agglomeration of provinces.

It is only natural that under these circumstances the linguistic acculturation of all parts of the Empire found no succor.

In A.D. 14, at the death of Augustus, the population of Italy is estimated as 6,000,000, that of the Empire as 54,000,000, of whom 26,000,000 lived in the predominantly Latin west, 28,000,000 in the predominantly Greek east.[23] In the city of Rome as many as 90 per cent are thought to have been of foreign, especially Greek and Near Eastern birth or ancestry. But also the rest of Italy and the provinces continue to undergo a considerable change in their population. "In a word, the whole of Italy as well as the Romanized portions of Gaul and Spain were during the Empire dominated in blood by the East."[24]

Under Septimius Severus (193–211) the Italians lose their majority in the Senate. Italy is deprived of a vast number of inhabitants during the catastrophic third century through wars, epidemics, and a general economic decline. The population of Italy had become so sparse and weak that it could not be counted upon to provide a defensive hinterland for the very capital of the Empire. Rome had not been under attack by foreign troops since the cry "*Hannibal ante portas*" arose. But under Aurelianus (270–275) it became necessary for the first time since those perilous days to fortify Rome with a wall of brick twenty feet high, twelve feet wide, and twelve miles in circuit, large portions of which, though restored, still stand today.

The army grows stronger in influence though not in numbers, having discovered the secret of making and breaking emperors. Between 235 and 285, no fewer than twenty-six Augusti are raised

---

[23] Beloch 1886, 507. There are no authoritative ancient statistics on demographic or economic matters (cf. Jones 1948, 1–10), and the estimates of modern scholars diverge greatly from one another, especially since in the Roman census the phrase *ciuium capita* 'number of citizens' can be interpreted differently at different times (cf. Beloch 1886, 315–319; Jones 1948, 3–4). Frank 1940, in sharp disagreement with Beloch, gives the total population of Italy in 28 B.C. as 14,000,000 of which 10,000,000 were freeborn citizens. For a severe, but just critique of all attempts, however ingenious, to estimate ancient populations, see Boak, Manpower, 1955, 4–8.

[24] Frank 1927, 216; 1927, 330; he finds among 1,854 occurrences of names of workmen on imperial inscriptions only 65 which are demonstrably those of freeborn citizens.

to the throne, mostly by the soldiery, and prevalently not out of political considerations but rather upon the incentive of donatives and promises of rewards. Indeed, no response to patriotic motives could be expected from mercenaries, including ever greater numbers of officers, who did not feel allegiance to the state as a whole but only to the general or politician who paid them.

In the city, and especially in the country, the poor grow poorer and the rich grow richer but fewer. Ever more Romans live on the dole, and ever more tax money is spent by emperors and officials to keep the populace entertained in the circus and the theater, with the number of yearly holidays increasing to two hundred and more. The Senate declines, the equestrians — that is, bankers, business-men, and capitalists — rise. The ponderous machinery of the state is kept in motion, not by elective or appointed officials, but by a pro-lific bureaucracy, which is self-perpetuating and self-glorifying (note the titles *clarissimus, eminentissimus, perfectissimus, egregius*), and withal incompetent. The old senatorial aristocracy, or what was left of it, languishes and expires, and is replaced by, or converted into, a fawning retinue of sycophant courtiers. The entire popula-tion of the Empire is now officially and bureaucratically divided into two classes, the *honestiores* and the *humiliores*. The first in-cludes the rich and the new aristocrats through wealth and favorit-ism who run and own everything, and also, at least by title, the soldiers and veterans who make emperors; the second comprises all the remaining mass of the people. The peasants groan under crush-ing taxes and are reduced to virtual serfdom since they are by law prohibited from leaving the land and seeking a different livelihood. The same is true of tradesmen and craftsmen and workers. Thus the *humiliores* are legally free, but actually their status is somewhere between a freedman and a slave. And the manpower shortage, partly a cause and partly a result of the general decline, becomes more and more severe.[25] The Empire is rapidly moving toward its demise. "Thus we find barbarians at the gates, barbarian troops holding those gates, vanishing figures on the throne, triumphant civil servants, and a population declining in number and in spirit. And people ask why the Roman Empire fell. Why did it last?"[26]

[25] Cf. Jones 1948, 14–19; Boak, Manpower, 1955.
[26] Glover 1953, 324.

CHAPTER XXIII

Spoken and Written Latin   Our history of the

Latin language has up to this point described its diffusion from
Latium over all of Italy in consequence of the conquest of the
country and its tribes by Roman arms. I shall now attempt, supported by the facts of socio-cultural history, to examine the significant facts of the history of Latin in Italy until the dissolution
of the Western Empire.

Hierarchy in human groups has been a reality throughout the
ages whose history we know. It may well be a timeless human universal; for even if a classless society were to abolish all social distinctions, a hierarchy of native endowment and intelligence would
assert itself, which, whenever we are dealing with a culture where
success is measured by material acquisitions, would quickly re-
establish economic and social differentiation. I have emphasized the
ingrained class structure of Roman society, which is fundamentally
and palpably twofold: the patricians (and knights) and the plebeians, the rich and the poor, the 'haves' and the 'have-nots,' the
honestiores and the *humiliores.*

Concomitant with this material division of society runs also
a distinction between the literate and the illiterate, the educated
and the non educated, again much more effectively and irreconcil-
ably and irrevocably separated from one another in the Roman than
in modern European states, to say nothing of the United States
where, stark though class differences may be, the individual's
mobility from one social or intellectual or financial class to another
is relatively easy.

The present chapter proposes to relate the kind of evidence
which entitles the linguist to postulate two types of language, the
written and the spoken (and I do of course not subscribe to the

view that written language is not properly language), to describe the sources, and to show how the two are related.[1]

As for the sources and records of the literary language little need be said. They are the works of Latin literature of all ages, in particular, as far as Classical Latin is concerned, those of the Golden Latinity of the end of the Republic and of the Augustan Age.

A discussion of records of the spoken language and their evaluation is somewhat more complex.[2] Every textbook of Romanic linguistics teaches that the Romanic languages are not really descended from Classical Latin but from Vulgar Latin. Quite apart from the questionable term 'descent,' which is at best metaphorical (I should rather say that the Romanic languages *are* modern Latin of one kind or another), the term Vulgar Latin in this context appears objectionable, for reasons I shall mention presently, and I want to replace it with Spoken Latin.

The great number of definitions proposed for Vulgar Latin mirrors the plurality of Vulgar Latin theories, which cannot all be correct.[3] Since all of them are based on the same records, the divergence of theories must spring from the interpretation and not the nature of the evidence.[4]

One may completely discard, as the majority of scholars have done, the idea that Spoken (Vulgar) Latin is the chronological successor to and a corruption of Classical Latin.[5] But the romantic and pedantic view that any linguistic divergence from a norm established by a period of classicism is necessarily a sign of decadence or decay dies hard.

Apart from this antiquated belief there are, roughly, two types of Vulgar Latin theories. First, there are those which propose that

[1] Much of the following discussion is based, by quotation or paraphrase, but with important changes and additions, on Pulgram 1950.

[2] For a chrestomathy see Rohlfs 1951.

[3] Sas 1937, 491, counts nineteen definitions. See also Löfstedt 1936, 8; Palmer 1954, 148–149.

[4] The difficulties were seen, or rather foreseen, nearly a century ago when Schuchardt 1866, 1. ix mentioned the complexities of the subject, "because the term 'Vulger Latin' strictly speaking signifies not one single language but a number of linguistic stages and dialects from the time of the first Roman to the time of the first Romanic literary monuments." See also *ibid*. 1.3.

[5] This too had already been said by Schuchardt 1866, 1.47: "The sermo plebeius is related to the sermo urbanus not ascendentally but collaterally."

there prevailed, especially during the Empire and the early Middle Ages, a linguistic unity of popular speech throughout the Roman and Romanized world. According to some scholars this unity dissolved in the fifth or sixth century of our era, according to others not before the end of the eighth or ninth centuries. Second, there are theories which insist on early dialectalization of Latin, or indeed maintain that there never existed, outside of early Latium, a single unified Latin, or anything but a number of local dialects, especially in the Romania outside of Italy. (And we know that even ancient Latium was not without its local Latin dialects.)

To what extent may our sources claim to represent spoken Latin? On our conclusions will depend our judgment of the various Vulgar Latin theories.[6] The largest and most varied source comprises inscriptions of all periods from Italy and the entire Romania. Besides, we have also literary texts, sacred and profane; political, juridical, historical, liturgical, and hagiographical documents; and, last but not least, the testimony of the grammarians and the glosses. All writing in Classical Latin is by its nature excluded.

Inscriptions are highly prized for determining popular speech, especially those referring to and made by common people. Official inscriptions are mostly stuffy, full of archaisms to enhance their solemnity. Their writers, of no matter what period, are consistently guided by a desire to write good, that is, Classical or at least urban, and urbane, Latin. More often than not, they have not mastered it, either because of geographical or chronological remoteness from Rome of the Golden Latinity, or for lack of education, or for both reasons. This does not apply to the type of Latin writing, especially outside of Rome, which preceded the rise of the Latin standard language, that is, which is older than the second or third century B.C. (see Chapter XXV). But our records of that early period are very scanty indeed. Yet in what we have of this preclassical era we can discern certain spoken dialectal variations which were not yet submerged by the spreading standard of Rome.[7]

But while mistakes and deviations from the literary language, from the socially permissible and recommendable norm, will be

---

[6] On the principles of evaluating written documents see Richter 1934, 4 ff.; a listing of sources may be found in Palmer 1954, 149–155.
[7] See below, Chapter XXIV, on local dialects.

significant in any written document, their presence does not yet make a document of this type an example of vulgar speech in intent or appearance: it is such only by default and only in spots. For even in the lowest form of literary activity, say, in scratchings on the walls of toilet and brothel (and we do have such so-called *graffiti*), the very fact of performing the intellectual act of writing, an accomplishment by no means as common even in the best time of Rome as it is today in Europe, leads even the most ignorant of writers to do somehow 'better' than he would in spontaneous speech. He cannot help it because, being schooled, however little and superficially, he has learned to write in the literary language only, according to certain rules of spelling and grammar. What he achieves may not always conform to those rules, but neither will it be a faithful rendering of what he would say. "We have no text which is a faithful record of even one mode of contemporary speech. The chisel of the stonemason, the pen of the loquacious nun, and the chalk that scribbles on the wall, disregard the tongue and move self-willed in traditional patterns. It is only through their occasional inadvertences, almost willy-nilly, that writers give us hints that their natural speech deviates from the language of the schoolroom which they are at pains to use." [8]

As for grammarians, their help in reconstructing an ancient popular form of speech is invaluable. When they point out, always disapprovingly, of course, deviations from the standard, one may trust their judgment, because by their profession they are a conservative if not reactionary lot. They are teachers, not of speech but of artful speech, of rhetoric; they are not recorders of currently prevailing customs, but self-appointed guardians of tradition. Unfortunately, they have a habit of copying one another over the centuries, so that it would be rash to construct a chronology of linguistic changes on their authority.

A very valuable source of knowledge for popular speech is the literary work of playwrights, especially of low comedy, and of some novelists, at least in passages of direct speech. In such instances Plautus (about 254–184 B.C.), Petronius (died A.D. 66), and Apuleius (of the 2nd century B.C., a native of Africa) give us honest spoken Latin. These three names practically exhaust the list, except for

[8] Palmer 1954, 149.

occasional words and phrases elsewhere, because Plautus' are the only truly popular comedies we know, and we have no Latin novels besides Petronius' *Satyricon* and Apuleius' *Golden Ass*. But, in the narrative passages of Petronius and Apuleius, too, the literary mind is at work; and the spontaneity of Plautine speech is inevitably inhibited by the use of the verse form.

Where an author wishes to render faithfully even the phonology of popular speech, the very requirement of having to write it down will pose difficulties, for, short of employing a phonetic transcription, which is impossible for authors who want their works read by a wide audience and which is moreover an unknown art in antiquity, the divergence between popular speech and the standard language can only be intimated by certain changes in spelling. These must be sufficiently evocative of non-standard pronunciation, yet at the same time not so radically removed from conventional orthography as to leave the reader exasperated by the difficulties of the deciphering. If a modern American realistic author writes, for example, "Ah sho' do lahk that li'l ol' b'ar" (and perhaps few writers would go that far), an American (though possibly not a British) reader will understand it to mean "I sure do like that little old bear." If, in addition, he can read it with the sounds and the intonation which the author wished to suggest, he does so, not because the approximate transcription is in any degree a sure guide, but only because he has guessed that it is supposed to represent some Southern American speech, and because he knows what that is like, perhaps not well enough for audible reproduction but well enough to imagine it properly enunciated.

When we are faced with a Latin text in which divergences from conventional spelling occur, deliberately or accidentally put there by the writer, we are in the position, not of the American reader described above, possibly not even in that of the British reader, but we are most likely faced by the difficulties that confront, say, a Frenchman who has learned English, that is, Standard English, and knows it well enough, but who, even after he has laboriously deciphered the English phrase I just cited, will have no idea how it actually sounds. True enough, and more is the pity, Latin writers who use popular speech never deviate from standard spelling to such a degree as did my example. But this, despite the consequent ease of decipherment on our part, only aggravates our problem of finding out just exactly how people did speak.

There are, in fact, scarcely any Latin literary works which furnish us an important amount of information on phonology. Deviations from spelling in professional authors who 'know better' are no doubt trustworthy guides to pronunciation, whether we can follow them or not, because they have been put there consciously, skillfully, and with the intent to convey nonstandard sounds, whereas the inscriptions and scribblings by semiliterate writers, while often clearly indicating the presence of a nonstandard phonation rather than mere ignorance of orthography, may not be adroitly enough respelled to give even a hint of the true sound, partly because the writer is too concerned with the 'correct' spelling, the prestige of which he had learned to esteem highly, partly because he has only a limited number of conventional letters to operate with and lacks the ingenuity to manipulate them as cleverly as does the expert.

However, phonological matters are by no means the unique or most important characteristics where popular speech may be distinguished from the cultivated language. Grammatical and stylistic variations, semantic changes, and choice of words are frequently more relevant, and these of course we can more often detect in writing of all types by both literary and naïve authors, in novels, poems, plays, and inscriptions of all types. Unlike popularisms on the phonological level, those on the morphological, syntactic, and lexical level require for proper notation no special alphabet, no particular spelling skill, but merely a good ear and the willingness to write what one hears, or indeed the inability to do otherwise.

As for political, juridical, historical, liturgical, and hagiographical records of late Antiquity and the Middle Ages, their authors were always literary or at least literate men who could read. It must not be forgotten that after the disappearance of the Roman public school system, which had been inadequate in any event, there was nothing to take its place for several centuries. Anything written was, therefore, necessarily intended for an élite; and since learning to read meant, in the absence of vernacular texts and because of the prestige of Roman culture, learning to read the Latin of Rome, authors had no reason or incentive to use another language. Writing, therefore, meant writing the best possible Roman Latin the author was capable of. But even so, if only we had texts in the original spelling and in the style of their first composition, we might fare better; instead we must be content with later copies, and mediaeval clerks are notoriously inaccurate copyists, particularly of models neither biblical nor classical, who not only impose their personal ways of writing upon their copy but also sometimes try to 'improve' on the original according to their own light.

For our purposes of discovering peculiarities of spoken Latin I should value much more highly a few direct statements on the state of the vernacular in Italy and other parts of the Romania. We have evidence of this sort in collections of vulgarisms such as the *Appendix Probi* (probably of the third century), the Glosses of Reichenau (probably of the ninth century), and similar compilations, from a variety of persons, not only grammarians. But they are mostly of a relatively late date and tell nothing about Latin speech of the Republic or the early Empire. They contain on the whole corrections of pronunciation, where the author consciously imitates in spelling a form he has heard; but nothing is said, of course, about the frequency of these 'errors' at any given time. This subtracts considerably from their value as evidence for speech. For grammatical and syntactical matters we may cite the observations of numerous persons, mainly grammarians, who unfavorably compare the *rusticitas* of someone's speech with the *urbanitas* of the educated classes of Rome, and who make explicit reference to dialectalization of various areas, to the change of speech in time, and to social differences — in other words to the horizontal (geographic), vertical (social), and chronological differentiation of language. What else could Hieronymus, for example, certainly an acute observer, have meant when he said: "Latin usage itself changes continuously according to place and time." [9]

In what relation do the written and the spoken language stand to one another? In an article on Demotic and Koptic, Sethe prints a sketch to illustrate the development of spoken and written Egyp-

---

[9] Hier. *ad. Gal.* 2.3.

tian (see Fig. 1).[10] Our knowledge of Egyptian extends over a much longer period than that of Latin, the Romanic languages included. Its history comprises, as the sketch shows, six different written or classical languages of successive eras. The steps on the sketch indicate these succeeding classical languages, whereas the straight sloping line represents the continuous change of the spoken idiom throughout the history of Egyptian. Each linguistic break that produces a step coincides roughly with an important political event in

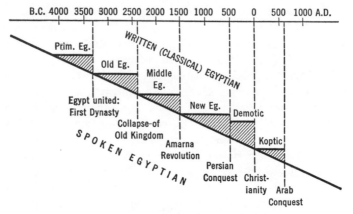

Fig. 1 (after Sethe 1925, 316, slightly revised)

Egyptian history, usually a catastrophe. Now while the spoken language of the masses moves along its undisturbed linear development, each classical language, from its inception, is held to a level standard, without major changes as long as the society which employs it remains stable. A breakdown of this society involves the breakdown of its classical language; and the new socio-cultural structure creates a new literary language out of the spoken language then current. In other words, the established classical tradition collapses with the culture which it represents, and a new one begins. Since each classical language is by nature and intent conservative, it continues, as it were, horizontally from its point of origin, whereas at the same time popular speech proceeds on

[10] Sethe 1925. My present sketch is copied from Pulgram 1950, 461, Fig. 1.

its accustomed natural course, that is, changes gradually with the passage of time.

In applying the same schematic principle to Latin (see Fig. 2),[11] obviously I can show no steps, because we have knowledge of but one classical era of that language. In the same horizontal di-

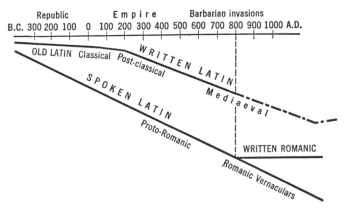

Fig. 2

mension I have reproduced 5000 years of Egyptian and only 1300 years of Latin history. But the larger scale permits a detail which could hardly appear on the Egyptian chart: at the end of what is strictly called the classical period of Latin letters, the line of written Latin bends downward, approaching though never quite reaching the lower sloping line of spoken Latin. This change of direction reflects the continued vulgarization of even the written language. Now it is precisely from this downward slanting part of the line that the so-called Vulgar Latin documents stem. There, and not on the lower line, we must place the writings of the Church Fathers, the *Mulomedicina Chironis* (of the fourth century), the *Peregrinatio Aetheriae* (probably of the fifth century), the Merovingian and Langobard documents, and the like.

In all periods of linguistic development, the written language, if one exists, differs from the spoken, except perhaps during that comparatively brief span of time when it is in the act of arising

[11] Copied, with some revisions, from Pulgram 1950, 462, Fig. 2.

from the vernacular, when it is just being codified. But divergences will emerge soon, because, as change lies in the nature of speech, so conservatism lies in the nature, is indeed one of the *raisons d'être*, of writing and spelling. An unstable orthography which changes too often and too radically defeats its purpose (regardless of whether this purpose is a valid one — as some linguists, but not I, maintain it is not). The relatively uniform language of our Latin texts from Italy and the Romania is but an administrative, learned, written language, propagated in Italy and the provinces by Roman civil and military administrators, by Roman exporting and importing merchants, by the clergy, and by the upper-class provincials, who all needed and used it as a sort of international language — much as Standard English has been used for similar ends in India. The same language was also spoken as a lingua franca; but this does not mean that it was any more the popular language of the entire Romania, or of any part of it, or that all its speakers used the same phonemes and grammar, than any of these characteristics are true of English in India, or even of Pidgin English in the South Pacific area. Moreover, even someone who was fully able to use first-rate classical or at least acceptably correct Latin in writing, may well have handled the language less properly, phonemically and grammatically, in speaking. A written text can be revised and corrected, the flow of speech cannot; people who do not write an unfamiliar language with a visible foreign accent, as it were, may well speak it with an audible one. If, therefore, the term Vulgar Latin is applied to the documents available from the post-classical period of Latin down to the ninth century, it should be made clear, as it generally is not, that this is mostly a *written* 'Vulgar Latin,' that it largely attempts to continue the tradition of Classical Latin, no matter how numerous the inroads of popular speech which point toward the Romanic languages — that, in short, it does indeed merit the description of a bad, vulgarized Classical Latin. Whether this idiom should still be called 'Vulgar Latin,' with the implication that the Romanic dialects originate from it, is another matter. I think not.

What, then, do we put on the sloping line of Spoken Latin, which follows an unbroken direct development, as do the generations of speakers themselves? I have already said that we have little to put there: Plautus, the passages of direct speech in Petronius and Apuleius, some inscriptions, some graffiti, and some glosses; that is about all. The truth is that we do not know how people of various periods actually talked Latin, except by inference and deduction.

In Old Latin times, the lines of written and spoken Latin converge. At that time, a written classical tradition was just emerging; that is, Roman literature is being created (almost exclusively on Greek models), and the linguistic evidence we have from the earliest times, though meager and fragmentary, confirms the view that the spoken and the written idiom have not yet diverged from one another very much. That Old Latin is in fact a tongue more akin to contemporary popular speech than the classical language, is not a new theory.[12]

Obviously, the blank space on Fig. 2 between the lines of written and spoken Latin is not a linguistic vacuum. First, there is a lively crossing of influences from one to the other; the slant of the later part of the written line is meant to indicate this. The vulgar features of the post-classical written language are, of course, derived from vulgar speech; if this were not so, the written documents would give us not even a clue as to the state of the vernacular. Fortunately they do, though in no orderly, chronological, exhaustive fashion. In spite of several investigations of 'Spanish' or 'African' Latin, it has not been possible to discover dialects of this written Latin, to say nothing of spoken dialects. On the other hand, the very existence of a literary tradition certainly influenced the development of popular speech, probably as a conservative, retarding factor because of its social prestige.[13] In a society like that of Rome and Italy, whose masses were so much less profoundly literate and educated than those of modern European and American states, the retarding momentum which the written language exercised was correspondingly weak. No exact

---

[12] Löfstedt 1936, 14 and *passim*; Richter 1911, claims that the Praenestine fibula (*DUENOS MED FHEFHAKED NUMASIOI*), the oldest Latin document in our possession (of the late seventh or sixth century B.C.), is already an example of popular Romanic speech because of its word order. See also Ettmayer 1916; Altheim 1951, 395–404.

[13] See the remarks on hyperurbanism (hypercorrection) by Spitzer 1949, 232–233.

measurements of this phenomenon are possible, and I put no trust in pretended measurements which prove that linguistic change proceeds at a regular, unvarying rate everywhere at all times. Why should language be the one cultural possession to obey such a fatalistic rule? Surely no one will maintain that nonlinguistic cultural change occurred no faster, say, during the last century, than in any given century of the palaeolithic age, or even in the century preceding the last.

Second, not all writing can be located precisely on a line; there are many shadings and degrees of urbanism and vulgarism and rusticism that may appear in writing as they do in speech, though not in the same degree.

Third, and most important, there cannot have been just two layers of language, because there are never just two strata of social classes.[14] Nonetheless, as I hope I showed in Chapter XXII, the stratification of Roman society into two basic classes, albeit with some overlapping and with a further breakdown of either of the principal groups, seems to have been enough of a reality to warrant both a social and a linguistic dichotomy. Of course one must not forget that a single speaker can vary his speech and his style of writing according to his surroundings and his purpose.[15] But this adaptability is open only to the literate speaker, because only he has a choice; the man who speaks the vernacular alone cannot, and is not called upon to, adjust his speech to the requisites of a rhetorical performance in the Senate or the courts of law. (However, it may occur that also a literate, educated man who has led a sheltered life and moved exclusively among the upper classes from childhood on is bereft of choice, being incapable of producing truly popular speech or a local dialect.) And that is perhaps one of the outstanding differences between the literate and non-literate speaker of a language: the former generally has several registers to play and to choose from, the latter has not.

Then, of the two theories concerning spoken Latin mentioned at the beginning of this chapter, I should choose the second, but

[14] Lot 1931, 98: "During the last century of the existence of the Western Empire (383–476), there were two languages, that of the people, spoken by the immense majority in the Empire, and that of the aristocracy." Lot is here over-simplifying. See Guérard 1947; Bloomfield 1933, 52.
[15] See Cicero's own words on this, below, p. 327.

with the proviso that the so-called dialectalization was not primarily a centrifugal movement away from Roman Latin through the agencies of time and distance, though these too played their part, but rather due to the imposition of Latin upon non-Latin speakers.

CHAPTER XXIV

The Dialects of Spoken Latin   It has been
shown that great obstacles impede an investigation of Spoken Latin.
If it were not for the existence of the Romanic dialects and the
certain knowledge that a language used by so many persons of
such varied social positions and intellectual accomplishments over
such a wide area and through so many centuries could not maintain itself unified and unaffected by changes normally wrought
by all these factors, the evidence alone as we possess it would give
us but a pale picture of the diversity of speechways that must have
existed.[1] In a further attempt to break down these linguistic
varieties of Latin into social and local dialects, the linguist has little
more to go on than a general knowledge of how languages behave,
a specific knowledge of the ultimate Romanic results, in particular of the dialects of Italy, and, last but not least, the history
of the speakers. Although we are bedeviled by a scarcity of records,
I have nonetheless thought it opportune to write this chapter and
impart to it the degree of factualness which the evidence warrants.
General systematic research on the correlation of social and linguistic classes is still outstanding. And work on the effects of
borrowing and bilingualism, which pertain to the social and
local dialectalization of language, has only begun.

This chapter is divided into two sections, dealing with the
social and local dialectalization. The division indicates the vertical
and the horizontal types of diversification, in which class differences are mainly, though not wholly, responsible for the first,
and geographic location for the second.

An intermediate position is held by linguistic borrowing and
various phenomena of bilingualism. It could be argued that,

[1] Cf. Brugmann 1884, 254; Schmidt 1871, 2. 186; Sittl 1882, 1; Hirt 1894, 40;
Hirt-Arntz 1939, 196, 209; Paul 1920, 46; Bloomfield 1933, 47.

since influence of foreign languages originating from foreign places is involved, this type of dialectalization should come under the local, horizontal heading. On the other hand, since in our instance we are examining these influences upon and within Italy, although this is not a linguistically homogeneous area to being with, a case can be made for giving it the social, vertical label, especially since during the period with which we are dealing, foreignisms, excepting learned and poetic Greek loans, are mainly due to the agency of low-class foreigners and appear to begin with in the lower social speech strata. Accordingly, one could also argue that substrata, which I put into the section on local dialects, should find their place in the section on social dialects, because thanks to the social prestige of Latin the disappearing idioms, such as Oscan, Messapic, and others, were retained longest by the uneducated lower classes. Whatever anyone's personal preferences may be, I have made my choice without implying any particular linguistic necessity for it. The truth is obviously that in matters of speech one cannot clearly and without overlapping and residue keep separate the two types of dialects.

SOCIAL DIALECTS

Since the Roman state originated as a small farming community of Latium, Latin speech will of course show rustic traits, it will bear "the mark of a farmer mentality." [2] This will be visible especially in the lexicon, idiomatic expressions, phrases, proverbs, and metaphors. If a language uses *delirare*, originally meaning 'to leave the furrow (while ploughing)' in the sense of 'to go mad,' or *laetus*, originally 'well manured' for 'glad,' or *egregius* 'outside the herd' for 'outstanding,' *pecunia* from *pecus* 'cattle' for 'money,' it is obvious that this is a manner of speaking invented by peasants.[3] But it is equally obvious that the perseverance of such traits in the vocabulary of the first century B.C. and thereafter is not necessarily indicative of a like cultural condition at that time (any more than such common American phrases as 'to stake out a claim,' 'to do a land-office business,' 'to go to town,' 'to strike it rich,' 'to pan out,' and many others, offer linguistic proof that *all*

---

[2] Marouzeau 1949, 8.
[3] Weise 1909, 14–20, *passim;* Devoto 1940, 101–102; Palmer 1954, 69–72.

of America is *today* a country of pioneers, cowboys, and gold-diggers); nor does it presage that the Latin lexicon will in any way remain lacking in an adequate nonrural vocabulary, since each language is supplied by the speakers with vocables and expressions for all the things they want to, need to, and are able to talk about. (Our modern civilization has supplied us with 'to step on it,' that is, 'to step on the gas,' that is, 'to step on the gas pedal of an automobile,' or 'to go into a tailspin,' or 'to strike out,' or 'to tune in,' expressions which, by the way, will no doubt be used long after the things that gave birth to them have been forgotten, and with them the original meaning of the phrase.[4]) I have had several occasions to mention the conservatism of Roman institutions and the prestige of the *mos maiorum*, that is, the durability of the basic farming culture with strong emphasis on the family and the clan. This fundamental attitude with its continued nostalgia for the good old, simple days lent its imprint also to the language, which for a long time, until it became permeated with Greek influence, retained this rough-hewn, lapidary, conservative character. Archaisms, especially in public anouncements and legal codification, were much sought after because they were thought to surround notable pronouncements with an aura of solemnity and authority.

With Rome's attainment of supremacy over Latium (338 B.C.), the other Latin tribes were reduced to subject allies. Consequently, also the language of the conqueror, Latin of Rome, became dominant throughout the confederacy. Within the speech of the city, in Rome itself, and wherever else it was carried, there were bound to arise social dialects corresponding to the classes of society, with the distinctions growing as the rift between the two principal classes widened. And since the political gains of the plebeians found but minimal reflection in the social and cultural field, except insofar as they permitted some plebeians to grow rich, the linguistic class distinction persisted also.

But as the educated classes of Rome concerned themselves more and more with Greek culture and Greek language, as they formed with the aid of Greek teachers and on the model of Greek

---

[4] On the pitfalls in concluding on national traits from linguistic features, see Pulgram 1954.

authors a Latin literary language (see Chapter XXV), and moved away from what they considered the linguistic crudeness of their ancestors in the direction of refinement and elegance both in manners of living and speaking, so the lower classes also became, albeit for different reasons and with different results, more and more alienated from the ancient *mos maiorum* in life and speech, a drift due, at least in part, to a cultural and ethnic permeation and pervasion with foreign elements, but without regard to aesthetic or artistic standards and without the deliberate choice that characterized the development of the literary language. We cannot pursue the progress of the linguistic development in the usual manner, owing to the lack of evidence, but we can see the results in the Romanic languages, which indicate quite unambiguously that the spoken language moved farther and farther away from the written language, to the point of mutual unintelligibility. As far as we can gather from the records, it would have been impossible and unnecessary for Romulus to attain the degree of linguistic sophistication which Cicero recommended, because no apposite socio-linguistic hierarchy existed, namely: "In my opinion one must not speak in the same style at all times, nor before all people, nor against all opponents, nor in defense of all clients, nor in partnership with all advocates. He, therefore, will be eloquent who can adapt his speech to fit all conceivable circumstances."[5] And even in Plautus' day we find that the colloquial language of his comic characters is not so far removed from contemporary formal language exemplified in the inscription recording the *Senatus consultum de Bacchanalibus*, as is the talk of Trimalchio and his boon companions in Petronius' novel from the well-turned phrases of Quintilian.

All societies which exhibit a class structure show corresponding divergent cultural features proper to each of the classes. Indeed, the division into classes becomes visible only in the diversity of the cultural traits of each class. This goes for clothing, housing, aesthetic preferences, sexual customs, educational goals, food and manners of eating, and, of course, words and ways of speaking. As for Latin social distinctions in speech, their traces have been largely obliterated through the standardizing pressure of written

[5] Cic. *Or.* 123 (LCL, trl. by H. M. Hubbell).

usage: even a man who is not reluctant to use low-class talk, or cannot do otherwise, becomes something of an intellectual and user of the written language, as we have seen, within the limits of his learning, as soon as he starts writing.

But clearly in a society so divided into castes as was the Roman, and so racked for centuries by struggles, possibly but not probably inflamed originally by ethnic animosities, between plebeians and patricians, between rich and poor, aristocrats and upstarts, Optimates and Populares, a man's manner of speaking must have identified him not only as one belonging to a certain educational level but also as a partisan, by birth or by choice, of one or the other principal political movements. For what other reason would the aristocrat Claudius choose to change his name to Clodius, thereby aligning himself with popular pronunciation that used *o* in the place of classical *au*, than to curry favor also onomastically with the masses and to identify himself linguistically with them? (He demagogically engineered, through the *Lex Clodia*, the banishment of Cicero, in 58 B.C.) It is certain that in popular circles an odium, albeit mingled with reluctant respect, attached to classical speech. It would have been infinitely more injurious to the ambitions of Claudius-Clodius, playing the ultra-democrat and wanting to be elected tribune of the people, to harangue his constituents in Ciceronian Latin than it would be for a candidate for the governorship in the state of Arkansas to make a campaign speech in Oxford English.

The breakdown of language in accordance with the social and educational stratification of a society is therefore a certainty, and is merely one of the several cultural exhibits testifying to this condition of society. And if we had, for Latin, even less than the scanty evidence we do possess, and no corroborating evidence from the Romanic languages, this is one assumption we could make in good conscience and with all the positiveness of proven fact.

I have said before that the Romans did not pursue a policy of assimilation, political, cultural, or linguistic, with regard to their conquests. Within Italy, the tribes and nations, including those as foreign to Latin ways as the Etruscans, Greeks, and Kelts, seem to have chosen, or at least been forced by circumstances toward, the path of acculturation, even while some of them were still allies of Rome and theoretically independent. This was inevitable because all of Italy grew inexorably to form a unit of common fate and common history, albeit under the hegemony of Rome. But as Roman arms carved new conquests out of the land beyond Italy's boundaries, this sentiment of a community of destiny among the vanquished nations could not come to the fore: partly because they were physically so far removed from the mother land, or rather the mother city (one must never forget that Rome was in effect the state), partly because their cultures, especially in the oriental regions, were altogether strange, often superior, and incompatible with the Roman culture, and finally because Rome continued not to press acculturation upon its subject peoples. As we have seen, the imperial idea, the sense of community of the whole Empire, did not make itself seriously felt until the second and third centuries.

Yet this preservation of un-Romanness outside of Italy would have remained of lesser importance for the cultural history of the Roman state if many of the persons concerned had not retained their foreignness also after they had settled in Italy and Rome. Of the two possibilities — full acculturation or cultural coexistence — it was the second that occurred most frequently, as we have seen from the historical evidence, even in so small an area as the city of Rome.

Linguistic evidence, however, does not in any detail show this foreign admixture, least of all in its stages of ingress into the Roman state. And even when contemplating the results — for example, Spoken Latin (as far as we know it) of the sixth or seventh century after Christ — one cannot often label a phenomenon a foreignism of one or the other geographic or national derivation, except for loan words whose origin can be easily determined through examining the lexicon of other idioms. Yet there can be no question but that the pervasive foreign influence must have exerted itself also on Latin speech if only to the point of speeding up its transformation and rate of change. It is also self-evident that, the more foreign an idiom is in sounds and structure to the borrowing language, the greater will be the changes the first wreaks upon the second — although it is well to remem-

ber that greater foreignness also increases the difficulties of borrowing to begin with.

When talking in detail about the growing influence of the
foreign element in Italy upon the culture and the economy of
the nation, I emphasized that there could be no question of this
phenomenon's being due to biological, racial causes, but rather
to the failure of the Roman world, for a variety of reasons, to
further consciously or unconsciously the acculturation of immigrants. Now, considering a particular part of this culture, the
language, the same view holds.

The acquisition of a new language is a cultural and mimetic,
not a biological process. Hence if the speech organs of a speaker
are normal and not deformed by disease or custom (for example,
wooden disks in the lips) there will be no physiological obstacle
to the mastery of a new language. In fact, if need be, also anatomical abnormalities can be compensated for in the articulation of
speech sounds. But since we are creatures of our own culture,
a certain gravitational pull is exerted by it and to a greater or
lesser degree distorts our efforts, no matter how sincere, to accul-
turate ourselves to new surroundings. It would be interesting to
measure the degree of difficulty in acquiring a new set of cultural
patterns. But even without having at hand the results of scientific
measurements, I daresay it is easier and quicker to learn how
to eat properly, that is, according to a model behavior, than how
to speak properly, that is, correctly according to a standardized
model speech and without a foreign accent. The pressure to do
one or the other thing 'properly' will vary according to the customs and exigencies of the society involved. Given the articu-
latory difficulty inherent in ridding oneself of a foreign accent and
in acquiring full native fluency in a language, the social pressures
which are to lead to complete linguistic acculturation must accordingly be very strong, stronger than some which are sufficient to
produce certain types of nonlinguistic adjustments.

Since Rome did not officially require from its subjects the
learning of Latin, and since the percentage of non-Latins of various
degrees of assimilation was rather high in Italy and especially in
Rome, it seems to follow that among the great mass of the population no important social stigma attached to linguistic for-

eignisms, and that therefore the pressure upon the common man to learn good Latin was not very powerful. Seeming reports to the contrary, such as the emperor Claudius' (41–54) refusal of citizenship to a man because of his bad grammar, are sporadic and most likely owe their being recorded precisely to their unusualness. It is probably true that a Greek accent on Rome's Palatine Hill was socially acceptable as is a French accent on Boston's Beacon Hill — provided they are the property of ambassadors or nobles or successful artists, that is, persons otherwise socially acceptable in any event. But it is equally true that an Oscan brogue in Rome and an Irish brogue in Boston are more studiously avoided and more discriminated against on the Hill, Palatine or Beacon, than by the river, Tiber or Charles. Yet apart from such special conditions one can probably say that in ancient Rome the premium set upon linguistic conformity was lesser than it is today in the United States, for example. In large part this difference is due to the fact that assimilation and absorption of the foreign element is a declared policy and governmental philosophy in the United States, which was not at all true of Rome, and in a perhaps smaller degree to our present tendency, for better or for worse, toward mass conformity (as an accompaniment of mass production), equally absent in ancient Rome, if our historic records give us at all a true picture of society. In addition, a comparison of educational levels yields the conclusion that the percentage of literate and educated persons is much higher in the United States than it was at any period of Roman history, that therefore an at least passive knowledge of the literary language is more widespread, and that consequently the social pressure to adhere to a linguistic standard is much greater today, and not only in the United States, than it was in ancient Italy. Combining all these influences and contemplating the state of Spoken Latin during the early Middle Ages, it becomes obvious that foreign influence upon Latin was capable of being, and was in fact, potent and successful.

This linguistic influence can be of two types. It may be a conscious adoption, with or without phonemic or morphemic alterations, of a foreign sound or form, as when in English we use *bureau* (a whole word with phonemic adjustments), or *phe-*

nomena (with a borrowed plural morpheme), or when Latin uses an accusative singular in *-n* on the Greek model. Or it may be the unconscious acceptance by native speakers of a trait that has originally come into the language as a nonstandard foreignism, as English *an apron*, which is really an illiterate misunderstanding of *a napron* from French *naperon*, or as standard Latin *lacrima* 'tear', which was originally a Sabinism for an inherited *dacruma*, as in Greek δακρύω 'I cry.' All these features may well be united, for want of a better term, under the title of linguistic borrowing, although "the metaphor is certainly absurd, since the borrowing takes place without the lender's consent or even awareness, and the borrower is under no obligation to repay the loan. . . . [But] no apter term has yet been invented." [6]

In view of the social conditions and the linguistic habits of the Roman people whose spoken language we are examining for evidence of dialects, the second class of loans will be of greater importance, that is, not foreign loans that are sought by the few sophisticated users of the language, but such as are attributable to what the purist would consider corrupting influences. Of course, the greater the number of the corrupters and the weaker the cultural resistance of the victims the more widespread and enduring the phenomena of linguistic transfer will be. A linguistic error, if made often enough and by enough people, after a while ceases to be one. It is quite feasible that the 'foreign accent' becomes through the sheer numerical weight of its practitioners the new standard of an area. This is at least in part responsible for the divergent development of the Romanic languages where Latin with a Gaulish or Dacian or Iberian or some other kind of local accent became the standard pronunciation.

In Rome and in Italy, in any event, the number of 'corrupters,' that is, foreigners who formed a large part of the lower classes, was enormous, and because of the absence of a governmental policy fostering nationalism and acculturation among them, no stigma attached to their foreignness. Hence the cultural resistance of the natives in turn was weak. The outstanding nonlinguistic example of this xenophilia is the readiness with which Roman cit-

---

[6] Haugen 1950, 211–212. This important article gives also a classification of types of borrowing.

izens embraced foreign religions and the insouciance with which the government, both of the Republic and the Empire, condoned these adoptions — provided they did not threaten, in the good old days, morality (see the injunction of the Senate against the orgiastic Bacchanalian rites in 186 B.C.) or, later on, seemed not to endanger the states or the emperor politically (see the singularly vengeful subjection of the Jews because they refused to accept the divinity of the monarch, or the persecution of the Christians whose Heavenly Kingdom appeared bent on diminishing the majesty of the secular one). Linguistic conditions would no doubt furnish similar evidence of foreign cultural borrowing if we but possessed the perquisite records.

If we had anywhere near the evidence for Latin that modern scholars have gathered from currently spoken idioms on borrowing and bilingualism,[7] we should surely obtain from it the same fundamental conclusions on the process and its results. One of them is that "the more structural a feature is, the less likely it is to be borrowed," from which follows that "the effects of borrowing on structure are likely to be small."[8] The classical example of English shows that, despite the large percentage of lexical borrowing from Romanic, English is still structurally a Germanic language. For Latin this would explain why the Italian dialects, and all Romance languages, are without exception structurally of the Latin type, regardless of the multitude of lexical borrowings. And, considering that the kind of Latin texts we have will be anything but hospitable to foreignisms to begin with, the virtually complete absence of foreign structural features (except for conscious poetic or learned adoption of Greek forms) and the relative scarcity of phonemic and lexical borrowings find a doubly sound explanation.

It is not likely, nor is there any evidence, that the type of foreigners who as slaves and freedmen and traders swarmed all over Italy, gathered anywhere in homogeneous groups so that we could find prevalently Thracian, or Gaulish, or Syrian settlements in any given localities, except that in Rome, as in New York or other large nationally heterogeneous cities, conationals

---

[7] See especially Haugen 1953 and Weinreich 1953.
[8] Haugen 1950, 225.

would congregate in certain quarters. It is therefore highly improbable that we should ever discover, even with the best linguistic evidence, borrowed items of either nonstructural or, even less likely, structural character in anything but a sporadic random distribution. Hence, such isolated finds as we manage to ferret out, we may possibly identify as to their sources; but their appearance at a given place can give us no trustworthy information on the precise nonlinguistic causes of their existence in this spot rather than elsewhere, on their persistence, and spread. In other words, these foreignisms do not enlighten us on the linguistic history of Italy or any part thereof beyond the general statements already made.

In the domain of Latin local dialects we are somewhat better, but far from satisfactorily and systematically informed. It has until now been impossible to construct a Latin dialect geography for Italy and the empire. Various attempts to isolate Spanish Latin, or African Latin, or Tuscan, Latian, Samnite Latin have on the whole failed, and have uncovered mere scattered instances of deviation from the Roman norm but without allowing of any systematic truly dialectological conclusions. We can draw no isoglosses for Latin in Italy or anywhere in the empire. To postulate local dialects of Latin is therefore possible only, as it was with social dialects, in consideration of general linguistic knowledge and as an inference from results attested in the Romanic dialects.

If we start again from the historic fact that Rome was but one of a number of Latin-speaking communities over which it eventually attained political and cultural hegemony, it will appear plausible enough that there should have existed a variety of Latin dialects of which Roman was one. It may seem at first odd that the extremely scarce inscriptional records until the year 200 B.C. give us a better idea of Latin local dialects than the profuse evidence of later centuries. But the paradox is of course easily explained by the fact that while, until the beginning of the second century B.C., writers and composers of inscriptions were uninhibited in using their local speech and wrote Latin by ear, as it were, the subsequent period saw the rise of the literary language and with it the suppression of dialects in writing by the increasing preponderance and prestige of Roman Classical Latin.

This phenomenon occurs also in written records of other nations and other times. To take two examples from the mediaeval Romanic field, our knowledge of non-Tuscan Italian and non-Parisian French dialects is better for the period preceding the predominance of Standard Tuscan Italian and Standard Parisian French than for the later era during which the supremacy and usefulness of the literary language squelched local dialects as a means of literary expression, except whenever an author used consciously and for the sake of realism, or because of ignorance of the norm, a local colloquial style. But this, as we have seen, happened rarely in Latin literature. (Or at least, if there ever was much of this writing, it would have been considered, and possibly was, trashy and not worth quoting or preserving.)

Hence, in the earliest Latin records which we possess and which are not all from Rome, linguists have been able to discover various local traits which distinguish the language from Roman Latin. The oldest Latin inscription, on the gold fibula of Praeneste, shows certain features which attest not merely corrupted Roman but genuine dialectal Latin.[9] Inscriptions from the Faliscan district show their own peculiarities, as do those from the Oscan, Umbrian, and other dialect areas.[10] In fact, apart from the badly mutilated inscription on a cippus under the so-called *lapis niger* on the Roman Forum, whose interpretation has been attempted by many and has produced many ingenuous but widely divergent solutions,[11] and the so-called Duenos inscriptions on a triple bowl, we are less informed about Roman Latin than about other dialects until the end of the third century B.C. We have some obviously very ancient Roman texts, like the *Carmen Aruale*,[12] which is the

---

[9] Plautus *Trin.* 609 and *Truc.* 691, and Quint. 1.5.56 also cite a number of Praenestinisms.

[10] For a linguistic description of these local features see Palmer 1954, 59–67. It is interesting to juxtapose, for example, the inscriptions CIL 1.2.366, from Spoleto in Umbria, and CIL 1.2.401, from Lucera in Apulia, both dealing with the same subject in very similar terms. But it is easy to see that the Spoleto inscription resembles urban Latin more closely than does the one from Lucera, which is strongly influenced by Oscan.

[11] One of the most recent, together with an extensive discussion and bibliography of earlier work, is that by Goidanich 1943.

[12] See Norden 1939.

ritual song of the *Fratres Aruales*, or the *Carmen Saliare*, or the law of the *Twelve Tables*, but in versions recorded at a date much later than their original composition. Whoever put the (then possibly seven-hundred-year-old) *Carmen Aruale* into the Proceedings of the Arval Brethren in A.D. 218, whence we know it, certainly had little idea of what it meant. Therefore we cannot be wholly certain of the genuineness of the apparent archaisms. Indeed, it did not take seven but less than three centuries for the Romans to be no longer able to recognize their own archaic language, as is disclosed by Polybius when he speaks of the treaty concerning sea traffic and trading between Rome and Carthage, concluded shortly after the establishment of the Republic in 509 B.C., whose original text was seemingly still preserved in Rome in Polybius' days in the middle of the second century B.C.: "I give below as accurate a rendering as I can of this treaty, but the ancient Roman language differs so much from the modern that it can only be partially made out, and that after much application, by the most intelligent men." [13] Possibly the dearth of authentic early Roman inscriptions is a result of the sack of Rome by the Gauls (390 B.C.), a catastrophe during which many primary sources valuable not only for linguistics but also for Roman history perished.

Whether certain discernible non-Roman but Indo-European traits in the language of Roman documents are due primarily to imports into Rome or to a non-Roman Italic substratum will have to remain a moot question as long as we know so little about the linguistic history of pre-Latin Rome.[14] I am rather inclined toward the thesis of importation since, apart from Sabine, we know, at least until now, of no other Italic dialect native, that is, relatively indigenous, on Roman soil. In other words, we have no evidence that some kind of Proto-Latin was not the first Indo-European idiom of this region.

Local dialect features maintain themselves against Roman Latin in inscriptions (from which we must not conclude upon their persistence in common speech) over varying lengths of time. An ingenuous analysis of the copy of the *Senatus consultum de Bac-*

[13] Polyb. 3.22.3. (LCL, trl. by W. R. Paton).
[14] Ribezzo 1930, 90–95, supports unqualifiedly the substratum hypothesis.

chanalibus of 186 B.C. which was found at Tiriolo in Calabria, disclosed that the first twenty-one lines are good Roman Latin, whereas from line twenty-two on the copyist or local author had his own linguistic way and the text becomes un-Roman in many traits.[15] If the writer was not a native speaker of Oscan or Greek, to whom Latin was a second or foreign language, he certainly was not up to date on the language currently in fashion in the capital. But even if the inscription had been wholly in Roman or wholly in Calabrianized Latin, any inference on the state of Latin in Calabria would be highly unwarranted — which serves as additional warning to those who would be rash in concluding from written evidence upon speech habits. Consider, on the other hand, an inscription from Furfo, a village in the Abruzzi (CIL 9.3513) of the year 58 B.C., when Ciceronian Latin was at its height in Rome, containing the text of a dedication of a temple to *Iuppiter Liber*. If this inscription exhibits quite an array of dialect forms, then surely the negative judgment is justified that at least someone in Furfo, and possibly, in view of the solemnity of the text which normally calls for carefully polished language, even many and important people, had not yet learned to use the language of the city folk.

In the discovery and discussion of the dialectal features in Latin texts of Italy it is important to distinguish rigorously between those which are native, that is, due to original differences between varieties of Latin, and those which are the effects of bilingualism, that is, caused by the changes wrought upon Latin by non-Latin speakers. Since the first type will of necessity be restricted to Latium, the cradle of Latin speech, and since our evidence of them is scanty, these dialects being the first and very early victims of Romanization because their area was first to come under Roman domination, such intra-Latin dialect features will be found rarely enough. But the second type will be at home in Italy wherever Latin was superimposed upon non-Latin, Italic or other, languages. But as these areas came under the sway of Rome and Latin mainly at a time when specifically Roman Latin was on its way to reign supreme and when a literary language was in the process of formation, there too, albeit for other reasons,

[15] Fraenkel 1932.

local linguistic habits have not much opportunity to unfold themselves before our eyes. So we repeat our customary regrets on the dearth of evidence of Spoken Latin.

I have said several times, however, that the attested ultimate results of the most spontaneous and least inhibited development of Latin — the Romanic, and more narrowly for our purposes, the Italian dialects — are apt to shed light upon the history for which we have no intervening records. We might therefore ask whether the modern Italian dialects, which have obviously not centrifugally developed out of the all-Italian literary language since its creation by Dante (we may in fact observe the opposite centripetal development), do not continue in some way and in some degree the local dialects of Latin, which in turn are due in some measure, as we have seen, to the changes produced in Latin by its non-Latin learners in the course of a period of bilingualism. Thus the causes of the dialectalization of Latin and Neo-Latin in Italy, and elsewhere, would have to be sought in the effectiveness of linguistic substrata, at least in part.

When I speak of a substratum [16] I refer to a linguistic, not to some mythical racial substratum, whose energies are thought by some to lie dormant for centuries, then suddenly arise to battle against foreign corruptions of speech and soul, with the miraculous result that people talk again like some remote ancestors whose speech had not been heard for centuries.[17] The reason for my view is that language is a social and not a racial phenomenon, that it is no part of human biology, hence not subject to heredity, that it does not exhibit that alleged feature of heredity which is commonly referred to as throwback. Furthermore inherited physical characteristics, especially those of the speech organs, do

---

[16] By substratum I mean a linguistic layer which is eventually superseded by the language that comes to predominate; in the same sense a superstratum is a linguistic layer on top of such a predominating language. Thus, for example, Keltic is the substratum of Latin in Gaul, while Frankish is its superstratum. The reason why I do not speak conversely of Latin, or Proto-Gallo-Romanic, as a substratum for Germanic in Gaul is that eventually Romanic and not Germanic predominated. In other words, what I call the sub- and superstrata are always idioms which provide the contributory and not the dominant features of a linguistic structure. Cf. Pulgram 1957.

[17] An extensive statement of principle on the substratum problem will be found in Pulgram 1949. Much of the following discussion is based on this article, quoted verbatim or paraphrased.

not necessarily cause a continuity of characteristics of enunciation, because all normal humans can learn to produce all human sounds and can under cultural pressure compensate for normal, and even abnormal, anatomic divergencies which may influence speech production. Hence even in a group of speakers who are provenly related by race, physical inheritance cannot be the cause of phonemic peculiarities.[18]

If this is so, then a claim for substratum influence cannot be based on racial arguments, nor even on linguistic evidence of congruence and similarities alone, but must be supported by non-linguistic cultural factors whose continuity makes a concomitant perseverance of linguistic traits plausible. In attempting to establish a case for the dialectalization of Latin through a consideration of the multiplicity of modern Italian dialects and their linguistic substrata, prehistoric and historic evidence such as was presented in several of the preceding chapters is indispensable and must be fully utilized.

In Chapters XIV to XVII, I described in detail the pre-Latin dialects of Italy; in Chapter V, I listed the dialects of modern Italy. If we could find that two superimposed maps of the ancient and the modern dialects were completely congruent, a thesis of the stability of Italian dialect boundaries would be all but proved. But, because of the long and checkered history of Italy, such a coincidence was not to be expected, and does not prevail. Yet the high degree to which at least the wider dialect areas of today and of two thousand years ago concur is a fact, and a surprising one. A bundle of isoglosses, running east and west from Lucca to Ancona, along the height of the Apennines, separates the Toscana in the south from the Emilia, Lombardy, Liguria, and Piedmont in the north. The last four provinces speak Gallo-Italian dialects; their area coincides with that formerly occupied by Kelts.[19] A linguistic boundary followed the same line for Latin also, as far as our records permit us to perceive it; to the north of it Latin showed peculiarities that can be connected with Keltic

[18] See Pulgram 1949, 243, n. 11.
[19] The boundary which separates the northern from the central dialects is roughly the La Spezia — Rimini line, separating also Eastern from Western Romanic dialects, of which I spoke in Chapter V above.

and Venetic phonology.[20] The line separating Venetian and Gallo-Italian coincides very well with the frontier of the country of the ancient Veneti. The Kelts of Gallia Cisalpina, like their relations in Gaul many years later, were not expelled or exterminated by their Roman conquerors, but merged with them peacefully, though slowly. That especially Gallia Transpadana remained for the Romans an essentially foreign land for a very long time may be seen from an act of official discrimination, whereby as late as 89 B.C. this part of Italy, unlike the rest of the country, was not granted the franchise, not Roman citizenship, but only Latin rights. It had to content itself with a complex and inequitable settlement in which cities were not accorded the privilege of *ciuitates*. This they obtained only under Caesar, through the *Lex Roscia* of 49 B.C., because of the strategic and logistic importance of the area for Caesar's conquests and wars. There seems to have been a continued Keltic tradition also after the Kelts had learned to understand and talk Latin, in spite of Polybius' story of their expulsion.[21] All these facts point to fertile ground for substratum influence; one cannot deny it categorically for that part of Italy. And if its effects are discernible in modern Italian dialects they must of course have been present in the Latin speech of the region also because, as we have seen, their reëmergence after a temporary lapse is out of the question. (It is curious that some opponents of a Keltic substratum speak nonetheless of 'Gallo'-Italian dialects.)

Whether or not the Etruscan language furnished a substratum for Latin and the modern Tuscan dialects is a much disputed problem. However, in view of the peculiar social and political position of the Etruscans in Etruria, who were not only foreigners but also a minority of most likely unpopular conquerors, it would not be surprising if one could discern but little influence of Etruscan upon Latin outside of lexical borrowing. It is difficult to say just how many speakers of Etruscan actually existed when Rome conquered Etruria. Reports on the sporadic survival of Etruscan speech as late as imperial times are in themselves an indication

[20] Whatmough 1933. See also Schuchardt 1866, and Sittl 1882.
[21] Polyb. 2.35.4. See Whatmough 1944, 82–85. For Keltic relics especially in northern districts (Switzerland) see Hubschmied 1938.

of the unusualness and oddity of the phenomenon rather than the contrary, and prove little concerning the true vitality of the idiom. In any event it does not seem likely that at the time of the conquest there were left many persons of the original invading Etruscan stock, whatever it may have been, after several centuries of living among the Italians and, it seems, without replenishment by new immigration. But we do not know how many of the Italians or of the mixed Italo-Etruscan population had learned Etruscan and actually spoke it.

The area of what is now called Tuscan Italian coincides surprisingly well with the country of the Etruscans, apart from their Campanian and Patavinian possessions. However, one of the most outstanding features of modern Tuscan often laid to an Etruscan substratum, the *gorgia toscana*, that is the aspiration and, outside of Florentine, the complete disappearance of intervocalic unvoiced stops, especially *k*, covers a much smaller area than Etruscan did.[22] But this does not seem a convincing argument against the working of an Etruscan substratum, because no one knows exactly in what district of their land the Etruscans were thickly enough settled, or where there lived speakers of Etruscan in large enough numbers, to modify local speech habits. It is more significant that Dante, when characterizing the dialects of the Tuscan cities in *De vulgari eloquentia* does not mention this striking peculiarity. An indulgent attitude on his part toward Florentine dialectal waywardness can hardly be assumed, and he also does not highly prize Tuscan speech in general. Hence it would be strange if he had overlooked or forgiven such a mannerism if it had actually been present in the language of his day.

However, such arguments *ex silentio* are not very telling, especially if the silence extends in fact to the Etruscan language itself. It seems wisest, then, to defer judgment on the Etruscan substratum for both Tuscan Latin and Tuscan Italian until we know the Etruscan language.

The substratists themselves, even the most enthusiastic and least critical among them, are surprised by the insignificant traces of Umbrian, if any, that they can discover in modern dialects of

---

[22] Rohlfs 1930, 49.

that area.[23] Many, also, have wondered at the scarcity of Umbrian inscriptions brought to light so far. This is probably not due to almost total illiteracy (at least after a rather early date), but rather, in contrast to the Keltic situation, to the small area occupied by speakers of ancient Umbrian, and, we may presume, to their slight number.[24] They did not inhabit the whole province now called Umbria but only the fringe of it, in particular the upper valleys of the rivers emptying into the Tyrrhenian on one side and into the Adriatic on the other. We may conclude this from the location of the cremation graves, whose area lay between the inhuming Etruscans in the west and the inhuming Picenes in the east. Probably the Italic Umbri to whom we owe the few Umbrian documents we have, notably the extensive Iguvine Tablets whose language we cannot with certainty date because their codification, as is the case with most ritual texts, does not necessarily render contemporary speech, were a relatively small and insignificant tribe which had little to do with the earlier non-Italic 'Umbri.' These Umbrian inscriptions, then, have assumed an importance to us far greater than any that they would have if we possessed equally rich finds of other tribes and cultures of that era. Since what we today term Umbrian may therefore have been no more than a local dialect of small geographic extent (some have therefore suggested that it be called Iguvine instead), and since we do not know other Umbrian dialects, our search for an Umbrian substratum for the Latin and Italian of Umbria must remain inconclusive.

The Oscan-speaking population of central and southern Italy covers, in contrast to the Umbrians, a much vaster area; it was surely more dense, and its dialect survived longer the leveling by Latin. These Oscans have left us numerous inscriptions, with dialectal variations, on different subjects. There are a number of features in the modern dialects of southern Italy which bring strongly to mind Oscan characteristics.

We may be sure that Romanization, as Christianization, became more and more superficial, less and less intense, as the distance

[23] Concerning the phenomenon most frequently connected with Umbrian, the substitution of -r- for -d-, see the exhaustive study by Wahlgren 1930.
[24] For the development of this thesis see Whatmough 1937, 194–196.

from Rome southward increased. "Christ stopped at Eboli," they say in Lucania, where Christianity even today is just another myth, full of the magic, spirits, superstitions, local divinities (now called local patron Saints), incantations (now directed to Saints specializing, as did the ancient gods, severally in the healing of various sicknesses, in influence upon the weather and the harvest), and where poverty-stricken, ignorant peasants till, as generations have tilled before them, a now depleted, barren, eroded land which they do not own. One is left to wonder how deep an imprint the ancient, mediaeval, and northern incursions of foreigners — Greeks, Phoenicians, Etruscans, Romans, Germans, Arabs, Normans — have left in this inhospitable land, where centuries seem to have passed without bringing changes. The cultural and ethnic continuity since pre-Roman days seems to have been but superficially disrupted. Why should the Latin language be a cultural good accepted and passed on *in toto*, without absorbing and retaining even traces of its predecessor?

Most of the work on the substrata of Italian, and with them Latin, dialects still needs to be done.[25] It will inevitably be hampered by a dearth of evidence; but, by employing the combination of linguistic and nonlinguistic, historic and prehistoric records, by applying the recent findings in bilingualism, and by eliminating racial preconceptions, much may yet be brought to light which will increase our knowledge of the dialects of Latin.

---

[25] It should be accomplished by a native Italian scholar who thoroughly knows at least several of the local dialects of the country (as well as ancient linguistic history); for this reason I must disqualify myself.

CHAPTER XXV

The Literary Language In Chapter VI, I spoke
of a literary language, modern Standard Italian, which is largely the
Tuscan of Dante, augmented and changed by subsequent historic
and linguistic developments. I said that a literary language is the
elevation of a dialect at a given period to the rank of a standard
language because of a certain prestige accrued to this dialect over all
the others of a language area. In the case of modern Italian, it was
Dante, together with Boccaccio and Petrarch, who conferred this
distinction upon Tuscan. In ancient Italy the standard 'classical'
language was the Latin of the educated classes of Rome, modeled
in particular on the writings of Cicero and Vergil and a few others.
We shall have to examine in some detail why, when, and how a
classical standard was established, and why, when, and how Roman
Latin of the two half-centuries before and after the birth of Christ
became the measure and the norm of literary excellence. Since the
two parts of the question are interwoven, I shall not try to answer
them separately.

In attempting to account as best I could for the causes, the
process, and the result of the spread of Latin in Italy I took as my
point of departure those historic facts which seemed to me especially
significant and enlightening for the story — colonization and communication. The aspect of Roman history which I choose as the
guiding thread for a history of the literary language shall be education, in the widest meaning of the word.

The preconditions for the development of a literary language
are economic and political unity of the region in which it is to become the standard, or at least a desire for such unity, and a favorable
educational climate. As for the first, the history of Rome speaks
for itself; in order to unite under one administration, one law, and
one economy, the multilingual inhabitants of Italy, the necessity for
some single means of communication, at least as an intertribal auxil-

iary language, imposed itself. That this language could be nothing but Roman Latin is self-evident. However, it might have been a kind of Pidgin Latin, fully sufficient to perform the daily business of the Romans with the other Italians and with the provincials. Instead, the development went farther, reaching finally the point where a highly cultivated classical language, taking its inception from Rome, became standard for all social and literate intercourse upon a higher level, responding not only to the mere exigencies of communication but also to the ideals of its users' aesthetic consciousness. That this second step was performed is due to the favorable educational, intellectual climate. Rome not only became big, but also wished to be great; it not only grew, but also tried to grow up; it not only developed a civilization, but also sought a style.

What I have just said concerning the necessity of a uniform language within the Roman state does not extend, as the preceding chapters have fully shown, to the spoken idioms and dialects of Italy and the Empire, but refers only to the koinë, the lingua franca of everyday intercourse of those persons who had intertribal or international business to attend to, orally or in writing. Such persons were comparatively few. Hence, Roman Latin, especially in its most highly developed classical form, but also as the vulgarized written Latin koinë, was not, as we have seen, in any sense the property of the masses.

My words concerning Roman growth and grandeur do not apply to the little village on the Palatine Hill, nor to the city of the Etruscan kings, nor even to the early Republic. In those remote days, the citizens were too much concerned with their livelihood, too much occupied with tilling the soil and defending it against enemies, with tending the hearth, and providing the table with the daily bread, to worry about niceties of language. And besides, there were no teachers. The Etruscans could have filled this role, and in some ways did. But they themselves, though enjoying a higher material culture, were lacking the external drive and the internal light which great civilizers, like the Greeks, must possess if they are to teach others. And although the Etruscans held the finest of all instruments of civilization, the art of writing — no invention of theirs and in no significant way changed or improved by them — their cultural influence upon Rome in this respect was merely

the gift of the alphabet. For even if the Etruscans had a literature, about which we know nothing, the Romans of the sixth,
fifth, and fourth centuries could in no wise avail themselves of
this model: first, because the two languages were so foreign to
one another; second, because only a few noble Etruscan families
mixed with the Romans, so that the Romans as a mass surely did
not know the Etruscan language and had little physical contact
with their strange neighbors, except in battle and after the Etruscan
decline had begun subsequent to their military defeats.

Also the Greeks of Magna Graecia seem to have exerted no
weighty influence upon earliest Rome. I have already mentioned
how the fall of Rome before the Kelts is described in Greece like
an event in some distant, unknown, and unimportant land.[1] After
all, Greek and Roman territories were not contiguous until the end
of the fourth century B.C., when Rome reached the fringes of
Campania in her fight against the mountaineers. A real acquaintance
between Greeks and Latins did not come about until the third
century, when Rome conquered Tarentum in the war against
Pyrrhus (272 B.C.), occupied Sicily after the defeat of the Carthaginians (241), and had to battle Hannibal during a campaign of
many years fought in Magna Graecia and Sicily. At the time of the
Second Punic War, however, more than a century after the death
of Alexander the Great and the division of his empire, the Greek
world had entered upon its period of decline politically and
culturally, though perhaps not materially, at least in Italy, where
Syracuse was a last splendid relic. But when the physicist and
engineer Archimedes fell there in 213 B.C. under the blows of a
Roman legionnaire, his death signaled the passing of the last
remnant of Greek culture on this side of the Adriatic.

Hence the Romans, until the third century, were culturally and
educationally pretty much on their own, if one disregards their
Italian neighbors, who were just as crude as they themselves. Some
will call this position of Roman civilization one of self-sufficiency
and applaud it, others one of isolation and deplore it. The verbal
slanting aside, there is truth in both judgments, and virtue in both
conditions.

Since the life of the Romans in the early Republic was drab

[1] See above p. 283.

and devoid of embellishments, the education of youth was determined by the physical requirements and geared to produce men, and women, who would be able to carry on the tasks of their forefathers and be satisfied with the simple life. All the traits of Roman education and Roman character, indeed of Roman tradition and religion, many of which persisted far into a period when there was neither necessity nor encouragement for them, were formed in these early days of harsh simplicity.

The education of the young started at home and was in the hands of the father, the *pater familias*, 'the father of the family,' or better, 'the master of the household.' The antiquity of this phrase together with the longevity of its peculiar semantic connotations of absolute mastery over everyone in the household, including power over life and death, can be seen from the ancient Indo-European genitive in -*as*, of which this is the only lasting remainder in Latin. The powerful position of the patriarch may have its roots in a time when the family was still the sole social and economic unit, and within it the oldest able-bodied male was father and master. This status of the father in early Rome found its cultural expression in filial piety and profound respect for the family ancestors. It also caused the whole state to become a tightly knit organization of families and clans, in which service for the fatherland was, next to family obligation, the supreme civic duty. Since all affairs of state were entered upon and dispatched according to the code of tradition accumulated in past generations, according to the *mos maiorum*, politics tended to be extremely conservative and changes came about, for better or for worse, slowly and tortuously. Since the *pater familias*, if he could look back upon a long line of ancestors, was also in possession of the inheritance passed down from them, which in a rural community was necessarily real property and land, we find in early Rome and nearly throughout the Republic, at least until the Gracchan period when a capitalistic system arose, a ruling aristocratic class of landowners. Whoever did not own land did not belong to that caste, he could not be a patrician and a senator (whose official title was also *pater*), but only a plebeian, though he may become a rich plebeian. The foremost concern and the paramount interest among the patricians was the welfare of the state, which was implicitly their own well-being, and the young Romans of this class were by education and precept imbued with this attitude. Consequently, apart from winning one's daily bread, public life was the most honorable of all careers, and preparation for it the most urgent task of the young men.

Such a public career did not need men versed in the niceties and amenities of a liberal education. Schooling had to be practical and utilitarian, not theoretical and intellectual. This view of what constitutes good education for a good Roman maintained itself for many centuries; and even when, in the last century of the Republic, preachings to this effect were mere lip-service, they served as an ideal, and as a brake. When in Cicero's treatise on the state Mucius asks, "What knowledge, then, Laelius, do you think we ought to acquire, in order to be able to accomplish the result you demand of us?," Laelius answers: "The knowledge of those arts which can make us useful to the state." [2] And in the same work, Scipio's judgment on the values of a solid upbringing at home as compared with book-learning is the very motto of education in the Republic: "[I am a Roman who], though provided by a father's care with a liberal education and eager for knowledge from boyhood, yet has been trained by experience and the maxims learned at home much more than by books." [3] And even the great Horace said without blushing that the best poet is the one "who has blended profit and pleasure, at once delighting and instructing the reader," [4] that is, the one who not only writes beautifully but also has a few practical things to say.

The intentional disregard for the beautiful, and the consciousness and the will for a mission to civilize the nations in a worldly, pragmatic way finds expression in the stately and, yes, beautiful lines of Vergil:

> *Excudent alii spirantıa mollius aera,*
> *Credo equidem, uiuos ducunt de marmore uoltus,*
> *Orabunt causas melius caelique meatus*
> *Describent radio et surgentia sidera dicent:*
> *Tu regere imperio populos, Romane, memento*
> *(Haec tibi erunt artes) pacique imponere morem,*
> *Parcere subiectis et debellare superbos.*

[2] Cic. *de re pub.* 1.20.33 (LCL, trl. by C. W. Keyes).
[3] Cic. *de re pub.* 1.22.36 (LCL, trl. by C. W. Keyes).
[4] Hor. *A.P.* 343-344.

Others, I doubt not, shall beat out the breathing bronze with softer lines; shall from marble draw forth the features of life; shall plead their causes better; with the rod shall trace the paths of heaven and tell the rising of the stars: remember thou, O Roman, to rule the nations with thy sway — these shall be thine arts — to crown Peace with Law, to spare the humbled, and to tame in war the proud.[5]

Obviously in a state in which educational utilitarianism reigned to such a degree, there can be no question of many persons seriously occupying themselves with the aesthetic aspect of the language and with grammatical rules.[6] All the more so because any literary endeavor, apart from ritual chants and possibly other occasional poetry, was completely absent. Whatever writing we have before the end of the third century B.C. is rough-hewn, uneven, laconic, and terse to the point of unintelligibility (for example, the Twelve Tables), but withal not lacking, for our sophisticated taste, the crude charm of folk art.

It may be of interest to point out that in the relative chronology of literary and political evolution Rome differed fundamentally from Greece. While the Greeks produced a Homer and a number of great poets and writers, and enjoyed a literary education, long before the political flourishing of their city-states (indeed several centuries before Athens' best days), Rome brought forth no literature and did not burden or gladden her youth with a literary and liberal education until the city and the state were firmly established in Italy and had entered upon the conquest of the Mediterranean basin, in the third and especially the second centuries B.C.

The early austere rusticity and frugality in the life and letters of Rome came to an end under the impact of Greek influence, which occurred to an important degree from the third century B.C. on, quite a while before Rome actually conquered Greece (in 146 B.C.). There was a rich depository of Greek civilization in Magna Graecia, although of a kind which would have angered or saddened an Athenian of the fifth century. But for the raw Romans it represented the apex of finesse and good taste. Numerous Greeks flocked to Rome from southern Italy and Sicily, as political ambassadors,

---

[5] Verg. *Aen.* 6.847–851 (LCL, trl. by H. R. Fairclough).
[6] I shall refrain from citing examples and texts. This internal stylistic and grammatical development can be learned from the handbooks listed in the bibliography. To illustrate the present chapter I recommend Palmer 1954, 95–147.

merchants, craftsmen, artists and, most important for us, as professional teachers. The last were not always free men but educated slaves, who were highly prized, and priced, as private tutors in wealthy families. The tenor and the aim of Roman education, at least among the leading houses, were thus transformed. True enough, the emphasis of the new Greek education on rhetoric training and preparation for a political career were neither unwelcome nor foreign to Romans. In matters of practical politics the Romans could learn nothing from the Greeks, their gifted and witty neighbors, whom with condescending affection they called *Graeculi* 'Greeklings,' and upon whom throughout their history they tended to look with the contempt which so-called hardheaded, practical men of action often have for artists and thinkers. But the novel practice of attaining this useful objective of political and electioneering skills by way of the Greek language and with considerable emphasis not only upon the effectiveness but also upon the pleasantness of discourse and polish of manners was a decidedly unwonted facet of education in Rome. For some persons this Greek influence was also unwanted, because they saw in it a dilution of the ancient Roman virtues, a softening of the moral fiber. Cicero, as late as the middle of the first century B.C., objects, sincerely or hypocritically, to the emphasis on Greek poets in the schools because "they represent brave men wailing" and sap the manliness of youth, especially since this type of instruction had come to be coupled with bad family discipline and a life of effeminate withdrawal instead of the lusty plunge into the clamor and excitement of the marketplace.[7] And a century later, when the Republic was all but forgotten and the *mos maiorum* 'the way of the forebears,' an empty phrase in the mouths of dubious patriots, the staid Romans were still shocked and alienated by their emperor Nero's appearing publicly as a singer and musician.

The greatest enemy of the invasion of all things Greek during the second century was Cato. But he was not alone. In 161 B.C. the Senate passed a law expelling from Rome all teachers of rhetoric and philosophy. Such a defensive decree is an indication of how much these teachers had become part of a changing system of education, how many students they had, and, by implication, how long

[7] Cic. *Tusc.* 2.11.26.

they must have been plying their trade in Rome. But Cato himself in the end learned the Greek language and occupied himself like all other Roman gentlemen with Greek literature, and the law to whose enactment the Senate had been prodded by Cato and perhaps some committee on un-Roman activities, was eventually forgotten without leaving traces of its existence upon the educational scene.

A number of Greek writers had great influence on nascent Roman letters, in fact they sowed the Greek seeds for a first Latin literary harvest (with consequences which in some aspects led to clashes of Greek literary form and Latin linguistic substance). I need only mention the names of Livius Andronicus (about 294–204 B.C., a Greek freedman from Tarentum, translator of Homer's Odyssey into Latin Saturnian verse, and of numerous other Greek works), Gnaeus Naevius (about 270–199 B.C., an Italian, more independent in the choice of subjects than Andronicus, noted especially for an epic poem in Saturnian meter on the First Punic War), and Ennius (239–169 B.C., a Messapian, author of the popular *Annales* which recount in eighteen books, of which but some six hundred lines are extant, the story of Rome from its foundation) in order to show the indebtedness of Latin literature to Greek models.

Also Latin drama developed under the aegis of the great Greek masters, but Italy was fortunate to produce at the very beginning of the native efforts a genius like T. Maccius Plautus (about 254–184 B.C.), an Umbrian, of whose numerous comedies only nineteen have come down to us. Although he derived his subjects from Hellenic mythology and Greek dramatic literature, his plays are in spirit, tone, and language (apart from the meter) wholly Italian. Even the Gaulish comic author Caecilius Statius (a younger contemporary of Plautus) copied Greek models. P. Terentius Afer (about 195–159 B.C.), a freed African slave, is also dependent on Greek models in his six plays, all of which have survived.

The tragic dramatists were less important and less great than the comedians, probably because their choice of subject and the exigencies of appropriate treatment gave them less freedom to Romanize their Greek material. Both Pacuvius (about 220–130 B.C.) and Accius (170– about 86 B.C.) were faithful and unimaginative imitators of Sophocles and Euripides. But contemporary Roman audiences were neither discriminating nor educated enough to appreciate classical tragedy, an art form which in Roman literature and entertainment remained singularly barren and unpopular. The Roman's favorite spectacles were then, and throughout Roman history, low comedy, the mimes, gladiators, and the circus.

Prose writing, was even more dependent on Greek models, and the first efforts at literary prose in Italy were authored in the Greek language. Around 200 B.C. Fabius Pictor wrote a history of Rome from its beginnings to the end of the just concluded Second Punic War. It was followed by various other Roman histories in the Greek language. But it is to Cato, the archfoe of Greek, that we owe the *Origines*, an historical work in Latin, which has not survived. Another book of his on agriculture has, and it is the oldest complete work in Latin prose that we possess.

The only genuine literary contribution of Rome was the genre of the Satire, commencing with Gaius Lucilius (180–102 B.C.).

I do not intend to tell the history of Latin literature, but rather, by citing its originators and early masters, to bring out its indebtedness to Greece. This brief literary exposé belongs among the aspects of Roman education for the very good reason that the practitioners of this new art fulfilled also, in matters of linguistic usage, the role of teachers. In view of the concern of the Greeks over the aesthetic and grammatically correct use of their language, it was inevitable that their Roman pupils and imitators also should feel compelled to seek a style, an elegance of diction and expression, and a standardization of 'correct' grammar, in other words, to strive for the mastery of all the paraphernalia by whose employment writing became a learnable craft as well as a form of art among professionals. Hence, it quickly devolved on education to provide the necessary instruction. Together with *mathesis*, *musike*, *geometria* and *philosophia* (school subjects were, as one might expect, commonly known under their Greek names), pupils were expected to study also *grammatike* and *rhetorike*.

Once more there arises xenophobic antagonism to this new, foreign kind of schooling, which again is futile. In 92 B.C. the censors Cn. Domitius Ahenobarbus and L. Licinius Crassus release an edict that is typical for the opposition: "It has been reported to us that there be men who have introduced a new kind of training, and that our young men frequent their schools; that these men have assumed the title of Latin rhetoricians, and that young men spend whole days with them in idleness. Our forefathers determined what they wished their children to learn and what schools they desired them to attend. These innovations in the customs and principles of our forefathers do not please us nor seem proper. Therefore it appears necessary to make our opinion known, both to those who have such schools and to those who are in the habit of attending them, that they are displeasing to us." [8] The admonition remained as fruitless as the fear was groundless.

I have repeatedly alluded to the existence of schools. Obviously the agricultural village on the Palatine boasted of no such institution any more than of private tutors, and under the patriarchic rule and the simplicity of instruction in the early Republic it was out of place. But it may be worthwhile to examine briefly when and in what manner schools started and how many young Romans were educated, especially according to the new Greek ways.

Above all one must keep in mind that a 'school' in republican Rome may have been not only privately conducted for the benefit of an exclusive clientèle, but indeed held under the patronage or in the very house of an eminent personage. Even what comes nearest to a type that Americans might call a public school resembled in many ways actually the British type of public school, that is, it was really a private school, admission to which was to a great extent contingent upon social position and ability to pay the fees.

The first elementary school of which we know is one established by Spurius Carvilius, freedman of a consul by the same name, between the First and the Second Punic Wars.[9] However, some may well have existed before;[10] possibly Spurius Carvilius was the first to open his establishment to the public and to charge fees. In

---

[8] Quoted by Suet. *Rhet.* 1 (LCL, trl. by J. C. Rolfe). The genuineness of this passage has been doubted, but Gwynn 1926, 61–66, makes a good case for its authenticity.

[9] Plut. *Quaest. Rom.* 59.

[10] Wilkins 1905, 23. The report by Plut. *Rom.* 6, that Romulus and Remus went to primary school at Gabii, is spurious in all respects. Similarly the tale that Virginia, with whom the Decemvir Appius Claudius, of 449 B.C., had fallen in love, was abducted on her way to school, which was on the Forum, is most likely quite unfounded.

any event, it seems that among the wealthy the system of private tutoring in the home continued to be preferred. As for the poor plebeians and the proletariat, it is doubtful whether they received any education at all at such an early date; indeed their schooling remained sketchy at best throughout Roman history, a situation which accounts for the lack of penetration of the written language among the masses.

At the time of the Second Punic War, when the Hellenizing influence started, the schools show a regular curriculum in which, after the Greek model, the study of letters and humanities attained an important role. Boys between the ages of seven and eleven or twelve attended primary schools where they were taught by the *magister ludi* (*ludus* being the technical term for elementary school, and *schola* reserved for the higher grades) or *primus magister*,[11] then progressed to secondary school under the *grammaticus* who instructed them in grammar.[12] In the second century B.C., under deepening Greek inspiration, the rhetorical school was added, where the youths between sixteen and twenty years of age were taught by the *rhetor*.[13] The first school of Latin orators was opened by L. Plotius Gallus, a client of Marius, in 93 B.C. (but closed again in the following year by the edict of Cn. Domitius Ahenobarbus and L. Licinius Crassus).

Except in the elementary schools, whose principal tasks were reading, writing, and arithmetic, the literary studies dealt above all with Greek works, partly in the original and partly in translation. Only in 26 B.C., a freedman of Cicero's friend Atticus, Q. Caecilius Epirota, decided to teach Latin poets on an equal basis with Homer and the other great Greeks. Also grammatical studies were at the outset concerned mainly with the Greek language, and the first work on Latin we owe to M. Terentius Varro (116–27 B.C.).

The teachers themselves were ill-paid and their social station was low. But this is probably no indication that the Romans' concerns with education were less heartfelt and worth less to them than they are to us. The best and most efficient teachers were the unpaid ones,

[11] Marrou 1948, 359–368.
[12] Marrou 1948, 369–379.
[13] Marrou 1948, 380–389.

those who belonged to a household as private tutors.[14] Plebeian tastes and interests were not served by the schools, and no efforts were made, of course, to raise the aspirations of the common people to a point where they would desire and profit from good public instruction, voluntary or compulsory. While Greek education had been a public business involving the state, in Rome the contrary held true. "Our people have never wished to have any system of education for the free-born youth which is either definitely fixed by law, or officially established, or uniform in all cases, though the Greeks have expended much vain labor on this problem, and it is the only point which our guest Polybius finds neglected in our institutions." [15] This reliance on rugged individualism in education may be a virtue, if it wishes to forestall undue bureaucratic influence upon subject and method of teaching, or a vice, if it is invented as a convenient pretext for precluding instruction for the lower classes. In Rome, and many other states since then, it was the second at least as much as the first. All of Quintilian's elaborate theory of education, for example, is patently devised for the children of the rich, not only in its physical requirements and suggestions (toy alphabets made of ivory, costly prizes for lessons well done, expensive private tutoring [16]) but also in its curriculum which dealt with subject materially and spiritually unsuited to the physical and intellectual conditions and ambitions of the majority of the citizens. The grand tour of the rich Roman youth to Greece and perhaps Asia Minor, with extended studies at Greek academies or universities and intercourse with learned men and good teachers, was an impossibility for most young men, being an incomparably more expensive enterprise than is a modern American student's sojourn in Europe.

Only from Vespasian (69–79) on does the state commence to concern itself earnestly with public education by subsidizing the teaching profession from public funds and by relieving its practitioners from the honorary *munera* 'civic obligations,' which, especially in the smaller communities, began to be a drain on energy and purse. This system of subventions was further extended, and finally

[14] Note that in republican days also attorneys were not officially permitted to charge their clients regular fees but derived their income from 'gifts.'
[15] Cic. *de re pub.* 4.3 (LCL, trl. by C. W. Keyes).
[16] Gwynn 1926, 189–191.

codified in the Justinian Code (534). Vespasian also endowed some chairs of rhetoric, and a number of professors were employed by the state. Trajan (98–117), a liberal and benevolent emperor of good sense and good heart, used the income accrued to the state from real estate to aid indigent students, especially by distribution of free food. Pliny the Younger (62–113) speaks in his letters of municipal schools which had sprung up throughout the Empire. Beginning in the middle of the second century, from the emperors of the Antonine family on, the state not only patronized, but also began to exercise control over the municipal schools and to influence the choice of the faculty. But this inroad of an inept bureaucracy, coupled with the growing authoritarianism of the later emperors, vitiated the gains which free education had at first made through official encouragement.

After about A.D. 100, education, though perhaps quantitatively benefitting more people than before, qualitatively entered upon a period of decline, presaging the imminent political decadence of the state. In literary education, emphasis continued to be on rhetorics, the art of public oratory and argumentation. Heretofore these skills had served the genuinely Roman goal of aiding in the attainment of public office and of preparing citizens for political and diplomatic careers. But, owing to the decline and fall of the Republic in the first century B.C., between Sulla and Augustus, which eliminated the participation of the people in balloting and practically abolished electoral offices, this important part of a literary education had outlived its usefulness. "Senatorial debate — except for a brief revival in 43 — came to an end when Caesar crossed the Rubicon. After that the sight of an unsheathed sword taught men to say their say briefly and to be done. . . . The schools were at a loss what to teach. They pretended still to be preparing their pupils for a public career through the art of declamation when everyone knew that a public career depended now more on judicious silence than on volubility." [17] And as oratory withdrew from the real business of the Forum and the Curia and the Comitia into the schools, it degenerated into mere factitious exercises and hollow declamations on contrived situations,[18] which

[17] Frank 1923, 328, 268.
[18] For examples see Sen. *Contr.* 1.6, 7; 2.2; 10.3, etc.

lent the term 'rhetorical style' the connotations of artificial bombast and unsincerity that it now has.

As this type of language and linguistic exercise became accepted and favored by the schools, it necessarily found its reflection also in the works of literature. The basis of the *elocutio noua* or 'new rhetoric' was "an artificial Latin acquired in school reading. . . . Into this went a condiment of recent colloquial expressions, while the imagery was apt to be floridly oriental." [19]

Roman education had come a long and not wholly fruitful way from its severe and utilitarian beginnings up to the time when Seneca admitted ruefully: "We do not learn for life but for the schoolroom." [20] And I have found at least one modern scholar who goes so far as to count the linguistic sterility and rigidity, accompanied by similar qualities of the spirit, and the linguistic inability to create appropriate terms and to think in them about the solution of pressing problems, among the reasons of the failure of the Empire.[21] There may be some truth in this, though I for one am more inclined to see in language an effigy, at best a catalyst, but only to a very small degree an agent of cultural and social change. Else our contemporary social scientists, so fertile in verbal effusiveness and in portentous neologisms, would be on the high road to lead us presently into the millennium — which I am afraid, or (*entre nous*) hope, they are not.

Roughly, then, one may distinguish four periods in the history of Roman education. First, until the middle of the third century B.C., it was wholly Roman, emphasizing the *mos maiorum*, with practical aims, and entirely in the hands of the family. Second, between 250 and 100 B.C. lies the period of the great transformation under Greek influence, bringing about a Hellenization of subject matter and aims, giving ever greater weight to the *artes liberales* and to the study of *humanitas*. Third, the period between 100

[19] Frank 1923, 504. For a detailed description of the 'new rhetoric' see Gwynn 1926, 153–179.
[20] Sen. *Ep.* 106.12.
[21] Bolgar 1954, 24: "Among the reasons why the Empire failed we ought probably to number the intellectual failure of its educated class. Hampered by their traditionalism and by the strict linguistic discipline which they imposed on their minds, the members of that class could not solve their immediate problems. They could not for a start suddenly invent after centuries of neglect the terms in which these problems might have been properly posed."

B.C. and A.D. 100, signals the final victory of Greek educational ideals, their acceptance by the Romans, and their greatest flowering in Italy. Fourth, from A.D. 100 on occurs a decadence which reaches its greatest depths after the fall of the Empire in the sixth and seventh centuries.

It is clear that the creation of a literary language must fall into the second period, and I have already mentioned the names of the writers who were instrumental in introducing the fundamental ideas and laying the literary and linguistic groundwork. The culmination of their endeavors was to be reached in the third period, and the undisputed masters of the language were Cicero in prose and Vergil in poetry (116–43, 70–19 B.C., respectively), around whom clustered and in whose footsteps followed the greatest writers Rome brought forth: Catullus, Horace, Lucretius, Ovid, Propertius, Tibullus, Livy, Sallust, Tacitus, Seneca, Quintilian, Martial, Juvenal, Suetonius. Not all of them were genuine Romans; they came from various parts of Italy, Gaul, Spain, and Africa. But it is significant that they all flocked to the capital and that they all wrote in the literary language of Rome, in the best Classical Latin. After Tacitus and Juvenal, good Latin literature terminates. No good work of literary criticism, no original philosophy, no first-class narrative in prose or verse, no learned works of value come afterward. "We cannot point to any period of history," writes Frank, "where such mental torpor continued through a long period of sound social and economic conditions." [22] The combination of mental torpor and sound social and economic conditions may seem somewhat surprising. In fact, Frank then continues to speak not only of a decadence in literature but also in the fine arts, in religion, in political administration and self-government; he cites the failing agriculture of the third century, the debasement of the currency, and oppressive taxation.[23] Obviously there is no more soundness in all this than there is in literature. And it is not surprising that, at least from the point of view of Classical Latin, the soundness of the language goes by the board too.

The early Latin writers, down to the middle of the second century, had converted rough, unpolished, and untutored Old Latin

[22] Frank 1927, 470.
[23] Frank 1927, 476–477.

into a language which was "a blend of colloquial speech with the archaic forms of the religious *carmina* and the formulae of the law, embellished with native cosmetics, with the *lumina* of Greek rhetoric, and the flowers of contemporary poetic diction." [24] What were the visible historical causes for the transformation of this semicultivated speech into Classical Latin? In general terms it can be put this way: "The centralization of government in organized states, the domination of a certain class, the prestige enjoyed by its social habits, of which not the least important is its mode of speech, result in the growth and imposition of a standard language." [25]

All of these factors can be found in the political and social history of Rome. I have already dealt with the centralization of government in the chapter on colonization and roads and the concomitant spread of Latin. The domination of a certain class is a permanent trait of Roman history illustrated revealingly by the system of voting which virtually keeps all citizens not living in Rome away from the polls, causes the people to lose its sovereign powers, and unabashedly favors the rising money-aristocracy and the diminishing senatorial nobility. The mode of speech of these Roman ruling classes was reformed in the course of the second century B.C. on Greek models. (Also in religion and the figurative arts the Romans were enormously indebted to Greece: the Greek pantheon was summarily appropriated, and Greek and Roman divinities of comparable attributes and spheres were simply identified with one another, with the blessing of the state, which interfered only when public morality and order seemed endangered; the Greek masterpieces of painting, sculpture, and the art-crafts, samples of which were brought to Rome by conquering heroes as part of the loot or through purchase, soon inspired native artists; and Greek architecture which, as a 'practical' art, was even closer to Roman genius, transformed the city of Rome.)

Since the Greek literary models were studied under the tutorship of expensive teachers and in costly schools, the resultant new fashion of speech became *ipso facto* the property of the wealthier classes. "Doubtless the rapid growth of the proletariat, with immi-

[24] Palmer 1954, 123.
[25] Palmer 1954, 119.

grants speaking dialects or broken Latin, stimulated the disdain and class-consciousness of the ruling aristocracy." [26]

Because of the peculiar socio-political history and the economic conditions which produced a rigidly bisected society, and because of an educational system which did not succeed in, nor even attempt the breaking down of these long-established barriers, not only wealth and influence but also good taste and good language according to Greek canons were and remained the jealously guarded property of the upper classes. Hence, the literary language, particularly in its classical form, was just another instrument of distinction which separated the masses from their oligarchic masters.

In a society as class-conscious as the Roman, a badge of class distinction so easily discernible as the classical language could not be a written idiom alone, but was of course exhibited in speech, even outside solemn senatorial or tribunal or courtly gatherings, by those who attached importance to being heard using it. In ancient Rome this particular kind of literary speech was given the name *urbanitas*, in distinction with *rusticitas*. The latter term did not necessarily bear the connotation of rustic peasant talk, but merely indicated a deviation from the suavity and the urban coloring of the cultured talk of the capital. " 'What do you mean by an urban coloring?' asked Brutus. 'I can't exactly say,' I replied; 'I only know that it exists. . . . In the words and pronunciation of our orators there is a certain intonation and quality which is characteristic of the city, and this is recognizable not in orators only but in others.' " [27] Quintilian describes urbanity of speech in this way: "*Urbanitas*, which I observe denotes language with a smack of the city in its words, accent, and idiom and further suggests a certain tincture of learning derived from associating with well-educated men; in a word, it represents the opposite of rusticity. . . . For my thinking urbanity involves the total absence of all that is incongruous, coarse, unpolished and exotic, whether in thought, language, voice, or gesture, and resides not so much in isolated sayings as in the whole complexion of our language, just as for the Greeks Atticism means that elegance of

[26] Palmer 1954, 123–124.
[27] Cic. *Brut.* 46.171 (LCL, trl. G. H. Hendrickson).

taste which was peculiar to Athens." [28] In other words, urbanity is a term which refers, as in English, not to language alone but rather to the attitude and behavior of the civilized gentleman and lady of the city. Of course, since this style of life bears the stamp of approval of the educated people of Rome, it must be imitated and cultivated. "As there is a particular accent peculiar to the Roman race and to our city, involving no possibility of stumbling or causing offense or unpleasantness or objection, no note or flavor of provincialism, let us make this accent our model, and learn to avoid not only the rustic roughness but also provincial solecisms." [29]

In the Roman state, the speech of Rome had no competition for being the standard for the whole empire. The *urbs* was the uncontested political and cultural center of Italy and, eventually, of the world. "Rome, my dear Rufus, Rome — stay there in that full light and live!",[30] Cicero, then proconsul in Cilicia, nostalgically counsels a friend. And all the great writers and practitioners of Classical Latin took the advice to heart.

It would obviously be an error to claim that whatever bears the stamp of *rusticitas* in the Roman view is 'Vulgar Latin' and therefore represents the spoken language. Indeed "certain people enjoy using a rustic countrified pronunciation, with the object that if their speech is in this tone it may seem to preserve a greater flavor of antiquity." [31] Hence anything that deviates from the highly fashionable and genteel can by a Roman be called 'rustic' without the term's bearing any meaning of local or social dialectalization.

It is curious that the rise of Classical Latin to its greatest heights coincides with the descent of the Republic to its lowest depths and its ultimate demise, and the birth of the monarchy. Both the last great republican, Cicero, and the first autocratic ruler, Caesar, are undisputed contemporaneous masters of the best Latin prose ever written. The reasons for this seemingly paradoxical simultaneity are contained in the history of the era. The social stratum whose members in other places and at other times (for example, in nineteenth-century France or in the United States of our own day) sustain

[28] Quint. 6.3.17; 6.3.107 (LCL, trl. H. E. Butler).
[29] Cic. *de or.* 3.12.44 (LCL, trl. H. Rackham).
[30] Cic. *ad. fam.* 2.12 (LCL, trl. W. G. Williams).
[31] Cic. *de or.* 3.12.42 (LCL, trl. H. Rackham).

the literary language both as consumers through reading it and, to a lesser extent, as producers through speaking and writing it, is a broad, deep layer of educated middle-class bourgeoisie. It is primarily domiciled in the cities, but not absent in the country, especially where schools, press, and radio carry the standard language also into farm homes, rich or humble. But in the fading Roman Republic this middle class was being ruined and extirpated in Italy, and its members relegated either into a vast, ignorant proletariat or, much more rarely, elevated into a thin crust of wealthy optimacy. The inevitable linguistic result was that the standard literary language, according to social opinion the best and noblest type of language, could become the property of but a relatively small number of persons who could afford the requisite schooling, for educational opportunities were restricted primarily to that class. Thus the small social élite of birth and wealth of Rome coincided with the élite of education which knew and used Classical Latin.

It may be idle to speculate on what would have been the future of Classical Latin if it had rested on a broader social foundation and had been mastered and propagated during the crucial period of its flowering and expansion by a greater number of persons, possibly by a majority rather than a small minority of the population. Perhaps then, thanks to its being more firmly anchored, it would have displayed such strength and durability that the Neo-Latin or Romanic languages would resemble it considerably more than they do, and thereby would also be more closely related and better intelligible to one another. They might still have retained, as does Modern German, a nominal declension of several cases, or a more elaborate system of synthetic (uncompounded) rather than analytic (compounded) tense forms and subjunctives, or a different vocabulary with fewer non-Latin borrowings. But it is impossible to make any assertions in this matter.

BOOK FOUR

MEDIAEVAL ITALY

Part Seven. The Abortive Germanization of Italy

CHAPTER XXVI

Historic Background, 300-800

By the end of the third century the Roman Empire had come upon a stage of severe internal and external difficulties. Especially the half century between 235 and 284 was fully catastrophic with its bloody struggles for the crown, mutinies of the army, repeated invasions of horde after horde of barbarians crushing the frontiers in various places, and epidemic diseases spreading over the devastated lands and reducing the population. Once more, as in the time of Caesar and Augustus, Roman economics and politics had reached that unfortunate impasse where the state can be saved from complete disintegration only by a strong, domineering personality wielding autocratic powers. But, at the same time, such a person, precisely because of these qualities and peculiar talents, contributes to the progressive degradation of the citizenry by depriving it increasingly of the will and the ability to seek the remedies for its ills in its own initiative.

Under the name of Diocletian (284–305), the Illyrian soldier Diocles shouldered the enormous burden of restoring the battered empire. With him the government became an undisguised autocracy, and the Principate of the previous emperors was converted into the Dominate. Under Diocletian and his successors the state enjoyed in some respects a partial recovery, but the dry rot had eaten too deep into the body politic to permit more than a stay of the ultimate collapse. For a little over a century, until 395, the empire remained at least one united state. But then occurred the division into an eastern and a western half. The latter, including Italy, crumbled in the course of the fifth century under the ceaseless onslaughts of German tribes, whose chieftains eventually managed to lodge themselves as shadow-emperors behind the legitimate heirs to the Roman throne, and who in the end bluntly and openly took in hand the reins of the government. The efforts of the eastern emperor Justinian (527–565) to reunite the east and the west were only partly and only temporarily successful.

In A.D. 568 the Langobards swarmed into Italy and eradicated the last vestige of Roman authority in the lands they occupied. The Romans were confined to Rome itself and the southern part of the peninsula, retaining for some time a toehold in the north, in Ravenna. Their position was further and disastrously weakened by the westward march of Slavic peoples who crossed the lower Danube and drove a powerful wedge of barbarism and heathendom between the eastern Byzantine empire and western Europe. Finally the tottering western Empire, which in any event no longer deserved the name, lost its last possessions outside of Italy when at the beginning of the seventh century the Visigoths took Spain.

During this time, when the secular authority lost prestige, power, and land, the nonbarbarian inhabitants of Italy found a rallying point in the Roman church. Indeed it was the church which filled the political vacuum and carried on the struggle of the western Empire against the Germanic peoples, although some of the latter had been converted to Christianity (with most of the Germans, however, becoming followers of Arianism which Rome condemned as a heresy). For over two centuries the ecclesiastical authorities succeeded in holding the Langobards of Italy in check by wielding the spiritual rather than secular goad, until Pope Stephen II finally persuaded Pipin, king of the Franks who were settled in Gaul and who were the first Germanic nation to embrace Christianity following their king Clovis (481–511), to subdue the Langobards by force of arms (754). In return for this and other favors, and for allowing the church to retain a large part of Italy stretching from Ravenna across Umbria to Rome (the duchy of Rome, generally known as the *Patrimonium Petri*), Pipin's son Charlemagne was crowned by Pope Leo III at Saint Peter's church in Rome in the year 800 and had bestowed upon him the title of Roman Emperor. Thus, in name at least, and piously fortified by the word 'Holy' in its name, the Roman Empire was tenuously restored. But its capital was far from Rome, few Italians were its subjects, little of Italy was among its vast lands, and its monarch was a German. Italy itself became a kingdom, the realm of the younger Pipin, Charlemagne's son (who preceded his father in death), in 781, a date marking officially the demise of the Langobard reign and the beginning of Italy's association with, and mostly subjection to, the new 'Roman' Empire.

What events and what conditions during these five centuries are of particular importance for the linguistic history of Italy? The first place, in both political and cultural respects, is held by the invasions of Germanic tribes, which, originating from various locations east and north of the Roman *limes*, roughly the Rhine-Danube frontier, moved in strong tribal or national contingents southward and westward, impinging upon the Roman border at different places, at various dates, and with unequal strength. It is difficult to determine what caused them to set out on their long treks. In some measure it may have been the desire of the underprivileged northerners to partake of the riches and pleasures of the civilized Roman Empire. But it also seems that they were the westernmost wave of a chain-reaction *Völkerwanderung* whose radiation center lay in Asia, hence the first breakers of a stormy sea of men which surged thundering against the wall of Roman fortifications. After them came Slavic peoples, and finally the Huns, the wave of easternmost origin that was to flood even Gaul before it receded to whence it had emerged. (At the same time, a southern wave of the Völkerwanderung taking its inception from the same central Asian focus, overran the Gupta Empire, about 375–475, of India.) What the ultimate impetus for the vast movement had been one can only surmise. Possibly it was due to one of the recurrent periods of desiccation of the steppes which force the nomadic peoples into onslaught against the adjacent agricultural areas. Such is, of course, the view of Toynbee, and also of the climatologists I mentioned before.[1] If this is so, then the Völkerwanderung of the early Middle Ages was an event comparable to the eruption, some three millennia before, of the speakers of Indo-European. But the crucial difference between the two seems to be that there is no evidence whatever that any ethnic 'Indo-Europeans' or 'Aryans' actually penetrated in large numbers into Italy, or Europe, while their dialects, borne forward through continued infiltration and diffusion, did; the mediaeval wanderers from the

[1] Cf. Chapter II above. See also Toynbee 1922, 339–342.

north and east, however, moved in closed, compact units, be they of Germanic, Slavic, or Mongolian speech, conquered temporarily parts of the Roman Empire and Italy, but they did not impose their dialects upon the speakers of Latin.

Just like their languages, so all but two of the Germanic successor states to the Roman Empire proved ephemeral, either exhausting themselves in fratricidal warfare (Franks versus Langobards, Burgundians, Visigoths; the wars of the Germanic invaders of Britain among themselves), or being crushed by a spasmodic revival of Roman strength (Ostrogoths), or succumbing to new non-Germanic rising powers (Visigoths and Vandals versus Moslems). The two Germanic states which have bequeathed Europe direct lineal descendants are the Frankish empire of Pipin and Charlemagne, now France, and Alfred's West Saxon kingdom, now England. And of these two only the second is of Germanic speech. *Tantae molis erat. . . .*

During the first and second centuries after Christ, and on sporadic occasions even in republican times, Roman arms had been able to ward off the foreign intruders. In the third century the strength of the Germans increased commensurately with the weakening of Rome. Manpower shortage reduced the Roman garrisons along the frontier, and whenever soldiers had to be rushed to support their fellows at some other point of assault their own positions were denuded of defenders and the dyke was pierced by the Germanic tide. And once the invaders had set foot upon Roman soil, they found little opposition because the Roman territorial army suffered from a lack of adequate mobile units with which to oppose them. How Germanic tribes overran and gobbled up the various provinces, or how the Romans assigned to them provincial land in order to buy them off after they threatened Italian soil (for example, the granting of parts of upper Pannonia to the Marcomanni who in 254 had advanced as far as Ravenna), or how the Romans hired them as *foederati* who for pay were supposed to protect the frontiers against other Germans (indeed, ironically, against themselves, as it were) does not concern us here. But German inroads into Italy do.

In the course of the later Principate it had become customary to strengthen the imperial army by the addition of barbarian auxiliary troops and by eventually admitting them to the ranks of the regulars and among officers. This led to a decline in military discipline and training, for the army was not able any more than the state as a whole, to assimilate foreigners and to make them integral and reliable functioning parts of the machinery. Other Germans, captives from among conquered tribes, were settled in Italy to provide needed agricultural labor. All these barbarians did not dangerously increase in numbers because of a high rate of infant mortality and low average longevity among them (especially among the soldiers who were pressed into military service at an early age and were by the field commanders considered more expendable than Italians). It would therefore be incorrect to imagine an ethnic Germanization of Italy or an important mixture of races. Those Germans who survived on the land were virtual serfs to whom Italy and the Roman Empire never could become a home, especially since, as I have said repeatedly, the Romans were traditionally unable and unwilling to absorb foreign populations culturally. No wonder that as strangers they gladly took every opportunity to rejoin their fellows, whether of the same tribe or not, who periodically irrupted into the Empire. These invaders themselves came as marauding bands, intent on looting and plundering, on short-term gains rather than on acquiring arable land and settling down. All in all, then, this kind of Germanic influx in Italy until the fourth century could do very little to change the culture of the native inhabitants.

Even in the fourth century, when the Germans began to attack the Empire as organized tribes rather than as desultory hordes, it seems that their actual fighting strength was surprisingly small — luckily for the Romans who had no great numbers of soldiers to put in the field against them. (In the battle of Strassburg, in 357, only 13,000 Roman legionnaires beat the Alemanni, whereas, a little later, the battle of Hadrianople, of 378, saw a not greater number annihilated by the rebellious Visigoths.[2]) But this, too, was soon to change.

When the Emperor Theodosius the Great died in 395 and the Empire was bisected, one of his sons, Honorius, then a boy of eleven, became the ruler of the West. The regent who had been

[2] Boak 1955, 100.

appointed by Theodosius himself and who became the real master of the state was one Stilicho, of the tribe of the Vandals. Though himself a German, he battled valiantly against various Germanic invaders, especially the Visigoths, who under Alaric had already overrun Greece, and whom subsequently he twice defeated in 401 and 403, when they attempted to set foot into Italy. But when Stilicho was murdered, in 408, in consequence of a plot by those who were jealous of his influence, Italy was deprived of its last capable defender. Honorius withdrew to Ravenna, and Alaric now moved southward virtually unopposed. Rome ransomed itself at enormous expense. But this time the Germans were not content to withdraw after having filled their pockets; in addition they wanted to be assigned land. Since Honorius, bolstered somewhat by troops of the Eastern Empire, proved untractable and turned a deaf ear to their demands, Alaric and the Goths marched upon Rome and pillaged the city ruthlessly for three days (410). Alaric's plans of advancing also into Sicily and Africa were foiled by the destruction of his fleet in a storm. Shortly thereafter he himself became sick and died in southern Italy, finding a legendary tomb near Cosenza in Calabria, at the bottom of the Busento River whose waters were diverted through a canal to permit the interment. Alaric's successor and brother-in-law, Ataulfus, then led the Goths into Gaul and married Honorius' sister, Placidia, who had been taken captive in Rome. Thus the Visigothic peril actually passed out of Italy, but the Goths did establish themselves firmly elsewhere on Roman soil, in Gaul and, later, in Spain.

Between 406 and 413 the Burgundians settled on the middle Rhine and Neckar, with their capital at Worms, where their royal house is remembered through the *Song of the Nibelungen:* Kriemhild, the sister of King Gunther, marries Siegfried, who is treacherously slain by Hagen at the instigation of the jilted Brunhild; in her burning desire to avenge her husband's murder, Kriemhild brings about a terrible blood bath at the court of Attila, king of the Huns, her husband in second marriage, where not only Hagen but also her brothers and compatriots perish. In 443 the Burgundians moved southward, occupying the valleys of the upper Rhone and Saône and the Italian slopes of the Alps down toward the Po plain, that is, part of the modern Piedmont. Their kingdom was conquered in 532 by the Franks under the two younger sons of Clovis. This northwestern corner of Italy remained in Frankish possession until the division of Charlemagne's empire.

Attila with his Huns invaded Italy, in 452. But, weakened as he was by earlier bloody battles in Gaul, by disease and starvation among his troops, and threatened by an army of the Eastern Empire, he could be induced to leave Italy without investing Rome. His death in the following year marked the decline of the Hunnish empire and the passing of this mortal danger.

Once more in the fifth century Rome was overrun. In 455, the Vandals, who had by then crossed the straits of Gibraltar (leaving a trace of their passage through Spain in the name of the province [V]andalusia) and had established an independent Germanic kingdom in northern Africa, landed at Ostia and descended under King Geiseric upon the city. Their merciless plundering of its treasures, albeit unaccompanied by a wanton destruction of the city's buildings and monuments, has bequeathed us the term vandalism. But the Vandals, too, left Italy again and withdrew to Africa, although they, like the Visigoths, might well have been able to stand their ground against Roman arms.

Though repeatedly invaded and pillaged, Rome and Italy had so far miraculously escaped a permanent occupation by foreign soldiery and populations. But the Empire's good fortune was about to run out.

Odoacar, the leader of the German auxiliary troops attached to the Roman legions in Italy, demanded that land be assigned to his troops in Italy just as it had been to the Germanic *foederati* in the provinces. When his request was rejected, the restive foreign mercenaries revolted, chased the last Roman emperor, Romulus Augustulus, from the throne, and Odoacar proclaimed himself ruler of the Western Roman Empire. He was eventually confirmed as imperial regent of Italy by the eastern emperor and governed monarchically from 476–493.

His rule was brought to an end in 493 by another German, Theodoric, chief of the Ostrogoths (the Dietrich von Bern, that

is, Verona, of German legend), a people formerly subject to the
Huns (it was Theodoric-Dietrich who, in the Niebelungenlied,
finally overpowered Hagen in the holocaust at Attila's court),
free since the death of Attila, and *foederati* of Rome in Pannonia.
The emperor Zeno, to divert Theodoric's ambitions from the east,
allowed him to attack Italy and to depose Odoacar. After two battles and a long siege of Ravenna, Theodoric and Odoacar came
to terms: they were to govern jointly the peninsula. But at a
banquet Odoacar and his followers were treacherously slain, and
Theodoric, king of the Ostrogoths, became officially the ruler of
Italy as a functionary of the Roman Empire. Soon (497) he received from the eastern emperor Anastasius the symbols of imperial
power which Odoacar had sent to Constantinople after the enforced
abdication of Romulus Augustulus, and became thereby an equal
and a colleague of the emperor of Byzantium.

The native population of the provinces and of Italy had to
come to some *modus uiuendi* with the barbarians, who, though
everywhere numerically inferior, were the real masters. In various
parts of the Empire various solutions were reached, more or less
favorable to the Roman citizens. In Italy, neither Odoacar nor
Theodoric changed the old administrative system, nor did they
on the whole replace Roman officials by men of their own choosing. A code of law which Theodoric published gave equal rights
and equal laws to Italians and Ostrogoths. The Ostrogoths received
allotments of land totaling one-third of the Roman real estate,
but since Italy was underpopulated and abundant state land available no confiscation of private property was necessary. The Roman
Senate, much debilitated but still an influential body although it
was far away from the new capital at Ravenna, supported Theodoric's policies.

The Goths, like most Germans, were adherents of Arianism,
which was proscribed by the Roman orthodox church. But Theodoric allowed complete religious freedom to the Roman Catholics
in his state, until Justinian, in 523, began to molest Arians in the
Eastern Empire and until a faction in the Roman Senate together
with the orthodox clergy of Italy became openly hostile to the
Arian heretics. Then Theodoric resolved to smash this politico-

religious uprising (the philosopher Boethius and other eminent Romans were at that time executed for treason), but his death, in 526, checked a general Catholic persecution.

Upon Theodoric's passing from the scene, opportunity seemed to smile upon a reconquest of Italy and a reunification of the Empire. Justinian (527–565) was successful at least for a time, thanks to the brilliance of his general Belisarius, in recovering Italy in addition to other parts of the Empire, and to make it a Roman province. But when Belisarius was withdrawn, owing to intrigues at the court, the Ostrogoths resumed their resistance under Totila and drove the Roman occupation troops from most of Italy. Belisarius, called back by the emergency, was able to regain only Rome. The resources of the Empire were severely overtaxed by a Persian war in the east, hence the redemption of Corsica, Sardinia, Sicily, and all of Italy, except a few strongholds, including Ravenna, had to be temporarily abandoned. Only in 552 and 553 did Narses, perhaps even a better general than Belisarius himself, subdue the Goths in two great battles in Umbria and in Campania. The Germans were allowed to leave Italy and to seek new homes beyond the Empire's frontiers. Also a dangerous attack by the Alemanni and the Franks was rebuffed by Narses (554), and Roman dominion was once more established.

But the price of the reconquest was so great and Italy so exhausted and devastated by years of warfare and all the accompanying misery that the political success of the emperor could not compensate for the economic castrophe it had wrought. When Justinian died he left an empire, true enough, but one that lay prostrate, its vitality drained.

Only a few years later, from 568 on, most of Italy was again lost, this time to the Langobards, who succeeded in establishing a kingdom that was to endure for over two centuries, until Pipin, king of the rising Frankish nation, champion of the papacy against Germans and Byzantines in Italy and against Moslems everywhere, brought it to an end. The Langobards, unlike their other Germanic predecessors, came as real conquerors, not as Roman soldiers or allies or *foederati*, not as mere pawns in the battle between Roman factions or between Romans and Germans. They wanted land, they wanted to remain, and they vanquished Italy to attain these ends. Their King Alboin, unlike Odoacar and Theodoric, did not wish to continue Roman institutions, he did not care to be an imperial official, he did not intend to come to terms or to respect and accept Roman culture for himself and his people. He came as conqueror and, if need be, as destroyer. He deprived Romans of their possessions, and he introduced Germanic law in Italy.

CHAPTER XXVII

Germanic Dialects in Italy Between 300 and
800, then, Germanic culture and Germanic speech gained a
foothold in Italy, and endured for long periods, notably under
the Langobards. Germans were actually the masters of the peninsula, especially its northern and central part. Yet at the end of this
era and after the political elimination of the Germans, we find
Italy in culture and language just as Roman under Charlemagne
as it had been under Diocletian. To explain why this was so it
will be necessary to spotlight some details of social and cultural
history.

As the main causes for the non-Germanization of Italy and
the ultimate Romanization of the Germans remaining there, I
should cite the relatively small number of German invaders, the
disunity of purpose among the Germans themselves, the reluctance of the Germans, up to the time of the Langobards, to destroy
the old culture, and the religious and cultural incompatibility of
Germans and Italians.

Whenever population figures are involved, we are, in ancient
and mediaeval history, treading on unsure ground, after A.D. 300
no less than before. But, while estimates on the size of German
contingents vary greatly in absolute figures, they all agree at least
that the number of invaders was always small in relation to the
natives. Indeed, had the Germans come in large hordes it is doubtful whether the Romans, themselves suffering from a crippling
manpower shortage, would have been able to stave them off as long
as they did and on occasion to beat them in pitched battle. It may
well be, judging by the success and duration of their occupation,
that the Langobards were numerically stronger than the preceding
Ostrogoths and these again stronger than the earlier Visigoths.
But nothing certain can be said about this. Most likely, Sforza is
more right than not when he deprecatingly speaks of certain starv-

ing tribes descending from Germany, which later through German vanity and a desire of the Italians to attribute their ills to an irresistible foreign assault rather than to internal dissolution of the state, were inflated into onrushing, incontrollable, powerful invading nations.[1]

In the absence of trustworthy figures, I do not think it illegitimate to deduce the small number of Germans from the demonstrable insignificance of their cultural contributions in Italy, and then to cite the small number as an explanation for the remarkable perseverance of Romanity. This is not, I believe, a circular argument.

The disunity of purpose among the Germans is blatant. They were organized in tribes and small nations, each having its own laws, administration, and dialect. They were not unaccustomed to wage intertribal war, and indeed indulged in sanguine intratribal feuds.[2] Communication among them was poor. Also, it was one of the policies of the fading Roman empire to play the German tribes against one another by bribing and blackmailing them alternately and employing them as mercenaries or *foederati* against their fellows. For all these reasons it is scarcely surprising that there should exist no German national sentiment which could be fruitfully channeled toward the concerted conquest of Italy and the Empire. Instead, the Romans were given an opportunity, which they desperately needed, to deal with the Germanic tribes piecemeal. This not only reduced the chance for success of Rome's enemies and shortened the sojourn of those who contrived to settle in Italy, but it also divested each tribe of the sense of security and superiority and of that quasi-missionary fervor which a people needs, consciously or not, to impose its culture upon another,

---

[1] Sforza 1949, 3.

[2] The kinship feud was a common Germanic institution. According to it, when a member of a clan was slain or injured or in any manner damaged, his kinsmen had the right and indeed the duty to commit blood revenge upon the evildoer himself or upon a member of his kindred. Such reciprocal revenge was bound to extend and prolong itself into incessant strife within the tribe, which is another reason for the difficulties the Germans experienced in attaining national identification and in pursuing common national goals. And even when vengeance could be remitted by payment of sums of money fixed in accordance with the gravity of the offense and the importance of the damaged person, these internal discords could not but hinder, throughout the Middle Ages, the establishment of peace and of a well-functioning government.

especially on one like the Latin Italians who looked back upon a millennium of power and prestige. In studying the history of the German tribes in Italy one cannot escape the impression that these barbarians, at least down to the Langobards, were overwhelmed by their surroundings, could not find their way in them, and forever felt like intruders whose business was regretfully temporary, and who were not only unable but reverently unwilling to destroy what they found and to impose themselves. The redoutable Odoacar, for example, the first Germanic ruler of Italy, named his son Caesar. But this is already part of the third and to my mind most important reason for their ineffectiveness culturally, including of course their failure to propagate their dialects.

I shall speak only of the three major German inroads in Italy which alone had a chance to become centers of cultural spread, those of the Visigoths, the Ostrogoths, and the Langobards.

In the early fifth century when the Visigoths marched into Italy after the murder of Stilicho, Alaric sought to come to terms with Honorius because he did not wish to undo the Empire or to destroy Rome. It seems that the sack of Rome in 410, into which the Visigoths were forced because their demands were not peacefully met, was not as brutal and catastrophical as the sources have it. Probably the conquest of Rome by barbarians was such a shock to the civilized world that the events were greatly magnified and distorted in the telling, until they assumed legendary proportions. And Alaric's successor, Ataulfus, supposedly said to the informant of the historian Orosius, from whom we have the tale, that "at first he, Ataulfus, had ardently desired that after the eclipse of Roman power he could make over all the Roman lands into the Empire of the Goths and so name them, that, to put it in popular terms, what had been Romania should be Gothia, and Ataulfus should become what had hitherto been Caesar Augustus; but as soon as he had found out through much experience that neither could the Goths, owing to their reckless barbarism, in any wise obey laws nor must a state be denied laws, without which in fact a state is not a state, he had at least chosen to seek his glory in restoring and strengthening the Roman dominion with the aid of the Goths, and in being remembered by posterity as the author of Rome's revival, since he had not been able to be its trans-

former." [3] And then Ataulfus, the barbarian, married Galla Placidia, the sister of the emperor Honorius, in a sumptuous wedding
according to Roman usage and rite. It is not to be expected that a
Germanic king and his people who are imbued with this reverential
attitude, can or intend to make much progress in reshaping Italy
after their image.

The king of the Ostrogoths, Theodoric, educated at Constantinople, is satisfied to be the vassal of the eastern emperor until
the latter breaks faith by persecuting Theodoric's fellow-Arians.
During his reign the administration of Italy is not changed. On
the contrary, the Germans themselves, once adherents of a com-
munistic form of tribal economy and governing themselves through
democratic councils, adjust themselves to the ways of Rome and
institute an absolute monarchy. And, although they continue
their judicial procedures and laws among themselves, they allow
the Romans to retain their own legal code. Whatever cultural rapprochement occurs is at the expense of the Goths.

Yet there can be no question of real coalescence. A law of A.D.
370 (*Cod. Theod.* 1.13.14) forbidding mixed marriages between
Romans and Germans under penalty of death, remains in force
until the middle of the seventh century, broken during this time
only for dynastic reasons. The Senate, in Rome, ostensibly legis-
lates for all of Italy, but in fact by now its actions are binding
neither on Goths nor on Italians. The Goths become no more
Roman citizens than the Italians turn into Goths. True enough,
Theodoric himself changes to Roman dress, his language and that
of the court and the offices is Latin, the education of German youth,
that is, of those few who receive an education, is thoroughly
Roman, and the royal house becomes closely related with the
Byzantine reigning family through intermarriage. A modern historian calls him "the most Roman of the barbarian kings." [4] But
the army remains Gothic, and Romans are excluded from it (although some of Theodoric's generals are Romans); the Arian service
in the church is Gothic and not Roman; and in Theodoric's own
family and among a nationalist faction arises resistance against his
too vigorous, albeit external, attempts at assimilation.

[3] Oros. 7.43. 5–6.
[4] Lot 1935, 165.

In short, while perhaps the upper classes recognize and seek the higher culture of their Roman subjects, the masses and the lower classes remain unassimilated and probably resent the cultural betrayal by their leaders. (The national sentiment was similar in England after 1066, when some of the native nobles, with the disapproval and to the disgust of their Anglo-Saxon compatriots, especially the common people, took up the ways of the Normans.)

The brief flourishing of Italy under Theodoric's beneficent rule is therefore not the rebirth of a new Germanic-Roman conglomerate civilization but the last flicker of the ancient Roman culture before its inexorable conversion into mediaeval Italian culture. Under such circumstances, the Germanization of Italy in culture and language is out of the question.

When the Ostrogoth Totila, between 541 and 546, after the recall of Belisarius, drove once again the Byzantine-Roman armies out of Italy, he was begged in a letter by General Belisarius to spare the city of Rome, which had only recently suffered cruelly in the year-long siege of 537–538. (Then the beleaguering Goths under Witiges cut the aqueducts which provided the city with water, thereby not only weakening their adversaries through unbearable thirst while at the same time converting their own camping grounds into an insalubrious swamp, but also making Rome virtually uninhabitable by anything but a shadowy fraction of its ancient population.[5]) "While the creation of beauty (wrote Belisarius to Totila) in a city which has not been beautiful before could only proceed from men of wisdom who understand the meaning of civilization, the destruction of beauty which already exists would be naturally expected only of men who lack understanding, and who are not ashamed to leave to posterity this token of their character. Now among all the cities under the sun Rome is agreed to be the greatest and the most noteworthy. For it has not been created by the ability of one man, nor has it attained such greatness and beauty by a power of short duration, but a multitude of monarchs, many companies of the best men, a great lapse of time, and an extraordinary abundance of wealth have availed

[5] Trevelyan 1920, 44; "By that one fatal deed [of cutting the aqueducts] the Goths did more to plunge Rome into the squalor of the Middle Ages than all their good government had done to avert it."

to bring together in that city all other things that are in the whole world, and skilled workers besides. Thus, little by little, have they built the city, such as you behold it, thereby leaving to future generations memorials of the ability of them all, so that insult to these monuments would properly be considered a crime against the men of all time; for by such action the men of former generations are robbed of the memorials of their ability, and future generations of the sight of their work. . . . If you should dismantle Rome, you would not have destroyed the possession of some other man, but your own city, excellent Sir, and, on the other hand, if you preserve it, you will naturally enrich yourself by possessing the fairest of all." [6] Thus Totila and his Goths, by flattery and browbeating, but mainly because they actually believed what Belisarius told them, were induced, for better or for worse, to spare Rome. Shortly afterward the returning Belisarius reconquered the city; and in 552 the brave Totila was killed in battle and the Goths had to leave Italy. Once more the reverence of the barbarians for the superior culture had deprived them of the full fruits of victory through their hesitancy to triumph fully over the vanquished. And again no fusion of the two cultures can be expected, and no important linguistic contribution of Ostrogothic to Latin speech, let alone complete Germanization, can be discerned.

The Langobards behave more like true conquerors than their predecessors. But they also suffer more than their forerunners from internal disunity and lack of a unified social and cultural purpose. In the occupied territory (comprising, at its greatest extent, all of the Western Empire except Istria, the cities on the northern Adriatic — Ravenna, Rimini, Fano, Pesaro, Senigallia, Ancona — the Duchy of Rome from Civitavecchia to Gaeta, Naples and Amalfi, Apulia, Calabria, Sicily, and Sardinia [7]) the conquerors appropriate all acreage owned by Romans and become sedentary. However, the land, after the murder of Alboin's successor in 574, is divided into three dozen loosely confederated dukedoms (strongest and most independent of which are those of Spoleto

[6] Proc. *D.B.* 7.22.8–16. These are, of course, exactly the reasons why Rome was declared an Open City toward the end of World War II, and thus was spared disfigurement or destruction.

[7] Cf. map in Trevelyan 1920, facing p. 56.

and Benevento) whose lords more often than not find themselves at cross-purposes and whose allegiance to the weak central government sitting in Pavia is rather tenuous. The Langobards do fight the Romans without reluctance wherever they want to and need to, but they do not emerge anywhere as a unified victorious nation.

Although the Langobards are converted from Arianism to Roman Catholicism in the course of the seventh century, their most implacable yet most impalpable enemy remains the Roman church whose interests had begun, since Gregory the Great (590–604), to broaden into the political field and whose popes wished to be heard in the councils of secular rulers. It cannot be charged that the Langobards, while still Arians, suppressed or persecuted the Roman Catholics. On the contrary, it is reported that in the time of King Rothari, the great legislator (636–652), almost all cities of the kingdom had two bishops, one Arian and one Catholic.[8] Nonetheless it was the pope who personally persuaded the Frankish king Pipin to break the Langobards' power in Italy, possibly because he feared that in the end, under their last and able king, Desiderius, the Langobards were about to reach their aim of founding a Langobard-Roman nation, in which the papacy would be relegated to a minor role. And, indeed, with the establishment, through Pipin and Charlemagne, of the Church State in Italy, the popes became a power that henceforth would challenge the emperors of the Holy Roman Empire themselves for centuries to come, and whose permanent policy it was to increase their possessions and their influence by restraining secular powers, be they Germanic conquerors, or Norman invaders, or Swabian emperors, from subjecting all of Italy and unifying it. This ecclesiastic policy proved successful, though disastrous for Italy, until the nineteenth century.

Unlike the short-lived Visigothic and Ostrogothic visitations of Italy, the Langobard kingdom lasted more than two hundred years. But where the former had failed, through lack of time, respectful reluctance, and ineptness, to leave a significant and permanent imprint on the life and the languages of Italy, the Langobards foiled the opportunity through political incompetence alone. And once their state was dissolved, the Langobards, deprived

[8] Paul. Diac. *H.L.* 4.42.

of their last unifying tie, however impotent it had been politically, were culturally absorbed by the Italians.

Two recent writers have suggested that one notable reason for the Germanic cultural failure in Italy was that the Germans were mainly rural settlers and feudal lords who underrated and ignored the force of municipal life in Italy, applying tribal, rural, and feudal conceptions in a country where the city, the arch-antagonist and eventual conqueror of feudalism, was everything.[9] This is, apart from its extremes, an attractive hypothesis, but it must remain just that, at least for the period before A.D. 800, not only because we have virtually no knowledge of the number of Germans in Italy but also since we know equally little of their distribution in city and country all over the peninsula.

Political supremacy over any region may be attained by force of arms, possibly in a single battle, without a subsequent physical occupation, sparse or dense, by the conquerors. Hence also the evidence of proper personal and local names, however fascinating its study, is inconclusive for our purposes, because the appearance of a Germanic name anywhere in Italy is no clue whatever as to the size and impact of the Germanic occupation. It merely shows that some Germans, and it may well be no more than one family, penetrated into a certain locality — and not even that is wholly certain because names can be borrowed and can travel, like items of vocabulary, without being carried the entire distance by native speakers of the dialect to which they belong, although, admittedly, this phenomenon may be rare.[10] There are also all over Italy, not only in Sicily but also in the center and north, many local names of Arabic origin. But no one would claim that all such names, even those which are not properly Arabic but only recall, in an Italian form, the presence of Moslems in the locality (such as compounds with *Saracen-*, *Saracinesco*, and so on), are indicative of permanent Moslem settlements in strength or of civilian colonization. Accordingly, there is no reason to found a similar thesis upon the occurrence of Germanic local names.

Moreover, apart from the Ostrogothic language known through

[9] Olschki 1949, 26–27; Sforza 1949, 4–5.
[10] The distribution of Germanic names in Italy is shown in Gamillscheg 1934, 3.208, map III.

Wulfila's translation of the Bible, our information on the early Germanic dialects in question is so scant that it is almost impossible to identify severally their contributions to the onomasticon of Italy. The best that can be said in many instances is that certain names are Germanic, without further specification as to tribe and date. This means that for our purposes of linguistic history the evidence is insufficient.

What about the influence, if any, of Germanic on Latin in sounds, forms, and syntax in general? [11] What has been said about the onomasticon and lexicon applies equally in these other realms. Phonemic peculiarities due to German are difficult to recover, unless one believes, as does von Wartburg, that the diphthongization of accented vowels is due in Italy to the Langobard superstratum (as it is in Gaul to a Frankish superstratum). The gradual weakening and disappearance of this linguistic phenomenon from north to south and its straddling of the potent La Spezia-Rimini dialect boundary correspond to the pattern of settlement of the Langobards.[12] The theory is attractive, but it would be more persuasive if we knew more about the phonemic habits of the Langobards. Syntactic borrowings, difficult of transfer in any two languages, may hardly be expected from German to Latin, whose interaction, because of the linguistic strangeness and cultural coolness and incompatibility of the speakers to one another, remained perforce superficial. At best one may hope to discover the type of linguistic borrowings for which a mere external relationship and a bare exchange of conversation among the people suffices, that is, lexical ones. Scholars have found some 70 Ostrogothic loans in Italian, 280 Langobard loan words,[13] altogether about 500 Italian words of Old Germanic provenance.[14] But detailed classification and conclusions on the linguistic history of Italy are difficult to derive from this evidence. Gamillscheg's ingenious research led him to believe that the distribution of Ostrogothic and Langobard loanwords coincides remarkably well with the distribution of the local names of each of the two dialects and con-

---

[11] See Migliorini 1953, 44–64.
[12] von Wartburg 1950, 117–146.
[13] Gamillscheg 1934, 2.17–24, 127–175.
[14] Gamillscheg 1939, 89. Cf. also Bertoni 1914.

sequently with the settlements of Goths and Langobards.[15] I have already mentioned the objections that can be raised against converting toponymic into ethnic evidence. The same is true, at the place and the time under examination, also for items of the general lexicon. Hence the alleged geographical congruence of onomastic and lexical loans is a priori suspect of being spurious. Besides, it is virtually impossible to say, without nonlinguistic, external evidence, at what time between 300 and 800 a German word found its way into Latin, because we have almost no evidence of the spoken language of the period; and a Germanic borrowing in the written Latin language is most likely learned and deliberate, and tells us nothing about the speech habits of the inhabitants of Italy. Dating of German loans with the aid of the relative chronology of sound change[16] is possible in but few instances since in most cases we do not know from what original form we should start, that is to say, we do not know with sufficient precision what most Germanic words in Italy could have been like at any given date within five and more centuries, in order to fit their phonemic development from a given point on into the chronology of Latin-Italian sound change. Gamillscheg proposes to separate direct loans, due to German settlers in Italy after 400, from indirect loans which reach Italy from Germans living outside of Italy both before and after 400. In a small total of five hundred lexical items this division will not only be difficult to accomplish but also — and this is important for us — even if it is accomplished without a major residue of uncertainties and doubts, and even though the history of each of the single items is of enormous importance and interest in the study of historical grammar, it will tell us but little about the total linguistic history of German dialects in Italy. Lexical borrowings, which can be due to such a great variety of causes and motives (psychological, semantic, local, personal, statistical, phonetic) simply are not apt instruments of investigation, at least not by themselves. And we have them only by themselves in this instance.

One thing is certain. Since the Germanic languages in Italy, including Langobard, the last and, in terms of speakers and dur-

---

[15] Gamillscheg 1934, 2.25–27, 175–176.
[16] Cf. Bertoni 1914, 29 ff.

ation, most powerful one, disappear in Italy as spoken idioms, their users must at one point have become bilingual during a state of transition. Whether only one generation or several were bilingual, and at what time bilingualism ceased in favor of Latin, we can only guess. No doubt, as in all such situations, people spoke their own dialects longest among themselves, and the foreign language earliest with the natives. Social and cultural pressure and lack of necessity of continuing Germanic speech reduced and finally eliminated it. We have some evidence, not altogether conclusive, that the Langobards had ceased to speak their dialects in the second half of the tenth century, at least in southern Italy.[17]

There is no indication that German was of any literary importance in Italy during these centuries. And it should be noted that the codification of Germanic law accomplished under the Langobard King Rothari and published in 643, the famous *Edictus*, was composed in Latin. (By this route a number of untranslatable Langobard terms found their way into Latin and eventually Italian.) This is due in part to the precedence and the models of Latin legal codes, especially the Theodosian Code, and in probably greater measure to the absence of a written standard Langobard language. As I have remarked repeatedly, the creation of a written language is an act of cultural standardization that requires strong personal or political motivation and a conscious effort. The Langobards of Italy did not produce the necessary impetus toward such a lofty goal.

Whatever few Visigoths, if any, had remained in Italy after Alaric's untimely death in 410, had probably been wholly absorbed, ethnically and linguistically, by the time the Ostrogoths arrived nearly a century later. If any of the latter were left when Langobards under Alboin crossed the Alps in 568, they may or may not still have spoken their original dialect rather than Latin, they may or may not have become speakers of Langobardic before they, together with the Langobards, changed to Latin. There may or may not be, then, among the so-called Langobardic loans a number of assimilated Ostrogothic ones in disguise.

[17] A passage of the *Chronicon Salernitanum* of about 978, quoted in MGH, Script. 3.489, mentions "the German language which the Langobards *spoke* at one time," that is, by implication, no longer spoke when the chronicle was written.

The Franks came not as a people in search of conquest and lands but merely as soldiers in order to assist the pope against the Langobards. No doubt they arrived as large enough an army, but not as colonizers. Having accomplished their task, the majority withdrew. And those who remained were by that date (toward the end of the eighth century) Romanized and Latinized, like their fellow-countrymen in Gaul, to such a degree that their linguistic influence in Italy could scarcely contribute to a Germanization of Latin. Moreover, their native Germanic vocabulary had already undergone some Romanization in Gaul and entered the speech of Italy together with other Romanic that is, palaeo-French items. Indeed we may wonder, though scarcely hope for an answer, how many of Pipin's and Charlemagne's 'Frankish' soldiers were not already native speakers of Latin.

Interesting is the case of the Burgundians whose territory corresponds remarkably well with the area of the modern Franco-Provençal dialects, straddling the western Alps and thus forming a speech area of northwestern Italy, notably the Aosta valley, in which a non-Italian dialect is at home. Although the so-called First Kingdom, of the original Burgundians, came to an end through conquest by the Franks in 532, and although the region later was subjected to numerous partitions, it nonetheless survived as a political concept. The Second Kingdom was founded in 933, and became better known as the Kingdom of Arles. In the fifteenth century the dukes of Burgundy, thanks to their conquests which reached as far north as the Netherlands and Belgium, became powerful figures in French politics, and in the Hundred Years War the English, at first supported by Burgundy, suffered irreparable damage from the withdrawal of their erstwhile allies. Only through the marriage of Mary, daughter of Charles the Bold, Duke of Burgundy, to the archduke and later emperor Maximilian I (1493–1519), did Burgundy fall to the house of Habsburg. But the small duchy of Burgundy proper, created in 877 by the emperor Charles II, was annexed to France and eventually became the province of Burgundy, or Bourgogne, with its capital at Dijon. It is impossible to determine at present the extent or longevity of the original Burgundian dialect. But the congruence of the First Kingdom with Franco-Provençal, and the tenacity of Burgundy both as a name and a political reality make it very tempting to believe in a linguistic continuity and to make Burgundian the superstratum responsible for the present Franco-Provençal dialects of southeastern France and northwestern Italy.[18]

All the historical evidence we possess indicates that, with the exception of the Langobards toward the end of their reign, the Germans who settled as conquerors upon Italian soil and among Latin-speaking Italians, were not culturally assimilated and absorbed (excepting, of course, the inevitable small but unknown number who early intermarried with the Italians), but either fled if they were serfs, or otherwise were annihilated or exiled from Italy in the course of Roman reconquests. But lest I be misunderstood, I want to make clear that ethnic and linguistic absorption and acculturation of all things Germanic could not fail to take place, and indeed did take place as soon as the Germans ceased to be the dominant political power. For at that moment, hostility and, with it, incompatibility were reduced, and eventually disappeared, because the native Italians no longer had to fear subjection and suppression from the Germans, and the remaining Germans were no longer obliged in the interest of prestige to maintain rule and superiority over the Italians. I daresay such a relationship of cultures, which for a time occupy the same territory, is indicative of a conscious refusal on both sides to enter into fraternization or amalgamation, until one side loses supremacy and the other loses apprehension.

It is fascinating to reflect on the possible linguistic consequences if the Germans, from their earliest appearance in Italy, had become assimilated and acculturated and fused with the Italians. I presume that their linguistic influence, nurtured perhaps by more friendly human relation and surely by an exchange of cultural goods, would have been incomparably greater, regardless of whether they were or were not the political rulers of the country. (The influence of Frankish on the Romanic speech in Gaul is far more profound and lasting precisely for these reasons.) Who knows but what modern Italian, while remaining a structurally Romanic language, might have as much Germanic substance as English, which is structurally Germanic, has Romanic substance. But these are hypothetical questions, and history should not be written in conditional clauses.

But what did happen to the spoken Latin language during

[18] Cf. von Wartburg 1950, 74–101.

these five centuries of political decadence and convulsion? The answer must be, unfortunately, simple and brief enough, for we possess little useful information. There can be no doubt that the language underwent a number of changes. We know this for certain not only because that is the way of language, but also because the results that emerge later cannot be explained by a sudden profound transformation, for such is surely not the way of language. Instead they must have been effected by previously existing forces, however invisible under the surface they may lie. The written language, that is, the documentation we possess, covers like an opaque sheet of ice on a brook the rushing and babbling current that runs underneath it and of which we catch only a glimpse and a sound every now and then, where the ice is thin, transparent, or broken.

What I have proved is, I hope, the reason why the waters of the stream of spoken Latin received remarkably little admixture from the many Germanic rivulets and torrents which at various times rippled or roared through Italy.

We have followed the history of the Western Empire over five centuries from the first ephemeral intrusions of Germanic bands, as allies or foes, upon Italian soil to the almost total and enduring subjugation of Italy by an organized German conquering nation. In the field of linguistic history we have seen how and, in some measure, why these repeated onslaughts and occupations did not lead to the Germanization of Italy and the Italians either in material civilization or in language. At the beginning of the ninth century the Germanic danger in Italy is overcome, although the peninsula will long remain the battleground of the continuous struggles in which the German emperors with their armies are heavily involved. But the intermittent political supremacy of the German crown over parts of Italy will occasion neither an extensive occupation by German civilians, nor a colonization, hence the culture and language of Italy will not again be faced with any struggle for survival against foreign intruders. The Latin inheritance, but slightly and externally affected by German imports, will evenly and placidly evolve into the Italian dialects.

Part Eight. The Italianization of Italy

Historic Background, 800-1250 After the defeat of the Langobards, the accords between the Throne and
the Holy See were such that they either divided the loyalty
of the Italians, which was unsatisfactory for both claimants to it,
or that they created partisanship for one and against the other:
the pope was politically dependent on the emperor, yet he had
independent territorial possessions and secular ambitions which
often clashed with the imperial ones; the emperor was dependent
on the spiritual approval of the pope and required to be crowned
by the prince of the church, yet he desired and needed independence without papal interference if his reign was to be just and
efficient. From this vague and tortuous division of power sprang
the contests between the papacy and the monarchy which were to
keep Europe in turmoil for centuries and make of Italy the long-
suffering battlefield upon which the contenders for the domination
of man's physical and spiritual allegiances exercised and deployed
for battle their costly and consuming armies.

Toward the end of Charlemagne's reign Italy was divided into
four principal spheres of dominion. First, the kingdom of Italy, that
is, the former Langobard kingdom, now in Frankish hands but
without the duchies of Spoleto and Benevento. Second the Church
State, *Patrimonium Petri*, grown out of donations to the papacy by
both Langobards and Franks, mainly at the expense of the Byzantine
possessions, and comprising the duchy of Rome, the exarchate of
Ravenna, the two pentapoles (the maritime: Rimini, Pesaro, Fano,
Senigallia, Ancona; the continental: Urbino, Fossombrone, Jesi,
Cagli, Gubbio), all under the *de iure* sovereignty of the Carolingian
emperors but *de facto* governed by the bishop of Rome. Third, the
duchies of Benevento and Spoleto, remainders of the Langobard
states, which the Carolingians were unable to subdue. Fourth, the
Byzantine holdings, consisting of Venice, the duchies of Naples,

Gaeta, and Amalfi, and Calabria. When death wrested the reins of government from Charlemagne's strong hands in 814, the emperor's successors and heirs were unable to hold the empire together. Nascent feudalism was a political and economic system which, especially in the absence of a very powerful personage at the summit of the social pyramid, favored the independence of the great feudatories and abetted the decline of imperial strength. The treaty of Verdun (843) sought to reconcile the various centrifugal factions and to satisfy local ambitions by providing for a judicious amount of autonomy among the component nationalities, but the discords kept nonetheless growing. The deposition of Charles the Fat, the last Carolingian ruler (887), brought about the complete and final dismemberment of Charlemagne's state into four kingdoms: Germany, France, Upper and Lower Burgundy, and Italy, with the imperial authority tending, after years of confusion, intrigue, and bloodshed, to settle in Germany, thus preparing the eventual emergence of the Holy Roman Empire of German Nation. This came officially into being under Otto I, of the house of Saxony, who was crowned emperor in Rome in 962. Henceforth the royal crowns of Italy and of Germany were united with the imperial crown, so that whoever was elected king of Germany was automatically, save for the formality of confirmation by the great feudatories and pending subjugation of rebellious Italian cities and factions, also king of Italy and emperor of the Holy Roman Empire. Nonetheless, the union was merely a personal one, with Italy retaining its own laws and institutions, and with the pope alone having the power to confirm the emperor by setting the crown upon his head. On the other hand, the emperor was instrumental in the nomination of the pope and the confirmation of his election (which was effected by the people of Rome, until the Lateran Council of 1059 transferred that function to the cardinals). It is evident that under such vague and circular arrangements of imperial and papal succession and division of authority the balance of power between the secular and spiritual sphere of influence was determined by the personality of the individuals who faced one another: either the pope or the emperor predominated, and changes in personnel almost inevitably led to political upheavals whose repercussions were apt to shake the world.

With the north and the center of Italy — the kingdom of Italy proper — in the hands of the emperor, and the Church State cutting a swath out of the peninsula between Ravenna and Rome, the south became more and more isolated from Europe. It was divided between the southern Langobards, whom no one had been able to dislodge but who could never live at peace among themselves, and the Byzantines, while a number of maritime cities (such as Amalfi, Naples, and Gaeta) gained, like Venice in the north, political and economic autonomy and played Benevento and Byzantium against one another according to their own needs and for their profit.

But such was the game of all southern Italian powers, and they severally even called on the Moslems of North Africa for assistance. These gladly obliged, and once under arms proceeded to conquer (between 827 and 902) and retain Sicily for themselves, making Palermo the capital of a quasi-independent Moslem state (831). They grew more daring every day, and the coasts of Italy had to be fortified against their audacious raids. Pope Gregory IV constructed a fortress at Ostia, fearing an attack upon the very heart of Christianity. This was not long in coming, occurring in 846, but the advance was halted at the church of St. Peter and St. Paul, not far from the walls of the city. Yet the continued discords between the emperor and the pope, and the Italian princes among themselves, permitted the Moslems to pursue with impunity their predatory forays upon Italy as far north as Gaeta and Monte Cassino. Finally, in 915 (or 916) an unforeseen and short-lived alliance of practically all Italians, Langobards, imperialists, papists, and Byzantines, beat them decisively in a pitched battle on the Garigliano River and forced them to withdraw to Sicily. Later in the century the Moslems once more, with the connivance of Byzantium, crossed the straits of Messina, were overcome in a first engagement by the emperor Otto I, but shortly thereafter inflicted on the imperial troops a crushing defeat (982). Henceforth the fortunes of war favored now the Moslems, now the Christians, but the infidels remained ever a menace at least to southern Italy, especially since the Christians themselves, divided as they continued to be into Byzantine, Langobard, imperial, and papist parties, plus newly arising independent communities such as Venice, Amalfi, and Naples, with each faction desiring its own aggrandizement at the expense of the others, were not able to face the aggressors with an energetic and organized opposition. The peninsula was prey to continuous assaults and depredations, while Sicily remained firmly in Moslem hands. It was only the Normans, under the brothers Robert Guiscard and Roger I, who finally brought peace to southern Italy, allowing the Moslems religious freedom there, an act of tolerance quite without equal at that period; and eventually, in 1091, Roger wrested Sicily from the enemy. The Moslems were not annihilated or driven out but remained as subjects of the new Norman kingdom and, though in separate units, became part of the united southern armies which the Normans fused into an admirable and efficient fighting force.

This new ethnic and political element in Italy, the Normans, made its first impressive appearance in Italy, it is said, when some forty pilgrims, returning from the holy places of Jerusalem, zealously and valiantly aided in the defense of Salerno against the Mohammedans (1016) and so distinguished themselves that the prince of Salerno invited a number of Normans to enter his service to help him against both the Moslems and the Byzantines. The Normans, originally a Scandinavian people, now at home in Normandy, and soon to cross the English Channel, were adventurous and gallant soldiers of fortune led by bold condottieri, and proved themselves able not only to comply with the requests of their Italian employer but also to carve out a kingdom for themselves in southern Italy and Sicily. Although divided at first, they eventually pooled their strength in Italy and quickly became a power to be reckoned with. Hence, Pope Gregory VII (1073–1085) secured their alliance in his long struggle against the emperor Henry IV (1056–1106). Henry, excommunicated for the second time (1080), besieged the pope in the Castle of St. Angelo at Rome and raised to the see Clement III as an anti-pope by whom he had himself crowned emperor. The Normans, under the command of Robert Guiscard, strengthened by various southern contingents and Moslem soldiers, defeated the imperial troops, freed the pope, and put the city to fire and sword (1084). But with Robert's death (1085), the unification and restoration of southern Italy commenced by him came to nought, his successful campaign against Byzantium and Venice was broken off by his two sons, Roger Borsa and Bohemund, who instead wasted their strength by contesting the paternal inheritance against one another. But when Bohemund was seized by religious fervor and embarked on the First Crusade (1096–1099, set in motion under universal enthusiasm by Pope Urban II, 1088–1099), his uncle Roger I, Robert Guiscard's younger brother, restored order and refounded the dynasty of the family. He was mainly responsible, as I just mentioned, for the final reconquest of Sicily in 1091 after two and one-half centuries of Mohammedan rule. When he died, in 1101, his widow became regent. After the premature death of his elder son, Simon, and that of his nephews and sons and heirs of Robert Guiscard, Roger Borsa and Bohemund, and of Roger Borsa's son William, the way to power was open for his own younger son who became king of Sicily. He was crowned at Palermo in 1130 as Roger II, and, after some disagreements with the pope, confirmed, in 1139, in his titles of King of Sicily, Duke of Apulia, and Prince of Capua. Determined to seek further conquests in the east, death cut short his brilliant career in 1154. He was followed by his son William I (1155–1166), and his grandson William II (1166–1189, whose mother was regent until 1171, when William reached the age of eighteen).

In Germany, in the meantime, Frederick I, called Barbarossa, of the House of Swabia, had been elected. During his long reign (1152–1190), the chief ambition of this forceful and intelligent ruler was the extension and strengthening of the imperial authority in Italy. In that endeavor his interests collided with those of the rising Italian Communes of the north, to whom independence and liberty were essential; with those of the papacy which as always was fearful of foreign political interference in Italy; with those of the Byzantine empire, which tenaciously defended its holdings upon Italian soil; and with those of the Norman monarchy, which was loath to surrender its domain. But Frederick's enemies could not agree upon a persistent and unified policy, being themselves justly unsure of their loyalties toward one another. After much shifting of alliances and varying fortunes of war, the two principal protagonists, Frederick I and William II, found themselves involved in the Third Crusade, undertaken against the Egyptian Sultan Saladin who had captured Jerusalem in 1187. Both William and Frederick met death in foreign lands, in 1189 and 1190, respectively. William, dying childless, bequeathed his kingdom to his aunt Constance, daughter of Roger II and last offspring of the Norman dynasty, and arranged for her marriage to Henry, son of Frederick Barbarossa, who afterward came to the throne as Henry VI (1190–1197). Thus, Sicily and southern Italy fell peacefully to the House of Swabia and became parts of the empire which, theoretically, now comprised all of Italy. Thereupon the popes, threatened in their secular power in Italy, turned to seek the support of foreigners elsewhere and eventually invited the French royal house of the Angevins to occupy southern Italy.

Henry VI encountered enormous difficulties in making good his claim to the Italian throne, especially in having himself acknowledged as legitimate successor to William II, the Norman. When he died, in 1197, his son and heir to the Norman kingdom, who was to become the great Frederick II, was but three years old. It was to Pope Innocent III, energetic champion of the supremacy of papal over imperial authority (to him is attributed the oft-quoted simile comparing the emperor with the moon and the pope with the sun, the former receiving his light and power from the latter), that Constance, Henry VI's widow, ironically entrusted the guardianship of her son Frederick. Hence in Germany many anti-papists favored the bypassing of Henry's heir, preferring either the Ghibelline Philip of Swabia, Henry's brother, or the Guelph Otto of Brunswick, the nephew of Richard the Lionhearted. Both were, in fact, crowned by opposing parties, with the pope supporting the latter. Accordingly, all of Italy was also divided into an imperial and a papist, a Ghibelline and a Guelph camp — but with many Italians, especially the citizens of the Communes, who did not care to be the creatures of either form of autocracy, wishing a plague on both their houses. When Philip suddenly was killed by a personal enemy in 1208, Otto was proclaimed king and crowned as Otto IV, in 1209, at St. Peter's. But once upon the throne, Otto IV could not but guard the interests of the crown, and of necessity, despite his indebtedness to the pope, became an anti-papist Ghibelline, bent upon strengthening imperial authority in Italy. The pope promptly excommunicated him in 1210 and now supported the election of his own ward Frederick, heir to the Norman throne, who had reached the age of nineteen. Otto IV was defeated and the way to the throne was free for the son of the Swabian father and the Norman mother. Frederick was crowned at Aix-la-Chapelle, Charlemagne's ancient capital, in 1215.

But the road Frederick II had to travel during his long reign (1215–1250) was anything but straight and smooth. The refractory Communes of the north, the worldly pope in the center, and the turbulent nobles of the south laid innumerable obstacles in his path, not only because of his imperial ambitions, but also because his tolerance of the Mohammedans in his entourage and his army, and the liberality and intellectuality of his court at Palermo rendered him suspect of un-Christian leanings in the eyes of the narrowly zealous. He was twice excommunicated by the pope. Called upon to rule realms so distant from and foreign to one another in all respects as Germany, northern and southern Italy, and Sicily, which could not be governed by the same policy during times so riotous and rebellious, Frederick in the end perished under the constant, relentless blows of numerous enemies, not all of whom he could please or reconcile or subdue.

Of his many sons, born of his many wives and concubines, Frederick chose Conrad as his successor in Germany, and the talented but politically inept Manfred for Italy. Conrad died in his twenty-seventh year (1253) and left as the only legitimate heir of his dynasty the infant Conradin. Manfred was recognized as regent for his nephew (1255). But when he usurped Conradin's imperial rights, he found himself opposed, not only by the pope but also by the German Imperial party. His reliance on Moslem troops as well as German mercenaries whom he called to Italy proved a mistake. The new pope, Urban IV (1261–1264), a Frenchman, invited Charles of Anjou, the brother of the French King Louis IX, to conquer, with papal aid and blessing, southern Italy, and Pope Clement IV (1265–1268), a Provençal, continued to organize a veritable crusade against Manfred, now an excommunicated heretic, and had Charles and his wife crowned king and queen of Italy at St. Peter's in January 1266. And when finally Charles' and Manfred's soldiers were joined in battle at Benevento in February 1266, Manfred's faithless nobles deserted him on the field, and his confused army was routed. Benevento was sacked amidst great slaughter and Charles brutally exterminated the Swabian house in Italy. This left only the young Conradin, who should soon come to a sorry end: defeated by Charles in the bloody battle of Tagliacozzo, near Lake Fucino, in 1268, he fled north, was captured in the Maremma, imprisoned at Palestrina, condemned by a sham court, and beheaded at Naples.

Charles of Anjou reigned over the south with cruelty and intolerance toward all that was not French and Catholic, applying a tyranny exactly the opposite of the enlightened rule of the Normans and Swabians. His ambitions were boundless, and his endeavors partly successful. But the election of Rudolf of Habsburg (1273-1291, after the lawless Interregnum 1256–1273) to the German throne, a succession of popes unfavorably inclined toward his projects of conquest, and the mutinous massacre at Palermo, known as the Sicilian Vespers (1282), followed by wars and great sea battles, proved his undoing. His antagonist, Pedro of Aragon, whom the Sicilian nobles had called in to assist them, became his successor on the throne of Sicily. Thenceforth the Spanish dynasty had great influence in southern Italy and Sicily.

In the history of Italy from the ninth to the thirteenth century an important role was played by the cities of northern and central Italy. During the tumultuous tenth century, abandoned to their fate by the feudal lords who retired to their castles and worried mainly about themselves, in the absence of a strong Italian government which could protect them against repeated sieges and sackings by invading Mohammedans and Hungarians (the latters' sojourn in Italy being brief enough and without consequence culturally), the Communes were thrown back upon their own resources and had to defend themselves as best they could. Each organized a city militia, fortified the town with walls and trenches, and gave itself a government that could function efficiently in an emergency without time-consuming and most likely futile recourse to higher authority. When the burghers had attained this degree of emancipation they were, of course, loath to surrender it again to autocratic claimants just because external enemies no longer threatened and the imperial government was in the saddle once more. In addition, thanks to the prosperity which the skill and industry of their artisans and the enterprise of their merchants had won for them, the citizens of such towns had also obtained a measure of economic autonomy. The cities normally belonging to the Eastern Empire, like Venice, Naples, Amalfi, and Gaeta, to which Constantinople had to grant, for fear of losing their allegiance altogether, political and economic concessions amounting almost to independence, showed by their example how an organized and proud community could stand on its own feet, even in defiance of its overlords.

During the twelfth and thirteenth centuries the growth of the Communes became more rapid. The trade with the east and the seven Crusades (between 1096 and 1270) contributed greatly to their prosperity, and with it went the abrogation of fealty from either or both dominant powers of Italy, the emperor and the pope. Cities might sympathize either with the imperialist Ghibellines or the papist Guelphs, but often followed their own inclination and advantage without becoming irrevocably involved on either side. Thus Venice, Pisa, and Genoa became important harbor cities and prominent sea powers, and Florence, Siena, Milan, Verona, and many others grew to be anyone's redoubtable foes or puissant friends, as popes and potentates were to learn. But unfortunately they also engaged in endless rivalries and armed strife among themselves, even to the extent of allying themselves occasionally with the common archenemy — the emperor — a cause of great loss and calamity to all. Also the rise of the affluent bourgeoisie of artisans and traders, joined by the lesser nobles who lived within the city, led to bitter internal conflict, on the one hand with the poor urban and rural working populace, on the other hand with the greater nobles who saw their feudal society and income threatened by a new social order. Yet through these stormy seas the Communes, under republican or pseudo-republican oligarchic governments, held their course serenely. In good time, owing in no small measure to the establishment of free communal in the place of the illiberal clerical schools, which had monopolized education for the purposes of the church, they should experience the exaltation of bringing forth from their citizenry and nurturing within their gates the great talents and geniuses who made the Italian Renaissance.

Among the Communes Rome occupied a very special position. It lay in the midst of the by then barren and depopulated Campagna, which was a hearth of fever and pestilence, a situation altogether unfavorable to trade and industry. Moreover, it housed, for the most time, the pope with his retinue of church dignitaries, and off and on the emperor with his court and armies. It was the spot on which papal and imperial interests clashed most violently, diplomatically or under arms, so that the people of the often embattled city could, for good causes, not bring themselves to place confidence wholly and lastingly in either of their would-be protectors and masters. Hence Rome, though spiritually the capital of the empire and of the Christian faith, was torn internally by too many conflicting forces and could not attain the cultural sway befitting its history, nor for the same reason assume the political sovereignty behooving the nominal home of both the Imperial Throne and the Holy See. The career of Arnold of Brescia who was originally a religious reformer, but whose endeavors led him inevitably into the political and diplomatic arena, for that was where the pope himself took his stand, and who was hanged (his body was then burnt and the ashes cast into the Tiber) in 1155, mirrors the Romans' desire, powerless, amorphous and vacillating though it was (they even sacrificed their champion Arnold to the pope), to liberate themselves of an unworthy papacy and of an emperor (Frederick I) whose hands were dripping with the blood of the citizens of the Communes of the north. For centuries the burghers of Rome, and with them many other Italians, were to be ground into submission and insensibility between the millstones of papacy and empire, of church and state. The concordate of 1929 is the latest, but scarcely the last act of the drama.

Florence, on the other hand, enjoyed a development which, although it suffered from the same internal discords between its various classes of citizens, was at least not convulsed by the cataclysmic collisions of world powers within its own terrain. Though its institutions and its flourishing can be viewed as typical for many another city, they are so at a higher degree and with greater intensity. Undoubtedly Florence is the queen of all the Italian Communes, especially after she had concluded, bloodily but victoriously, her life and death struggle with Pisa. She put herself thereby politically and economically at the head of all Tuscany, and also managed to enlarge her real territorial possessions. Having been at first governed by Consuls and the urban nobility, the city later (1250) was divided into two administrative domains — one being the Commune headed by a *Podestà*, the other being the *Popolo* under a Captain of the People. In 1293, through the great republican reform called the *Ordinamenti di Giustizia*, the nobles were completely excluded from the government of the city, and the *Arti Maggiori*, or Greater Guilds (the professions — judges, lawyers, notaries — and primary and lucrative industries), and *Arti Minori*, or Lesser Guilds (secondary industries, trades, and shops) received their final constitution. Also the peasantry of the surrounding countryside was fully liberated from serfdom or near-servitude, the pertinent law of 1289 speaking of personal liberty as "a natural and therefore inalienable right," in terms reminiscent of nothing less than the American Declaration of Independence.

But Florence would not be Florence, and Italy not Italy, if all had remained sweetness and light. Internal factions and quarrels arose again. Guelphs and Ghibellines (though these names no longer meant the same everywhere in Italy) rent the city and its government by their unending disputes. When the Guelphs won they split into a White and a Black faction. The Blacks, supporters of the papacy, were victorious, Charles of Valois entered Florence in 1301, and the Whites, among whom one Dante Alighieri, were driven from the city. It might have been difficult in any event, regardless of external pressures, to maintain an island or islands of republican freedom in a churning sea of warring monarchies and autocracies. The tendency in Florence, as in other cities, veered more and more toward the tyranny of powerful, rich men who usurped the government, though in Florence the process was slower than elsewhere. Indeed in 1378, in the *Tumulto dei Ciompi* the populace triumphed once more. But the fifteenth century witnessed the rise of the Medici family to the Lordship.

CHAPTER XXIX

From Latin to Italian Charlemagne saw himself
not merely as the restorer of the Roman Empire in politics but also
as the resuscitator of ancient culture. These endeavors of his, at
least partly successful, are spoken of as the Carolingian Renaissance.[1] To put it briefly, he encouraged learning and a revival of
the civilization of Roman antiquity. But a revival of something
dead, even if it is merely a set of behavior patterns, and even though
a mighty and intelligent emperor, counseled by the Northumbrian
Alcuin, former master at York, one of the most learned and wisest
men of the period, lends his hand and his mind, is an impossible task.
Charlemagne's efforts were rewarded by less success than they
deserved, and for a short time only.

Similar to what I have previously noted for preceding centuries, our evidence for the spoken Latin language in Charlemagne's
time is again unsatisfactory. In fact it bodes to be worse, since
an emperor and an era bent on a restoraton of things classical
would apply their efforts at reform not only to a restitution of
classical but also to a conscious repression of unclassical speech.
The decay of Latin in contemporary writing was palpable to anyone who could read Classical Latin, who, in other words, could
read. Regardless of whether Charlemagne himself was a well-
educated person (some say he could not write), his intention and
the advice of his learned courtiers counseled a linguistic reform,
now that the neglect and the ignorance of Classical Latin had
reached what seemed unbearable proportions even within the
clergy.[2] In a letter from Charlemagne to Abbot Baugulfus, written in the year 787, "for the establishment of schools," the linguistic reform was put, according to the spirit of the times and in

[1] See Bolgar 1954, 106–129.
[2] Cf. Bede, *Epistola ad Egbertum*, PL 94.659. I am again following, but dis-
connectedly, passages from Pulgram 1950.

order to make it more palatable to the devout, on a religious basis, and usage of good Classical Latin was urged upon Christians "so that those who strive to please God by a decorous life, would not neglect to please Him also by decorous speech. . . . We exhort you to study letters . . . precisely with the aim that you may be able to penetrate more easily and more accurately into the mysteries of the Holy Scriptures." [3]

The religious argument for the restoration of Classical Latin is not a very cogent one. And if Charlemagne had known, or had wished to take to heart, the view of at least two other good Christians of no mean learning and piety, he may well have come to the opposite conclusion on the godly virtues of the proper use of Latin. Several centuries earlier, Saint Augustine (354–430) wrote that "it is better that the grammarians should chastize us than that the people should not understand us." [4] And it was none other than Gregory the Great, Bishop of Rome from 590–604 (under whose occupancy the episcopal chair of St. Peter officially became the papacy, and the term *papa* 'priest' was restricted to the successor of St. Peter in Rome), who wrote in a letter concerning his own Latin style: "I have disdained to observe the rules of rhetoric which the instruction in secular disciplines is trying to put over. For as the style of this very letter indicates, I do not shrink from the shock of metacismus,[5] I do not avoid the mixing in of barbarisms, I despise the observance of position and trope and the cases of prepositions, because I consider it unbecoming in the extreme that I should subject the words of the heavenly oracle [6] to the rules of [the grammarian] Donatus." [7] Gregory harbored a deep Christian hatred for the profane Roman culture; he proscribed Roman letters and was much responsible for their oblivion from the seventh century on, until their resurrection in the Renaissance; and he reprimanded clerics who devoted themselves to the study of classical antiquity.[8]

[3] Mabillon 1739, 25.64. See also Lehmann 1927, 8–9.
[4] Aug. *En. in Ps.* 138.20.
[5] *metacismus* 'a frequent repetition of the letter *m*, the pronunciation of *m* at the close of a word before a word beginning with a vowel.'
[6] *oraculum* here 'the mercy-seat,' the place in the tabernacle in which the presence of God becomes manifest.
[7] PL 75.516.
[8] Cf. Manacorda 1913, 2.144–159.

Charlemagne's endeavors on behalf of Classical Latin show that his attempted linguistic reform is a political maneuver at least as much as an act of piety, designed to enforce the revival, at least for courtly and churchly use, of 'good' old Roman speech (which was dead) in the new Roman Empire (which was the Frankish state plus parts of Italy as mere appendages) under the new Roman Emperor (who was a German). Charlemagne knew before he died that his noble political dream was doomed and that his empire would be falling to pieces because of its own irreparable internal contradictions. No wonder that a linguistic reform, always far too weak a mortar for joining together heterogeneous cultural bricks and rocks, not only was ineffective in maintaining the continued coherence of the empire, which disintegrated soon after Charlemagne's death, but also was in itself an experiment whose ill outcome was a foregone conclusion, unless it were supported by popular cultural demands and pressures for a Latin revival. These of course could not possibly be forthcoming at that period.[9]

The common people quite naturally continued their speechways, and a plan for the reintroduction among them of Classical Latin did not enter the heads of even the most optimistic and devoted revivalists. Nor was it possible to eradicate the vernacular by monarchic fiat. But what and how exactly this popular language was, we still do not know.

However, light was to be thrown before long unto these dark pages of linguistic history. It should come, at least mediately, from a very unexpected source. While Charlemagne may have hoped that among the literate and learned the study and knowledge of Classical Latin would find, under his prodding, new strength and would actually lead them to a better knowledge of the Bible and consequently to a better life, he and the church also could not help realizing that this type of linguistic approach to a religious awakening was out of the question as far as the ignorant masses were concerned. It was unfortunately true that most people could not read the Bible, either in Latin or in Greek, since few enough could read at all. Moreover, they also could not speak or even understand Classical Latin. This state of affairs is implied by the recognition in 813, in France, of the so-called *sermo rusticus*, the 'rustic speech,'

[9] Manacorda 1913, 141-61.

as a legitimate idiom, acceptable even to the church for use in the cult: not, of course, in the liturgy and in reciting the Scriptures, but for the sermon. There lies behind this acceptance of what was universally considered a low, vulgar type of language, a resigned recognition that one cannot talk to people either about politics or about religion in a language they have long ceased to understand, that Latin was no longer an apt instrument to teach and guide the common people as subjects of the state and members of the church.

But it should not be thought that the lower clergy, the parish priests, were in the knowledge of Latin far ahead of their flock. Boniface (about 680–753) was horrified by hearing a priest baptizing a child *in nomine Patria et Filia et Spiritu Sancta* (the grammatically correct form being *In nomine Patris et Filii et Spiritus Sancti*) and worried whether a sacrament thus ungrammatically bestowed was valid in the eyes of God.[10]

The elevation of the vernaculars of the empire to at least partial ecclesiastic dignity was bound to clothe them in a mantle, albeit scant and threadbare, of respectability. It was hardly to be expected that presently works written in the popular language would pour forth in great quantities. But there was opened a break in the dyke, and no amount of shoring by scholars and grammarians could close the hole or indeed prevent its progressive enlargement. We shall shortly enter, then, upon a period when we are suddenly confronted with written evidence of the spoken language, however meager and however much under the oppressive tutelage of written Latin.

The relative suddenness of this phenomenon has induced some scholars to propound the theory of the sudden breakdown of a unified Vulgar Latin into the various Romanic languages. But it seems to me that they misinterpret the evidence.

Let us consider Fig. 2 on page 319. In the opinion of those who believe in an abrupt eighth-century conversion of a hitherto uniform Vulgar Latin into Romanic, a break in the upper line and its continuation on a lower level about A.D. 800 would represent this precipitous change.[11] According to the chart, this is out of the

[10] Cf. Tangl 1916, 1.190. The requirement that prayers and incantations be recited to the letter, lest they be inefficacious or indeed provoke the wrath of the divinity, is common to many religions and rites.

[11] See especially, Muller 1921, 1929, 1945; Taylor 1924; Pei 1932, 1937, 1945.

question, because the upper line, while containing the primary
sources of most scholarly studies on Vulgar Latin, at no time
actually represents speech.[12] There is but one thing such a break
could indicate: a step like those in the Egyptian chart, that is, the
terminus of a classic era (classic here in the wider sense, not in that
of Latin literary history). One really should be able, therefore, to
begin a new horizontal line emanating from the slanted line at that
point or thereafter.

But here complications set in which did not exist for Egyptian
at comparable points. The lower line should really flare out quite
early into several branches to indicate early dialectal differentiation
resulting in the different Romanic vernaculars, caused by varying
distances, cultural and geographical, from Rome, different times
and types of occupation and colonization, and different linguistic

---

Politizer 1949, assigns the French language a 'birthday' (126), at which occurred
"the suddenness of the removal of the restraining influence of Classical Latin
from the popular language" (130), and wishes to find out, from the written
testimony, exactly when "the cleavage of Latin and Romance was accomplished"
(130). *What* cleavage? See also the review of Muller 1929 by Marouzeau 1930.

Pei 1937, 243, writes as follows: "A single sporadic occurrence of a Romance
feature in the midst of hundreds of classical forms is to this school of thought
[which rejects the uniformity of Vulgar Latin throughout the empire down to
the ninth century] conclusive evidence of the fact that the Romance feature in
question held undisputed sway in the spoken tongue, instead of being accepted
as evidence of the fact that the language was beginning to change. . . ." I agree
with the school attacked, because if the ancient and mediaeval writers had known
Classical Latin they would not have written an unclassical form (cf. Jud 1914,
58; Schuchardt 1866, 1.82); and an intellectual's ignorance on such matters presupposes general, profound, long-established popular ignorance. A mediaeval Latin
writer is no linguistic trail-blazer. And Politzer's "suddenness of the removal of
the restraining influences" occurs in writing, in the documents, while in the
speech of the masses there were no restraining influences to be removed, least
of all suddenly.

[12] Taylor 1949, 96: "Mr. Muller [see n. 11 above] demonstrated that the
scribes wrote what they spoke and heard. . . . He found no significant differences
in the Latin throughout Romania up to the ninth century and therefore no evidence of dialectalization or the formation of Romance languages before the ninth
century." Naturally one does not find such things in mediaeval books; and
that scribes, especially mediaeval ones, wrote what they spoke and heard is
absurd, because no scribe ever does, not even today, not even so learned and
linguistically sophisticated a scribe as a professor of linguistics. A more moderate
view is expressed by Sas 1949, 134: "It must be stated . . . that the desire to write
as one spoke was generally confined to narrative writing, sermons, *Lives of the
Saints*, that is, to materials directed to an audience untutored and uneducated by
all former standards." But in this pre-Carolingian era the conjectured recipients
of such writing, untutored and uneducated, could read "as one spoke" no better
than they could read Classical Latin, which is not at all.

substrata and superstrata.[18] I left this undone for the sake of simplicity. The upper line, however, that of the written language, does not so flare out in a definite number of dialects: although localisms may be discerned in it, reflected by the downward 'vulgarizing' slant of the line, it continues the classical tradition. No wonder, then, that those who consider only what is written marvel at the uniformity and the lack of dialectalization of the language throughout the empire down to the eighth century — a uniformity which contradicts all sensible expectations and all that we know of the ways of human speech, whose outstanding quality is change, notably that of disintegration of an idiom through the agencies of longevity, expansion, and superimposition upon multiple linguistic substrata.

If a linguist were to look, some fifteen hundred years hence, at the written documents of Italian and other Romanic languages now current, he would be making an elementary error if he assumed that what he was reading represented the vernacular of each region or nation, only because it diverged more or less from the written language of a still earlier period. Except for consciously imitative passages of direct speech and for dialectal literature, a piece of Italian writing of our days, no matter how many single popular features it exhibits, does not represent fully or truly any dialect or speechway now popularly used. There is no reason to believe that matters stood differently in spoken and written Latin, within and without Italy.

On my sketch I have put the break from Written Latin to Written Romanic about 800, the date around which the stigma of inferiority is at least partly removed from the vernaculars and after which the first texts in the various Romanic languages appear, sporadically and hesitantly. In Italy also, as in France under Charlemagne, a Latin renaissance takes place, though it appears

---

[18] See above, Chapter XXIV. Here Meillet 1922, 151, errs in believing that even as early as "the third century after Christ there was still one single Latin, spoken only with accents slightly varying from one province to another," if he means to say that this was the only Latin current in the provinces. It was, rather, a *koinë*, which, says Meier 1940, 181, "lay like a blanket upon an already existing local differentiation." The *koinë* is the lingua franca of international communication and commerce, it is the written and standardized spoken language of the so-called Vulgar Latin documents of all periods and belongs to the upper rather than the lower line in the chart.

somewhat later and seems less spectacular than in France because it is not sponsored by a great personage. In 825 eight royal schools are created (in Turin, Ivrea, Pavia, Cremona, Vicenza, Cividale, Florence, and Fermo), and the recommendations of the Roman Council of 826, ratified by Pope Eugenius II, stress the need for local schools in bishoprics and in parishes. While in Roman times schools had been sponsored by private persons or by the state, with the fall of the Roman Empire all teaching enterprises devolved upon the church, and diocesan control of schools became the established pattern. Wherever a school was not owned outright by the church, its existence and curriculum had to be licensed by the bishop. The primary aim, therefore, of all instruction and learning was the education of able propagators and upholders of the faith. Naturally the idiom in which this was accomplished could be nothing but Latin, the language of the Bible and the clerics, whose preservation and, if possible, improvement according to classical standards seemed thereby assured literally with God's help, at least among the clergy and the learned.

Latin, of one kind or another, was still thought the real and living language of Italy and the church. But with a better and more widespread knowledge of good standard Latin came also the quick and probably dismaying realization that what had hitherto been merely thought bad and vulgarized Latin had, in the mouths of the masses, in fact ceased to be Latin and had removed itself so far from the language at which the revivalists and reformers aimed that a restoration and imposition of Classical Latin for everyday usage, even among those able and willing to learn, was out of the question. The result of the educational reform on Fig. 2 was not that the line of the spoken language could be made to rise toward the level of the written but that the downward trend of the written language was halted, and even reversed, so much so that, during the eras of Humanism and Renaissance, a better Latin, nearer the classical norm, should emerge in the documents, and that, given requisite skill and instruction, a classical scholar of our days can attempt with fair success to imitate Cicero's style. The new written Romanic vernaculars, however, took their origins, as one would expect, from the stage of the spoken language prevalent at the period of their incipient codification, giving rise to the phenomenon, on my chart, of the new step (or rather several steps in depth each representing one kind of Romanic writing), similar to the several successive examples in the sketch on Egyptian.

From the tenth century on we have both direct and indirect evidence of the use of an Italian vernacular in writing. And a passage of a penitential from Cassino of the tenth century [14] advises that "the confession of the sinners should be received in the rustic [i.e. Italian] language," a concession which parallels fully the recognition of the vernacular in France, in 813, as a language admissible in some phases of the cult, sermons in particular.

To lay preachers and church services in the vernacular, making more of the religion intelligible to more people, is no doubt due also the liveliness of the religious revival at that period, the success of the different sects, and the flourishing of the monastic movement, which, had Latin been its only linguistic vehicle, could not have attained such enormous expansion and influence and popular appeal.[15]

The oldest monument in the vernacular, which we may well call Italian now, is the so-called *Indovinello veronese*, the 'Veronese riddle.' [16] At this stage of linguistic development and documentation it is only appropriate that there exists some doubt as to whether the author of the riddle wrote from memory Latin hexameters into which he introduced, without his knowledge and will, numerous vulgar elements, or whether he on purpose composed verses in the popular language. The problem thus contains in a nutshell a piece of linguistic history and the question of linguistic classification. At what point in its history does a language cease to be itself and become another? And how different do two linguistic systems have to be in order to merit different names?

Next in date are the so-called *Placiti cassinesi*, the 'Agreements of Cassino,' of 960 to 963, stemming from three monasteries subordinate to Monte Cassino — at Capua, Sessa, and Teano. They are the court records on a dispute over real estate in which the scribe, or secretary, reports the proceedings in the best Latin he knew, which as usually is not very good, but where he inserts

---

[14] *Cod. Cassin.* 451, quoted by Migliorini 1953, 26.
[15] Cf. Olschki 1949, 77–78.
[16] The oldest Italian texts are conveniently accessible in, among others, Monaci 1912; von Wartburg 1946; Monteverdi 1948; Dionisotti–Grayson 1949.

verbatim the deposition of a witness in the vernacular, probably to lend the authenticity of a *procès verbal* to the document, and to give everyone an opportunity to understand at least this crucial part of the testimony. This was, after all, also the intention of the authors and recorders of the Oaths of Strassburg, of 843, the first properly French document in our possession, in which the oaths which the grandsons of Charlemagne pronounced in front of the assembled soldiers and people, were read and chronicled not only in Latin but also in German and French, so that everyone ignorant of Latin, as no doubt the majority of the audience were, could understand what was happening, and would remember it.

After the *Placiti* there is a gap of about a century in our evidence in Old Italian, which does not signify that nothing was actually written in the language. But it does no doubt mean that the output was rather meager. Around the middle of the eleventh century we find two Sardic and three central Italian texts. From here on, documentation increases rapidly, so as to give a fairly satisfactory picture of linguistic, including dialectal, developments.

When I discussed the succession of the written languages of ancient Egypt, I suggested that the disappearance of each successive classical norm and the concomitant rise of a new one could be aligned with some major historical, cultural break. It is therefore legitimate to ask what break accompanies the emergence of the Romanic vernaculars shortly after A.D. 800. It would be ideal if one could connect the phenomenon with the fall of the Roman Empire. But the Roman Empire did not really fall, or collapse, least of all around A.D. 800, but rather dragged itself on in a long agony, and no historian would set a precise date for its demise: there is no single crushing defeat by foreign enemies, no internal revolution which marks an end and a beginning. Hence our search for a precise date of linguistic expiration and renewal is likely to be idle also. Also, as concerns Figs. 1 and 2, the comparative scales of the Egyptian and Roman charts are such that whatever appears as a sudden break in the former could, on the scale of the latter, not be so radically marked. Hence, what appears as a vertical break on the more telescoped Egyptian chart corresponds to several centuries, from the fourth to the ninth, on the more detailed Latin one, and the required historical and cultural catastrophe on the latter is contained in the overextension, the weakening, and the end of the Roman Empire. The convenient neatness of the Egyptian situation is further obscured for Latin because the written classical tradition never actually came to an end: throughout the Middle Ages, and also in modern times, Latin remained a used, albeit not a living language which, though for some time it deteriorated, eventually experienced a reform. For all these reasons one should not expect the line of Classical Latin to terminate at a particular point and thus create the picture of a step.

On the other hand, according to our direct and indirect evidence on the state of the written language in Italy and the Romania, we are well justified in choosing a date around A.D. 800 for the beginnings of a new *written* language in Italy, which one can no longer call Latin, but at best Neo-Latin, or Italian. A similar phenomenon shows itself in other parts of the Romania at approximately the same time. Just as Spoken Latin and Classical Latin start at the same point in my sketch, so Spoken Italian and Written Italian at the time of the inception of the latter are still much the same. The date for Italian that corresponds to the century of Cicero and the great classics who gave Rome its classical tongue, is the age of Dante, Boccaccio, and Petrarch, who performed the same service some fourteen hundred years later.

The other outstanding features of the history of Italy between 800 and 1250 are the renewed or continued domination of parts of Italy by foreigners (Germans, Moslems, Normans), and the permanent and ingrained political disunity of the peninsula. The first of these phenomena remains linguistically unproductive, that is, in spite of it there occurs no disturbance of the persistent integrity of Romanic speech in Italy, wherein foreign elements are only external borrowings lacking the strength to induce structural changes in the language. The second phenomenon is productive; it enhances the long established dialectal variegation of the speechways of Italy, with no central authority and prestige gathering in and reversing the centrifugal forces of linguistic separatism.

As for the Germans in Italy, their presence after A.D. 800 is mainly due, not as before to the appearance of land-seeking or looting invaders, but merely to the fact that the Roman emperor is a German prince who, in order to validate his claims against anti-imperial forces, finds it necessary to import German troops and administrators who win and run the country for him. No statistics on the number of Germans in Italy are available, but it is a safe guess that there were few at any time and that no more than an insignificant fraction of them, if any, became permanent settlers and colonizers who mingled with the Italian population. Whatever linguistic borrowed items penetrated into the Italian language bear out this fact of superficiality even more than those of Gothic and Langobard and Frankish times.

The Moslems came to Italy as conquerors, and in force. But also their linguistic contributions to the patrimony of Latin are small and concern chiefly the lexical and onomastic inventory. Sicily has numerous Arabic local (and some personal) names, and there are many also in southern Italy, and a few strays in the rest of the country. There seems to have taken place at times, thanks to the exceptional policy of tolerance under some of the Norman rulers and Frederick II, a good deal of ethnic mixture (and some think that Arabic traits are still discernible in the physical aspect of the modern southern population). But there is certainly less cultural and physical interpenetration between Christians and Moslems in Italy than in Spain, partly because the occupation did not last so long, partly because the Latin-Romanic culture in Italy was more deeply rooted and had not been recently disturbed to a significant degree, as indeed it had been in Spain through the extensive and lasting occupation by the Visigoths, and partly because, as we can be certain despite the absence of statistics, the Romanic population of Italy was both relatively and absolutely more numerous than that of Spain. It is symptomatic, I believe, that architectural remains of Mohammedan culture are very insignificant in southern Italy and Sicily as compared with the magnificent edifices of Moslem art in Spain: in Granada (the Alhambra), in Córdoba (the Mosque), in Seville (the tower of the Cathedral and the Alcazar), and in many other places. Nothing even approaching this oriental splendor appears in Italy and Sicily.

If in Spain the linguistic imprint of Arabic and other dialects is restricted to vocabulary and toponomastics, and, although it is considerable, not as extensive in either as one might expect after seven centuries of occupation, it is not surprising that in Sicily, under Mohammedan dominion for only two and one-half centuries, influences of the Islamic idioms are even less profound and notable. In southern Italy, which was never permanently occupied by Moslems, they are lacking completely.

The Moslems were not only foreigners and a minority in both Italy and Spain; they were strange and unwanted ones upon whom lay the odium of heathendom and against whom all Christianity had been incensed to the point of blind and hateful fanaticism by the Crusades and the battle for the Holy Sepulcher. Hence, Moslem culture and language not only encountered the normal barrier of cultural inertia in the face of innovation, but were actively combated by religious zeal and narrowness.

The Normans came to Italy as a mere handful of adventurers, in much smaller numbers than to France, and later, to England. Their domination of Sicily and southern Italy was mainly a personal one, in the hands of a few leaders and autocrats. Again statistics are unavailable, but the sources have nothing to say about a continuous increment of new settlers sailing from the English Channel to the straits of Messina. At the time of their Italian adventure the Normans spoke, of course, a Romanic dialect which they had acquired in France and which they eventually exported also to England. But, whereas enough Normans moved to England to impose upon Anglo-Saxon a decidedly Romanic stamp in vocabulary — though not in the structure of Old English — there were obviously not enough newcomers in Sicily to produce anywhere near equal results. In addition, whereas they entered in England upon an island which was not long removed from barbarism and whose resistance to the blandishments of a superior, no matter how alien a culture was correspondingly weak, especially among the upper classes of society, the Normans had nothing to offer in Sicily and southern Italy, lands drenched to saturation by a plethora of great civilizations — Phoenician, Greek, Roman, Moslem — nothing which the inhabitants would find worth desiring or emulating. They did bring the force of freshness, strength, and initiative, which availed them the throne and the political supremacy over the natives. But it did not suffice to conquer the Italians' spirits and tongues.

As for the political disunity of Italy, little more need be said.

Italy was torn not only by the great powers — Byzantium, the emperor, the pope, the Normans — but also by the rivalries among its kingdoms and duchies and counties and municipalities, which no strong central power transformed into a union with common interests and purposes until the nineteenth century. Consequently, there is no progress to be recorded on linguistic standardization and amalgamation, and on the weakening of dialectal boundaries.

When speaking of the rise of Florentine as the standard literary language, as Italian *tout court*, I emphasized the part that Dante, and also Boccaccio and Petrarch played. That these Three Great should be Tuscans is, of course, a coincidence and proves nothing for the superiority of the Tuscan dialect. However, I have noted that a case can be made for the relative nearness of Tuscan to Classical Latin; thereby its aptitude for being, not a lingua franca, but a model for the literary language of Italy was, if not determined, at least accentuated. By comparing certain pertinent features of the histories of Rome and Florence, certain facets were brought out which very likely aided the exaltation of Florentine among the sister dialects, though again without Dante they may have produced no durable results.

The capital of the Roman Empire and of Christendom had recovered somewhat from the depopulation and devastation suffered in the Gothic and later Germanic wars, but it remained far from doing justice to so august a title.[17] The plague of 1167, which had conveniently defeated the army of Frederick Barbarossa encamped at the gates of Rome, proved also the city's and the Campagna's scourge, leaving them together, in 1198, we are told, a population of about 35,000.[18] In 1230, a terrible flood of the Tiber swept over the low-lying parts of Rome and the Leonine City at the foot of the Vatican Hill, drowning thousands of persons and leaving famine and pestilence in its wake. In 1241, a priest writes the following discouraging letter to a colleague who plans to attend a council in Rome: "How can you enjoy safety in the city, where all the citizens and the clergy are in daily strife for and against both disputants? The heat is insufferable,

---

[17] On the physical decay of Rome see Showerman 1924, 348–373, the chapter entitled "A thousand years of ruin."

[18] Showerman 1924, 369.

the water foul, the food is coarse and bad; the air is so heavy that it can be grasped with the hands, and is filled with swarms of mosquitos; the ground is alive with scorpions, the people are dirty and odious, wicked and fierce. The whole of Rome is undermined, and from the catacombs, which are filled with snakes, arises a poisonous and fatal exhalation." [19] The language may be exaggerated, but the substance is true.

But the worst was yet to come during the residence of the popes outside of Rome, in Avignon, between 1305 and 1378. In a letter entreating Pope Urban V to return the papacy to Rome, Petrarch describes the desolation of the city in the Holy Year, 1350, thus: "The city is forever plagued by wars, civil or foreign, her houses are falling, her walls crumbling, the temples in ruin, the sacred things in contempt, the laws ignored, justice trodden under, and the unhappy people weeps and howls. . . . The Lateran is falling in ruins, and the church which is the Mother of them all, stands without a roof and is a prey to wind and rain; the sacred dwellings of Saint Peter and Saint Paul are tottering, and where once rose the holy temple of the Apostles one now sees nothing but rubble and ruins whose shapeless aspect would move to tears a man with a heart of stone." [20]

"The city of Rome," writes the anonymous author of the *Life of Cola di Rienzo*, the popular leader of Rome (1313?–1354), "was in the most profound distress. There were none to govern her; fighting occurred every day; robbery happened everywhere; in places holy to the Virgin blasphemy was rife; there was no safe place to hide; they carried off little girls and outraged them; the wife was snatched from her husband's side right out of the bed; the workingmen, when they went out to work were robbed — where? at the very gates of Rome; the pilgrims who came to the holy churches for the salvation of their souls were not protected, but were knifed and robbed; the priests were evil-doers. There was every vice, every evil, no justice, and no restraint; there was no longer any remedy; everyone perished; he who had the stronger sword had the better right. There was no other redress than self-defense with the aid of relatives and friends; every day

[19] Quoted by Showerman 1924, 369–370.
[20] Petr. *De reb. sen.* 7.1.

there occurred gatherings of armed men. The nobles and the barons did not dwell in Rome." [21]

And Dante himself bewails the fate of the city:

> *Vieni a veder la tua Roma che piagne,*
> *Vedova, sola, e dì e notte chiama:*
> *"Cesare mio, perchè non m'accompagne?"*

'Come see thy Rome that weeps, widowed, alone, and calling day and night, "Caesar, my son, why art thou not by my side?" ' [22]

Proud though the name, and glorious the history, Rome had fallen on evil times. She was poor, ill, torn by the factions within and the strife of the great world of which she no longer was an integral part. Her mighty buildings lay in ruins, her citizens suffered, her population was decimated. Is it any wonder that the tongue of this shadowy city could not compete, despite the magic of its name, with those of the flourishing, rich Communes of Tuscany and Lombardy and Emilia and Venezia?

Rome had no university until 1303, long after Bologna, Padua, Naples, and other cities had graced themselves with institutions of higher learning. The historiography of Rome was neglected, city archives were wanting: the Roman Senate did not entrust to anyone the task of composing a continued narrative or chronicle of the city's history, and Rome did not find, as did Florence, a Giovanni Villani, or even, as many other cities did, an ordinary citizen, patriotic and curious enough to set down her story. Possibly it was too dangerous to do so because one or the other of the great powers would inevitably think itself offended or put in a bad light by an independent historian intent on stating the facts.

Literature lay fallow in Rome, both in Latin and in the *lingua vulgare*. Northern Italy had its poets writing in the Provençal language, in Sicily a school of poetry in a new literary language flourished at the court of the Hohenstaufen emperors. Bologna, Tuscany, Umbria brought forth their poets and troubadours. But Rome had no voice.

When Dante described the dialect of Rome as the vilest of

[21] Anon. 1928, 14–15.
[22] Dante, *Purg.* 6.112–114.

all Italian speeches, he added that this was "no wonder, because the Romans seem to stink above all other Italians through the baseness of their morals and customs." [23] In connecting causally the aesthetic impression he received from the Roman dialect with the cultural conditions of Rome, Dante gave vent to prejudice. But his opinion on Roman unworthiness in politics and therefore in language is nonetheless significant for the common view which must have prevailed in Italy and surely poisoned the mind of the people against the possibility that Roman speech might become standard Italian.

Even if there had been no Dante and no Boccaccio and no Petrarch in Florence, it is more than doubtful that Rome of the thirteenth and fourteenth centuries, during the crucial period of the formation of Italian, or Rome of any century since the fifth, could have mustered the prestige and the power necessary to persuade other Italians that Rome was still or could remain their capital. The glory of the past was not enough. Cultural and political leadership passed therefore from Rome to a more worthy model, and Florence became the capital of a renascent Italy, of the Italian Renaissance. The city of Dante became also the mother-city of the Italian language.

[23] Dante, *De vulg. el.* 1.11.

BIBLIOGRAPHY

BIBLIOGRAPHY

PERIODICALS AND ABBREVIATIONS

AA	*American Anthropologist*
ArA	*Archiv für Anthropologie*
AAA	*Archivio per l'Alto Adige*
AAAH	*Acta Academiae Aboensis Humaniora*
AC	*L'Antiquité classique*
ACIE	*Atti del ... Congresso internazionale etrusco*
ACIL	*Atti del ... Congresso internazionale dei linguisti*
	Actes du ... Congrès international de linguistes
ACIPP	*Atti del ... Congresso internazionale di preistoria e protostoria mediterranea*
ACISL	*Atti del ... Congresso internazionale di studi liguri*
ACISS	*Atti del ... Congresso internazionale di scienze storiche*
ACNE	*Atti del ... Congresso nazionale etrusco*
ACNSR	*Atti del ... Congresso nazionale di studi romani*
ACSB	*Atti del ... Congresso di studi bizantini*
AER	*American Economic Review*
AFC	*Accademia fiorentina di scienze morali, La Colombaria*
AGI	*Archivio glottologico italiano*
AHR	*American Historical Review*
AJA	*American Journal of Archaeology*
AJP	*American Journal of Philology*
AJPA	*American Journal of Physical Anthropology*
AK	*Archiv für Kulturgeschichte*
AL	*Acta linguistica*
ALMA	*Archivium Latinitatis Medii Aevi; Bulletin Du Cange*
AO	*Archiv orientalni*
APL	*Archvio di preistoria levantina*
AR	*Archiv für Religionswissenschaft*
ARo	*Archivum Romanicum*
A(R)AI	*Atti della (Reale) Accademia d'Italia*
A(R)AL	*Atti della (Reale) Accademia dei Lincei*
A(R)AN	*Atti della (Reale) Accademia di Napoli*
A(R)IV	*Atti del (Reale) Istituto Veneto*
AS	*American Speech*
ASc	*American Scholar*
ASCL	*Archivio storico della Calabria e della Lucania*
ASNS	*Archiv für das Studium der neueren Sprachen*
ASSNP	*Annali della Scuola superiore normale di Pisa*
Ampurias	
Anthropos	
Die Antike	

Antiquitas	
Antiquity	
Athenaeum	
Ausonia	
BCA	*Bullettino della Commissione archeologica del governatorato di Roma*
BJ	*Bonner Jahrbücher*
BPI	*Bullettino paletnologico italiano*
BSGI	*Bollettino della Società geografica italiana*
BSL	*Bulletin de la Société de linguistique de Paris*
BzN	*Beiträge zur Namenforschung*
CJ	*Classical Journal*
CL	*Comparative Literature*
CN	*Cultura neolatina*
CQ	*Classical Quarterly*
CRAIBL	*Comptes-rendus, Académie des inscriptions et belles-lettres*
La Cultura	
ED	*Ephemeros Dacoromana*
Emerita	
Eranos	
GA	*Geistige Arbeit*
GR	*Geographical Review*
GRM	*Germanisch-romanische Monatsschrift*
La Geografia	
Glotta	
Gnomon	
HSCP	*Harvard Studies in Classical Philology*
Hermes	
Historia	
History	
ID	*Italia dialettale*
IF	*Indogermanische Forschungen*
Italica	
JHS	*Journal of Hellenic Studies*
KZ	*Kuhns Zeitschrift; Zeitschrift für vergleichende Sprachforschung*
Klio	
Language	
MA	*Monumenti antichi*
MAAR	*Memoirs of the American Academy in Rome*
MAGW	*Mitteilungen der Anthropologischen Gesellschaft in Wien*
MAH	*Mélanges d'archéologie et d'histoire*
MAIBL	*Mémoirs, Académie des inscriptions et belles-lettres*
MH	*Museum Helveticum*
MLR	*Modern Language Review*
MOIG	*Mitteilungen des Oesterreichischen Instituts für Geschichtsforschung*
M(R)ASB	*Memorie della (Reale) Accademia di scienze dell'Istituto di Bologna*

MSL	*Mémoirs de la Société de linguistique de Paris*
Minos	
NA	*Nuova antologia*
NC	*La nouvelle Clio*
NJADB	*Neue Jahrbücher für antike und deutsche Bildung*
Orbis	
PBA	*Proceedings of the British Academy*
PP	*La parola del passato*
PPS	*Proceedings of the Prehistoric Society*
PSQ	*Political Science Quarterly*
PZ	*Prähistorische Zeitschrift*
Pannonia	
Phoenix	
QJE	*Quarterly Journal of Economics*
RA	*Rivista di antropologia*
RAr	*Revue archéologique*
RAL	*Rendiconti dell'Accademia dei Lincei*
REA	*Revue des études anciennes*
REL	*Revue des études latines*
RF	*Romanische Forschungen*
RFIC	*Rivista di filologia e d'istruzione classica*
RIGI	*Rivista indo-greco-italica*
RIL	*Rendiconti dell'Istituto lombardo*
RLiR	*Revue de linguistique romane*
RM	*Römische Mitteilungen; Mitteilungen des deutschen archäologischen Instituts, Römische Abteilung*
RhM	*Rheinisches Museum*
RR	*Romanic Review*
RSL	*Rivista di studi liguri*
Renaissance	
SBAW	*Sitzungsberichte der Bayerischen Akademie der Wissenschaften, Philologisch-historische Klasse*
SE	*Studi etruschi*
SHAW	*Sitzungsberichte der Heidelberger Akademie der Wissenschaften, Philologisch-historische Klasse*
SM	*Scientific Monthly*
ST	*Scienza e tecnica*
Scientia	
Speculum	
TAPA	*Transactions of the American Philological Association*
TZ	*Techmers Zeitschrift*
VR	*Vox Romanica*
WaG	*Welt als Geschichte*
WJA	*Würzburger Jahrbücher für die Altertumswissenschaft*
WS	*Wörter und Sachen*
Word	
ZA	*Zeitschrift für Assyriologie*
ZCP	*Zeitschrift für celtische Philologie*
ZDMG	*Zeitschrift der Deutschen Morgenländischen Gesellschaft*

ZM	*Zeitschrift für Mundartforschung*
Z(O)NF	*Zeitschrift für (Orts-) Namenforschung*
ZRP	*Zeitschrift für romanische Philologie*
ZV	*Zeitschrift für Volkskunde*

Other abbreviations

CAH	Cambridge Ancient History
CIL	Corpus Inscriptionum Latinarum
LCL	Loeb Classical Library
MGH	Monumenta Germaniae Historica
PID	R. S. Conway, S. E. Johnson, J. Whatmough, *The Prae-Italic dialects of Italy* (Cambridge, Mass., 1933).
PL	Jacques Paul Migne, *Patrologiae cursus completus. Series latina* (Paris, 1844–1904).
PW	Pauli — Wissowa, *Real-Encyclopädie der classischen Altertumswissenschaft* (Stuttgart, 1893ff.).

ANCIENT AND MEDIAEVAL AUTHORS AND WORKS CITED

Amm. Marc.	Ammianus Marcellinus	*ca.* 330–400	Historian
App.	Appianus	*fl* A.D. 140	Historian
	B.C. = *Bellum ciuile*		
Aug.	Aurelius Augustinus (Saint Augustine)		
	Ciu. Dei = *De ciuitate Dei*	354–430	Church father
	En. in Ps. = *Enarratio in Psalmum*		
Bede	Bede	672/3–735	Historian, theologian
Cic.	Marcus Tullius Cicero	106–43	Lawyer, philosopher
	Ad. fam. = *Epistolae ad familiares*		
	Agr. = *Orationes de lege agraria*		
	Brut. = *Brutus*		
	De or. = *De oratore*		
	De re pub. = *De re publica*		
	Off. = *De officiis*		
	Tusc. = *Tusculanae disputationes*		
Claud.	Claudius Claudianus	*fl.* A.D. 400	Poet
	Nupt. Hon. et Mar. = *De nuptiis Honorii et Mariae*		
Col.	Lucius Iunius Moderatus Columella	*fl.* A.D. 50	Farmer, author on agriculture
	De re rust. = *De re rustica*		
Dante	Dante Alighieri	1265–1321	Poet
	De vulg. el. = *De vulgari eloquentia*		
	Purg. = *Divina Commedia, Purgatorio*		
Diod. Sic.	Diodorus Siculus	*fl.* under Caesar, Augustus	Historian
Dion. Hal.	Dionysius of Halicarnassus	*ob.* 7 B.C.	Rhetorician, historian
Flor.	Lucius Annaeus Florus	*fl.* A.D. 140	Historian
Her. Pont.	Herakleides Ponticus	*ca.* 390–310	Philosopher
Her.	Herodotus	*ca.* 484–425	Historian

Hier.	Eusebius Hieronymus (Saint Jerome)	348–420	Church father
	ad. Gal. = ad Galaticos (Commentary)		
Hor.	Quintus Horatius Flaccus	65–8 B.C.	Poet
	Car. = Carmina		
	A.P. = Ars poetica		
Liv.	Titus Livius	59 B.C.–A.D. 17	Historian
Lucr.	Titus Lucretius Carus	94–55	Poet, philosopher
Or.	Paulus Orosius	*fl.* A.D. 415	Presbyter, historian
Paul. Diac.	Paulus Diaconus	*ca.* 720–800	Historian
Petr.	Francesco Petrarca	1304–1374	Poet
	De reb. sen. = De rebus senilibus		
Plautus	Titus Maccius Plautus	*ob.* 184 B.C.	Writer of
	Trin. = Trinummus		comedies
	Truc. = Truculentus		
Plin.	Gaius Plinius Secundus	23/4–79	Official, author
Plut.	Plutarchus	*ca.* 46–127	Philosopher,
	Quaest. Rom. = Quaestiones Romanae		biographer
	Rom. = Romulus		
Pol.	Polybius	*ca.* 203–120	Historian
Proc.	Procopius	*ob.* A.D. 565	Official, author
	D. B. = De bello		
Sen.	Marcius Annaeus Seneca	55 B.C.–A.D. 37/41	Rhetorician
	Cont. = Controversiae		
Sen.	Lucius Annaeus Seneca	5/4 B.C.–A.D. 65	Philosopher,
	Ep. = Epistulae		tragedian
Serv.	Servius	*fl.* fourth cent. A.D.	Grammarian, commentator
Sil.	Tiberius Catius Asconius Silius Italicus	26–104	Poet
Strabo	Strabo	64/3 B.C.–A.D. 21	Geographer, historian
Suet.	Gaius Suetonius Tranquillus	*ca.* 69–140	Biographer
	Ner. = Nero		
Sulp. Sev.	Sulpicius Severus	*ca.* 350–425	Christian writer
Tac.	Cornelius Tacitus	*ca.* 55–119	Historian
Theoph.	Theophrastus	*ca.* 372/69–288/5	Philosopher
Val. Max.	Valerius Maximus	*fl.* A.D. 26	Historian
Varr.	Marcus Terentius Varro	116–27	Philologist, writer on
	De re rust. = De re rustica		agriculture
	L. L. = De lingua latina		
Verg.	Publius Vergilius Maro	70–19 B.C.	Poet
	Aen. = Aeneis		
	Geor. = Georgica		

BIBLIOGRAPHY

PART ONE. INTRODUCTION TO ITALY

Cited

Franz Altheim, *Römische Geschichte*, vol. 1: *Die Grundlagen* (Frankfurt, 1951).
Annuario Statistico Italiano.
Arthur E. R. Boak, *Manpower shortage and the fall of the Roman Empire in the west* (Ann Arbor, Mich., 1955).
C. E. P. Brooks, *Evolution and climate* (London, 1922).
Max Cary, *The geographic background of Greek and Roman history* (Oxford, 1949).
J. C. Curry, "Climate and migration," *Antiquity* 2(1928) 292–307.
Daremberg — Saglio, *Dictionnaire des antiquités grècques et romaines* (Paris, 1875–1919).
Wilhelm Deecke, *Die Falisker* (Strassburg, 1888).
Pericle Ducati, *L'Italia antica* (3rd ed., Verona, 1948).
Tenney Frank, "Agriculture in early Latium," *AER* 9(1919) 267–276.
——— *An economic history of Rome* (2nd ed., Baltimore, 1927).
Ellsworth Huntington, *Mainsprings of civilization* (New York, 1945).
W. H. S. Jones, *Malaria: a neglected factor in the history of Greece and Rome* (Cambridge, 1907).
——— *Malaria and Greek history* (Manchester, 1909).
Friedrich Klingner, "Italia: Name, Begriff und Idee im Altertum," *Antike* 17(1941)89–104.
H. Koch, E. von Mercklin, C. Weickert, "Bieda," *RM* 30(1915)161–303.
Oswald Menghin, *Weltgeschichte der Steinzeit* (2nd ed., Vienna, 1941).
Konrad Miller, *Itineraria romana* (Stuttgart, 1916).
John L. Myres, *Geographical history in Greek lands* (Oxford, 1953).
Heinrich Nissen, *Italische Landeskunde* (Berlin, 1883–1902).
Leonard Olschki, *The genius of Italy* (New York, 1949).
Ettore Pais, *Storia dell'Italia antica e della Sicilia per l'età anteriore al dominio romano* (2nd ed., Turin, 1933).
Francesco L. Pullè, *Italia: genti e favelle* (Turin, 1927).
Franz Rauhut, "Italia," *WJA* 1(1946)133–152.
Francesco Ribezzo, "Il nome 'Italia,'" *RIGI* 4(1920)99–100.
Ellen C. Semple, *Geography of the Mediterranean region* (New York, 1931).
Giuseppe Sergi, "Gli Etruschi e la loro lingua," *RA* 25(1922–23)3–11.
Jules Sion, "Italie," in: Vidal de la Blache, 1927, vol. 7, part 2 (1934).
Sorre — Sion, "La Méditerranée," in: Vidal de la Blache, 1927, vol. 7, part 1 (1934).
United Nations Statistical Yearbook.

A. W. Van Buren, "Newsletter from Rome," *AJA* 60(1956)389-400.
P. M. J. Vidal de la Blache, ed., *Géographie universelle* (Paris, 1927-48).
Luigi Visintin, *Atlante geopolitico universale* (Novara, 1947).
Joshua Whatmough, *The foundations of Roman Italy* (London, 1937).
Erik Wikén, *Die Kunde der Hellenen von dem Land und den Völkern der Apenninenhalbinsel bis 300 v. Chr.* (Lund, 1937).
Erik Wistrand, "Per la storia del nome d'Italia nell'antichità," *Mélanges . . . Karl Michaëlsson*, 469-481 (Göteborg, 1952).

Additional

Atlante Fisico Economico d'Italia. Consociazione Turistica Italiana (Milan, 1940).
Karl Julius Beloch, *Kampanien* (2nd ed., Breslau, 1890).
C. E. P. Brooks, *Climate through the ages* (2nd ed., New York, 1949).
Angelo Celli, "Malaria e la colonizzazione dell'Agro romano dai più antichi tempi ai nostri giorni," *AAL* ser. 6, vol. 1 (1925)77-468.
Carleton S. Coon, *The races of Europe* (New York, 1939).
Ernest E. A. Desjardins, *La table de Peutinger* (Paris, 1869).
E. G. Gardner, ed., *Italy — a companion to Italian studies* (London, 1934).
Hugo Hassinger, *Geographische Grundlagen der Geschichte* (2nd ed., Freiburg, 1953).
H. Stuart Hughes, *The United States and Italy* (Cambridge, Mass., 1953).
Ellsworth Huntington, *Civilization and climate* (3rd ed., New Haven, Conn., 1924).
—— "Climatic change and agricultural exhaustion as elements in the fall of Rome," *QJE* 31(1917)173-208.
—— *The human habitat* (New York, 1928).
J. H. G. Lebon, *An introduction to human geography* (London, 1952).
S. F. Markham, *Climate and the energy of nations* (London, 1944).
John L. Myres, *Mediterranean culture* (Cambridge, 1944).
Gerhard Rohlfs, "Streifzüge durch die italienische Onomastik," *ASNS* 184(1944)103-129.
Frances E. Sabin, *Classical associations of places in Italy* (Madison, Wis., 1921).
Carlo Sforza, *Italy and the Italians* (New York, 1949).
Friedrich Vöchting, *Die italienische Südfrage* (Berlin, 1951).

PART TWO. THE ITALIAN LANGUAGE
(See also Bibliographies for Parts Seven and Eight.)

Cited

Giovanni Alessio, "Gli imprestiti dal latino nei relitti bizantini dei dialetti dell' Italia meridionale," *ACSB* 5. 1936 (Rome, 1939) 341-390.
—— "Nuove indagini sulla grecità dell'Italia meridionale," *RIL* 77(1943-44)27-106.
—— "Nuovi grecismi nei dialetti del Mezzogiorno d'Italia," *RFIC* 18(1941)256-263, 20(1942)47-53.

――― "Nuovo contributo al problema della grecità nell' Italia meridionale," *RIL* 72(1938–39)109–172, 73(1940–41)631–706, 77(1943–44)617–706, 79 (1945–46)65–92.

――― "Il sostrato latino nel lessico e nell'epotoponomastica della Calabria meridionale," *ID* 10(1934)111–190.

Carlo Battisti, "Ancora sulla grecità in Calabria," *ASCL* 3(1933)67–95.

――― "Appunti sulla storia e sulla diffusione dell'ellenismo nell'Italia meridionale," *RLiR* 3(1927)1–91.

――― "Nuove osservazioni sulla grecità nella provincia di Reggio Calabria," *ID* 6(1930)57–94.

Gioacchino Belli, *Sonetti romaneschi*, ed. Morandi (Città di Castello, 1906).

Giulio Bertoni, "La vecchia e nuova 'questione della lingua,'" *NA* 73(1938)121–131.

Frederick Bodmer, *The loom of language* (New York, 1944).

Julian Bonfante, "L'origine des langues romanes," *Renaissance* 1(1943)573–588.

Dante Alighieri, *De vulgari eloquentia*, ed. Marigo (Florence, 1938).

Giacomo Devoto, *Profilo di storia linguistica italiana* (2nd ed., Florence, 1954).

Robert A. Hall, Jr., *The Italian questione della lingua* (Chapel Hill, N. C., 1942).

Paul Oskar Kristeller, "The origin and development of the language of Italian prose," *Word* 2(1946)50–65 (translated into Italian in *CN* 10.1950).

Thérèse Labande-Jeanroy, *La question de la langue en Italie* (Paris, 1925).

Nunzio Maccarrone, "Romani e Romaici nell'Italia meridionale," *AGI* 20(1926)72–96.

Bruno Migliorini, "Dialetto e lingua nazionale a Roma," *RLiR* 9(1933) 370–382.

――― *Lingua e cultura* (Rome, 1948).

――― "Primi lineamenti di una nuova disciplina: la linguistica applicata o glottotecnica," *ST* 6(1942)609–619. (Reprinted in: B. M., *Saggi linguistici* [Florence, 1957] 307–317.)

――― "La questione della lingua," in: Momigliano, 1948, 3.1–75.

――― "Storia della lingua italiana," in: Momigliano, 1948, 2.57–104.

――― (Manuscript of forthcoming book *The Italian language*).

Attilio Momigliano, ed., *Problemi ed orientamenti critici di lingua e di letteratura italiana* (Milan, 1948–49).

Giovanni Morosi, "Dialetti romaici del mandamento di Bova in Calabria," *AGI* 4(1878)1–99.

――― "L'elemento greco nei dialetti dell' Italia meridionale," *AGI* 12(1890–92)76–96.

――― *Studi sui dialetti greci della terra d'Otranto* (Lecce, 1870).

L. R. Palmer, *The Latin language* (London, 1954).

Gerhard Rohlfs, "Autochthone Griechen oder byzantinische Gräzität?," *RLiR* 4(1928)118–200.

—— "Griechischer Sprachgeist in Süditalien. Zur Geschichte der inneren Sprachform," *SBAW* 1944–46, Heft 5 (Munich, 1947).

—— "Mundarten und Griechentum des Cilento," *ZRP* 57(1937) 421–461.

—— "Die Quellen des unteritalienischen Wortschatzes," *ZRP* 46(1926) 135–164.

—— *Scavi linguistici nella Magna Grecia* (Rome, 1933).

Adriano Tilgher, *La poesia dialettale napoletana, 1880–1930* (Rome, 1930).

Herbert H. Vaughan, "Italian and its dialects as spoken in the United States," *AS* 1(1926)431–435, 2(1926)13–18.

Walther von Wartburg, *Einführung in die Problematik und Methodik der Sprachwissenschaft* (Bern, 1943).

Additional

G. I. Ascoli, "L'Italia dialettale," *AGI* 8(1882–85)98–128.

Gertrud Baer, *Zur sprachlichen Einwirkung der altprovenzalischen Troubadourdichtung auf die Kunstsprache der frühen italienischen Lyriker* (Dissertation, Zürich, 1939).

Carlo Battisti — Giovanni Alessio, *Dizionario etimologico italiano* (Florence, 1950 ff.).

Giulio Bertoni, *Profilo linguistico d'Italia* (Modena, 1940).

Benedetto Croce, "A. Manzoni e la questione della lingua," in: *La letteratura della nuova Italia* (Bari, 1914) 1.151–160.

Alberto D'Elia, *A bibliography of Italian dialect dictionaries* (Chapel Hill, N. C., 1940).

Karl von Ettmayer, "Die historischen Grundlagen der Entstehung der italienischen Sprache," *MOIG* 48(1934)1–21.

Alfred Ewert, "Dante's theory of language," *MLR* 35(1940)355–366.

Karl Jaberg — Jakob Jud, *Sprach- und Sachatlas Italiens und der Südschweiz* (Zofingen, 1928–40).

Alberto Menarini, *Profili di vita italiana nelle parole nuove* (Florence, 1951).

Bruno Migliorini, *Lingua contemporanea* (3rd. ed., Florence, 1943).

—— *Pronunzia fiorentina o pronunzia romana?* (Florence, 1945).

Mario A. Pei, *The Italian language* (New York, 1941).

Sever Pop, *La dialectologie* (Louvain, 1950), vol. 1.466–618: L'italien.

Barbara Reynolds, *The linguistic writings of Alessandro Manzoni* (Cambridge, 1950).

Gerhard Rohlfs, *Etymologisches Wörterbuch der unteritalienischen Gräzität* (Halle, 1930).

—— *Historische Grammatik der italienischen Sprache und ihrer Mundarten* (Bern, 1949–54).

—— "Sprachgeographische Streifzüge durch Italien," *SBAW* 1944–46, Heft 3.

—— *La struttura linguistica dell'Italia* (Leipzig, 1937).

Alfredo Schiaffini, "Le origini dell'italiano letterario e la soluzione manzoniana della lingua dopo G. I. Ascoli," *ID* 5(1929)129–171.

Walther von Wartburg, *La posizione della lingua italiana* (Florence, 1940).

PART THREE. PREHISTORIC BACKGROUND

Cited

(Anon.) Editorial notes, *Antiquity* 27(1953)193–195.

Ugo Antonielli, "Due gravi problemi paletnologici: l'età enea in Etruria — Incinerazione ed inumazione nell'Italia centrale," *SE* 1(1927)11–60.

—— "Le origini di Roma alla luce delle scoperte archeologiche," *ACNSR* 1928(Rome, 1929)1.27–42.

M. F. Ashley-Montagu, *An introduction to physical anthropology* (2nd ed., Springfield, Ill., 1951).

Piero Barocelli, "Terremare, Palatino, orientazione dei *castra* e delle città romane," *BCA* 70(1942)131–144.

Karl Julius Beloch, "Le origini cretesi," *Ausonia* 4(1910)219–237.

David Bidney, *Theoretical anthropology* (New York, 1953).

Franz Boas, "Changes in bodily form of descendents of immigrants," *AA* 14(1912)530–562.

John Bradford, " 'Buried landscapes' in southern Italy," *Antiquity* 23 (1949) 58–72.

—— "Etruria from the air," *Antiquity* 21(1947)74–83.

John Bradford — P. R. Williams-Hunt, "Siticulosa Apulia," *Antiquity*, 23(1949)58–72.

Edoardo Brizio, *Epoca preistorica* (Milan, 1898).

C. E. P. Brooks, *Evolution and climate* (London, 1922).

Miles Burkitt — V. G. Childe, "A chronological table of prehistory," *Antiquity* 6(1932)185–205.

Max Cary, *The geographic background of Greek and Roman history* (Oxford, 1949).

V. Gordon Childe, *The Aryans* (New York, 1926).

—— *The Danube in prehistory* (Oxford, 1929).

—— "The Danube thoroughfare and the beginnings of civilization in Europe," *Antiquity* 1(1927)79–91.

—— *The dawn of European civilization* (4th ed., London, 1947).

—— "Is prehistory practical?," *Antiquity* 7(1933)410–418.

—— *Prehistoric migrations in Europe* (Oslo, 1950).

—— *Progress and archaeology* (London, 1945).

—— "Races, peoples and cultures in prehistoric Europe," *History* 18(1933)193–203.

John G. D. Clark, *Prehistoric Europe: the economic basis* (New York, 1952).

G. A. Colini, "Intorno all'origine della civiltà della prima età del ferro in Italia," *BPI* 23(1908)35–39.

—— "Il sepolcreto di Remedello Sotto nel Bresciano e il periodo eneolitico in Italia," *BPI* 24(1898)1–47, 88–110,206–260,280–295, 25(1899)1–27,218–295, 26(1900)57–101,202–267, 27(1901)73–132, 28(1902)5–43.

Robert S. Conway, "Italy in the Etruscan age," in: *CAH* vol. 4, chs. 12, 13 (Cambridge, 1926).

C. S. Coon — S. M. Garn — J. B. Birdsell, *Races* (Springfield, Ill., 1950).

Glyn E. Daniel, *A hundred years of archaeology* (London, 1950).

Christopher Dawson, *The age of the gods* (London, 1928).

Alessandro Della Seta, *Italia antica* (2nd ed., Bergamo, 1928).

Giacomo Devoto, "Agli inizi della storia etrusca," *SE* 19(1946–47)285–300.

—— *Gli antichi Italici* (1st ed., Florence, 1931: 2nd ed., Florence, 1951).

—— "Le fasi della linguistica mediterranea," *SE* 23(1954) 217–228.

—— "Protolatini e Protoitalici," *SE* 21(1950–51)175–184.

—— *Storia della lingua di Roma* (Bologna, 1940).

Pericle Ducati, "La civiltà villanoviana a sud e a nord dell'Appennino," *BPI* 52(1932)59–68.

—— *L'Italia antica* (3rd ed., Verona, 1948).

—— *Le problème étrusque* (Paris, 1938).

—— *Storia di Bologna,* 1: *I tempi antichi* (Bologna, 1928).

Friedrich von Duhn, *Italische Gräberkunde,* 1 (Heidelberg, 1924).

G. F. Scott Elliot, *Prehistoric man and his story* (London, 1920).

Edward Eyre, ed., *European civilization, its origin and development* (London, 1935–39).

C. Franke, *Die mutmassliche Sprache des Eiszeitmenschen* (Halle, 1913).

J. Fraser, "Linguistic evidence and archaeological and ethnological fact," *PBA* 12(1926)257–272.

Giuseppe Furlani, "Lingua e razza nell'Asia Anteriore antica," *AGI* 22/23 (1929)12–22.

A. W. Gomme, "The Roman republic," in: Eyre 1935, 2.1–158.

Albert Grenier, *Bologne villanovienne et étrusque* (Paris, 1912).

Christopher F. C. Hawkes, "From Bronze Age to Iron Age: Middle Europe, Italy, and the North and West," *PPS* n.s. 14(1948)196–218.

—— "Chronology of the Bronze and Early Iron Ages, Greek, Italian and Transalpine," *ACIPP* 1(1950)256–264.

Hugh Hencken, "Future aims and methods in research in prehistoric Europe," *AJA* 50(1946)341–344.

—— *Indo-European languages and archaeology* (American Anthropological Association, Memoir No. 84, 1955).

Gustav Herbig, "Kleinasiatische und etruskische Namengleichungen," *SBAW*, 2. Abhandlung (Munich, 1914).

Gertrud Hermes, "Das gezähmte Pferd im neolithischen und frühbronzezeitlichen Europa," *Anthropos* 30(1935)803–823, 31(1936)115–129.

Melville J. Herskovits, *Franz Boas; the science of man in the making* (New York, 1953).

Harry Hoijer, "Linguistic and cultural change," *Language* 24(1948)335–345.

Léon Homo, *L'Italie primitive et les débuts de l'impérialisme romain* (Paris, 1925).

Earnest A. Hooton, *Up from the ape* (2nd ed., New York, 1946).

Bedřich (Friedrich) Hrozný, *Ancient history of Western Asia, India and Crete* (Prague, 1953).

—— "Etruskisch und die 'hethitischen' Sprachen," *ZA* N.F. 4 (1928)171–184.

Antonio Jatta, *La Puglia preistorica* (Bari, 1914).

Frederick Johnson ed., *Radiocarbon dating. A report on the program to*

432   BIBLIOGRAPHY FOR PART THREE [pp. 69–136]

aid in the development of the method of dating (Memoirs of the Society
for American Archaeology, no. 8, 1951).

Guido Kaschnitz-Weinberg, "Italien mit Sardinien, Sizilien und Malta," in: *Handbuch der Altertumswissenschaft* 6.2.1, Handbuch der Archäologie 2.1. 309–402 (Munich, 1950).

Augustus H. Keane, rev. by A. H. Quiggin — A. C. Haddon, *Man — past and present* (Cambridge, 1920).

Clyde Kluckhohn — William Kelly, "The concept of culture," in: Ralph Linton ed., *The science of man in the world crisis*, 76–106. (New York, 1945).

Wilhelm Koppers, *Primitive man and his world picture* (London, 1952).

Hans Krahe, "Das Problem der 'ägäischen Wanderung' in sprachwissenschaftlicher Beleuchtung," *GA* no. 18, 1–2. (September 20, 1938).

—— *Die Indogermanisierung Griechenlands und Italiens* (Heidelberg, 1949).

Paul Kretschmer, *Einleitung in die Geschichte der griechischen Sprache* (Göttingen, 1896).

Nino Lamboglia, "La Liguria antica," in: *Storia di Genova dalle origini al tempo nostro*, 1 (Milan, 1941).

Gabriel W. Lasker, "Migration and physical differentiation," *AJPA* 4(1946) 273–300.

Pia Laviosa-Zambotti, *Le più antiche civiltà agricole europee. L'Italia, i Balcani, l'Europa centrale durante il neoeneolitico* (Milan, 1943).

—— "Nuovi orientamenti del metodo in paletnologia," in: *Reinecke Festschrift* 102–107 (Mainz, 1950).

—— "La successione delle gravitazioni indoeuropee verso il Mediterraneo e la genesi della civiltà europea," *AFC* 16(1947–50)107–157.

J. H. G. Lebon, *An introduction to human geography* (London, 1952).

H. M. R. Leopold, "L'età del bronzo dell'Italia centrale e meridionale," *BPI* 52(1932)22–39.

—— "Le sale del Museo Preistorico Luigi Pigorini contenenti oggetti delle palafitte e delle terramare della Valle Padana," *BPI* 50/51(1930–31) 148–174.

—— "La sede originaria dei Terramaricoli," *BPI* 49(1929)19–31.

Oswald Menghin, "Grundlinien einer Methodik der urgeschichtlichen Stammeskunde," *Hirt Festschrift* (Heidelberg, 1935)1.47–67.

Gero von Merhart, "Donauländische Beziehungen der früheisenzeitlichen Kulturen Mittelitaliens," *BJ* 147(1942)1–90.

Franz Messerschmidt, *Bronzezeit und frühe Eisenzeit in Italien* (Berlin, 1935).

Oscar Montelius, *Die vorklassische Chronologie Italiens* (Stockholm, 1912).

Jacques de Morgan, *Prehistoric man* (London, 1924).

John L. Myres, "A history of the Pelasgian theory," *JHS* 27(1907)170–225.

—— "The ethnology and primitive culture of the Nearer East and the Mediterranean world," in: Eyre 1935, 1.83–177.

Massimo Pallottino, "Appunti di protostoria latina ed etrusca," *SE* 14(1940) 27–32.

R. Paribeni, "La steatopigia in figurine preistoriche, e una recente opinione del Senatore Mosso," *BPI* 34(1908)68–75.

Giovanni Patroni, "Due punti fondamentali delle dottrine di Edoardo Brizio alla luce delle più recenti indagini," *SE* 14(1940)11–25.

—— "Espansioni e migrazioni," *AGI* 32(1940)21–69.

—— "L'indoeuropeizzazione dell'Italia. A proposito di recenti teorie," *Athenaeum* 17(1939)213–226.

—— *Le origini preistoriche dell'Italia e il suo destino storico* (Milan, 1927).

—— "Il paese delle terremare nei rispetti delle inondazioni," *Historia* 6(1932)533–538.

—— *La preistoria* (2nd ed., Milan, 1951).

—— "I problematici *Anamares* (*Ananes*) alla luce della 'etnogenesi fluviale' e della 'Lex Kossinna,'" *RAL* ser. 7, vol. 4 (1943)110–123.

—— "Voci e concetti classici arbitrariamente applicati alle 'terremare.'" [A review of H. J. Rose, *Primitive culture in Italy* (London, 1926)] *Athenaeum* 8(1930)425–451.

Thomas Eric Peet, "Italy and Sicily," in: *CAH* vol. 2, ch. 21, part 1. 563–574 (Cambridge, 1924).

—— *The Stone and Bronze Ages in Italy* (Oxford, 1909).

André Piganiol, *Essai sur les origines de Rome* (Paris, 1917).

Luigi Pigorini, "Le più antiche civiltà dell'Italia," *BPI* 29(1903)189–211.

—— "La terramara Castellazzo di Fontanellato nella provincia di Parma," *MA* 1(1892)121–154.

Giovanni Pinza, *Storia delle civiltà antiche. Paletnologia d'Italia* (Milan, 1923).

Vittore Pisani, "Studi sulla preistoria delle lingue indoeuropee," *AAL* ser. 6, vol. 4 (1931)547–651.

Richard Pittioni, "Die Urnenfelderkultur und ihre Bedeutung für die europäische Geschichte," *ZCP* 21(1938)167–204.

Ernst Pulgram, "On prehistoric linguistic expansion," *For Roman Jakobson*, 411–47 (The Hague, 1956).

—— "Names and realities in prehistoric linguistics of Italy," *Gedenkschrift . . . Kretschmer* 2. 99–108 (Vienna, 1956–57).

David Randall-MacIver, *The Iron Age in Italy* (Oxford, 1927).

—— *Italy before the Romans* (Oxford, 1928).

—— "Modern views on the Italian terremare," *Antiquity* 13(1939)320–323.

—— *Villanovans and early Etruscans* (Oxford, 1924).

Ugo Rellini, "La civiltà enea in Italia," *BPI* 53(1933)63–96.

—— *Le origini della civiltà italica* (Rome, 1929).

—— *La più antica ceramica dipinta d'Italia* (Rome, 1934).

—— "Il problema degli Italici," *NA* 68(1 settembre 1933)71–87.

—— "Sull'origine della civiltà del ferro in Italia," *SE* 12(1938)9–16.

Francesco Ribezzo, "La originaria unità tirrena dell'Italia nella toponomastica. Carattere mediterraneo della più antica toponomastica italiana," *RIGI* 4(1920)83–97.

—— "Sulla originaria unità linguistica e culturale dell'Europa mediterranea," *ACIPP* 1(1950)185–194.

Gösta Säflund, "Bemerkungen zur Vorgeschichte Etruriens," *SE* 12(1938) 17–55.

—— Le terremare delle provincie di Modena, Reggio Emilia, Parma, Piacenza (Lund, 1939).
G. Scabia, Sul tipo etnico degli Etruschi (Volterra, 1910).
Johannes Schmidt, Die Verwandtschaftsverhältnisse der indogermanischen Sprachen (Weimar, 1872).
Wilhelm Schmidt, "Primitive man," in: Eyre 1935, 1.1–82.
Giuseppe Sergi, Arii e Italici (Turin, 1898).
—— Italia: le origini (Turin, 1919).
—— Le prime e più antiche civiltà (Turin, 1926).
H. L. Shapiro, Migration and environment (Oxford, 1939).
Ernst Sittig, "Entzifferung der ältesten Silbenschrift Europas, der kretischen Linearschrift B," NC 3(1951)1–40.
Grafton Elliot Smith, The migrations of early culture (Manchester, 1915).
E. A. Speiser, "The ethnic background of the early civilizations of the Near East," AJA 37(1933)459–466.
J. Sundwall, "Villanovastudien," AAAH 5(1928)1–120.
Eugen Täubler, "Terremare und Rom," SHAW 22(1931–32)no. 2.
Griffith Taylor, Environment, race, and migration (Chicago, 1937).
Lily Ross Taylor, Local cults in Etruria (Rome, 1923).
Benvenuto Terracini, "Per la storia dell'Italia antica. Linguistica ed archeologia. Lettera aperta a Giacomo Devoto," Cultura 12(1933)735–750.
Alfredo Trombetti, "Saggio di antica onomastica mediterranea," SE 13(1939) 263–310, 14(1940)183–260.
Michael Ventris — John Chadwick, "Evidence for Greek dialect in the Mycenaean archives," JHS 73(1953)84–103.
—— "Greek records in the Minoan script," Antiquity 27(1953)196–206.
Paul Vouga, "The oldest Swiss lake-dwellings," Antiquity 2(1928)387–417.
Franz Weidenreich, "The human brain in the light of its phylogenetic development," SM 67(1948)103–109.
J. S. Weiner, "Skeletons: some remarks on their value to the Human Biologist," Antiquity 28(1954)197–200.
Joshua Whatmough, The foundations of Roman Italy (London, 1937).
—— "The Lepontic inscriptions and the Ligurian dialect," HSCP 38(1927)1–20.
Leslie A. White, The science of culture (New York, 1949).
Georg Wilke, "Die Herkunft der Italiker," ARA 45(1919)162–180.

Additional

Nils Aberg, Bronzezeitliche und früheisenzeitliche Chronologie (Stockholm, 1930–35).
Piero Barocelli, "L'ultimo decennio di studi preistorici in Italia: discussione, problemi, bibliografia," BPI n.s. 8(1947–50)92–159.
—— "L'ultimo trentennio di studi paletnologici in Italia, 1910–1940," BPI n.s. 5/6(1941–42)3–42.
V. Gordon Childe, Man makes himself (London, 1936).
—— What happened in history (New York, 1946).
G. A. Colini, "La civiltà del bronzo in Italia," BPI 29(1903)53–103, 211–237, 30(1904)155–199,229–304, 31(1905)18–70.

Robert J. Forbes, *Man the maker. A history of technology and engineering* (New York, 1950).

Christopher F. C. Hawkes, *The prehistoric foundations of Europe* (London, 1940).

Harry Hoijer, "The relation of language to culture," in: A. L. Kroeber ed., *Anthropology today. An encyclopedic inventory*, 554–573. (Chicago, 1953).

Clyde Kluckhohn, *Mirror for man: the relation of anthropology to modern life* (New York, 1949).

Pia Laviosa-Zambotti, "La ceramica della Lagozza e la civiltà palafitticola italiana vista nei suoi rapporti con le civiltà mediterranee ed europee," *BPI* n.s. 3(1939)61–112, 4(1940)83–164.

—— *Civiltà palafitticola lombarda e civiltà di Golasecca* (Como, 1940).

—— "Correnti culturali etniche in Italia durante l'età del rame e del bronzo," *RA* 37(1949)3–83.

—— *Il Mediterraneo, l'Europa, l'Italia durante la preistoria* (Turin, 1954).

—— *Origini e diffusione della civiltà* (Milan, 1947).

Claude Lévi-Strauss, "Language and the analysis of social laws," *AA* 53(1951)155–163.

—— *Race and history* (UNESCO, Paris, 1952).

R. H. Lowie, *An introduction to cultural anthropology* (2nd ed., New York, 1947).

Oscar Montelius, *La civilisation primitive en Italie* (Stockholm, 1895–1910).

—— "Wann begann die allgemeine Verwendung des Eisens?" *PZ* 5(1913) 289–330.

Giuseppe Sergi, *The Mediterranean race* (London, 1901).

Michael Ventris — John Chadwick, *Documents in Mycenaean Greek* (Cambridge, 1956).

PART FOUR. THE INDO-EUROPEANIZATION OF ITALY

Cited

Nils Aberg, *Bronzezeitliche und früheisenzeitliche Chronologie*, 1: *Italien* (Stockholm, 1930).

Ake Akerström, *Der geometrische Stil in Italien* (Uppsala, 1943).

—— *Studien über die etruskischen Gräber* (Uppsala, 1934).

Franz Altheim, *Geschichte der lateinischen Sprache* (Frankfurt, 1951).

—— *Italien und Rom* (2nd ed., Amsterdam, 1941 ?)

—— *Römische Geschichte* (Frankfurt, 1951–53).

—— *Der Ursprung der Etrusker* (Baden-Baden, 1950).

F. Altheim — E. Trautmann, *Italien und die dorische Wanderung* (Amsterdam, 1940).

—— "Nordische und italische Felsbildkunst," *WaG* 3(1937)83–118.

—— "Orthia" *WaG* 7(1941)360–368.

Alphons A. Barb, "Noreia und Rehtia," *Festschrift . . . Egger* 1.159–174 (Klagenfurt, 1952).

Madison S. Beeler, "The relation of Latin and Osco-Umbrian," *Language* 28(1952)435–443.

—— The Venetic language (Berkeley, Calif., 1949).

Karl Julius Beloch, Der italische Bund unter Roms Hegemonie (Leipzig, 1880).

Jean Bérard, La colonisation grècque de l'Italie méridionale et de la Sicile dans l'antiquité: l'histoire et la légende (Paris, 1941).

Luigi Bernabò Brea, "Civiltà preistoriche delle isole eoliche," APL 3(1952) 69–85.

—— "La Sicilia prehistórica y sus relaciones con Oriente y con la Península Ibérica," Ampurias 15/16 (1953–54) 137–235.

André Berthelot, "Les Ligures," RAr 2(1933)72–120, 245–303.

Vittorio Bertoldi, "Contatti e conflitti di lingue nell'antico Mediterraneo," ZRP 57(1937)137–169.

—— "Fra latino e prelatino," AGI 37(1952)69–81.

Albrecht von Blumenthal, "Osci und Volsci," ZNF 13(1938)31–33.

Axel Boëthius, "Livy 8.10.12 and the warrior image from Capestrano," Eranos 54(1956)202–210.

Giuliano Bonfante, "Quelques aspects du problème de la langue rétique," BSL 36(1935)141–154.

—— "Tracce di terminologia palafitticola nel vocabolario latino?" ARIV 97.2(1937–38)53–70.

—— "Who were the Philistines?" AJA 50(1946)252–262.

Willy Borgeaud, Les Illyriens en Grèce et en Italie (Dissertation, Geneva, 1943).

Pedro Bosch-Gimpera, "Le relazioni mediterranee postmicenee ed il problema etrusco," SE 3(1929)9–41.

Gino Bottiglioni, Manuale dei dialetti italici. (Osco, umbro e dialetti minori.) (Bologna, 1954).

Wilhelm Brandenstein, ed., Frühgeschichte und Sprachwissenschaft (Vienna, 1948).

—— Die Herkunft der Etrusker (Leipzig, 1937).

Alfonsina Braun, "Stratificazione dei linguaggi indoeuropei nell'Italia antica," ARIV 93(1933–34)989–1057.

Carl D. Buck, Comparative grammar of Greek and Latin (Chicago, 1933).

—— A dictionary of selected synonyms in the principal Indo-European languages: a contribution to the history of ideas (Chicago, 1949).

Giulio Buonamici, "Dubbi e problemi sulla natura e la parentela dell'etrusco," SE 1 (1927)239–253.

Albert Carnoy, "La langue étrusque et ses origines," AC 21(1952) 289–331.

Rhys Carpenter, "The alphabet in Italy," AJA 49(1945)452–464.

Gordon V. Childe, The Aryans (New York, 1926).

—— Progress and archaeology (London, 1945).

Ugo Coli, Saggio di linguistica etrusca (Florence, 1947).

Giuseppe A. Colini, "La civiltà del bronzo in Italia," BPI 29(1903)53–103, 211–237, 30(1904)155–199,229–304,31(1905)18–70.

Robert S. Conway, Ancient Italy and modern religion (Cambridge, 1933).

—— "Italy in the Etruscan age," in: CAH, vol. 4, chs. 12, 13 (Cambridge, 1926).

Wilhelm Corssen, Ueber die Sprache der Etrusker (Leipzig, 1874–75).

S. P. Cortsen, "Zur etruskischen Sprachkunde," *Symbolae . . . Danielsson* 43–61 (Uppsala, 1932).

G. Cultrera, "La fase di transizione dal periodo villanoviano al periodo orientalizzante," *SE* 11(1937)57–75.

Ernesto Curotto, *Liguria antica* (Genoa, 1940).

Wilhelm Deecke, *Corssen und die Sprache der Etrusker. Eine Kritik* (Stuttgart, 1875).

Wilhelm Deecke — Carl Pauli, *Etruskische Forschungen und Studien* (Stuttgart, 1881–84).

Giacomo Devoto, "Agli inizi della storia etrusca," *SE* 19(1946–47) 285–300.

—— *Gli antichi Italici* (2nd ed., Florence, 1951).

—— "Contatti etrusco-iguvini," *SE* 4(1930)221–247.

—— "Etrusco e peri-indoeuropeo," *SE* 18(1944)187–197.

—— "Illiri e Tirreni," *Pannonia* 4(1938)22–31.

—— "Illiri Tirreni Piceni," *SE* 11(1937)263–269.

—— "Protolatini e Protoitalici," *SE* 21(1950–51)175–184.

—— *Storia della lingua di Roma* (Bologna, 1940).

Georges Dottin, *Les anciens peuples d'Europe* (Paris, 1916).

Pericle Ducati, "La civiltà villanoviana a sud e a nord dell'Appennino," *BPI* 52(1932)59–68.

—— *Preistoria e protostoria dell'Emilia* (Rome, 1942).

—— *Le problème étrusque* (Paris, 1938).

—— *Storia di Bologna*, 1: *I tempi antichi* (Bologna, 1928).

Friedrich von Duhn, *Italische Gräberkunde*, 1 (Heidelberg, 1924).

—— "Das voretruskische und etruskische Bologna," *PZ* 5(1913)472–497,601.

Georges Dumézil, *Jupiter, Mars, Quirinus*. 2. *Naissance de Rome* (Paris, 1944).

Hortensia Dumitrescu, "L'età del bronzo nel Piceno," *ED* 5(1932)198–330.

Vladimir Dumitrescu, *L'età del ferro nel Piceno* (Dissertation, Bucarest, 1929).

Karl von Ettmayer, "Zu den Ortsnamen Liguriens," *Festschrift . . . Kretschmer* 23–24 (Vienna, 1926).

Edward Eyre, ed., *European civilization, its origin and development* (London, 1935–39).

Margit Falkner, "Epigraphisches und Archäologisches zur Stele von Lemnos," in: Brandenstein 1948, 91–109.

Eva Fiesel, "Die Bedeutung der relativen Chronologie für die etruskische Sprachforschung," *ACIE* (1929)187–188.

—— "Etruskisch," in: *Geschichte der indogermanischen Sprachwissenschaft*, 2. Teil, Band 5, Lieferung 4 (Berlin, 1931).

J. Fraser, "Linguistic evidence and archaeological and ethnological facts," *PBA* 12(1926)257–272.

Jean Gagé, *Huit recherches sur les origines italiques et romaines* (Paris, 1950).

Ernst Gamillscheg, *Romania Germanica* (Berlin, 1934–36).

I. J. Gelb, *The study of writing* (Chicago, 1952).

Vladimir Georgiev, "L'état actuel du problème de l'origine et la langue des Étrusques," *ACIPP* (1950)409.

—— "L'origine degli Etruschi come problema della storia delle tribù egee," SE 20(1948)101-108.

—— Die sprachliche Zugehörigkeit der Etrusker (Sofia, 1943).

Emil Goldmann, Beiträge zur Lehre vom indogermanischen Character der etruskischen Sprache (Heidelberg, 1929-30).

Albert Grenier, Bologne villanovienne et étrusque (Paris, 1912).

—— Les Gaulois (Paris, 1945).

—— "Ligures et Italo-Celtes. De d'Arbois de Jubainville à Camille Jullian," Mélanges . . . Ernout, 159-169 (Paris, 1940).

—— Les religions étrusque et romaine (Paris, 1948).

Eric P. Hamp, "Albanian and Messapic," Studies . . . Whatmough 73-89 (The Hague, 1957).

—— "The relationship of Venetic within Italic," AJP 75(1954)183-186.

Wolfgang Helbig, Die Italiker in der Poebene (Leipzig, 1879).

—— "Ueber die Herkunft der Iapyger," Hermes 11(1876)257-290.

George Hempl, Mediterranean studies, 4: Etruscan (Stanford, Calif., 1932).

Gustav Herbig, "Indogermanische Sprachwissenschaft und Etruskologie," IF 26(1909)360-381.

Gertrud Hermes, "Das gezähmte Pferd im neolithischen und frühbronzezeitlichen Europa" Anthropos 30(1935)803-823, 31(1936)115-129.

Jacques Heurgon, Recherches sur l'histoire, la religion, et la civilisation de Capoue préromaine des origines à la deuxième Guerre Punique (Paris, 1942).

Hermann Hirt, Die Indogermanen (Strassburg, 1905-07).

—— (ed. Helmut Arntz), Die Hauptprobleme der indogermanischen Sprachwissenschaft (Halle, 1939).

Henry M. Hoenigswald, "South Etruscan and Cypriote writing," AJA 56(1952)174.

—— Review of Slotty 1952, Language 29(1953)183-186.

Louise Adams Holland, "The purpose of the warrior image from Capestrano," AJA 60(1956)243-247.

Earnest A. Hooton, Up from the ape (2nd ed., New York, 1946).

Eduard Hrkal, Der etruskische Gottesdienst. Dargestellt nach den Agramer Mumienbinden (Vienna, 1947).

Bedřich (Friedrich) Hrozný, Ancient history of Western Asia, India and Crete (Prague, 1953).

—— "Etruskisch und die 'hethitischen' Sprachen," ZA 38(1928)171-184.

—— "Etruskisch und die hethitischen Sprachen," ACIE (1929)189-191.

Mary A. Johnstone, Etruria: past and present (London, 1930).

Camille Jullian, "L'époque italo-celtique. De son existence," REA 18(1916) 263-276.

Ulrich Kahrstedt, "Die Geschichte der Elymer," WJA 2(1947)16-32.

Guido Kaschnitz-Weinberg, "Italien mit Sardinien, Sizilien und Malta," in: Handbuch der Altertumswissenschaft 6.2.1, Handbuch der Archäologie 2.1.309-402 (Munich, 1950).

Hans Krahe, "Der Anteil der Illyrier an der Indogermanisierung Europas," WaG 6(1940)54-73.

—— "Beiträge zur illyrischen Wort- und Namenforschung," IF 57(1939) 113-133, 58(1941-42)131-152,209-232.

—— "Das früheste Griechentum in sprachlicher Beziehung," *GA* (1938) 6.3–4.

—— "Die Illyrier in ihren sprachlichen Beziehungen zu Italikern und Griechen," *WaG* 3(1937)119–136,284–299.

—— *Die Indogermanisierung Griechenlands und Italiens* (Heidelberg, 1949).

—— "Ligurisch und Indogermanisch," *Festschrift . . . Hirt* 2.241–255. (Heidelberg, 1936).

—— "Die Ortsnamen des antiken Apulien und Kalabrien," *Z(O)NF* 5(1929)3–25,139–166,7(1931)9–33,13(1937)20–31.

—— "Die Ortsnamen des antiken Lukanien und Bruttierlandes," *Z(O)NF* 15(1939)72–85, 110–140, 17(1941)127–150, 19(1943)58–72,127–141.

—— *Die Sprache der Illyrier* (Wiesbaden, 1955).

—— *Sprache und Vorzeit. Europäische Vorgeschichte nach dem Zeugnis der Sprache* (Heidelberg, 1954).

Paul Kretschmer, "Die antike Punktierung und der Diskus von Phaistos. Eine schriftgeschichtliche Untersuchung," *Minos* 1(1951)7–25.

—— "Die Etruskerfrage und die Inschriften von Magrè," *Symbolae . . . Danielsson*, 134–142 (Uppsala, 1932).

—— "Die frühesten sprachlichen Spuren von Germanen," *KZ* 69(1948) 1–25.

—— "Die Herkunft der Umbrer," *Glotta* 21(1932)112–125.

—— "Das *nt*-Suffix," *Glotta* 14(1925)84–106.

—— "Die protindogermanische Schicht," *Glotta* 14(1925)300–319.

—— "Sprache," in: A. Gercke — E. Norden, *Einleitung in die Altertumswissenschaft*, 1 (3rd ed., Leipzig, 1927).

—— "Die vorgriechischen Sprach- und Volksschichten," *Glotta* 28(1940)231–279, 30(1943)84–218,244–246.

Nino Lamboglia, "La Liguria antica," in: *Storia di Genova dalle origini al tempo nostro*, 1 (Milan, 1941).

Pia Laviosa-Zambotti, "Intorno alle origini e alla espansione degli Indoeuropei," *Festschrift . . . Tschumi*, 9–17 (Frauenfeld, 1948).

—— "La successione delle gravitazioni indoeuropee verso il Mediterraneo e la genesi della civiltà europea," *AFC* 16(1947–50)107–157.

Michel Lejeune, "La position du latin sur le domaine indoeuropéen," *Mémorial . . . Marouzeau*, 7–31 (Paris, 1943).

—— "Sur les inscriptions de la Vénétie préromaine," *CRAIBL* (1952) 11–15.

Ferdinand Lot, *La Gaule* (Paris, 1948).

Yakov Malkiel, Review of Menéndez-Pidal 1952, *Speculum* 29(1954)588–594.

Ludolf Malten, "Aineias," *AR* 29(1931)33–59.

Margherita N. Margani, *Sprazzi di luce sulla lingua etrusca* (Comiso, 1951).

—— *La stele pelasga di Lemno* (Comiso, 1954).

Jules Martha, *La langue étrusque* (Paris, 1913).

Friedrich Matz, "Die Indogermanisierung Italiens," *NJADB* 1(1938)367–383,385–400, 2(1939)32–47.

Maximilian Mayer, *Apulien. Vor und während der Hellenisierung* (Leipzig, 1914).

Ramón Menéndez-Pidal, *Toponimia preromanica hispana* (Madrid, 1952).

Gero von Merhart, "Donauländische Beziehungen der früheisenzeitlichen Kulturen Mittelitaliens," *BJ* 147(1942) 1–90.

Piero Meriggi, "Der indogermanische Charakter des Lydischen," *Festschrift . . . Hirt*, 2.283–290 (Heidelberg, 1936).

—— "Der Indogermanismus des Lykischen," *Festschrift . . . Hirt*, 2.257–282 (Heidelberg, 1936).

Reinhold Merkelbach, "Spechtfahne und Stammessage der Picentes," *Studi . . . Enrico Paoli*, 513–520 (Florence, n.d. [1956]).

Clemente Merlo, "I. Tracce di sostrato ligure nella regione che già fu dei Leponzi. II. L'invasione dei Celti e le parlate odierne dell'Italia settentrionale," *Antiquitas* 1/2(1946)74–80.

Franz Messerschmidt, *Bronzezeit und frühe Eisenzeit in Italien* (Berlin, 1935).

Gordon M. Messing, Review of van Windekens 1952, *Language* 30(1954) 104–108.

Basile Modestov, *Introduction à l'histoire romaine* (Paris, 1907).

Theodor Mommsen, *Die unteritalischen Dialecte*, (Leipzig, 1850).

A. C. Moorhouse, *The triumph of the alphabet* (New York, 1953).

Hans Mühlestein, *Ueber die Herkunft der Etrusker* (Berlin, 1929).

John L. Myres, "The ethnology, habitat, linguistic, and common culture of Indo-Europeans up to the time of the migrations," in: Eyre 1935, 1.179–244.

—— *History of Rome* (London, 1914).

G. Nicolucci, "La stirpe ligure in Italia nei tempi antichi e nei moderni," *ARAN*, Scienze fisiche e matematiche, ser. 1, vol. 2(1863) 225–234.

Heinrich Nissen, *Italische Landeskunde* (Berlin, 1883–1902).

Eduard Norden, *Alt-Germanien* (Leipzig, 1934).

Biagio Pace, *Arte e civiltà della Sicilia antica* (Milan, 1935ff.).

Antonino Pagliaro, "La lingua dei Siculi," *ACIL* 3(1935)151–159.

—— "Siculi e Liguri in Sicilia," *Scritti . . . Trombetti*, 365–373 (Milan, 1938).

Ettore Pais, *Storia dell'Italia antica e della Sicilia per l'età anteriore al dominio romano* (2nd ed., Turin, 1933).

Massimo Pallottino, *Elementi di lingua etrusca* (Florence, 1936).

—— "Erodoto autoctonista?" *SE* 20(1948)11–16.

—— *Gli Etruschi* (2nd ed., Rome, 1940).

—— *Etruscologia* (3rd ed., Milan, 1955).

—— "Nuovi orientamenti nello studio dell'etrusco," *AO* 18.4 (1950)159–165.

—— *L'origine degli Etruschi* (Rome, 1947).

—— "Le origini storiche dei popoli italici," *ACISS* Roma 1955, Relazioni, 2(1955)1–60.

—— "Il problema dei Liguri nella formazione dell'*ethnos* italico," *ACISL* 1,1950 (1952)83–97.

—— "Gli studi sulla lingua etrusca nelle loro condizioni attuali," *AGI* 32(1940)1–20.

L. R. Palmer, *The Latin language* (London, 1954).

Luigi Pareti, "Come uno storico risolve il problema delle origini etrusche," *ACNE* (1926) II.31–50.
———— *Le origini etrusche* (Florence, 1926).
Edeltraut Passler, "Die Buchenfrage," in: Brandenstein 1948, 155–161.
Giovanni Patroni, "Espansioni e migrazioni," *AGI* 32(1940)21–69.
———— "Noterelle di preistoria," *Historia* 8(1934) 346–353.
———— *La preistoria* (2nd ed., Milan, 1951).
Thomas E. Peet, "Italy and Sicily," in: *CAH* 2, ch. 21, pt. 1. 563–574 (Cambridge, 1924).
Mario A. Pei, "Etruscan and Indo-European case endings," *Italica* 22(1945) 73–77.
Giovanni B. Pellegrini, "Divinità paleovenete," *PP* 6(1951) 81–94.
André Piganiol, *Essai sur les origines de Rome* (Paris, 1917).
Vittore Pisani, "La lingua degli antichi Reti," *AAA* 30(1935) 91–108.
———— "Il linguaggio degli antichi Liguri," in: *Storia di Genova dalle origini al tempo nostro*, 1.383–396 (Milan, 1941).
———— *Le lingue dell'Italia antica oltre il latino* (Turin, 1953).
———— "Il problema illirico," *Pannonia* 3(1937)276–290.
———— Review of Krahe 1955, *Gnomon* 28(1956)442–445.
———— "Studi sulla preistoria delle lingue indeuropee," *ARAL* ser. 6, 4 (1931)547–651.
———— "Zur Sprachgeschichte des alten Italiens," *RhM* 97(1954)47–68.
Richard Pittioni, "Die Urnenfelderkultur und ihre Bedeutung für die europäische Geschichte," *ZCP* 21(1938)167–204.
Julius Pokorny, "Zur Urgeschichte der Kelten und Illyrier," *ZCP* 20(1935) 315–352, 20 [sic] (1936)489–522, 21(1938)55–166.
Ernst Pulgram, "Family tree, wave theory, and dialectology," *Orbis* 2(1953) 67–72.
———— "Linguistic expansion and diversification," *Studies . . . Whatmough*, 239–252 (The Hague, 1957).
———— "Names and realities in prehistoric linguistics of Italy," *Gedenkschrift . . . Kretschmer* 2. 99–108 (Vienna, 1956–57).
G. Quispel, "Gli Etruschi nel Vecchio Testamento," *SE* 14(1940)409–425.
David Randall-MacIver, "Forerunners of the Romans," *Antiquity* 2(1928) 26–36, 133–146.
———— *The Iron Age in Italy* (Oxford, 1927).
———— *Italy before the Romans* (Oxford, 1928).
———— *Villanovans and early Etruscans* (Oxford, 1924).
———— "Who were the Etruscans?" *AJA* 47(1943)91–94.
Franz Rauhut, "Italia," *WJA* 1(1946)133–152.
Otto Reche, *Rasse und Heimat der Indogermanen* (Munich, 1936).
Ugo Rellini, "La civiltà enea in Italia," *BPI* 53(1933)63–96.
Marcel Renard, *Initiation à l'Étruscologie* (2nd ed., Brussels, 1943).
Francesco Ribezzo, "Popolo e lingua degli antichi Piceni," *SE* 21(1950–51) 185–207.
———— "Preistoria, protostoria e glottologia. Indoeuropei e Preindoeuropei nel bacino del Mediterraneo," *AGI* 35(1950)46–64.
Gisela M. A. Richter, *Ancient Italy. A Study of the interrelations of its people as shown in their arts* (Ann Arbor, Mich., 1955).

Helmut Rix, "Bruttii, Brundisium, und das illyrische Wort für 'Hirsch,' "
    BzN 5(1954)115–129.
———— "Picentes-Picenum," *BzN* 2(1951)237–247.
Paolo Ettore Santangelo, *L'origine del linguaggio* (Milan, 1949).
———— *Fondamenti di una scienza della origine del linguaggio e sua storia
    remota* (Milan, 1955).
Fritz Schachermeyr, *Etruskische Frühgeschichte* (Berlin, 1929).
———— "Wanderungen und Ausbreitung der Indogermanen im Mittelmeer-
    gebiet," *Festschrift . . . Hirt* 1.229–253 (Heidelberg, 1936).
Carla Schick, Review of van Windekens 1952, *AGI* 38(1953)210–216.
Carl Schuchhardt, "Die Etrusker als italisches Volk," *PZ* 16(1925)109–123.
———— "Die Indogermanisierung Griechenlands," *Antike* 9(1933)303–319.
Adolf Schulten, "Die Etrusker in Spanien," *Klio* 23(1930)365–432.
Wilhelm Schulze, *Zur Geschichte der lateinischen Eigennamen* (Berlin,
    1904).
Giuseppe Sergi, *Arii e Italici* (Turin, 1898).
———— *Da Alba Longa a Roma* (Turin, 1934).
———— "Gli Etruschi e la loro lingua," *RA* 25(1922–23)3–11.
———— *The Mediterranean race* (London, 1901).
———— *Origine e diffusione della razza mediterranea* (Rome, 1885).
Friedrich Slotty, *Beiträge zur Etruskologie*, 1. (Heidelberg, 1952).
Felix Staehelin, *Die Schweiz in römischer Zeit* (3rd ed., Basel, 1948).
Hans Stoltenberg, "Der Vertragsstein von Perugia," *ACIPP* (1950) 405–408.
Edgar H. Sturtevant, *A comparative grammar of the Hittite language* (New
    Haven, Conn., 1951).
Benvenuto A. Terracini, "Spigolature liguri," *AGI* 20(1926)122–160.
Paul Thieme, "Die Heimat der indogermanischen Gemeinsprache,"
    AAWLM, 1953, no. 11 (Wiesbaden, 1954).
Jules Toutain, *The economic life of the ancient world* (New York, 1930).
Arnold J. Toynbee, *A study of history* (Oxford, 1933–39).
Alfredo Trombetti, *La lingua etrusca* (Florence, 1928).
———— "La lingua etrusca e le lingue pre-indoeuropee del Mediterraneo,"
    SE 1(1927)213–238.
———— "Sulla parentela della lingua etrusca," *MRASB* vol. 2, Classe di
    scienze morali, ser. 1, vol. 2, Sezione di scienze storico-filologiche, fasc.
    2 (1909)167–221.
N. S. Trubetzkoy, "Gedanken über das Indogermanenproblem," *AL* 1(1939)
    81–89.
Emil Vetter, *Handbuch der italischen Dialekte* (Heidelberg, 1953).
———— "Die Herkunft des venetischen Punktiersystems," *Glotta* 24(1936)
    114–133.
———— "Süd-Pikenisch," *Glotta* 30(1943)38–41.
Vilhelm Wanscher, *La langue étrusque renaît* (Copenhagen, 1951).
Joshua Whatmough, *The dialects of ancient Gaul* (Ann Arbor, Mich.,
    1949–51).
———— *The foundations of Roman Italy* (London, 1937).
———— "Inscriptions from Magrè and the Raetic dialect," *CQ* 17(1923)61–
    72.
———— "Κελτικά," *HSCP* 55 (1944)1–85.

—— "The Lepontic inscriptions and the Ligurian dialect," *HSCP* 38 (1927)1–20.
—— "On the name 'Ligurian,'" *HSCP* 55(1944)77–80.
—— *Poetic, scientific, and other forms of discourse* (Berkeley, Cal., 1956).
—— "The Raeti and their language," *Glotta* 22(1934)27–31.
—— "'Tusca origo Raetis,'" *HSCP* 48(1937)181–202.
Erik Wikén, *Die Kunde der Hellenen von dem Land und den Völkern der Apenninenhalbinsel bis 300 v. Chr.* (Lund, 1937).
A. J. van Windekens, *Le pélasgique. Essai sur une langue indoeuropéenne préhellénique* (Louvain, 1952).

Additional

Ugo Antonielli, "Due gravi problemi paletnologici: l'età enea in Etruria. Incinerazione ed inumazione nell'Italia centrale," *SE* 1(1927)11–60.
Carlo Battisti, "Liguri e Mediterranei," *RSL* 9(1943)79–95.
—— "Osservazioni sulla lingua delle iscrizioni nell'alfabeto etrusco-settentrionale di Bolzano," *SE* 18(1944)198–236, 19 (1946–47)249–276.
Raymond Bloch, *L'art et la civilisation étrusques* (Paris, 1955).
Tristano Bolelli, "Unità italica e unità italo-celtica," *ASSNP* 9(1940)97–119.
Carl D. Buck, *A grammar of Oscan and Umbrian* (2nd ed., Boston, 1928).
Giulio Buonamici, *Fonti di storia etrusca. Tratte dagli autori classici* (Florence, 1939).
Albert Carnoy, *Les Indo-Européens* (Brussels, 1921).
Robert S. Conway, *The Italic dialects* (Cambridge, 1897).
George Dennis, *The cities and cemeteries of Etruria* (London, 1907).
Giacomo Devoto, "Italo-greco e italo-celtico," *AGI* 22/23(1929)200–240.
Pericle Ducati, *Storia dell'arte etrusca* (Florence, 1927).
R. A. L. Fell, *Etruria and Rome* (Cambridge, 1924).
Hugh Hencken, *Indo-European languages and archaeology* (American Anthropological Association, Memoir No. 84, 1955).
Richard Heuberger, *Rätien im Altertum und Frühmittelalter* (Innsbruck, 1932).
Historia 6(1957)1–132, articles by Pallottino, Säflund, Devoto, Olzscha, Bloch, Heurgon, Mazzarino, Herbig.
Johannes Hubschmid, *Praeromanica* (Zurich, 1949).
Richard von Kienle, "Italiker und Kelten," *WS* 17(1936)98–153.
Hans Krahe, *Die alten balkanillyrischen geographischen Namen auf Grund von Autoren und Inschriften* (Heidelberg, 1925).
—— *Lexicon altillyrischer Personennamen* (Heidelberg, 1929).
—— "Die sprachliche Stellung des Illyrischen," *Pannonia* 3(1937)291–312.
Winfred P. Lehmann, *Proto-Indo-European phonology* (Austin, Tex., 1952).
Mario Lopes Pegna, *Saggio di bibliografia etrusca* (Florence, 1953).
Maximilian Mayer, "Alt-Italiker auf der Südwanderung," *Klio* 25(1932)348–402.
—— "Die Morgeten," *Klio* 21(1927)288–312.
Ernst Meyer, *Die Indogermanenfrage* (Marburg, 1948).
Antonino Pagliaro, "La lingua dei Siculi," *ACIL* (1935)151–159.

444   BIBLIOGRAPHY FOR PART FOUR [pp. 137–236

Massimo Pallottino, *Etruscan painting* (Geneva, 1952).

—— *Testimonia linguae etruscae* (Florence, 1954).

Giovanni Patroni, "L'indoeuropeizzazione dell'Italia," *Athenaeum* 17(1939) 213–226.

Vittore Pisani, "Geolinguistica e indoeuropeo," *ARAL* ser. 6, 9(1940)113–378.

Richard Pittioni, "Urgeschichtliche Stamm- und Sprachgeschichte," *ZM* 21 (1953)193–197.

Julius Pokorny, "Substrattheorie und Urheimat der Indogermanen," *MAGW* 66(1936)69–91.

Walter Porzig, *Die Gliederung des indogermanischen Sprachgebiets* (Heidelberg, 1954).

David Randall-MacIver, *The Etruscans* (Oxford, 1927).

Franz Rauhut, "Italia," *WJA* 1(1946)133–152.

Francesco Ribezzo, "La originaria unità tirrena dell'Italia nella toponomastica. Caratterre mediterraneo della più antica toponomastica italiana," *RIGI* 4(1920)83–97.

—— Unità italica ed unità italo-celtica," *RIGI* 16(1932)27–40.

Anton Scherer, "Das Problem der indogermanischem Urheimat vom Standpunkt der Sprachwissenschaft," *AK* 33(1950)1–16.

Benvenuto A. Terracini, "Per la storia dell'Italia antica. Linguistica ed archeologia," *Cultura* 12(1933)735–750.

Alois Walde, *Ueber älteste sprachliche Beziehungen zwischen Kelten und Italikern* (Innsbruck, 1917).

Joshua Whatmough, Review of Hubschmid 1949, *Language* 26(1950)298–299.

Joseph Wiesner, "Italien und die grosse Wanderung," *WaG* 8(1942)197–243.

PART FIVE. THE LATINIZATION OF ITALY
(See also Bibliography for Part Six)

Cited

Nils Åberg, *Bronzezeitliche und früheisenzeitliche Chronologie*, I: *Italien* (Stockholm, 1930).

Franz Altheim, "Patriziat und Plebs," *WaG* 7(1941)217–233.

Ugo Antonielli, "Le origini di Roma alla luce delle scoperte archeologiche," *ACNSR* (1929)1.27–42.

Karl Julius Beloch, *Der italische Bund unter Rom's Hegemonie* (Leipzig, 1880).

—— *Römische Geschichte* (Berlin, 1926).

Raymond Bloch, *Les origines de Rome* (Paris, 1946).

Arthur E. R. Boak, *A history of Rome to 565 A.D.* (4th ed., New York, 1955).

Giuliano Bonfante, "Civilisation indo-européenne et civilisation hittite," *AO* 11(1939–40)84–90.

—— "Sobre el vocabolario céltico y latino," *Emerita* 2(1934)263–306.

G. Boni (On Forum excavations), *NS* (1902)96–111, (1903)123–170, 375–427, (1905)145–193, (1906)5–46, 253–294, (1911)157–190.

Carl D. Buck, "The general linguistic condition in ancient Italy and Greece," *CJ* 1(1906)99–110.

Giuseppe Cardinali, *Le origini di Roma* (Rome, 1949).
Max Cary, *The geographic background of Greek and Roman history* (Oxford, 1949).
Wilhelm Deecke, *Die Falisker* (Strassburg, 1888).
Giacomo Devoto, *Storia della lingua di Roma* (Bologna, 1940).
Pericle Ducati, *Le problème étrusque* (Paris, 1938).
Friedrich von Duhn, *Italische Gräberkunde* (Heidelberg, 1924).
Georges Dumézil, *Jupiter, Mars, Quirinus. II. Naissance de Rome* (Paris, 1944).
Edward Eyre, ed., *European civilization, its origin and development* (London, 1935–39).
Plinio Fraccaro, "I fattori geografici della grandezza di Roma," *La Geografia* 14(1926)84–100.
Tenney Frank, *An economic history of Rome* (2nd ed., Baltimore, 1927).
Einar Gjerstad, "Stratigraphic excavations in the Forum Romanum," *Antiquity* 26(1952)60–64.
Josef Göhler, *Rom und Italien. Die römische Bundesgenossenpolitik von den Anfängen bis zum Bundesgenossenkrieg* (Breslau, 1939).
Pier Gabriele Goidanich, "Varietà etniche e varietà idiomatiche in Roma antica," *ACSNR* (1929) 2.396–414.
A. W. Gomme, "The Roman republic," in: Eyre 1935, 2.1–158.
Hans F. K. Günther, "Indogermanentum und Germanentum, rassenkundlich betrachtet," *Festschrift . . . Hirt* 1.317–340 (Heidelberg, 1936).
Louise Adams Holland, *The Faliscans in prehistoric times* (Rome, 1925).
—— "Septimontium or Saeptimontium?" *TAPA* 84(1953)16–34.
Richard W. Husband, "Race mixture in early Rome," *TAPA* 40(1910)63–81.
Ernst Kornemann, "Coloniae," *PW*, s.v. (Stuttgart, 1933).
J. Lacour-Gayet, ed., *Histoire du commerce* (Paris, 1950–52).
A. K. Lake, "The origins of the Roman house," *AJA* 41(1937)598–601.
Pia Laviosa-Zambotti, *Origini e diffusione della civiltà* (Milan, 1947).
Maxime Lemosse, *Le commerce antique jusqu'aux invasions arabes*, in: Lacour-Gayet 1950, 2.1. 1–187.
Giuseppe Lugli, "Les débuts de la romanité à la lumière des découvertes archéologiques modernes," *Eranos* 41(1943)8–27.
—— "Tradizione e realtà delle origini di Roma," *NA* 16 (aprile 1937) 375–387.
Bruno Migliorini, "Sull'origine del nome di Roma," *ACSNR* (1929) 2.427–433.
Massimo Pallottino, *Gli Etruschi* (2nd. ed., Rome, 1940).
—— *Etruscologia* (3rd ed., Milan, 1955).
André Piganiol, *Essai sur les origines de Rome* (Paris, 1917).
Vittore Pisani, *Le lingue dell'Italia antica oltre il latino* (Turin, 1953).
Salvatore M. Puglisi, "Gli abitatori primitivi del Palatino attraverso le testimonianze archeologiche e le nuove indagini stratigrafiche sul Germalo," *MA* 41(1951)1–98.
Ernst Pulgram, "On prehistoric linguistic expansion, *For Roman Jakobson* 411–417 (The Hague, 1956).
—— "The origin of the Roman nomen gentilicium," *HSCP* 58/59(1948) 163–187.

David Randall-MacIver, *Italy before the Romans* (Oxford, 1928).

Francesco Ribezzo, "Roma delle origini, Sabini e Sabelli," *RIGI* 14(1930) 55–99.

William Ridgeway, "Who were the Romans?" *PBA* 3(1907)17–60.

Edward T. Salmon, "Rome and the Latins," *Phoenix* 7(1953)93–104, 123–135.

Wilhelm Schulze, *Zur Geschichte der lateinischen Eigennamen* (Berlin, 1904).

Inez G. Scott, "Early Roman traditions in the light of archaeology," *MAAR* 7(1929)7–118.

Grant Showerman, *Eternal Rome* (New Haven, Conn., 1924).

Bertha Tilly, *Vergil's Latium* (Oxford, 1947).

A. W. Van Buren, *Ancient Rome, as revealed by recent discoveries* (London, 1936).

Joshua Whatmough, *The foundations of Roman Italy* (London, 1937).

Additional

Julius Beloch, *Die Bevölkerung der griechisch-römischen Welt* (Leipzig, 1886).

——— "Die Bevölkerung Italiens im Altertum," *Klio* 3(1903)471–490.

Franz Bömer, *Rom und Troia. Untersuchungen zur Frühgeschichte Roms* (Baden-Baden, 1951).

A. Budinszky, *Die Ausbreitung der lateinischen Sprache über Italien und die Provinzen des römischen Reiches* (Berlin, 1881).

Alberto Davico, "Ricostruzione probabile dell'abitazione laziale del primo periodo del ferro secondo le testimonianze dello scavo sul Germalo," *MA* 41(1951)125–134.

Pericle Ducati, *Come nacque Roma* (Rome, 1939).

A. Ernout — A. Meillet, *Dictionnaire étymologique de la langue latine* (3rd ed., Paris, 1951).

Plinio Fraccaro, *La storia romana arcaica* (Milan, 1952).

Pier Gabriele Goidanich, "Rapporti culturali e linguistici tra Roma e gli Italici. Origine antica della cultura di Roma," *ARAI*, ser. 7, 3(1943)317–501.

Charlotte E. Goodfellow, *Roman citizenship. A study of its territorial and numerical expansion from the earliest times to the death of Augustus* (Dissertation, Bryn Mawr, Pa., 1935).

Mason Hammond, "Ancient imperialism; contemporary justification," *HSCP* 58/59(1948)105–161.

Ulrich Kahrstedt, *Geschichte des griechisch-römischen Altertums* (2nd ed., Munich, 1952).

Wilhelm Kroll, "Die Entwicklung der lateinischen Schriftsprache," *Glotta* 22(1934) 1–27.

Giuseppe Lugli, *Roma antica. Il centro monumentale* (Rome, 1946).

Frank B. Marsh (rev. by H. H. Scullard), *A history of the Roman world from 146 to 30 B.C.* (2nd ed., London, 1953).

H. M. D. Parker, *A history of the Roman world from 138 to 337* (London, 1935).

Jacques Perret, *Les origines de la légende troyenne de Rome* (Paris, 1942).

Edward K. Rand, *The building of eternal Rome* (Cambridge, Mass., 1943).

H. J. Rose, *Primitive culture in Italy* (London, 1926).

Mikhail Ivanovich Rostovtzeff, *Studien zur Geschichte des römischen Kolonates* (Leipzig, 1910).

Edward T. Salmon, *A history of the Roman world from 30 B.C. to A.D. 138* (2nd ed., London, 1950).

Howard H. Scullard, *A history of the Roman world from 753 to 146 B.C.* (London, 1935).

Alois Walde — J. B. Hofmann, *Lateinisches etymologisches Wörterbuch* (3rd ed., Heidelberg, 1930–55).

PART SIX. THE HISTORY OF LATIN
(*See also Bibliography for Part Five*)

Cited

Franz Altheim, *Geschichte der lateinischen Sprache* (Frankfurt, 1951).

Julius Beloch, *Die Bevölkerung der griechisch-römischen Welt* (Leipzig, 1886).

Leonard Bloomfield, *Language* (New York, 1933).

Arthur E. R. Boak, *A history of Rome to 565 A.D.* (4th ed., New York, 1955).

——— *Manpower shortage and the fall of the Roman Empire in the west* (Ann Arbor, Mich., 1955).

R. R. Bolgar, *The classical heritage and its beneficiaries* (Cambridge, 1954).

Karl Brugmann, "Zur Frage nach den Verwandtschaftsverhältnissen der indogermanischen Sprachen," *TZ* 1(1884)226–256.

Giacomo Devoto, *Storia della lingua di Roma* (Bologna, 1940).

Karl von Ettmayer, "Vulgärlatein," in: *Grundriss der indogermanischen Sprach- und Altertumskunde* 1.2.1 (Strassburg, 1916).

Eduard Fraenkel, "Senatus consultum de Bacchanalibus," *Hermes* 67(1932) 369–396.

Tenney Frank, *An economic history of Rome* (2nd ed., Baltimore, 1927).

——— *A history of Rome* (New York, 1923).

——— *Rome and Italy of the Empire. Economic survey of ancient Rome*, vol. 5 (Baltimore, 1940).

T. R. Glover, *The ancient world* (London, 1953).

Pier Gabriele Goidanich, "Rapporti culturali e linguistici tra Roma e gli Italici. Origine antica della cultura di Roma. L'iscrizione arcaica del foro romano e il suo ambiente archeologico. Suo valore giuridico," *ARAl* ser. 7, vol. 3(1943)317–501.

Albert Guérard, "Ten levels of speech," *ASc* 16(1947)148–158.

Aubrey Gwynn, *Roman education from Cicero to Quintilian* (Oxford, 1926).

Einar Haugen, "The analysis of linguistic borrowing," *Language* 26(1950) 210–231.

——— *The Norwegian language in America* (Philadelphia, 1953).

Hermann Hirt, "Die Verwandtschaftsverhältnisse der Indogermanen," *IF* 4(1894)36–45.

Hermann Hirt (ed. Helmut Arntz), *Die Hauptprobleme der indogermanischen Sprachwissenschaft* (Halle, 1939).

J. U. Hubschmied, "Sprachliche Zeugen für das späte Aussterben des Gallischen," *VR* 3(1938)48–155.

Arnold H. M. Jones, *Ancient economic history* (London, 1948).

Ernst Kornemann, *Weltgeschichte des Mittelmeerraumes. Von Philipp II. von Makedonien bis Muhammed* (Munich, 1948–49).

Einar Löfstedt, *Philologischer Kommentar zur Peregrinatio Aetheriae* (Uppsala, 1936).

Ferdinand Lot, "A quelle époque a-t-on cessé de parler latin?" *ALMA* 6(1931)97–159.

Jules Marouzeau, *Quelques aspects de la formation du latin littéraire* (Paris, 1949).

H. I. Marrou, *Histoire de l'éducation dans l'antiquité* (Paris, 1948).

Eduard Norden, *Aus altrömischen Priesterbüchern* (Lund, 1939).

L. R. Palmer, *The Latin language* (London, 1954).

Hermann Paul, *Prinzipien der Sprachgeschichte* (5th ed., Halle, 1920).

Ernst Pulgram, "Language and national character," *QJS* 40(1954)393–400.

——— "Linguistic expansion and diversification," *Studies . . . Whatmough* 239–252 (The Hague, 1957).

——— "On prehistoric linguistic expansion," *For Roman Jakobson* 411–417 (The Hague, 1956).

——— "Prehistory and the Italian dialects," *Language* 25(1949)241–252.

——— "Spoken and written Latin," *Language* 26(1950)458–466.

Francesco Ribezzo, "Roma delle origini, Sabini e Sabelli. Aree dialettali, iscrizioni, isoglossi," *RIGI* 14(1930)59–99.

Elise Richter, "Beiträge zur Geschichte der Romanismen," ZRP, Beiheft 82(1934).

——— "Der innere Zusammenhang in der Entwicklung der romanischen Sprachen," ZRP, Beiheft 27(1911).

Gerhard Rohlfs, *Sermo vulgaris latinus. Vulgärlateinisches Lesebuch* (Halle, 1951; 2nd ed., Tübingen, 1956).

——— "Vorlateinische Einflüsse in den Mundarten des heutigen Italien?" *GRM* 18(1930)37–56.

Louis F. Sas, *The noun declension system in Merovingian Latin* (Paris, 1937).

Johannes Schmidt, *Zur Geschichte des indogermanischen Vokalismus* (Weimar, 1871–1875).

Hugo Schuchardt, *Der Vokalismus des Vulgärlateins* (Leipzig, 1866–68).

Kurth Sethe, "Das Verhältnis zwischen Demotisch und Koptisch und seine Lehren für die Geschichte der ägyptischen Sprache," ZDMG 79 (1925)290–316.

V. G. Simkhovich, "Rome's fall reconsidered," *PSQ* 31(1916)201–243.

Karl Sittl, *Die lokalen Verschiedenheiten der lateinischen Sprache mit besonderer Berücksichtigung des afrikanischen Lateins* (Erlangen, 1882).

Leo Spitzer, "The epic style of the pilgrim Aetheria," *CL* 1(1949)225–258.

Bruno Stech, "Senatores Romani qui fuerint inde a Vespasiano usque ad Traiani exitum," *Klio*, Beiheft 10(1912).

Ernst G. Wahlgren, *Un problème de phonétique romane* (Uppsala, 1930).

Uriel Weinreich, *Languages in contact* (New York, 1953).

Joshua Whatmough, *The foundations of Roman Italy* (London, 1937).

—— "Κελτικά," *HSCP* 55(1944)1–85.

—— "Quemadmodum Pollio reprehendit in Liuio Patauinitatem," *HCSP* 44(1933)95–130.

Oscar Weise, *Language and character of the Roman people* (London, 1909).

Augustus S. Wilkins, *Roman education* (Cambridge, 1905).

Additional

Giovanni Alessio, "Suggerimenti e nuove indagini sul problema del sostrato mediterraneo," *SE* 18(1944)93–157.

—— "I dialetti romanzi e il problema del sostrato mediterraneo," *ARo* 25(1941)140–183.

Franz Altheim, *Römische Geschichte* (Frankfurt, 1951–53).

Carlo Battisti, "Aspirazione etrusca e gorgia toscana," *SE* 4(1930)249–254.

Vittorio Bertoldi, "Problèmes de substrat," *BSL* 32(1931)93–184.

Reinier Boulogne, *De plaats van de paedagogus in de romeinse culture* (Utrecht, 1951).

Carl Darling Buck, *Comparative grammar of Greek and Latin* (Chicago, 1933).

Max Cary, *A history of Rome, down to the reign of Constantine* (London, 1935).

M. L. Clarke, *Rhetoric at Rome* (London, 1953).

J. F. Dobson, *Ancient education and its meaning to us* (New York, 1932).

Alfred Ernout, *Les éléments dialectaux du vocabulaire latin* (Paris, 1909).

Tenney Frank, "Race mixture in the Roman Empire," *AHR* 21(1916)689–708.

Pier Gabriele Goidanich, "Varietà etniche e varietà idiomatiche in Roma antica," *ACSNR* (Rome, 1929), 2.396–414.

Charles H. Grandgent, *An introduction to Vulgar Latin* (Boston, 1907).

Martin Hammer, *Die locale Verbreitung frühester romanischer Lautwandlungen im alten Italien* (Halle, 1894).

Herbert Hill, *The Roman middle class in the republican period* (Oxford, 1952).

J. B. Hofmann, *Lateinische Umgangssprache* (2nd ed., Heidelberg, 1936).

Johannes Hubschmid, *Praeromanica* (Bern, 1949).

Roland G. Kent, *The forms of Latin* (Baltimore, 1946).

—— *The sounds of Latin* (3rd ed., Baltimore, 1945).

Ernst Kieckers, *Historische lateinische Grammatik mit Berücksichtigung des Vulgärlatein und der romanischen Sprachen* (Munich, 1930–31).

Wilhelm Kroll, "Die Entwicklung der lateinischen Schriftsprache," *Glotta* 22(1934)1–27.

Jules Marouzeau, "Le latin, langue de paysans," *Mélanges . . . Vendryes* 251–264 (Paris, 1925).

—— "Notes sur la formation du latin classique," *MSL* 17(1912) 266–280, 18(1913)146–162, 20(1918)77–88, 22(1921)174–181.

Frank B. Marsh (revised by H. H. Scullard), *A history of the Roman world from 146 to 30 B.C.* (2nd ed., London, 1953).

Antoine Meillet, *Esquisse d'une histoire de la langue latine* (5th ed., Paris, 1948).

Clemente Merlo, "Del sostrato delle parlate italiane," *Orbis* 3(1954)7–21.

450   BIBLIOGRAPHY FOR PART SIX   [pp. 289-362

―――― "Il sostrato etnico e i dialetti italiani," *ID* 9(1933)1-24.
Christine Mohrmann, *Latin vulgaire. Latin des chrétiens* (Paris, 1952).
Max Niedermann, *Historische Lautlehre des Lateinischen* (3rd ed., Heidelberg, 1953).
Eduard Norden, *Die antike Kunstprosa* (Leipzig, 1923).
H. M. D. Parker, *A history of the Roman world from 138 to 337* (London, 1935).
André Piganiol, *Histoire de Rome* (Paris, 1939).
Vittore Pisani, *Grammatica latina storica e comparativa* (Turin, 1948).
―――― *Testi latini arcaici e volgari* (Turin, 1950).
Ernst Pulgram, "Accent and ictus in spoken and written Latin," *KZ* 71 (1954)218-238.
Francesco Ribezzo, "Reliquie italiche nei dialetti dell'Italia meridionale," *ARAN*, n.s., 1.2. (1910)151-169.
Edward T. Salmon, *A history of the Roman world from 30 B.C. to A.D. 138* (2nd ed., London, 1950).
Howard H. Scullard, *A history of the Roman world from 753 to 146 B.C.* (London, 1935).
A. N. Sherwin-White, *The Roman citizenship* (Oxford, 1939).
Ferdinand Sommer, *Handbuch der lateinischen Laut- und Formenlehre* (4th ed., Heidelberg, 1948).
E. H. Warmington, ed., *Remains of Old Latin* (Cambridge, 1940).

PART SEVEN. THE ABORTIVE GERMANIZATION OF ITALY [pp. 363-388]
   (See also Bibliographies for Parts Two and Eight)

Cited

Giulio Bertoni, *L'elemento germanico nella lingua italiana* (Genoa, 1914).
Arthur E. R. Boak, *Manpower shortage and the fall of the Roman empire in the west* (Ann Arbor, Mich., 1955).
Ernst Gamillscheg, *Romania Germanica. Sprach- und Siedlungsgeschichte der Germanen auf dem Boden des alten Römerreiches* (Berlin, 1934-36).
―――― "Zur Geschichte der germanischen Lehnwörter des Italienischen," *ZV* 10(1939)89-120.
Ferdinand Lot, *Les invasions germaniques. La pénétration mutuelle du monde barbare et du monde germanique* (Paris, 1935).
Bruno Migliorini, *Tra il latino e l'italiano. Primordi della lingua italiana.* (Lezioni tenute nell'Anno Accademico 1952-53.) (Florence, 1953).
Leonard Olschki, *The genius of Italy* (New York, 1949).
Carlo Sforza, *Italy and the Italians* (New York, 1949).
Arnold J. Toynbee, *The Western question in Greece and Turkey* (London, 1922).
Janet Penrose Trevelyan, *A short history of the Italian people from the barbarian invasions to the attainment of unity* (New York, 1920).
Walther von Wartburg, *Die Ausgliederung der romanischen Sprachräume* (Bern, 1950).

Additional

Nils Åberg, *Die Franken und Westgoten in der Völkerwanderungszeit* (Uppsala, 1922).
—— *Die Goten und Langobarden in Italien* (Uppsala, 1923).
Karl Julius Beloch, *Bevölkerungsgeschichte Italiens* (Berlin, 1937–40).
Carlo Cipolla, "Della supposta fusione degli Italiani coi Germani nei primi secoli del medioevo," *RAL* ser. 5, vol. 9(1900)329–360,369–422,517–563, 567–603.
Edward Eyre, ed., *European civilization, its origin and development* (London, 1935–39).
Ernst Gamillscheg, *Immigrazioni germaniche in Italia* (Leipzig, 1937).
Ferdinand Gregorovius (ed. F. Schillmann), *Geschichte der Stadt Rom im Mittelalter* (Dresden, 1926).
Pietro Gribaudi, "Sull'influenza germanica nella toponomastica italiana," *BSGI* 39(1902)523–539,597–621.
Thomas Hodgkin, *Italy and her invaders* (Oxford, 1892–99).
Léon Homo, *Rome médiévale, 476–1420* (Paris, 1934).
Ferdinand Lot, *Les invasions barbares et le peuplement de l'Europe* (Paris, 1937).
Clemente Merlo, "L'Italia linguistica odierna e le invasioni barbariche," *ARAI* ser. 7, 3(1941)63–72.
S. N. Miller, "The Church, the Later Empire, and the Barbarians," in: Eyre 1935, 2.599–672.
G. Romano — A. Solmi, *Le dominazioni barbariche in Italia, 395–888* (Milan, 1940).
Pasquale Villari, *Le invasioni barbariche in Italia* (4th ed., Milan, 1928).
Ferdinand Wrede, *Ueber die Sprache der Ostgoten in Italien* (Strassburg, 1891).

PART EIGHT. THE ITALIANIZATION OF ITALY
(See also Bibliographies for Parts Two and Seven)

Cited

(Anon.) *Vita di Cola di Rienzo*, ed. Alberto M. Ghisalberti (Florence, 1928).
R. R. Bolgar, *The classical heritage and its beneficiaries* (Cambridge, 1954).
Dante Alighieri, *De vulgari eloquentia*, ed. Aristide Marigo (Florence, 1938).
C. Dionisotti — C. Grayson, ed., *Early Italian texts* (Oxford, 1949).
Jakob Jud, "Probleme der altromanischen Wortgeographie," *ZRP* 3(1914) 1–75.
Paul Lehmann, "Fuldaer Studien. Neue Folge," *SBAW* (1927).
Jean Mabillon, *Annales ordinis Sancti Benedicti* (Lucae, 1739–45).
Giuseppe Manacorda, *Storia della scuola in Italia* (Milan, 1913).
Jules Marouzeau, Review of Muller 1929, *REL* 8(1930)384–387.
Harri Meier, "Ueber das Verhältnis der romanischen Sprachen zum Lateinischen," *RF* 54(1940)165–201.

Antoine Meillet, "L'unité romane," *Scientia* 31(1922)149-153.
Bruno Migliorini, *Tra il latino e l'italiano. Primordi della lingua italiana.* (Lezioni tenute nell'Anno Accademico 1952-53) (Florence, 1953).
Ernesto Monaci, *Crestomazia italiana dei primi secoli* (Città di Castello, 1912).
Angelo Monteverdi, *Testi volgari italiani dei primi tempi* (2nd ed., Modena, 1948).
Henri F. Muller, *A chronology of Vulgar Latin*, ZRP Beiheft 78 (Halle, 1929).
—— *L'époque mérovingienne. Essai de synthèse de philologie et d'histoire* (New York, 1945).
—— "When did Latin cease to be a spoken language in France?" *RR* 12(1921)318-334.
Leonard Olschki, *The genius of Italy* (New York, 1949).
Mario A. Pei "Accusative or oblique? A synthesis of the theories concerning the origin of the oblique case of Old French and the single-case system of other Romance languages," *RR* 28(1937)241-267.
—— *The language of the eighth century texts in northern France* (New York, 1932).
—— "Reflections on the origin of the Romance languages," *RR* 36(1945) 235.
Robert L. Politzer, "On the emergence of Romance from Latin," *Word* 5(1949)126-130.
Ernst Pulgram, "Spoken and written Latin," *Language* 26(1950)458-466.
Louis F. Sas, "Changing linguistic attitudes in the Merovingian period," *Word* 5(1949)131-134.
Hugo Schuchardt, *Der Vokalismus des Vulgärlateins* (Leipzig, 1866-68).
Grant Showerman, *Eternal Rome* (New Haven, Conn., 1924).
M. Tangl, *Die Briefe des hl. Bonifatius* (Berlin, 1916).
Pauline Taylor, *The latinity of the Liber Historiae Francorum* (New York, 1924).
—— "Henri François Muller," *Word* 5(1949)95-99.
Walther von Wartburg, *Raccolta di testi antichi italiani* (Bern, 1946).

Additional

C. Battisti — G. Alessio, *Dizionario etimologico italiano* (Florence, 1950 ff.).
Giulio Bertoni, *Il duecento* (2nd ed., Milan, 1930).
Joseph Brüch, *Der Einfluss der germanischen Sprachen auf das Vulgärlatein* (Heidelberg, 1913).
Edmund Curtis, *Roger of Sicily and the Normans in Lower Italy. 1016-1154* (New York, 1912).
F. D'Ovidio — W. Meyer-Lübke, *Grammatica storica della lingua e dei dialetti italiani* (Milan, 1932).
Ernst Gamillscheg, "Germanische Wörter im Vulgärlatein," *RF* 61(1948) 212-224.
Charles H. Grandgent, *From Latin to Italian* (Cambridge, 1940).
B. Migliorini — A. Duro, *Prontuario etimologico della lingua italiana* (Turin, 1950).
Henri Pirenne, *Histoire économique de l'occident médiéval* (Bruges, 1951).

G. Prati, *Vocabolario etimologico italiano* (Milan, 1951).

Gerhard Rohlfs, *Historische Grammatik der italienischen Sprache und ihrer Mundarten* (Bern, 1949–54).

———— *Romanische Philologie, Zweiter Teil* (Heidelberg, 1952).

———— *Sermo vulgaris latinus. Vulgärlateinisches Lesebuch* (Halle, 1951; 2nd ed., Tübingen, 1956).

Pasquale Villari, *L'Italia da Carlo Magno alla morte di Arrigo VII* (Milan, 1910).

SUBJECT INDEX

NAME INDEX

SUBJECT INDEX

NAME INDEX
HISTORIC, LITERARY

SCHOLARLY